SEX AND SECTS

American Spirituality
Matthew S. Hedstrom and
Leigh Eric Schmidt, Editors

SEX AND SECTS
The Story of Mormon Polygamy, Shaker
Celibacy, and Oneida Complex Marriage

Stewart Davenport

University of Virginia Press • *Charlottesville and London*

University of Virginia Press
© 2022 by the Rector and Visitors of the University of Virginia
All rights reserved
Printed in the United States of America on acid-free paper

First published 2022

9 8 7 6 5 4 3 2 1

Library of Congress Cataloging-in-Publication Data

Names: Davenport, Stewart, author.
Title: Sex and sects : the story of Mormon polygamy, Shaker celibacy, and Oneida complex marriage / Stewart Davenport.
Description: Charlottesville : University of Virginia Press, 2022. | Series: American spirituality | Includes bibliographical references and index.
Identifiers: LCCN 2021042969 (print) | LCCN 2021042970 (ebook) | ISBN 9780813947051 (hardcover) | ISBN 9780813947068 (paperback) | ISBN 9780813947075 (ebook)
Subjects: LCSH: Sex—Religious aspects—Christianity. | Shakers—History. | Oneida Community—History. | Mormon Church—History. | United States—Church history—19th century. | United States—Religious life and customs.
Classification: LCC BT708 .D3835 2022 (print) | LCC BT708 (ebook) | DDC 261.8/350973—dc23/eng/20211014
LC record available at https://lccn.loc.gov/2021042969
LC ebook record available at https://lccn.loc.gov/2021042970

Cover art: Typography and design by David Drummond/Salamander Hill Design

For Mary, of course
(we have sex)

A great Christian empire, divided into a thousand little kingdoms, all inclosed in the bowels of a great republic, and each contending for the mastery. America exulting in her health, the liberty and equality of her members, and yet full of worms, biting and devouring one another, each pursuing a distinct course to which he presumes all others must finally give way.
—RICHARD MCNEMAR, *The Kentucky Revival; or, A Short History of the Late Extraordinary Outpouring of the Spirit of God in the Western States of America*, 1807

CONTENTS

Acknowledgments		xi
Prologue: The Perfectionist Snow-Bound Funeral Orgy of 1839 and What This Book Is Not About		1
Introduction		7

Part I. Context and Ideas — 17

1	More	19
2	Metanarrative	27
3	Marriage	38

Part II. Geneses — 53

4	Spiritual	57
5	Sexual	75
6	Institutional	92

Part III. Early Crises — 119

7	Shaker Family Drama	123
8	Polygamy and Persecution at Nauvoo: The Mormons, 1842–1844	130
9	"A Scatteration at Oneida"	150
10	Succession, Relocation, and Proclamation: The Mormons, 1844–1852	159

Part IV. Practices and Enforcements — 177

11 Selfishness and Status — 185
12 Control — 194
13 Revival — 207
14 Gender — 219
15 Children — 235

Part V. Sectarian End Times — 247

16 The Shakers, from Revolution to Refuge — 251
17 The Triumph of Bread and Butter at Oneida — 259
18 The War on Polygamy and the Temporal Salvation of the Mormon Church — 273

Epilogue — 289

Notes — 297

Index — 339

ACKNOWLEDGMENTS

THIS IS my favorite part of writing a book: getting to thank all those who made it possible. First, I have to express my gratitude to the Communal Studies Association (CSA) for being committed to community not just as a topic of study but as a scholarly and human practice. The conferences and conversations were invaluable in making this book a reality. In particular I would like to thank Martha Bradley-Evans, Kathleen M. Fernandez, Lawrence Foster, Christian Goodwillie, Matt Grow, Susan Love-Brown, Timothy Miller, Don Pitzer, and Marc Rhorer for the encouragement, critiques, and insights that have shaped my understanding of this subject of our shared inquiry.

I would also like to thank Pepperdine University for the institutional support over the many years of working on this book. I am particularly grateful for the sabbaticals that allowed me to launch and complete this project, the course releases, and the generous support of the Blanche E. Seaver Professorship from 2011 to 2016.

I am tremendously indebted to a number of individuals who helped me turn an unwieldly manuscript into a published book. At the Huntington Library I would especially like to single out Michael Alexander, Mark G. Hanna, and Dana Velasco Murillo for their invaluable advice on the publishing process. At the University of Virginia Press I have been incredibly fortunate to work with Eric Brandt. He is a consummate publishing professional: knowledgeable, supportive, and focused in his critiques. I honestly could not have asked for a better editor. I similarly could not have asked for a better reviewer than Christopher Grasso. Thank you for your fair and brutal treatment of the manuscript. It is much improved as a result of that refining process. Any imperfections that remain are my own.

Speaking of imperfection, now would be a good time to talk about my marriage. I began this project back in 2008, a year after getting married and the same year that Californians voted to deny same-sex couples that right. Proposition 8 has since been overturned and Mary and I have somehow made it through cancer, six years of infertility, and about a million and a half other challenges—all positive developments in my opinion. Mary lived with this project as a resident in our home for over a dozen years, committed to seeing it completed as a book even when that meant real sacrifices of time and money. I am forever grateful for your love, support, and understanding. In addition to being a wonderful mother to Shiloh, you are a best friend and were an unfailing advocate during this often-excruciating process. Monogamy itself is imperfect but you sure make it fun. I just like holding your hand as we both get fat and old. You know, the sexy stuff.

SEX AND SECTS

PROLOGUE

The Perfectionist Snow-Bound Funeral Orgy of 1839 and What This Book Is Not About

I LOVE this story.

In December 1839 a member of a Perfectionist sect in Newark, New Jersey, died. Fellow Perfectionists arranged a funeral at a nearby "country estate," when a winter storm blew up and the mourners found themselves "snow-bound for two days at the hospitable mansion." We do not know precisely what happened during those two days, but one sympathetic historian reports that there was "much unedifying talk and loose behavior" as well as "much singing of 'Babylon Is Fallen,'" a rousing hymn about the triumph of God's kingdom over the powers of this world.[1]

This "climax of wantonness" had apparently been brewing for some time. Although a small sect, the Newark Perfectionists were themselves "split into three parties": legalists, antinomians, and a third faction that "was attempting to steer clear of both" extremes. In the fall of 1839, unsurprisingly, "the antinomian party were in the ascendant." "Whenever Perfectionists met," this scholar explains, "it was expected that they would kiss." As radical followers of the Bible, they took seriously the injunction to "Greet one another with an holy kiss,"[2] although they started interpreting that injunction more liberally. "Some went so far as to bundle [sleeping together fully clothed], and one couple lived as man and wife nearly a year before they were married. Heart-burnings and jealousies resulted." And then came the Perfectionist snow-bound funeral orgy of December 1839, after which the owner of the "country estate" had second thoughts, "experienced a reaction toward legality," and "swung clear over to Shakerism"—presumably meaning that he (temporarily) embraced abstinence and a more negative theological perspective on human bodies and human sexuality.[3]

I love this story not for its salacious content, but for what it reveals in microcosm about the human condition. That hermetically sealed "hospitable mansion" was an almost perfect religio-sexual-sociological experiment. Take a bunch of people who fervently believe that they are perfect—that nothing they do on earth can separate them from the love of God in heaven—confine them in accommodations that are likely much nicer than their own homes back in Newark, give them nothing else to do but contemplate mortality and keep warm, and one pretty much has all the ingredients necessary for "much unedifying talk and loose behavior."

I also love this episode for what it reveals about the power of religious ideas, and in particular religious stories. By far the most important variable in what took place in December 1839 were the stories of eternity that filled the minds and souls of the believers, and gave them parts to play as characters in a cosmic drama that included life and sex, but that also continued into the hereafter. What they believed about the afterlife informed how they acted in this life. The owner of the estate, for instance, changed his mind first—from antinomianism to legalism—and consequently changed the way he lived as a sexual being. In other words, if one were to keep the setup the same but switch out the historical actors or their beliefs, one would have very different results.

A party of mourning snow-bound Shakers, for instance, would not result in two days of so-called "loose behavior." Founded by Mother Ann Lee, the Shaker sect believed that sex was the most sinful of sins, and indeed the root of sin. In a vision in 1770 Lee witnessed Adam and Eve in flagrante delicto, and received a revelation that this, and not eating the apple, was the origin of human depravity. As Lee taught her followers both in England and soon in America, true disciples of Christ must resist all temptations to lust, believe the Shaker version of the Christian story, and ascetically strive for the kingdom of God on earth as it is in heaven. Clearly devout, a group of Shakers stuck in a mansion for two days might also have sung "Babylon Is Fallen" as a way to express their sectarian contempt for the world and its worldly churches, but there would be no "wantonness" among them. Imitating Christ and the apostles, they embraced celibacy and looked forward to being rewarded for their earthly sacrifices in the life to come.

A party of snowed-in Mormon polygamists would also have acted differently because of their different beliefs about life, sex, and the afterlife. Although Joseph Smith and the Latter-day Saints came to believe in plural marriage as a newly revealed commandment from God, they—along with most nineteenth-century Americans—still believed that sexual activity should take place only within the institution of marriage, whether monogamously or polygamously defined. Joseph Smith and those who followed him into the practice of polygamy, in fact, were always sensitive to the charge of adultery. "And as ye have asked concerning adultery," the revelation that sanctioned plural marriage reads, "if he have [sic] ten virgins given unto him by this law, he cannot commit adultery, for they belong to him, . . . therefore he is justified."[4] Yes, the men in these relationships had multiple sexual partners, but the relationships themselves were both hallowed by this new revelation and were, in fact, required—or at the very least encouraged—for Mormon men and women to attain the highest level of exaltation in the afterlife.

Instead of just life and death, heaven or hell, Mormons have their own story of eternity, with the institution of marriage and the obligation of reproduction through sex at the center of that story. Unlike many other Western religions, Mormons believe in a premortal phase of existence in which unborn spirit children anxiously wait to receive physical bodies that can only be granted to them when men and women on earth procreate, which these revelations refer to as being "enlarged," or having "an increase."[5] Furthermore, Mormons believe that after death immortal souls do not merely face judgment individually but as eternal family units, "sealed" in the everlasting covenant of the appropriately named "celestial marriage." And finally, when it comes to eternal rewards and punishments, there are not just the standard binary options of heaven or hell, but rather "three heavens or degrees; And in order to obtain the highest, a man must enter into . . . the new and everlasting covenant of marriage." Marriage in Mormonism therefore comes with exceedingly high eternal stakes. If adherents want to be spiritually superlative, they have to have their marriages "sealed upon their heads. . . . Then shall they be gods, because they have no end." Marriages properly sealed on earth will endure as procreative units into eternity, and the more celestial wives a man might have, the more opportunity for "a fulness [sic] and a continuation of the seeds forever."[6]

So-called "wantonness" would therefore not describe Mormon polygamists stuck in a mansion for two days. Rather, the husbands would likely retire with one of their plural wives, perhaps have sexual intercourse, and hope that the act would result in a pregnancy that would provide a material body for an awaiting spirit child and further bless the father with "an increase." Sexual pleasure and connubial intimacy mattered, but procreation mattered most, and all sexual activity would be within the confines of "sealed" plural matrimony. "Behold," the revelation on plural marriage proclaims, "mine house is a house of order, saith the Lord God, and not a house of confusion."[7] And nor would be any "hospitable mansion" in which devout Mormon polygamists might find themselves. Although the surrounding Gentile (non-Mormon) world would ridicule and persecute them for "the principle" of plural marriage—and while "living the principle" was more emotionally painful and sacrificial than it was pleasurable or easy for polygamous men and women—the Saints continued to do so because, like the Shakers, they believed that their actions were helping build up a righteous kingdom on earth while securing rewards for themselves and their family in eternity.

So what about those other Perfectionists, John Humphrey Noyes's Oneida Perfectionists, who also expanded the institution of marriage beyond its traditional, monogamous bounds? Would they be guilty of the "loose behavior" of their 1839 Perfectionist peers? Yes and no is arguably the best answer. On the one hand, yes, they would probably have engaged in sexual activity that outsiders would consider scandalous. But on the other hand, no, that activity would hardly have been unbridled "wantonness." In fact, rather like Mormon polygamists, Noyes and his Perfectionists believed in keeping "a house of order, . . . and not a house of confusion."

John Humphrey Noyes struggled to maintain order in virtually every aspect of his life and his followers' lives. With his highly disciplined mind, in the 1830s Noyes turned his attention first to religion and soon to marriage and sex, rewriting both the story of the early Christian church and then the rules that were to govern sexual partnerships. Hating the exclusivity of monogamous marriage after he was rejected by a young woman for another suitor—a situation he could not control—he decided to abolish the institution, or at least redefine it: replacing the world's "simple" or monogamous marriage with his godlier, polyamorous version that he called "complex marriage."

Rather than a Saturnalia, complex marriage was itself highly controlled. Prospective sexual partners had to arrange their liaisons—or "fellowships" as they called them—through the ministrations of a third party, sleep separately after the fellowshipping had concluded, and strive not to have the same partner too often in order to prevent the relationship from becoming exclusive. Most controlling of all was what happened during intercourse itself. In order to enjoy the intimacy of sex but avoid the consequences that would accompany pregnancies, Noyes required the men at Oneida to practice a form of birth control that he called "male continence," or intercourse without ejaculation. Thus, if Noyes and company had been guests at a snowed-in mansion, those two days would have looked like any other two days at their own mansion in Oneida, New York. Mediated by a third party, the lovers would pair off, "fellowship" without risking pregnancy, sleep separately, and perhaps "fellowship" with someone else later if the spirit so moved, and the partner and arbitrator consented.

This, however, was the way Noyes's religio-sexual regime operated in its most mature phase, between roughly 1848 and the Community's collapse in 1881. Both the sexual liberty that Oneidans enjoyed as well as the obvious constraints were the outcome of the stories that Noyes told, and it took him years to refine those stories and develop means of reinforcing them with accompanying institutions and a disciplinary apparatus, which is why what happened in 1839 was truly aberrant. In 1839, the nascent Perfectionist movement was still in a time of trial and error, with the funerary "climax of wantonness" definitely in the "error" category. In fact, the historian who recorded the episode, George Wallingford Noyes, was John Humphrey Noyes's nephew, which is why I describe him as "sympathetic"—sympathetic to his uncle's life and labors, but not to those who bastardized his ideas and used them for sexual license.

As John Humphrey Noyes slowly constructed his religious metanarrative and institutional supports, some wanted to race ahead to the sexual freedom that they believed was theirs as Perfectionists. In this antinomian faction, which was "in the ascendant" in 1839, "there were no leaders, no rules, no regular meetings. . . . Dreams, impressions, and impulses were thought to be the voice of God, and social [i.e., sexual] relations were governed by them." Noyes, whose ideas influenced the third, moderate faction, would have none of it. Yes, he opposed the "legality of the churches on one side"—this is what made him a sectarian—but he also opposed antinomianism on the other for its obvious tendency to drift into community-destroying anarchy.[8]

Different religious stories clearly inspire people to engage in different sexual behavior: celibacy, monogamy, plural marriage, complex marriage, and "wantonness." But those stories, in order to endure, also need "leaders," "rules," "regular meetings," and sources of authority that are more reliable and consistent than the "dreams, impressions, and impulses" that governed these antinomian Perfectionists in 1839. One would not have to swing all the way over to the "legality of the churches" to endure, but one would have to supplement the thrill of religious revelations and ecstatic worship with rules and routines. Zeal never lasts. The original animating ardor of a religious belief or practice always fades with time, age, and changed circumstances, and has to be bolstered—for better or for worse—by rituals and institutions that are decidedly more mundane.

This book is going to tell the story of both: the exciting religious visions and the more plodding process of institution-building and maintenance. Shaker communal celibacy, Mormon plural marriage, and Oneida complex marriage were all institutions in the same way that monogamous marriage is an institution. What follows is a story about how those institutions changed over time, emerging out of the highly original religious stories of their sectarian founders to become countercultural establishments in their own right. Those establishments did not last forever, which is the final part of the story, but they had a more lasting impact on American society and American religious life than the leaderless and ruleless Perfectionist snow-bound funeral orgy of 1839. In what follows there are almost no episodes like it. To invoke another religious cosmology, it was literally the Dionysian exception to the Apollonian rule, including among Perfectionists.

INTRODUCTION

We humans are strange, hybrid creatures. "A minority in the realm of being," Abraham Heschel wrote, mankind "stands somewhere between God and the beasts. . . . Our existence seesaws between animality and divinity, between that which is more and that which is less than humanity."[1]

Sex might be the human activity that reveals our human nature the most, in all its glory and its horror, inspiring in even the most rational of people the most irrational of behaviors, attitudes, and actions. Sexual misconduct, for instance, has done incalculable damage and rightly ended the careers of politicians, pastors, news anchors, Hollywood moguls, Old Testament prophets, and university professors, just to name a few. Sex also has the power to unify and express physically the emotions that lovers hold for one another. Sex can therefore be either selfish, abusive, and forced; or selfless, salubrious, consensual, and mutually fulfilling. But no matter the manifestation, sex is an intimate human act of unparalleled power that can be used either to heal or to harm, and many things in between.

How are religious people—earthbound but eternity-conscious—supposed to live in light of this most powerful of human drives? This is an especially difficult question within the Christian tradition because Jesus Christ, the Apostle Paul, and countless other saints never married and are presumed never to have had sex. In the war between the flesh and the spirit, their "spiritual" side reigned supreme, setting an example for all would-be followers to go and do likewise. Paul famously wished that "all men were even as I myself," and yet knew full well that most human beings were not. "But if they cannot contain, let them marry," he wrote, "for it is better to marry than to burn."[2] Marriage was the institution in which the fire of lust would be safely enclosed—a compromise with humankind's animal instincts, but one that the more spiritual were willing to tolerate.

In the early American republic, however, all things seemed new and possible, and many things were tried. With a revolution behind them, a continent before them, and the First Amendment protecting them, religious pioneers were free to strike out on their own, breaking with tradition and the orthodoxies of the past. In the process they not only reinterpreted biblical texts and stories but often wholly reimagined them, reconceptualizing God, God's material Creation, and the self's role within that Creation.

This book is going to tell the story of three religious groups that—for a variety of reasons—focused their spiritual energies on the ambiguities of human sexuality. The Shakers followed the ascetic path. Mastery of the sexual self was thus only part of their wholesale rejection of earthly pleasures in favor of more important spiritual realities. For the Oneida Perfectionists mastery of the sexual self came through the joyful acceptance of sex as a gift from God, but only if that gift was also vigilantly controlled by the individual and regulated by the broader community. For the Mormons, sex and marriage were redefined in light of new religious revelations that also fundamentally redefined God, humankind, spirit, and matter. These are the varying theological perspectives—all of which will be described in detail—behind each of these group's sexual innovations: Mormon polygamy, Shaker celibacy, and Oneida complex marriage. Still, for all of their countercultural originality it needs to be noted that these religious radicals were creatures of their time, assuming both heterosexuality as the norm and that sexual activity should be regulated by and within an institution.

From a more earthly and historical perspective, sex became a powerful way for the Mormons, Shakers, and Oneida Perfectionists to reinforce their sectarian identity as strangers in a strange land. And if one is looking for this book's thesis, that would be it: for these nineteenth-century American religious groups, sex became a means of reinforcing sectarian identity. Thus the title "Sex and Sects." In pursuing this argument, I will explain why they focused so much attention on sex in the first place, and then what happened as they radically and provocatively departed from the norm of Christian monogamy. In particular—and corresponding to the book's organization—I will trace how they introduced their sexual innovations, the obstacles they had to overcome in their implementation, how those innovations operated once fully institutionalized, and how all three either had failed or were failing before the end of the nineteenth century. These religio-sexual innovations shared a common four-phase life-cycle over the course of that century: childhood, adolescence, maturity, and decline. One can also think about these novel sexual/marital institutions as following the trajectory of a narrative arc. Thus the book's subtitle: "The *Story* of Mormon Polygamy, Shaker Celibacy, and Oneida Complex Marriage."

Religious beliefs and practices do not drop down from heaven fully formed but rather develop historically and often according to recognizable processes. This is just as true for the great Western "religions of the book" (Judaism, Christianity, Islam) as it is for these much smaller American sects. Jesus and Mohammed, for instance, told radically new stories that attracted followers who eventually coalesced into religious communities. Joseph Smith, Mother Ann Lee, and John Humphrey Noyes all did the same, their followers eventually calling themselves Mormons, Shakers, and Perfectionists. There is, in other words, an identifiable pattern by which religious stories turn into religious movements, and then those religious movements—under the right set of historical circumstances—can transition into more stable religious institutions. This pattern gives the book its organization: Part 1 elucidates the stories themselves and the context in which they found a receptive audience; part 2 describes how those stories became movements; part 3 how those movements struggled to institutionalize; part 4 how those mature institutions functioned; and part 5 how those institutions succumbed to both external hostility and internal waning commitment.

Focusing on these sexual practices also gives the book a clear stopping point. Mormonism, for instance, is clearly alive and well today with (in 2020) over sixteen million Saints worldwide.[3] The story of Mormon polygamy as an official LDS Church–sanctioned practice, however, ends in 1890, when the Church bowed to the federal government's pressure and abandoned the principle of plural marriage. Many defiant Saints continued (and continue today) to practice plural marriage, but 1890 was still a turning point, and for this book an endpoint. The legal, political, and cultural environment in which Mormon polygamy, Shaker celibacy, and Oneida complex marriage had all emerged and flourished had turned from tolerable to toxic. The Oneida Community had disbanded in 1881, nine years earlier, and in that same decade of the 1880s the Shakers were far down a demographic death spiral from which they never recovered.

Much had changed in America in the half-century from 1830 to 1880, and one of this book's aims is to make clear the role of historical context in either encouraging or discouraging sectarianism. In the 1830s the federal government was weak, the American frontier seemingly endless, and the opportunities for sectarian start-ups equally boundless. In the 1880s the federal government was strong and getting stronger, the frontier was rapidly disappearing, and the majority of Americans were increasingly intolerant of sexual/marital arrangements that they believed corroded the nation's morality. What is fascinating in retrospect is the relative simultaneity of those sectarian sexual practices' rise and fall. Although at different paces and with different starting points, Mormon polygamy, Shaker celibacy, and Oneida complex marriage followed strikingly similar paths over the course of the nineteenth century—emerging, struggling, institutionalizing, and declining in tandem.

Scholars have been interested in these groups for some time, although no book comparing all three of them has been published in forty years, and no book has ever told their story as a story. The two most important monographs on the subject are Lawrence Foster's *Religion and Sexuality: The Shakers, the Mormons, and the Oneida Community,* and Louis J. Kern's *An Ordered Love: Sex Roles and Sexuality in Victorian Utopias—The Shakers, The Mormons, and the Oneida Community.* Both were published in 1981 and both are excellent works of scholarship, although their methodology and organization leave room for further study. Noticeably, both rely on the social sciences to elucidate the communities: Foster utilizing "Anthropological Perspectives," as he puts it; while Kern employs psychology to help explain them. As with all interpretive lenses, these "perspectives" clarify some things and distort others. In this book I have attempted to build on their many insights while moving beyond the places where their use of social scientific theories is out of step with the historical facts. Organizationally, both studies have somewhat of a reference-book-like feel to them. Foster and Kern introduce their interpretive schemes at the beginning and then revisit them in their conclusions, but in the body of the text they treat each of the three sects separately, in enormous descriptive chunks—an organization that minimizes the possibility of comparative insight and almost completely fails to pay attention to change over time.[4]

What caused these sexual innovations to rise and then fall primarily over the course of the nineteenth century and almost exclusively within the confines of the new American republic? Rather than view them through a social-scientific lens as these past treatments have done, this book emphasizes the power of religious stories to move people and the power of narrative structure to make complex phenomena comprehensible. In order to better understand these historical actors' seemingly unintelligible actions we have to see them within a context that was not static as social scientists assume, but constantly changing. Narrative, which historian John Lewis Gaddis calls "one of the most sophisticated of all methods of inquiry," carefully tracks change over time, distinguishes "*between the immediate, the intermediate, and the distant*" in terms of causality, and reveals how a particular context influenced the people living within it.[5]

When it comes to telling a story about religion, however, arguably the most important context is invisible. William James defined "the life of religion" as "the belief that there is an unseen order, and that our supreme good lies in harmoniously adjusting ourselves thereto."[6] I would tweak James's definition slightly and say that religious people believe in and adjust themselves to a *story* in which they see themselves as characters. It does not matter whether they are major characters such as Joseph Smith, Ann Lee, and John Humphrey Noyes, or minor ones; they let the story, which they take on faith, define them and direct their actions. These stories, which will be referred to as metanarratives, motivate individuals and define whole communities. Once a person assents to a particular religious story as true, that person is included in the religious community. Whenever a person ceases to believe that the story truly accounts for "the reality of the unseen," he or she usually departs the community, either voluntarily or through excommunication. This book is going to take these religious metanarratives very seriously, so much so that part 1 is devoted almost entirely to explaining them. Only after we have toured those stories for ourselves, beholding and perhaps appreciating their beauty and complexity, can we begin to make sense of the radical sexual innovations of Mormon polygamy, Shaker celibacy, and Oneida complex marriage. The stories provide the context in which the actions become intelligible.

One of the implicit goals of this book is to promote toleration for beliefs, actions, and communities that might seem strange and perhaps even threatening to us. In order for one to tolerate a religious system and its adherents, however, one has to know something about them—to listen before speaking, or "to walk a mile in their shoes" as the saying goes, before judging. That is why this book begins with a part 1 that lays out the fascinating metanarratives of each of the three sects. These are the dramas that were playing continuously in the heads and hearts of the believers, shaping their identities as characters within them and often directing their actions, including what to do with their bodies. When it comes to what they believed they should do with their sexuality in particular, the story is both a strange and a beautiful one: foreign to modern monogamous minds and yet familiar in its universal humanness.

Nineteenth-century Mormons, Shakers, and Oneida Perfectionists were people just like us—asking questions about God and the cosmos while at the same time longing for human intimacy. They just happened to reach different conclusions. In this book I have tried neither to agree nor disagree with them, but simply to understand them and, I hope, to make them understandable.

There are limits to toleration, however, and there will be value judgments in the pages that follow, especially when abuse is involved. Many nineteenth-century contemporaries hated the Mormons, Shakers, and Perfectionists, and wanted them either removed from their shared environs or destroyed outright. In their crusades against these sects, those unhappy neighbors often spread salacious stories in order to gin up hostility. Many of those stories are simply untrue—the product of overactive imaginations, cynical mob manipulation, or both—but not all of them are untrue. As they institutionalized, the Mormons, Shakers, and Oneida Perfectionists all built power structures to enforce religious uniformity and communal discipline, and they did indeed abuse the power that they had granted themselves. Those episodes will not be skipped or sugarcoated but will be shown for what they were: morally indefensible acts that exploited the less powerful members of the various communities. Unsurprisingly, most often the victims in those instances were women and teenage girls.

Making these kinds of value judgments and exposing those lamentable incidents is especially difficult when treating the Mormons. Unlike the Oneida Perfectionists who disbanded in 1881, or the Shakers who (in 2020) count only three surviving members, the Church of Jesus Christ of Latter-day Saints boasts over sixteen million adherents spread literally around the globe. All of those Saints revere Joseph Smith as their faith's founding prophet and revelator. He was also, however, profoundly and inescapably human; not divine and sinless as Christians believe Jesus Christ to be, or the model possessor of moral virtues as Muslims believe Mohammed to be. Joseph Smith had definite flaws and made many costly mistakes, which—thanks to a more complete historical record—scholars can see clearly and identify as such. None of this is intended to erode modern-day Mormons' faith in their prophet, but when the record is clear and the actions less-than-virtuous, they will be given the attention that, sadly, they deserve. Joseph Smith's (as well as Brigham Young's) abuses of power will not be the primary focus of the sections on Mormon polygamy, but neither will they be avoided.

It also bears mentioning that while the historical record on Joseph Smith is substantial and illuminating, it is nevertheless also frustratingly incomplete and sometimes intentionally vague, especially when it comes to plural marriage. From the late 1820s until his death in 1844, Smith wrote and recorded much: the entire *Book of Mormon,* scores of other revelations, and hundreds of letters and personal correspondences. On the subject of plural marriage, however, aside from the official revelation of July 1843, Smith wrote very little. As Richard Bushman, the renowned biographer of Joseph Smith, puts it: in the mid-1830s, precisely when he took his first plural wife, the "image of Joseph Smith shifts and goes out of focus. We know the facts of his life . . . but not his personality or attitudes."[7] Bushman, a practicing Mormon himself, is not intentionally avoiding the unsettling issues here. He is speaking as authoritatively as he can, based on the historical sources at his and other scholars' disposal. He is therefore not being merely humble, but also correct when he says that Smith's "personality" and "attitudes" are essentially unknowable. When it comes to discerning Smith's motivations for starting and spreading plural marriage, scholars (including this one) ultimately reach a dead end.

John Gaddis, in speaking about the difficulty and messiness of the historian's craft, particularly biography, confesses that "the mind of another person is at least as inaccessible as the landscape of the past." He also adds that social scientific theories, which deal with "collective human behavior," have "no way of accounting, say, for Buddha, Christ, and Mohammed." With them and people like them, the "actions of a single individual can, under certain circumstances, *shift standards of rationality,* and hence appropriate behavior, for millions of others."[8] This is exactly what happened with Joseph Smith and his introduction of plural marriage to the LDS Church. This is also what happened with Ann Lee's insistence on celibacy, and John Humphrey Noyes's institution of complex marriage. They all shifted "*standards of rationality,* and hence appropriate behavior." In many ways, this book is a telling of why and how they shifted those standards, the "certain circumstances" that allowed them to do so, and the sexually "appropriate behavior" that they redefined.

The historical actors investigated in this book all lived out their lives on a rather unique historical stage. Because of the First Amendment, the United States of America has no established church, while also protecting the free exercise of religion. This created a wide-open religious marketplace in which spiritual vendors were free to offer their goods and services, and spiritual consumers were free to choose their cosmologies and communities. As the first parts of this book will narrate, many people found this choice more confusing than liberating. Which one was right? Joseph Smith, Ann Lee, and John Humphrey Noyes all solved this problem with acts of sectarian defiance and creativity that both satisfied them personally and turned out to be appealing to those in the market for a new religious identity.

Much of their distinction and appeal in this crowded religious marketplace came from the intensity of their sectarianism. Speaking theologically, scholars often describe a sect as a religious group that splits, splinters, or branches off from an already established religious tradition. Rather than being sui generis, a sect is somewhat derivative, related to the tradition from which it sprang, but also positing an interpretation of that tradition so new and potentially controversial as to warrant a separate classification. Speaking sociologically, scholars define a sect as a protest group, fulminating against both the world and its worldly churches. Ernst Troeltsch, the great German scholar of religion, stated that sects "always appeal to the Gospel and to Primitive Christianity, and accuse the Church of having fallen away from its ideal." In contrast to the dogmatic purity of the sect, Troeltsch continued, "the Church," as a longstanding institution, "knows . . . how to attain her end only by a process of adaptation and compromise," compromises with the world that sectarians are always quick to identify and pillory.[9] Those compromises, it should be added, are almost always in response to some historically unique dilemma that "the Church" has to navigate, and ultimately does navigate but only after surrendering (adapting, compromising) some essential part of itself and its values in order to survive as an institution. Sectarians consider those compromises anathema and long instead for the original purity of "the Gospel" and "Primitive Christianity."

Scholars also regularly use the word "tension" to describe sects and how they operate. Stephen J. Stein, the preeminent historian of the Shakers, succinctly asserts that "Sectarians, by definition, live in tension with their host culture; they seek to turn the world upside down."[10] Sociologist of religion Meredith B. McGuire likewise describes the "sectarian orientation" as one that "thrives on a sense of opposition . . . because they typically enjoy greater cohesion and sense of purpose when they feel their values and goals are under attack."[11] In short, sectarians do not feel at home in the world, but rather "live in tension" with it. As passionate religious believers, oriented primarily toward the unseen reality of their faith, they judge the world and its compromised churches, and actively seek to distance themselves from both. And when they cannot literally distance themselves from worldliness, they symbolically distance themselves from it through practices such as wearing unique attire, eating according to strict dietary regulations, singing and worshipping in distinct ways, et cetera. All of these exercises reinforce their identity as a people set apart. For the Mormons, Shakers, and Perfectionists, their unique sexual beliefs and practices set them apart the most, constructing obvious sectarian boundaries with their monogamous host culture, while also intensifying tension with that culture.

Although according to one perspective "the Church" is the trunk from which sectarians branch off, sectarians consider themselves to be a holy vestige, more closely akin to the roots than the diseased trunk between them. Thus, while sectarians are doing something new and risky, they often claim to be doing it in the name of something old and venerable, reconnecting to and perhaps restoring an "ideal" that has become corrupted over time. Chapter 2, "Metanarrative," will describe in detail the sectarian theologies of the Mormons, Shakers, and Oneida Perfectionists, as well as their versions of early Christian history and how their movements claimed to be reorienting a church that had long since lost its way. Chapter 1, "More," will describe the kind of religious seeker who found those bold claims appealing in the first place.

PART I
CONTEXT AND IDEAS

1
More

FOR SOME antebellum Americans the intensity of evangelical revivals was not enough and they wanted *more*.

From approximately 1790 to 1830, the Second Great Awakening reinvigorated established churches on the East Coast, created thousands of new churches on the frontier, and swept back and forth across the "Burned-over District" of upstate New York, inspiring both traditional and novel forms of devotion. Longstanding denominations such as the Congregationalists and Presbyterians, and more fledgling ones such as the Baptists and Methodists, all grew exponentially in these decades, from hundreds of churches with thousands of members to tens of thousands of churches with millions of members.[1]

Historians are generally agreed about what created this hyperactive religious environment. Starting with the American Revolution and the protections granted by the First Amendment, the new United States was primed for an era of religious creativity and expansion. After disestablishment, religious institutions could no longer rely on the state for support. Now dependent on voluntary contributions for their financial lifeblood, religious leaders were forced to attract and retain loyal and regularly tithing members.

This seismic shift in the structure of American religious life around 1790 led to two interrelated shifts in religious culture. The most important was the redefinition of religious authority itself. Until the early nineteenth century, Protestants vested the authority to interpret the Bible in a minister's education. Knowing theology and the original biblical languages was deemed a prerequisite for accurate scriptural exegesis, and subsequent ordination and congregational submission. While definitely reading the Bible for themselves, members of American churches before 1790 would generally defer on theological matters to the greater knowledge and training of the pastor. In the aftermath of the American Revolution, however, the widespread "crisis of authority" affected not just churches but the entire, newly launched American republic. "Respect for authority, tradition, station, and education eroded" for every so-called learned professional, the historian Nathan Hatch writes, whether in medicine, law, or the ministry. The medical and legal professions eventually won their battles against post-Revolutionary egalitarianism through the exclusive institutions of the American Medical Association and American Bar Association, but religious leaders entirely reconstructed "the foundations of religious authority" in a way that resonates down to the present.[2]

If the first cultural shift after 1790 was the "crisis of authority," the second was the redefinition of religious authority along populist lines. To quote Hatch again: "authority depended not on education, status, ordination, or state support, but on the ability to move people and retain their confidence," a definition of authority that is fundamentally populist. Some antebellum religious leaders—including those investigated in this book—claimed to receive their spiritual authority directly from God through revelation, inspiration, visions, or special knowledge. But virtually all antebellum religious leaders, Hatch continues, "rested their claims to authority on the validity of lay proclamation." In other words, any inspired individual could claim divine authority, but if he or she failed to move anyone, then the movement itself would fail, as many did during this era of spiritual trial and error. If no potential follower could identify and assent to any vestige of authority in an aspiring religious leader, then that religious leader had no authority. This complex relationship between leader and led has shaped American religious life ever since. Paradoxically, the United States' egalitarian culture nevertheless creates authoritarian religious leaders to whom liberty-loving people willingly and often totally submit.[3]

This dynamic, which is best described using political terms such as "populism," "egalitarianism," and "authoritarianism," is part of a system that is best described using an economic term—the American religious marketplace. Once multiple denominations had moved into a given territory, the previously dominant church lost its local monopoly and had to depend for its continuance on fickle and occasionally unforgiving American religious consumers. This turned the laity into spiritual shoppers and religious leaders into competitive salespersons and entrepreneurs for their particular brand of religious truth. Individuals, movements, and whole institutions would either succeed or fail based almost entirely on their ability to attract a following. This permissive context changed as the nineteenth century rolled on and the American government, economy, and culture became less tolerant of religious experimentation, but in the beginning there were virtually no limits to the possibilities of creative religious leaders and restless religious seekers.

In large part there were no spiritual limits because there were no spatial ones. The seemingly unending American frontier provided adequate room for the dozens of religious and communal experiments that were launched in the first half of the nineteenth century. While not literally blank slates, these tracts of land were blank enough for the various communities to find a safe environment in which to experiment and grow outside of the reach of hostile or competitive forces. And if the host society did become hostile, the religious experimenters could either fight back with the First Amendment's "free exercise" clause, or move again, at least until 1890, when the frontier closed and there was nowhere ungoverned left to go. But before 1890, and especially before the Civil War, wherever one finds the dislocating phenomena of both a frontier setting and a rapid transition to market-capitalism, one has two of the most crucial ingredients for creating a society primed for religious awakening and innovation.

In no place was American society more primed and the religious soil more fertile than in the Burned-over District. Filled with recent immigrants, upstate New York was as fresh and unsettled as any new Western state. The completion of the Erie Canal in 1825 brought in even more settlers, new kinds of jobs, and dozens of new and radical religious ideas and practices. Religious seekers who longed for meaning and an identity-forging cause and community could easily find them among the myriad choices that the Burned-over District offered. Some, however, were overwhelmed by so great a spiritual selection. For them, the ability to choose was a double-edged sword, providing religious shoppers with plenty of options, but nevertheless confusing them with their competing and mutually exclusive truth claims.

So how exactly did the Mormons, Shakers, and Perfectionists manage to succeed in this overcrowded religious marketplace? As mentioned in the introduction, much of their appeal came from the intensity of their sectarianism. In addition to recognizing that their religious environment was chaotic, each of these groups also judged it harshly according to an uncompromising sectarian standard. To their minds, even with all of their evangelical zeal, antebellum Christians were hopelessly compromised, and these sectarians wanted to return to the purity of the early Church. What counted for Christian life in their antebellum present, they judged, was merely the latest manifestation of a Church that had lost its way centuries ago, and sometimes as early as the second or third generation after Christ. All three sects therefore had powerful stories to tell of Christian corruption that had derailed the original intentions of Jesus and the apostles. As the next chapter on "Metanarrative" will make clear, each group described the precise cause and date of this corruption differently, but they nevertheless all shared in a common critique of a Christian tradition gone awry, and one that they believed they were restoring to its original glory.

Coexisting with this sectarian critique of worldly churches was the sectarian longing for *more:* more intense and frequent spiritual experiences, more radical doctrines, more separation from the world, and more demanding individual sacrifices. The Second Great Awakening had raised the level of religious enthusiasm throughout the antebellum North to a new high. In such an environment it was difficult for intense religious seekers to distinguish themselves further from the awakened masses. For all kinds of reasons, the people investigated in this book deemed the standard options in their religious marketplace to be insufficient and they wanted *more*—a kind of spiritual satisfaction that would come only after they had embraced the most extreme form of religious expression, or as they called it at the time, the most "ultra" form of "ultraism."

This spiritual dissatisfaction and desire for *more* was true for both the religious leaders of these new sects and their followers. Both were confused by and critical of the cacophony of religious voices around them, and both sought answers that went beyond the orthodoxies of their day. The only real difference between the leaders and the led is that the leaders claimed to have found those answers and the followers assented to them. Both, however, shared the same intense spiritual longing that could only be satisfied once they had separated themselves thoroughly from the so-called nominal believers around them.

In Mormon history, Joseph Smith's formative years illustrate this point precisely. As he records it in his 1838 "History," soon after his family moved to Palmyra, New York, in 1816: "there was in the place where we lived an unusual excitement on the subject of religion. . . . Some were contending for the Methodist faith, some for the Presbyterian, and some for the Baptist; . . . Priest contending against priest, and convert against convert."[4] This passage describes perfectly the religious excitement, competition, and confusion of a Burned-over District town in the midst of the Second Great Awakening. Energized denominational leaders preached salvation and fought for converts, but the overall effect on some—Smith included—was perplexity. "In the midst of this war of words, and tumult of opinions," he continued, "Who of all these parties are right? Or are they all wrong together?"[5] Smith's answer was that they were indeed "all wrong together," but he did not reach this conclusion through personal Bible study. His answer to the question of which denomination was right came directly from God.

In 1820, when Smith was only fourteen years old, he received his "First Vision" in what Mormons now refer to as the "Sacred Grove" near his home in Palmyra. In this vision, both God the Father and Jesus the Son appeared to Smith in a blaze of light, responding to his queries about "which of all the sects was right" with the command to "join none of them, for they were all wrong."[6] By divine fiat Smith was now denied any traditional, denominational option in his search for spiritual answers and had to rely on other sources. Over the rest of the 1820s those answers came slowly but surely through visitations from the angel Moroni, the discovery of the Golden Plates, and the translation of the *Book of Mormon,* subjects that will be treated in detail in chapter 4, "Spiritual."

The story of John Humphrey Noyes's early spiritual formation likewise reveals a dissatisfaction with antebellum Christendom, and a desire for something *more* than the standard denominational offerings. After graduating from Dartmouth in 1830 and preparing for a career in law, Noyes was converted at a revival in Putney, Vermont, in September 1831 and began his religious studies in earnest. "John, like his mother, could do nothing by halves," one early biographer perceptively writes. Accordingly, Noyes committed himself to both perpetual "ardor" and a life-long search for religious truth.[7]

But unlike Joseph Smith, the farm boy who received guidance from visions, revelations, and entirely new sacred texts, Noyes took a more traditional route for someone of his socioeconomic background, matriculating first at Andover Theological Seminary and then Yale. But as with Smith, and in spite of their educational differences, Noyes also "lost confidence in the religion around me, and saw more and more the need there was of . . . an internal reformation of Christendom." Thus, like Smith, Noyes was unsparing in his critique not just of worldly "irreligion," but of "ordinary sinful religion" from which "believers in their primary state" need further rescue. In other words, they needed *more*—in this case a second conversion that would take them from what he deemed their sinful "'double-minded' state" into the so-called "higher stage of experience," which for him was sinless Perfectionism. Only in this "stage,"

Noyes argued, would the believer be spiritually satisfied and fully united with God.⁸

For the Shakers, while it is difficult to identify what Ann Lee thought because she was illiterate and thus left no documents of her own, it is possible to see the continuity of their sectarian priorities in other Shaker documents. In 1808, more than thirty years after Lee's death in 1774, Shaker leaders published a six-hundred-page tome that, in the words of historian Stephen J. Stein, "functioned as a theological norm."⁹ In one chapter, simply titled "Worldly Christians Contrasted with Virtuous Believers in Christ," the author "sum[s] up the whole matter" with an indictment of "the Christian world" as irredeemably and "universally corrupt."¹⁰ Similarly, in 1790 when the Shakers published their first attempt at systematizing their beliefs, they gave it the unconcise title *A Concise Statement of the Principles of the Only True Church, According to the Gospel of the Present Appearance of Christ, As Held and Practiced upon by the True Followers of the Living Saviour.*¹¹ Most revealing of their sectarian understanding of themselves, obviously, are the terms "*the Only True Church*" and "*the True Followers of the Living Saviour.*"

Religious groups often think that they have a monopoly on truth and that all other groups deviate from that truth. The point of these three separate but similar critiques was for each sect to establish itself as the guardian and restorer of the one true faith. Animated by this powerful sense of right and righteousness, each of the three called upon the "worldly Christians" in their midst to quit their confusion, abandon their "ordinary sinful religion," and join them in the vanguard of this new and thrilling godly movement.

Context, however, was still crucial for the success of all three sects. The Shakers, for instance, made many converts in Ohio and Kentucky in the early 1800s. Very much like the Burned-over District of New York, the Ohio Valley was a recently settled frontier where competing religious groups found receptive audiences for their various messages. In particular, this is the time and place of the famous Cane Ridge Revival of 1801, when tens of thousands of recent settlers came together for one of the largest camp meetings in American history.

Competing with evangelical preachers at places like Cane Ridge, the Shakers won converts on the margins of the great revivals. Thomas Brown, an early convert to Shakerism (although later an apostate), describes perfectly how Shaker elders sought out people who were similarly "dissatisfied with all other denominations," and who also had the all-important "unfavourable opinion of sexual intercourse."[12] This is precisely the kind of antebellum seeker who found the standard religious options unsatisfying and wanted *more.* This is also the kind of person who eventually filled out the ranks of all three sects. These individuals were in the market for something above and beyond the typical evangelical church, and the Shakers, Mormons, and Perfectionists gave them what they were looking for. The language that each sect used reveals very small but very important keys to understanding how they conceived of themselves and their mission, and how their stories then resonated with the right kind of potential convert.

To be more specific, these sectarian emphases show up in the kinds of adjectives they used to describe themselves. Shakers, for instance, constantly talked about the requirement that "the *true* followers of Christ" keep "the faith in a *full* cross," in order to obtain "*complete* salvation and redemption" by following Mother Ann Lee, who was the first to have "taken up a *full* cross against the carnal gratifications of the flesh."[13] This crucial phrase, sometimes expanded to the "*full and final* cross" is a constant refrain in Shaker rhetoric and apparently an effective one, as it found its way from the writings of leaders into the vocabularies of converts when they recounted their testimonies.[14]

These same kinds of ideas and adjectives pepper the writings of Mormons and Perfectionists as well. For all of them the common theme is that there is something sadly incomplete in the traditional Christian story that they are going to finish and make whole. For example, sounding like the Shakers but using an unconventional spelling, Mormons often refer to the "fulness" that can be experienced only in the Mormon Church. In the 1833 *Book of Commandments,* the first Mormon effort at a systematic theology, it is written: "Thou shalt preach the *fulness* of my gospel which I have sent forth in these last days; . . . until the *fulness* of my scriptures are given."[15]

Like the Shakers and Mormons, John Humphrey Noyes also highlighted the incompleteness of the Christian story up to that time, and the need for its fulfillment. "While we assert that the New Covenant *began* to take effect at the first coming of Christ," Noyes argued in an early Perfectionist publication, "we believe its principles and powers were not *fully* developed till his second coming."[16] But writing years after both the Shakers and the Mormons, and thoroughly immersed in the already extreme environment of a spiritually awakened America, Noyes went even further. "We agree with *the most ultra* class of Perfectionists," he wrote, "that whoever is born of God is altogether free from sin."[17] In some ways, Noyes had to "out-ultra" the other "ultraists" around him, which went hand in glove with his belief in Christian Perfectionism.

In what follows in the rest of this book, it is argued that these three sects were among the most radical or "ultraist" religious groups of their day because they rejected one of the most sacred conventions of their day—monogamous sexual relations. While others among the antebellum awakened sought and achieved their spiritual bona fides by taking on other causes (alcohol consumption, prison reform, slavery, private property), these three groups laid the axe to the root of the most unquestioned orthodoxy in the Christian West by willingly violating the sexual mores of monogamous marriage.

And perhaps most radically, they violated those mores in the name of Christ. The Shakers, Mormons, and Oneida Perfectionists were not freethinking socialists like Robert Owen or Charles Fourier—reformers who also critiqued monogamy. And they were definitely not in the same camp as the later sex radicals who viewed marriage as a coercive and patriarchal institution ripe for destruction.[18] Instead, they wanted a more demanding sacrifice for their Lord and, eventually, they found it in their loins. For those seeking moral and spiritual perfection, the human sex drive was still one of the most serious impediments to holiness. True discipleship demanded nothing less than an application of spiritual truths to even these most earthly and private of human affairs.

This focus on sex also removed these three groups further from their antebellum religious counterparts, bolstering their sectarian identity as a people set apart. In such an environment of heightened and widespread religious sensibilities, how could one distinguish oneself and one's community as being the "true" Church, comprised of Christ's "perfect" disciples, entrusted with the "full" gospel of God's final revelation? Rethinking the Christian tradition's understanding of sex and marriage and then implementing alternative practices and institutions was clearly one way to stand out from the crowd.

2
Metanarrative

THERE IS a debate among scholars about the best way to define religion. Those who hold to a "substantive" definition want to explore what a particular religious tradition *is*. Those who adhere to a "functional" definition want to explore what that religious tradition *does*.[1] While the subject of this book is sex—something people either do, or refrain from doing—one of its central claims is that in religious communities people's beliefs inform and often inspire their actions. What the religious tradition *is*, in other words, leads to what the adherents of that tradition *do*. There are always exceptions of course, but my general contention is that beliefs precede actions. The majority of this book (parts 2 through 5) tells the story of those beliefs in action: their origins, struggles, practices, and declines. This chapter is going to introduce as thoroughly as possible the religious metanarratives of the Mormons, the Shakers, and the Oneida Perfectionists.

These are the stories in which both the leaders and the followers in these movements cast themselves as characters. As sectarians, they embraced a unique understanding of the world's past, present, and eternal future and of the role they could play in the unfolding drama. As moral actors suspended between the beginning and the end, they could help shape the outcome through lives of devotion, obedience, discipline, and sacrifice. For us to understand them and their unique sexual practices, we must therefore first understand their stories.

What Mormons, Shakers, and Oneida Perfectionists emphasized in reconceptualizing the sacred past might be surprising. Since all three claimed to be a new revelation within the broader Christian tradition, one might expect for them to focus on Jesus and the New Testament. One might also expect them to spend time reflecting on God and God's properties. But what instead seemed to matter greatly to these sects was matter itself. Inspiring as much reflection and theological innovation as the mysteries of God were the mysteries of materiality. Where did matter come from? What were its properties? How should the immortal and immaterial soul relate to the perishable and material world? Was matter created by God, or did it predate God? What was matter's story? What was its history, and what was its relationship to the divine? These are the kinds of questions that Mormons, Shakers, and Oneida Perfectionists confronted with radical and unsettling answers.

For Shakers, the story of humankind's Creation and Fall generally follows the outline set forth in the first three chapters of Genesis, with one very important plot twist. Everyone knows that humanity's parents failed their first test in obedience, but Shakers add a fascinating explanation for why it turned out that way. "It was not an apple," Frederick W. Evans wrote dismissively: "Have we sinned eating apples? . . . The Fall of Man consists in disorderly social [i.e., sexual] relationship. . . . The serpent, according to the original, was the sensuous nature of man—the passions—that was the serpent."[2] *The* original sin, Shakers believe, was sex, with "the serpent"—a thinly veiled metaphor for a penis—being "the sensuous nature of man." This is the foundation of Shaker theology, beginning with Ann Lee's 1770 revelation, and still powerfully informing the community a full century later when Evans wrote these words in 1871. The details of this radical theological innovation, however, needed to be both spelled out and defended over the course of those hundred years in more formal theological iterations.

An important question for Shakers lingered: *why* was sex the original sin? As we will see in part 2 on "Geneses," Ann Lee had very traumatic experiences with sex and childbirth. These personal and psychological origins of Shaker sexual doctrines have been known and speculated about since the founding of the community. Theologically speaking, though, how exactly did Shakers explain why sex was not just a sin, but *the* sin? Part of the answer has to do with their Manichean outlook on life, with sex as a powerful human drive, rivaling God, and orienting His would-be followers (starting with Adam and Eve) away from spiritual worship and toward sensual, animal self-indulgence.

The other major reason why Shakers anathematize sex, however, has to do with the dual function of sex: procreation and pleasure. As the Shakers articulated it more clearly over the years, the true and God-given purpose of sex was procreation and procreation alone. In some ways they were forced to maneuver into this theological stance because critics often asked them what they were to make of God's prelapsarian command to Adam and Eve to "be fruitful and multiply,"[3] obviously implying that God approved of their having sex before the Fall. Shakers responded that "the power of generation was given to man solely for the purpose of procreation, and not for the gratification of his animal nature."[4] Humankind's conflicted, dual purpose for sex—species procreation and sensual gratification—reflected their conflicted, dual nature: spiritual on the one hand, and animal on the other. The problem, therefore, was not with God's command but with Adam and Eve's inability to heed their superior spiritual side, and thus be obedient to the command. In this sense the Shakers rescued themselves from making God the author of evil: ordering His creatures to engage in the very sinful act that He forbade. Instead they shifted the blame to humanity's all-too-human first parents, an interpretation that moved them closer to the Judeo-Christian tradition's "orthodox" answer to the problem of evil, but one that differed greatly from the Mormon metanarrative.

Mormon cosmology is intricate, beautiful, and utterly fascinating. As the Mormon historian Richard Bushman puts it, "No other nineteenth-century religious imagination filled time and space with stories like these."[5] If the Shakers took the familiar Creation story from Genesis and reinterpreted it, the Mormons almost completely rewrote it. This rewriting took many years to flesh out, but in the end the Latter-day Saints adhered to a radically different understanding of God, man, and matter and of how the three have related in both time and eternity.

On April 7, 1844, a mere two and a half months before his death, Joseph Smith crystalized the Mormon metanarrative in his *King Follett Discourse,* a funeral oration for a prominent elder who had died in a random and tragic accident. For "the consolation of those who mourn for the loss of their friends," he exhorted, "it is necessary that we should understand the character and being of God and how he came to be so; for I am going to tell you how God came to be God."[6] This was the story—God's story—that Smith dared to tell. In order to do this, though, he had to take his listeners "back to the beginning—to the morn of creation."[7] And then he surprised everyone, boldly pushing Latter-day Saint theology far outside of anything American Christians had ever seen or believed before. "*God himself was once as we are now, and is an exalted man,*" Smith explained, "*and sits enthroned in yonder heavens! That is the great secret.*"[8] As the Mormon prophet Lorenzo Snow expressed it even more succinctly and memorably: "As man now is, God once was; as God now is, man may become."[9]

It is impossible to overstate the importance of this Mormon belief in eternal progression—in God's prior humanity, and in humankind's potential advancement to divinity after death. One obvious implication is that instead of being radically different—the divine Creator and the earthly created—God and human beings share a common nature and even a common materiality. As Smith had recorded in a revelation on April 2, 1843: "The Father has a body of flesh and bones as tangible as man's."[10] And as he had once stated even more adamantly: "there is no other God in heaven but that God who has flesh and bones. . . . We came to this earth that we might have a body and present it pure before God in the Celestial Kingdom. The great principle of happiness consists in having a body."[11] This belief in a common materiality, or common bodies, also had important implications for Mormon beliefs about what God and human beings should do with those bodies, including having sex. There were many ways to be obedient, in other words, and progress in divinity. Sex, it turns out, was one of the most important ways, not merely because bodies and the sex drive are powerful instruments that need to be stewarded responsibly, but because they hold within them the divine power of procreation.

These Mormon beliefs about bodies, materiality, sexuality, exaltation to godhood, and procreation as a crucial part of that exaltation all relate to the Mormon doctrine of Creation. "In the beginning," Smith explained in the *King Follett Discourse,* "the head of the Gods called a council of the Gods; and they came together and concocted a plan to create the world and people it." But what matters at least as much as Joseph's departure from monotheism is what he says about the primordial act of Creation itself. The "word *create*," he explained, "does not mean to create out of nothing; it means to organize; the same as a man would organize materials and build a ship. Hence we infer that God had materials to organize the world out of chaos—chaotic matter, which is element, and in which dwells all the glory. Element had an existence from the time he had."[12] Matter is just as eternal as the omnipotent God. The Judeo-Christian tradition posits an immutable, uncreated, and eternal God who brought the universe into existence out of nothing, or ex nihilo. Mormons, on the other hand, believe that it is instead the universe's raw materials, "element, . . . in which dwells all the glory," that had always existed. The divine being who ultimately became "the head of the Gods" with all of the powers thereunto appertaining, had also always existed, but was not always omnipotent. Instead, God the Father achieved that preeminent status and those enhanced divine powers through the process of organizing eternal matter into the universe as it currently exists. God therefore has a history, changing over time to become God. Human beings likewise can change over time through the very same processes of obedience, organization, and procreation to one day become gods as well. Thus, rather than an unbridgeable divide between the divine, spiritual Creator and the human, material creature, Mormons see a continuum, with both sharing eternal life, a material substance, and a set of valued activities, just in different degrees rather than of different kinds.

In addition to believing that matter, or "element" is eternal—and this is highly significant—Mormons likewise believe that human souls, also referred to as "intelligences," are eternal and have an existence prior to their earthly connection to mortal human bodies. "Ye were also in the beginning with the Father," Smith proclaimed. "Intelligence, or the light of truth, was not created or made, neither indeed can be."[13] Like both the matter that makes up the universe, and "the head of the Gods" who organized that matter into the universe, individual human souls have always existed and always will. They were not created, neither are they capable of being destroyed.

This belief in the preexistence of the human soul is part of the elaborate Mormon "plan of salvation" and requires some explanation. When it comes to the inert, but still eternal material universe, the overall story looks like this:

Eternal/Uncreated Matter + God's Organization → Universe

When it comes to living, similarly eternal human souls, the overall story looks like this:

Premortality

Eternal/Uncreated Human Intelligences + Spiritual Procreation between Heavenly Father and Heavenly Mother → Spirit Children in Spirit Bodies

Getting to Earth

Physical Procreation between an Earthly Father and Mother allows Spirit Children to Inhabit Physical Bodies and Exercise Agency in Mortal Life on Earth

Earthly Probation and the Afterlife

Spirit Children in Physical Bodies with Agency + Obedience and the Temple Ordinances → Rewards in One of the Three Eternal Kingdoms (Celestial, Terrestrial, Telestial)

The Mormon metanarrative is more complicated than these schematics make out. There are, for example, no fewer than five temple ordinances required for exaltation in the Celestial Kingdom: baptism, confirmation, priesthood ordination for men, the endowment ceremony, and marital sealing.[14] Similarly, some of the doctrinal details of this metanarrative (the existence of Heavenly Mother in particular) were added later, including some after Joseph Smith's death.

In this "plan of salvation," in time immemorial, uncreated human "intelligences" shared their eternal preexistence with the foremost divine intelligence who would in time become God. Heavenly Father and Heavenly Mother then have to procreate and provide these intelligences with spirit bodies, which will allow them to progress to the next stage of their premortal existence. As the Mormon scholar Charles R. Harrell writes in a substantial exposition of this religious belief: "The doctrine that God, through a procreative act involving a heavenly mother, is the literal father of our spirits expresses *the most fundamental and important relationship between God and humankind in LDS theology.*"[15] Obviously this unique LDS belief about God's procreative—rather than merely creative—activity will be important for understanding Mormon beliefs about sex.

In the next phase of the plan of salvation, just as the intelligences need divine procreation to inhabit spirit bodies, so they need human procreation to inhabit physical bodies and continue their journeys. Being able to inhabit physical bodies is important because, as Mormons believe, mortal existence is a test, the life-long placement exam for the hereafter. It is where individuals, exercising their personal agency and behaving either obediently or not, decide for themselves how they will spend eternity. This is what Mormons refer to as the "second estate" of an individual soul's journey, the "first estate" being premortal life as intelligences and spirit children.

Adam and Eve are still major characters in this story and this overall "plan of salvation," but not in the way one might expect. Surprisingly, it is actually *through* their original sin that humankind received its agency. Thus rather than bewailing his disobedience and its resulting curse, Adam exults: "Blessed be the name of God, for *because* of my transgression my eyes are opened, and in this life I shall have joy."[16] This fortunate fall was God's intention from the beginning. "And it *must needs be*," *Doctrine and Covenants* 29 records, "that the devil should tempt the children of men, or they could not be agents unto themselves; for if they never should have bitter they could not know the sweet."[17] And in the most beautiful and succinct summary of the beginning of the plan of salvation, the *Book of Mormon* reads: "Adam fell that men might be; and men are that they might have joy."[18] Rather than being humankind's momentous ur-tragedy, Adam and Eve made a heroic choice, disobeying the "lesser law" of God's prohibition on the Tree of Knowledge, "in order to comply with a higher law" that would allow for human agency, "joy," and the "bitter" as well as "the sweet" of mortal human life.[19]

Perhaps most significantly, Adam and Eve's original sin also allowed them to have children. "And now, behold, if Adam had not transgressed," the *Book of Mormon* proclaims: "they would have had no children; wherefore they would have remained in a state of innocence, having no joy, for they knew no misery; doing no good, for they knew no sin." While free from the possibility of spiritual death, life before the Fall was static and incapable of procreation. Because of their disobedience, Adam and Eve were now capable of having biological children who would provide God's spirit children with the mortal bodies they needed to advance to exaltation through the righteous exercise of their agency. Again, rather than grieving her sin, the Eve of the LDS Creation narrative is "glad, saying: Were it not for our transgression we never should have had seed, and never should have known good and evil."[20] It is through Adam and Eve that human beings received the agency by which they choose either good or evil, and likewise received the bodies that would allow them a mortal and procreative life of obedience or disobedience, and an eternal afterlife of either alienation from God or exaltation to godhood.

If the place to begin understanding the Mormons and Shakers is with their doctrine of Creation and Fall, for the Oneida Perfectionists it is with their doctrine of Christ's Second Coming. Prodded by his seminary studies at Yale but inspired even more by intense personal Bible study, John Humphrey Noyes reached the conclusion that Christ had already returned in glory to usher in the final dispensation of the kingdom of God on earth. Reflecting further, Noyes came to understand that the precise date of Christ's Second Coming was the Romans' destruction of Jerusalem in A.D. 70.

According to Noyes, what exactly transpired in A.D. 70 was Christ's "primary resurrection and judgment of the spiritual world."[21] The destruction of Jerusalem not only violently ended the Jewish dispensation and inaugurated the Christian one, but also judged and split the Church into two parts: "Visible Christendom," which was imperfect, compromised, and ripe for judgment; and the "Resurrection Church," which although invisible, was perfect and was coming back into view through Noyes and his doctrine of Christian Perfectionism. Sometime soon, he warned, Christ would return to finish the judgment that He had started. Those in "Visible Christendom" would suffer wrath while his sectarian "Resurrection Church" would be rewarded for its faithfulness.

This radical rewriting of the Christian metanarrative was the theological wellspring from which the rest of Noyes's ideas flowed. Noyes himself admitted that he "did not at once perceive with much distinctness the bearings which this discovery was to have on the whole range of my theological views,"[22] but the "discovery" did powerfully affect all of them. As his nephew and biographer, George Wallingford Noyes, would later sum up: "Noyes's theory of the second coming was the key to his theology and consequently a most powerful factor in shaping his career."[23] Armed with this novel insight, Noyes continued his debate with orthodoxy and "Visible Christendom." Later he would go public with his doctrines of Perfectionism, biblical communism, and complex marriage, but they all originated from and fit within the context of his revised understanding of Jesus' return in A.D. 70 to judge and divide the Church.

Regarding the Church, all three sects made early Church history central to the stories they told about themselves. In particular all three adhered to a common sectarian plot: that while Jesus and the disciples were on the right path (at least as reported in the gospels and book of Acts), something went terribly wrong soon after the New Testament witness concluded. This now corrupted and incomplete version of Christianity had sadly eclipsed God's real intention for His Church for nearly 1,800 years. Not even the Protestant Reformation in the sixteenth century had returned Christians to the purity of the early Church. Instead, it was up to these new religious leaders and communities to fulfill God's long-lost plan for humanity, and restore the "full," "true," and "complete" gospel. Each leader also grounded his or her claim to personal religious authority in the ability to clearly perceive—whether through divine revelation or mere perspicacity—what this "pure" and "spiritual" Church was supposed to look like. The "primitive church" as they often called it, was for them both their authority and their model for building the kingdom of God on earth. All three therefore had in common a desire to return and restore. All three differed, however, in their understanding of where the early Church had gone wrong and in what they thought modern believers needed to do to regain the primitive Church's closeness with God.

Of the three, the Mormon narrative of unfaithfulness—called unsparingly the "Great Apostasy" in modern LDS theology—is by far the most complicated and involved. The precise nature of this first-century apostasy is not spelled out in great detail in either Joseph Smith's writings or today. At its most vague it is described as "a period of gospel perversion, spiritual darkness, and loss of priesthood authority." At its most specific, Mormon scholar Todd Compton writes, "some have put the blame exclusively on Greek philosophy and the influence of philosophy on Gnosticism for the rise of the great apostasy," but apparently even this is disputed.[24]

What matters is that there was a profound deviation from God's plan, a corresponding loss of divine authority, and most importantly a reestablishment of that plan and that authority through a series of divine revelations to Joseph Smith in the early nineteenth century. Thus in addition to being complex, this alternate narrative is also intertwined with the life and experiences of Joseph Smith, and in particular with the reestablishment of the authority of the Aaronic and Melchizedek priesthoods, a crucial part of the story that will be told more thoroughly in the fourth chapter, "Spiritual."

The Shakers are even more emphatic in their declension narrative, and definitely more precise. For centuries, according to their version of the story, Christ's followers were so faithful that they could serve as spiritual exemplars for modern believers. "Let Christians look back to the history of primitive Christianity as recorded in the New Testament," Richard McNemar exhorted in 1807, "the plain and native simplicity which shines out there; . . . and let them pant to breathe that native air."[25] Then, of course, things went wrong. Some early Christians departed from the truth in both their beliefs and their behavior, and tragic consequences followed. Exactly like the Mormons, the Shakers linked early Church faithfulness to God's blessings. When the former stopped, so did the latter. "When the primitive church fell and lost the revelation of the Holy Spirit, and blended their doctrines with the principles of the world, the power of the true gospel of Christ was withdrawn from it."[26] Again, thus far the Shaker morality tale about the early Church sounds very much like that of the Mormons.

But unlike the Mormons, the Shakers are far more exact about when and why the early Church lost its way. As former Shaker Hervey Elkins summarized in 1853: "The Shakers believe that Christ, or the divine unction, left the earth at the union of Church and state under the dominion of Leo the Great, about 450 years after the Christian era."²⁷ Leo I, or Leo the Great, was bishop of Rome from 440 to 461 during two important transitions in the life of the young Church. The first was presiding over the Eternal City while the powers of the state crumbled around him. In between the sack of Rome in 410 and the Visigoths' final nail in the coffin in 476, the Church had to take over more mundane functions as the empire lost the ability to do so. Thus, from the Shaker perspective, it was not the Christianization of the empire under Constantine in 313 that was so reprehensible, but the imperialization of the Church under Leo. That is when Christians first tasted worldly power and the corruptions that accompanied it.²⁸

But Shakers also believed that Pope Leo I presided over an even more despicable theological development that has misled Christians ever since. The Council of Chalcedon in 451 (Shakers mistakenly focus on 457) resolved the debate in Christology about how the divine and human natures are combined in Jesus Christ. The "Definition of faith" that emerged from Chalcedon and that has become orthodox doctrine ever since is that there are two natures in one person and that Jesus is both perfect in divinity and perfect in humanity.²⁹ For the Shakers, what was most unacceptable was the affirmation that Jesus possessed a material body. "Every discerning person will doubtless acknowledge that the flesh is a clog to the spirit," Shaker theologians proclaimed, "that the body is a clog to the soul."³⁰ The Shakers therefore anathematized the idea that Jesus was sullied with such a physical "clog." As the second edition of the Shakers' *Summary View* explains: "Here we find the origin of this antichristian doctrine of *two distinct natures in Christ*, so generally maintained by the reputed orthodox professors of Christianity, not from Christ, but from Leo, the first sovereign prince of Antichrist."³¹ Under Pope Leo I, the "real reign and dominion of Antichrist then commenced," not to be broken until the advent of Ann Lee in the late eighteenth century.³²

Like the Shakers, Noyes was admirably specific about when he thought things started to go wrong for the Church—A.D. 70—and which more pristine era modern Christians should look to for answers. In some ways Noyes and the Perfectionists elevated this romanticized "primitive church" from being a mere model of religious life into being one of their ultimate authorities, almost equal with the Omnipotent. As he praised it: "The invisible primitive church is, in reality, what the Roman church falsely pretends to be,—holy, apostolic, catholic, mother-church." It is in other words the one true Church with him as its high priest. He even gave his 1847 manifesto, *The Berean,* the subtitle *A Manual for the Help of Those Who Seek the Faith of the Primitive Church,* concluding its five hundred pages with an exhortation that readers endeavor to "*Open communication with the Primitive Church.*" Those who want to change the world for Christ, he enjoined, should not look to reform visible institutions like the church, the law, or slavery, but should instead unite themselves with the invisible, perfect, and ultimately authoritative primitive church. Thus, like the Shakers and the Mormons, John Humphrey Noyes discredited the authoritative claims of both Catholicism and Protestantism, carving out instead a sectarian identity legitimated by its connection to the unsullied early Church. As one especially in touch with that early and now lost Church, John Humphrey Noyes—like Joseph Smith and Mother Ann Lee—was thus spiritually qualified to teach, to lead, and to discern "the 'deep things of God,'" with marriage, sex, and the family among the deepest mysteries of all.[33]

3

Marriage

Now the stage is set to get to the heart of the matter. Only after we have entered into the mental worlds of these three sects—their spiritual hunger for *more* and their elaborate religious *metanarratives*—do their unorthodox sexual practices make sense. In fact, I hope that after this thorough contextual introduction, their sexual practices will make perfect sense. This chapter will simply explain what each of the three sects believed about the specific subjects of marriage, the family, the sex act, and the sex organs.

Of the three, the Mormons held marriage and the family in the highest esteem. As the historian Lawrence Foster writes: "To an almost unparalleled extent, the Mormon religion really was *about* the family; earthly and heavenly family ideals were seen as identical."[1] While important, the other institutions of this earth—cities, nations, even LDS meetinghouses and temples—will all pass away. Families, however, will endure for eternity. In Joseph Smith's most mature theological articulations not long before his death, the picture of heaven was neither individual nor even ecclesiastical, but familial instead.

This familial vision of heaven created powerful earthly incentives for Latter-day Saints. Mormons would not spend eternity worshipping their Creator, but would rather become divine creators and rulers themselves. Sharing in the godlike power to procreate, or "enlarge" as the 1843 revelation on celestial marriage puts it, was the highest degree of exaltation a Saint could hope to enjoy—a greatest good that obviously required Mormon men and women to partner with one another in marriage.[2] While individuals would experience salvation, the "fulness" of exaltation was only for the eternally married, whether monogamously or polygamously. "Then shall they be gods," Joseph recorded, "because they have no end."[3] The Church has officially abandoned plural marriage for monogamy, but the doctrine of eternal marriage is still central to LDS orthodoxy and orthopraxy. Marriage and family are as foundational to Mormon faith and life today as they were in the 1840s, imbued with both eternal significance and a certain earthly urgency.

In the Mormon metanarrative mortal life is a probationary period, with marriage being one of the most important items in the pre-exaltation checklist. Although Mormon marriages endure into the afterlife, it is only during life on earth that people can be united, or eternally "sealed" in the institution of celestial marriage, thereby ensuring for themselves the highest degree of exaltation. The sealing ceremony is a physical ordinance that must be conducted between partners in the flesh, preferably in a physical Mormon temple. Joseph Smith agreed with Jesus' words in Luke 20:35, that those worthy to obtain "the resurrection from the dead, neither marry, nor are given in marriage." (As we will see, this verse was even more foundational for the Shakers and Oneida Perfectionists.) After death one cannot enter into marriage. Good Mormons must therefore experience the all-important ordinance of sealing in this life only. Marriage not just for time but for eternity was the means by which they could become gods.

Unsurprisingly, when it came to plural marriage this vision of the afterlife inspired a kind of otherworldly ambition, especially in men. One earnest but hapless Saint, for instance, "had heard it said frequently by the high-priests, that if a man could not rule his earthly kingdom, he would never be fitted to be a king in the world to come. As he was very ambitious for regal honors, he was in great grief, and much perplexed, how to govern two unruly, contentious, and exasperated women."[4] In other cases, "Some of the Mormon brethren are so anxious to increase their kingdom that they frequently have very old ladies sealed to them."[5] As further evidence will show, Mormon men from Joseph Smith until the abandonment of polygamy in 1890 sought through their plural marriages a worldly status that would translate into even greater heavenly rewards.

Many Mormon women also thought about plural marriage with a combination of otherworldly ambition and fear. If the enticement of becoming heavenly royalty was not enough to convince some hesitant women, there was always the threat of punishment and God's displeasure. Orson Pratt, the foremost apologist for plural marriage after its announcement in 1852, made sure to include "a few words to unmarried females in this church . . . you can never obtain a fulness of glory without being married to a righteous man for time and for all eternity."[6] Other Mormon men were overtly threatening. Joseph Smith's revelation on plural marriage in 1843 calls out by name his first wife Emma, admonishing her that "if she will not abide this commandment she shall be destroyed saith the Lord."[7] Brigham Young likewise wooed one of his wives with the warning that "if she married anyone else she would be damned." Instead, he assured her: "If you marry me, I will save you, and exalt you to be a queen in the celestial world; but if you refuse, you will be destroyed, both soul and body."[8] There were obviously high eternal stakes for Mormon marriages. Like mortal life itself, marriage was a test that one could either pass or fail.

But in addition to being an eternal institution, marriage was also an earthly one in which the partners could demonstrate either their obedience or their selfishness. Plural marriage was an even greater sacrifice, demanding that women abandon any exclusive claim to their husbands. "It tried my spirit to its utmost endurance," one woman wrote in 1884 about her husband's decision to take a second wife, "but I always believed the principle to be true, and felt it was time we obeyed the sacred order. The Lord knew my heart and desires, . . . and assisted me to overcome the selfishness and jealousy of my nature."[9] Chapter 14, "Gender," will describe the turmoil both women and men experienced as they wrestled with, but ultimately "obeyed the sacred order" as this Saint did. What this passage illustrates most clearly, however, is the injunction against selfishness, and the countervailing admonition to do one's religious duty. "The argument was lucid, and it appealed to the grandest sentiment of humanity—self-abnegation," one ex-Mormon lamented. In spite of the "women who viewed with the most searching jealousy the wandering of her idol's love, . . . it was *her duty* to make her life a sacrifice." The purpose, or "*duty*," of marriage was to procreate, and thus provide physical bodies for the spirit children "anxiously waiting" in the premortal realm.[10]

The institution of marriage for Mormons, therefore, was an earthly means to several spiritual ends. Through their sealed and eternal unions, partners could ensure for themselves the promise of exaltation; while through their sexual activity they could ensure for premortal souls the bodies they needed to enter the second estate of existence and begin their earthly probation. "God is very anxious that these spirits should be provided with bodies," former Mormon Maria Ward explained, "and as the spirits themselves are very anxious to get down here, it became the duty of all true believers to lend their aid and produce bodies as fast as possible."[11] When compared to such lofty, ultimate, and eternal spiritual aims, the more mundane concerns of romantic fulfillment, sexual satisfaction, and selfish personal happiness clearly paled in comparison. Although there is an emphasis within Mormonism on human happiness and joy, there is a stoic side to the faith as well. As later chapters will illustrate, as the nineteenth century progressed, duty increasingly replaced joy as a motivation to marry polygamously.

Regarding sex in particular, the Saints argued that the "lusts and desires of the flesh are not of themselves unmitigated evils." Consistent with their roots in Judeo-Christianity, Mormons believed that sex should only take place within the context of marriage. As they saw it, providing a legitimate place for sexual partnership is one of marriage's most important functions. But by far *the* most important function of sex—for clearly stated theological reasons—is procreation.[12]

Defenders of plural marriage were therefore always quick to point out that male lust was never the motivation outside critics claimed it was. In contrast to the sensationalist images of "the Mormon seraglio" and "licentious intercourse" that enemies of the Saints employed to gin up hostility,[13] Mormon leaders such as Brigham Young countered that the purpose of plural marriage had always been to "raise up a holy nation," and "not to gratify lustful passion in the least."[14] The purpose of sex with multiple partners was to increase and multiply, not indulge. Even some of the more neutral non-Mormon observers of polygamy reported that the practice hardly resembled the "oriental" harems that people might imagine. In 1852 Army Lieutenant J. W. Gunnison reported that LDS leaders in Utah strongly encouraged plural marriage to be "a pure and holy state; and religious motives or a sense of duty, should alone guide; and that for sensual gratifications it is an abomination."[15] Lieutenant Gunnison still had misgivings about polygamy, but his analysis was ultimately charitable, fair, and largely accurate. While sexual attraction clearly played a role in Mormon men's decision to take an additional wife or wives, the main motivations were religious: the desire to experience exaltation in the Celestial Kingdom; the desire to provide physical bodies to premortal spirit children; and the desire to raise up a "righteous seed" while on earth.

Whereas the Mormons were more interested in marriage and family as eternal procreative institutions, the Shakers and Oneida Perfectionists focused more directly on the sex act and the sex organs. At first glance there are obvious and profound differences between the Shakers and the Perfectionists. The former esteemed asceticism so much that they felt uneasy about even the most trifling of worldly pleasures. If an activity was not overtly spiritual it was often condemned. The Oneida Perfectionists, on the other hand, valued worldly pleasures as gifts from God, and embraced sex in particular as a means of spiritual rather than carnal fellowship. But these differences in worldview and lifestyle belie some truly fascinating similarities.

As radical Protestants, both the Shakers and the Perfectionists had many of the same theological foundations. Both took the Bible very seriously. Both also longed passionately to bring heaven down to earth. In fact, scripturally speaking, it is safe to say that *the* theological starting point for each community can be found in Jesus' words in the Lord's prayer: "Thy kingdom come, Thy will be done in earth, as it is in heaven."[16] Both sects referenced this verse in the Gospel of Matthew as the raison d'être of their radical biblical communities, sometimes giving special emphasis to the phrase "IN EARTH."[17] Even John Humphrey Noyes himself lumped the two very different communities together with this common spiritual denominator, writing "that the Shakers, like the Bible Communists [the Oneida Community], have attempted to realize *here, now, on earth*, what they believe to be the social order of the heavens."[18]

Shakers and Oneida Perfectionists actually agreed on the institution of marriage as well, and used the same biblical passages to reach their conclusions. For starters, they reasoned, neither Jesus Christ nor the Apostle Paul ever married. Equally important is what both Jesus and Paul said about marriage. In Luke 20:27–40 the Sadducees confront Jesus with the scenario of a woman who had married seven brothers before her death. "Therefore in the resurrection whose wife of them is she?" they ask. Jesus' response is the foundational scripture for both the Shakers' and the Perfectionists' understanding of marriage: "The children of this world marry, and are given in marriage: but they which shall be accounted worthy to obtain that world, and the resurrection from the dead, neither marry, nor are given in marriage."[19] That was as straightforward a proof text as anyone could hope to find, and both the Shakers and the Oneida Perfectionists referenced it often in defending their decision to abolish the institution of monogamous marriage. In the Christian world to come, they argued, there are no marital unions. Therefore neither should there be in this world. As Noyes put it bluntly in a pivotal early document: "When the will of God is done on earth as it is in heaven, there will be no marriage."[20]

Precisely why the Shakers and Oneida Perfectionists disliked marriage so much is a bit surprising. The two obviously differ on the subject of sex, but when it came to monogamy, both judged it harshly according to a shared standard. Rather than seeing monogamous marriage as a lifelong institution that can potentially prune away one's selfishness as one learns to love and sacrifice for one's partner, the Shakers and Perfectionists saw it instead as the very pinnacle of selfishness, or as Noyes memorably called it, "Egotism for Two."[21] One mid-century Shaker best explained the rationale for this condemnation. "Natural man first loves himself," he wrote: "then his wife,—his children,—his neighborhood,—his state,—his country,—his race. But when he receives the love of God in Christ, his love extends to all the intelligent creation of God, whether in or out of the body. Love leads him to 'hate his wife, his children, and his own life also.' (See Luke, xiv.26.)"[22] In this scheme, the love of the "natural man" is a set of concentric circles, anchored in the self and then radiating out to include first the man's wife and family, and only then to larger bodies of people, becoming not only less intimate but also presumably less caring as the circles expand. Having spent so much energy on the self and the innermost circles, the natural man's love dissipates with distance, like heat diminishing the farther one steps from a fire. Christian love, however, is supposed to reverse this arrangement. Moving from the outside in, the follower of Christ is called first and foremost to a universal love of "all the intelligent creation of God," and then not just to a diminution of special loves (spouse, children, self) but to an outright repudiation of them. Indeed, as the referenced passage from Luke makes clear, the Christian man is called instead to "hate" the closer he gets to the self's center: "his wife, his children, and his own life also." This is, without a doubt, one of the harder sayings of Jesus, and for their part the Shakers loved it.

John Humphrey Noyes was similarly unsparing in his assault on "the selfish family spirit." "There is no point on which the gospel of Christ is more at variance with the ideas and spirit of the world," he maintained, "than in regard to the family relation."[23]

Over and over again he laid out his dichotomous view of the selfish and individualistic powers of this world versus the unselfish and communistic kingdom of God. In Christianity, the "*I-spirit*" is supposed to be replaced by the "*we-spirit.*"[24] Marriage is obviously a partnership—a "we" and not an "I"—but Noyes concluded that "marriage itself is only egotism for two—the same thing on a little larger scale."[25] Only in Christian communism, Noyes held, where the individual's exclusive claim to both property and persons has been abolished and absorbed into the group, are the true followers of Christ liberated to experience fully the selfless and universal love of the kingdom of God.

Thus far Noyes recognized the striking similarities between his community and the Shakers. "In respect to their estimate of marriage," he commended, "we think that the Shakers nearer right than the popular churches. We agree with them in regard to the necessity of its abolishment." If—as all good Christians presumably should—one begins with the desire to see God's kingdom come "on earth as it is in heaven"; and if one believes that the scriptures are clear about the absence of marriage in heaven; then one must conclude that neither should marriage exist on earth. Only the Shakers and Perfectionists, Noyes argued, and decidedly not "the popular churches," have had the courage to make this dramatic move and abolish the ancient, selfish institution. The obvious question that then arose, however, was what to do about sex, and on this the Shakers and Perfectionists went in dramatically different directions.

"We would now seriously ask, Whence proceeds all this shame?" the 1823 Shaker *Summary View* asked.[26] As this important early Shaker document explained: "*shame . . . is generally found to be inseparable from the act of sexual coition.*" That was the Shaker conclusion on the matter: sex and shame are "*inseparable.*" Because sex has its beginning in animal lust rather than godly obedience, it is simply incapable of being part of the life of faith. Nor does the institution of marriage sanctify the sex act. "Is there any real difference between the married and the unmarried?" the *Summary View* continues. "If so, why is not the shame removed from the action?" This is why sex, even within marriage, takes place "in the shades of darkness,"[27] and why, after their disobedience, Adam and Eve hid their sex organs from each other, themselves, and their God. And the same has been true of men and women ever since: "That the works of the flesh are an abomination, all men of common decency bear witness, by scrupulously concealing them."[28] Sex, whether inside or outside of marriage breeds shame: shame about both the sex act and the sex organs.

The Shakers went a step further, however, in their understanding of sexual shame, singling out the sex organs for special treatment. The origin of sin was lust, and the bodily origin of that lust were male and female genitalia. As a consequence, in their ongoing war of the spirit against the flesh, Shakers sometimes literally targeted the sex organs of people in their communities. For example, one early Shaker apostate reported on "the mother's pounding and beating the private parts of both men and women in her discipline"; while another "young man" ordered "his father to strip in the midst of a large room full of people both men and women, then seizing him by his private members, hauling him this way and that by them, chastising him aloud for his old heavens and lust, and then taking him up and setting him upon his head and shoulders, heels upwards, then by force wrenching his naked thighs apart and taking him again by his members, and handling them in the view of all present, every way exposing his father to the utmost shame."[29] Although this sensationalist account of early Shaker sadism comes from a biased source, the historian Stephen J. Stein concludes that it is nevertheless credible. "The Shaker obsession with overcoming lust may have led the Believers to practice severe forms of public mortification," he writes. "In that context the charge that Ann Lee pummeled the private parts of her followers as a frenzied act of ascetic discipline cannot be dismissed."[30]

This Shaker war on genitalia also took on masochistic tones. Reuben Rathbone, an eighteenth-century apostate, wrote that in their efforts "to mortify the flesh . . . some were so violent in their labors . . . that there was not much power of erection in the parts of generation." But sadly, whatever this "arduous work" was that male Shakers were practicing, it still did not yield the fruit they desired, and "they were more subject to involuntary evacuations than they were before." Presumably the young men of his Shaker community were experiencing nocturnal emissions, or "wet dreams" as they are called today. In addition to being somewhat salacious, this window into an eighteenth-century Shaker community reveals both the intensity with which the Believers struggled against their flesh, and the outright loathing they had for their bodies (penises in particular) and most revoltingly to them, their semen: that "most unclean and hateful of any thing in the natural creation." These "involuntary evacuations" were warnings—terrifying reminders—that they were not winning the war against the flesh.[31]

This Shaker hatred of penises also informed their theology. Shakers made an understandable connection between circumcision and "the full and final cross" of celibacy. Submitting to circumcision was doubtlessly a painful physical ordeal for male Israelites. This sacrificial practice, however, was only a physical foreshadowing of what would happen spiritually with the full revelation of God's plan in Christ. Under the old covenant, God's people were called to mutilate their penises. Under the new covenant, they were called to abandon using them for sex entirely. "This seal of the typical covenant made with Abraham," the 1823 *Summary View* explained, "was the most lively figure ever given to man, of the mortification of the very source of iniquity." The "spiritual work of Christ," however, is to entail "the complete destruction of that carnal pleasure received from that source, in the act of sexual coition. . . . This is the very foundation of the true cross of Christ, and the separating line between 'the children of this world'" and the real followers of Jesus.[32]

This undeniably difficult "true cross of Christ," or "circumcision of Christ in the heart," is also why Shakers believed they were right and all the other churches were wrong. The life and ministry of Jesus Christ, the Shakers reminded their detractors, "has left us the example of total abstinence from sexual intercourse."[33] This is a hard teaching, and one that the compromised members of "the various sects and denominations of the so-called Christian world" clearly could not abide.[34] Displaying obvious disdain for the ecclesiastical order of their day, the Shakers condemned "all those preachers of the various denominations who approbate that work [marriage and procreation], as being consistent with Christianity."[35] They "may be called Presbyterians, Episcopalians, Baptists, Methodists, or what not," the *Summary View* seethed, "yet so long as they live in the works of the first Adam, and follow his example, they do not follow Christ."[36]

Being included among "the true followers of Christ," Shakers maintained, entailed one thing and one thing only: "a full and final cross against their lustful passions."[37] Shaker documents emphasize this over and over again, and testimonies from both practicing and lapsed Believers repeat the phrase, making it clear that they had internalized the mantra. "Here then is the substance of the true virgin life," the *Summary View* concluded: "Here is the hatred which constitutes a true christian [sic] disciple, and the blessing which follows it. A full and final cross against the carnal nature of the flesh, and a hatred of that life, with all those affections and lusts which have a natural tendency to indulge and gratify it."[38] Notice again the centrality of "hatred" to the Shakers' sectarian definition of what "constitutes a true christian [sic] disciple." The root problem was not with marriage but with sex. The United Society of Believers abolished both, but sex was the more spiritually threatening of the two. Marriage, which one Shaker sardonically called "the most darling practice of the world," was precisely that—worldly—and not a spiritual safe haven for the lust-enslaved. Not even that supposedly God-ordained institution could blot out the original, ubiquitous, and unconquerable sin of concupiscence. Marriage instead was a calamity, the world's fatal and now legally protected compromise with lust. The only possible remedy, as always, was in "a full and final cross against the indulgence of that same fleshly lust, and the final destruction of that nature which leads to it."[39]

To say the least, John Humphrey Noyes was less severe when it came to sex. Also, having launched his community half a century after the founding of the Shakers, he often directly contrasted his views with theirs. Both took seriously Christ's teaching that there would be no marriage in the resurrection. Noyes maintained, however, that the biblical passage "does not exclude the sexual distinction, or sexual intercourse, from the heavenly state, but only the world's method of assigning the sexes to each other." In other words, there will be sex in heaven, but unlike in the world where partners pair off into exclusive life-long couples, in heaven all the saved are united to one another in what Noyes called "*complex marriage*," or "pantogamy," a step above and beyond the world's "simple" and selfish monogamous institution.

Noyes viewed sex positively because he viewed pleasure, the body, and matter itself as the good creations of a good God. "We like to see the body honored," he wrote, addressing the Shakers directly: "It was made to be the temple of God and was created for his pleasure. It is the true helpmeet of the soul in every good work. It must be confessed, however, that the general effect of the Shaker doctrines is to dishonor the body. . . . They take the ground that it is philosophically impossible for matter to be spiritualized, and then form the Bible into agreement."[40] Whereas Shakers saw matter and spirit as irreconcilable, Perfectionists believed that matter could in fact be "spiritualized." As a result they viewed the body as "the true helpmeet of the soul in every good work," and viewed sex as being one of the most powerful and important of those good works. "It is the ascetic and Manichean philosophy," Noyes made clear, and emphatically "not the Bible, that despises the senses and matter. Of all the pleasures of the senses, sexual intercourse is intrinsically the most spiritual and refined; for it is intercourse of human life with human life."[41] In contrast to the Shakers, Noyes dared to sing the praises of all these supposedly dirty and unspiritual things: matter, bodies, penises, pleasure, and sex.

In many ways, the central thesis of Noyes's experiment is this: sex is spiritual. Rather than being base and carnal—the flesh that wars against the spirit—sex was instead a means of approaching God and having "SPIRITUAL FELLOWSHIP" with God's people.[42] By using all-caps here, he gives as much emphasis as possible to his countercultural sexual theology. "The sentiment that the sexual organs are unclean, and that sexual intercourse is something shameful and degrading, impregnates the atmosphere of the whole world," he lamented.[43] This should not be. Noyes instead wrote of sex as a sacrament, an outward and visible sign of an inward and invisible reality. "With pure hearts and minds," he encouraged, "we may approach the sexual union as the truest Lord's supper" and "in its nature the most perfect method of 'laying on of hands.'"[44] Shame, therefore, should have no place in the Christian's understanding of sex and the body.

As Noyes understood it, sex was the most intimate means of Christian fellowship. Through sex Christians minister to one another, experiencing together God's gift of physical pleasure. The problem—barring the possibility of Christian orgies—is that sexual partners have to pair off and exclude others. Monogamous marriage is the traditional place for such pairing off, but Noyes found the institution unsatisfactory, unnatural, and positively unchristian. "Variety," he asserted, "is, in the nature of things, as beautiful and useful in love as in eating and drinking." "The fact that a man loves peaches best," he famously added, "is no reason why he should not, on suitable occasions, eat apples, or cherries." Noyes was obviously frustrated by the incongruity that existed between human beings' "natural" appetite for sexual variety on the one hand, and the "arbitrary" restrictions of monogamous marriage on the other.[45]

But more important than merely enjoying sexual variety, having multiple sexual partners was a way of sharing love and happiness rather than hoarding them. Shifting from a culinary metaphor to a commercial one, Noyes considered monogamous sexual unions "as unwise as it would be to say that all the business in New York city [sic] must be done in firms of two.... I believe that a vastly greater amount of happiness could be produced by large corporations than by individual pairs."[46] Not only was this communal sexual arrangement more just and inclusive, it was also what sex would be like in the eschaton.

Noyes nevertheless admitted that human sexuality was still affected by the Fall, and was thus not an unequivocal good. "I take the ground that there are two kinds of sensuality," he explained, "the godly and the ungodly—carnal sensuality and spiritual sensuality." The first "deserves all the odium" commonly heaped upon it, but the latter "is beautiful and good, and falls in with and increases the flow of soul toward God."[47] Basically, Noyes believed that human sexuality needed to be redeemed rather than condemned. Working toward this redemption was the only way, he argued, of "Ministering to the Whole Man," sex drive and all.[48] The passions are governable, he maintained; they can be rightly "*organized.*"[49] "The only way to do it," however, "is to introduce godly sensuality; and this is the job before us as moral reformers."[50] Precisely how Noyes recommended introducing that "godly sensuality" to the world warrants a thorough explanation.

In order to clearly identify the fine line between godly and ungodly sexual activity, Noyes analyzed sexual intercourse in great detail. Most fundamentally, he concluded that sex had two primary functions: pleasure and procreation, or as he called these, "two branches, the amative and the propagative." Noyes considered the amative function of sex to be the more important and spiritual of the two. After all, God had made woman in the Garden of Eden "for social, not primarily for propagative purposes."[51] In both the prelapsarian world of Adam and Eve, and in the resurrected world to come, sex is about pleasure, the "SPIRITUAL FELLOWSHIP" of the two partners. Unlike Mormons, Noyes believed that sex for procreation was in Eden "a *secondary* object," and in the resurrection will have no place whatsoever. In fact, while Noyes had nothing but positive things to say about the amative function of sex, he expressed almost entirely negative opinions about sex's propagative function. Employing another commercial analogy, he described amativeness as "being the profitable part, and propagation the expensive part of the sexual relation. . . . If expenses exceed income, bankruptcy ensues."[52] The question then became how, in the single act of sexual intercourse, to separate out the amative from the propagative function, and to this Noyes had a rather unique solution that he called "male continence."

Before explaining male continence—and this gets a little graphic—it is important to know that while Noyes had inspirational things to say about sex and the sex organs, he had almost hostile thoughts and feelings about ejaculation. "Ordinary sexual intercourse," he lamented in a passage that is laden with the personal turned theological, "(in which the amative and propagative functions are confounded) is a momentary affair, terminating in exhaustion and disgust. If it begins in the spirit, it soon ends in the flesh; i.e., the amative, which is spiritual, is drowned in the propagative, which is sensual. The exhaustion which follows, naturally breeds self-reproach and shame, and this leads to dislike and concealment of the sexual organs."[53] That was his understanding of "ordinary" and sinful sexual intercourse. Thus while he disagreed with the Shakers by valuing sex and maintaining a place of honor for it in the religious life, he nevertheless concurred that there was still something unclean about it. Noyes, however, relocated this "exhaustion and disgust," "self-reproach and shame" from sex and the sex organs in general to ejaculation in particular. In his quest to discern godly from ungodly sensuality, he seems to have found it in this distinction between the amative and propagative functions of sex.

Noyes's solution to the problem of procreation–basically the challenge of birth control—was "male continence." In sexual intercourse, to put it bluntly, ejaculation was the problem—Noyes even once referred to it as "the grand problem"—in that it is what led to the possibility of pregnancy. There were other attempts at a remedy, but Noyes's revulsion to semen made him reject them all. He was especially disgusted by coitus interruptus, or "Onanism" as it was called at the time after the biblical story of Onan in Genesis 38 who "spilled his seed on the ground," calling it "unnatural, filthy, and even more wasteful of life." Using condoms, what he called "the French method—the use of sacks" was a close second in terms of revolting Noyes; and he rejected outright "Madame Restell's system of producing abortions."[54]

Noyes was also no fan of masturbation, calling it the real "disreputable branch of the same seed-wasting business."[55] He believed that a man's semen was a vital life fluid that when expelled resulted in "shame," "exhaustion and disgust." This expulsion could take place either in sex with a partner, or alone in masturbation. Either way, Noyes had complex thoughts about ejaculation, and used the example of masturbation to reinforce his distinction between godly and ungodly sexual activity. Although male masturbation clearly does not lead to the possibility of pregnancy, Noyes still condemned it due to the man's loss of vitality in his ejaculate; and more importantly because masturbation "is not essentially social, since it can be produced in solitude."[56] While physically self-gratifying, masturbation did nothing to enhance the pleasure of a partner, or the love, unity, and fellowship of the community. Love, unity, and fellowship, without the burden of children, is precisely what Noyes wanted the sexual freedom of his Oneida Community to effect, and male continence was the way to do it.

Simply put, male continence was the union of man and woman in sexual intercourse without the man ejaculating. As Noyes described it in a famous passage that bears quoting in full:

> We begin by *analyzing* the act of sexual intercourse. It has a beginning, a middle, and an end. Its beginning and most elementary form is the simple *presence* of the male organ in the female. Then usually follows a series of reciprocal *motions*. Finally this exercise brings on a nervous action or ejaculatory *crisis* which expels the seed. Now we insist that this whole process, up to the very moment of emission, is *voluntary,* entirely under the control of the moral faculty, and *can be stopped at any point.* In other words, the *presence* and the *motions* can be continued or stopped at will, and it is only the final crisis of emission that is automatic or uncontrollable....

The situation may be compared to a stream in the three conditions of a fall, a course of rapids above the fall, and the still water above the rapids. The skillful boatman may choose whether he will remain in the still water, or venture more or less down the rapids, or run his boat over the fall. But there is a point on the verge of the fall where he has no control over his course; and just above that there is a point where he will have to struggle with the current in a way which will give his nerves a severe trial, even though he may escape the fall. If he is willing to learn, experience will teach him the wisdom of confining his excursions to the region of easy rowing, unless he has an object in view that is worth the cost of going over the falls.[57]

After much reflection, trial, and error, Noyes concluded that a man might engage in the first two parts of intercourse (sexual union and "reciprocal *motions*") but refrain from the third ("ejaculatory *crisis*"). In other words, the "skillful boatman" in his aquatic analogy may enjoy an outing in both placid waters and even some exhilarating rapids, while avoiding the point of no return after which the current carries him over the falls. While perhaps at first giving "his nerves a severe trial," such a man could eventually master the technique through both willpower and experience, and be entirely in control of his sexual fellowship—enjoying and sharing the union and pleasure of amative sex, while not risking the expensive consequences of propagative sex.

As a final and related note, Noyes disagreed vehemently with the charge that the Oneida Community's practices of male continence and complex marriage were motivated by licentiousness. Most obviously, male continence was an act of self-denial rather than self-gratification, a "subordination of the flesh to the spirit."[58] But neither was having multiple sexual partners in complex marriage a libertine experience. As the rest of this book will make clear, sexual intercourse at the Oneida Community was in some ways less frequent, and definitely more controlled, than among many monogamously married couples. Noyes therefore reacted fiercely to the charge that Oneida was a playground for "free love." "Our Communities are *families*," he emphasized over and over again. As a result, the pantogamous unions of complex marriage are "permanent," communal in their shared ownership of property, and responsible for both the well-being of sexual partners and children. Free love is none of these. It is temporary, individualistic, irresponsible, and driven predominantly by the sensuality of the partners. In short, it is ungodly, whereas complex marriage and male continence are spiritual in their origin, their practice, and in their salubrious effects.[59]

Noyes's complex marriage, however, was nevertheless distinct from Mormon polygamy in crucial ways. "The Mormons," he wrote, "representing polygamy, stand on the letter of the Old Testament. The Shakers, representing celibacy, stand on the letter of the New Testament. Bible Communists, representing the unselfish organization of mature Christianity, stand on the spirit of the whole Bible."[60] This passage perfectly summarizes what Noyes considered to be the right and godly sexual order. In addition to being superior to the world's selfish institution of monogamous marriage, as well as superior to the secular libertinism of free love, complex marriage was also superior to the other two religio-sexual experiments of his time. To him, both Mormon polygamy and Shaker celibacy were outdated. Only in complex marriage would seekers find the full sexual realization of "mature Christianity," and only in Bible communism would religio-sexual pioneers find the support they needed in their "fellowship with resurrection-life."[61] In other words, only within his particular religious metanarrative would male continence and complex marriage make sense, and only there, Noyes warned, could they be practiced safely.

PART II
GENESES

"Geneses" will tell the story of how it all started: how each sect began; how each leader developed his or her unique understanding of marriage and sexuality; and how each one then institutionalized those sexual innovations among often-dubious followers. Broaching these radical sexual ideas and practices was not easy. As they turned their backs on monogamy and guaranteed ostracism from their host society, followers had to be convinced of the religious truth of what they were about to do.

This is therefore the most appropriate place to highlight the powerfully charismatic personalities of Ann Lee, Joseph Smith, and John Humphrey Noyes. To begin to describe their characters, scholars often employ William James's concept of the "religious genius," and they are right to do so.[1] Possessing "extraordinary emotional susceptibility," James writes, the religious genius "is liable to fixed ideas and obsessions. His conceptions tend to pass immediately into belief and action; and when he gets a new idea, he has no rest till he proclaims it, or in some way 'works it off.'" This passage is especially descriptive because it highlights the primacy of ideas and their enhanced power when mixed with the "ardor and excitability of character" in a certain kind of religious leader. Ann Lee, Joseph Smith, and John Humphrey Noyes did indeed have "extraordinary emotional susceptibility," as well as the tendency both to fixate on "ideas and obsessions," and then turn them from beliefs into actions. Part 2 is going to tell the story of how, as James added, when "their ideas possess them, they inflict them, for better or worse, upon their contemporaries or their age." In particular it will highlight the personal origins of those ideas and the first instances of their inflicting them, with great success, on an already saturated American religious marketplace.[2]

Two other points about Mormon polygamy and Oneida complex marriage need to be made before starting in earnest. The first is that polygamy and complex marriage were both initiated *years* after the founding of these religious groups. In other words, the metanarrative came first, then the communities, and only then the risky departures from monogamy, which is why the chapter on "Spiritual" precedes the chapter on "Sexual." The second point is that these sexual experiments did not have to happen. There is nothing inherently built into the fabric of either Mormonism or Perfectionism that leads inevitably to polygamy or complex marriage. The underlying religious metanarratives described in part 1 do allow for these sexual experiments, but they do not make them foregone conclusions. Polygamy required the Mormon metanarrative, but the Mormon metanarrative did not require polygamy—at least not at first. And the same was true for complex marriage and Perfectionism. Why they were initiated *when* they were in the early life of these communities will be explained thoroughly in this part.

Ann Lee and the first generation of Shakers are different. Her metanarrative, community, and demanding sexual practices developed more simultaneously than seriatim. Thus when it comes to treating Lee and the early Shakers, the subjects of the first two chapters on the "Geneses" of the United Society of Believers are more chronologically condensed than spread out as they are with the Mormons and Perfectionists. As we will see in this section's final chapter, "Institutional," however, toward the end of this first life phase, the leaders of all three sects sensed a need for order in their belief systems and in their communal life together, and thus each developed institutional supports to undergird their religious movements and perpetuate them into the future.

4
Spiritual

It is difficult to get a clear picture of Ann Lee's early life due to scant historical records. It is also a challenge to disentangle fact from fiction in her biography: what the documentary evidence reveals about her life versus the hagiographic and perhaps made-up stories that later generations of Shakers told about her. For instance, according to one important source, even "in early youth" Ann "had a great abhorrence of the fleshly cohabitation of the sexes; and so great was her sense of impurity, that she often admonished her mother against it; which coming to her father's ears he threatened and actually attempted to whip her."[1] Whether such episodes took place is uncertain. What is clearer is that Ann Lee was born to John Lee (her mother's name was not recorded) in Manchester, England, on February 29, 1736, the second of eight children; and was baptized on June 1, 1742, at the age of six. Growing up the daughter of a poor blacksmith, Ann worked in the local textile trade and received next to no formal education. She was not taught to read and remained illiterate her entire life.[2]

The 1760s would prove to be a pivotal and traumatic decade for Lee. On January 5, 1762, at the age of twenty-five, she married Abraham Standerin (alternately spelled Standley and Stanley), who was a blacksmith like her father. Some sources describe the marriage as an abusive one, with Abraham "much given to inebriety." Without a doubt, the marriage was sexually consummated—Lee got pregnant at least four times—but with tragic results. One source claims that the deliveries were "occasioned by hard labour; her last child was extracted by forceps; after which, for several hours, she lay with but little appearance of life."[3] While this sad and intimate scene is speculative, it is certain that each of Ann's four children died in infancy or early childhood, a fact to which later commentators point as the psychological source of her hatred of all sex. At the very least, it is safe to say that whether or not the young Ann Lee disliked the carnality of sex, she would have understandable negative associations with the procreative consequences of it.

As Lee suffered the loss of one child after another during the 1760s, she grew in religious devotion as part of a sect that was eventually called the Shakers. As early perhaps as 1747, James and Jane Wardley, a couple from neighboring Bolton, began gathering followers into an informal worshipping community. They preached the imminent judgment of Christ, called followers to lives of strict religious discipline, and engaged in ecstatic worship during which they jerked and shook in the spirit of the Lord. By 1769 these unusual public displays of religious devotion attracted the attention of outsiders and earned them the name Shaking Quakers, or Shakers. According to historian Stephen Stein, scholars disagree about the "formative influences on the Shaking Quakers," but most attribute their inspiration to the Quakers and the French Prophets, a group of radical Calvinists, known in France as the Camisards, some of whom had moved to England in the early 1700s to escape persecution. Although there is no scholarly consensus about the Wardleys' own religious background, two points are nevertheless clear: that the original community was built around their charismatic leadership; and that they "challenged their disciples to live by inspired principles in tension with the surrounding culture."[4] For Ann Lee, this group gave her a community and a purpose. Along with other members of her family, Ann had begun following the Wardleys perhaps as early as 1758, sharing in their beliefs, their commitments, and their sufferings.

By the early 1770s the Shaking Quakers' radical religious devotion and condemnation of worldliness had turned into outright conflict with the powers that be. Like the Quakers a century before them, they especially despised the established church, often interrupting Anglican services to castigate both clergy and congregation alike for their errant beliefs and lukewarm piety. Also like the Quakers, these provocations landed the Shakers in prison. Many of the Wardleys' followers were arrested and punished in the early 1770s, including Ann Lee and several members of her family. Lee herself was fined and incarcerated numerous times, spending usually only a few days in prison. Later Shaker hagiographies make much of these episodes of Mother Ann's suffering for her beliefs. In one story that has a special place in Shaker lore, the cruel warden not only incarcerated Ann but also refused her food and drink in an effort to starve her into submission. Fellow believers came to her aid and in a memorable scene employ a long-stemmed pipe through which milk "was conveyed to her through the key hole of the door."[5] Both the reality of the Shakers' sufferings and the later romanticized accounts of them illustrate that persecution was central to their identity. In fact, it is safe to say that they invited it and valued it. This was true of both the Warldleys' original community in England, and later of the community that coalesced around Ann Lee in America. They saw in their persecutions—no matter how self-incurred those persecutions might have been—the world's disapproval, and by sectarian-minded deduction the approval of God.

According to Shaker tradition, it was also while in prison in 1770 that Ann Lee received God's "full revelation of the root and foundation of human depravity," and gradually rose to be a leader in her own right. Prior to this prison revelation, "she had continued to yield obedience to James and Jane Wardley, as her superiors." Afterward, "Mother took the lead of the Society, and was received and acknowledged, as the first pillar of the Church of God upon earth."[6] The "candle of the Lord was in her hand," another source recounts, and "she was able by the light thereof, to search every heart and try every soul among them."[7] The inner dynamics of the Shaking Quakers during this time are difficult to penetrate, but it does seem that Ann Lee's religious authority had been established, conferred upon her by God, her followers believed, in order that she might bear "an open testimony against the lustful gratification of the flesh, as the source and foundation of human corruption."[8] However it happened, this was a turning point both in the life of Ann Lee and in the development of the Shaker movement. Lee's sufferings in the 1760s were followed by personal spiritual clarity and enhanced community status in the early 1770s. In 1774, after years of more persecution and discouragement in their proselytizing in England, Ann Lee, her husband, Abraham, her brother William, and a handful of other determined believers set sail for what they hoped would be the more fertile spiritual soil of revolutionary America.

Like Ann Lee, Joseph Smith hungered for *more* than what his spiritual surroundings could offer, and he similarly struck out on his own; first to find religious answers and then to lead a community based on what he had discovered. But whereas Lee had condemned her established Anglican church—not the only church in eighteenth-century England but still culturally and politically dominant—the young Smith wrestled with the multiplicity of religious voices in the Burned-over District and their mutually exclusive truth claims.

Joseph Smith grew up at the height and in the heart of America's Second Great Awakening. He was born in 1805 in Sharon, Vermont, and after residing for a while around Lebanon, New Hampshire, his family moved in 1816 to Palmyra, New York, where the young Joseph Jr. lived until 1831. These fifteen years, from roughly age ten to twenty-five, were obviously formative. They were also literally foundational for the Church of Jesus Christ of Latter-day Saints.

Also like Ann Lee, Joseph Smith grew up a poor and poorly educated religious outsider. Later enemies of Mormons would use these facts as rhetorical weapons against them, claiming that the Smith family "were laboring people, in low circumstances," "indolent," gullible seekers of "hidden treasure," and superstitious tellers of "stories about ghosts, hobgoblins, caverns, and various other mysterious matters."[9] While these evaluations are clearly pejorative and polemical, they are not groundless. "Money-digging was epidemic in upstate New York," Richard Bushman explains, with the Smiths being every bit "as susceptible as their neighbors to treasure-seeking folklore."[10] In short, belief in supernatural forces outside of so-called Christian orthodoxy was commonplace in the Burned-over District.

The charge that the Smith family was poor is undeniable. Joseph Smith Sr. and Lucy Mack Smith did not rise with the tide of antebellum fortunes. Financially ruined in a failed mercantile venture in 1803, two years before Joseph Jr. was born, the family descended the socioeconomic ladder from landowners to tenant farmers, moving in Vermont half a dozen times in search of opportunity, before settling in Palmyra in 1816. The Smiths were able to purchase land there in 1820 but they eventually lost the title and had to become tenant farmers again in 1825.[11]

Spiritually speaking, everything began for Joseph and the LDS Church in the 1820s. Prior to this decade, the young man showed no real signs of religious interest or imagination. Another wave of revivals had hit Palmyra from 1816 to 1817, precisely when the Smiths arrived, and along with the rest of his community Smith contemplated his sins and his relationship with God. He found, however, no answers and no certainty in the competing claims of his local religious institutions.

Smith's confusion was only amplified within his own family. His mother, Lucy, eventually joined the Presbyterians, but Joseph Sr. never joined any church, preferring instead the life of a spiritually homeless seeker and visionary. After 1818, his mother had begun taking three of the children to the Presbyterian church; but his father, and the other three children—Joseph Jr. included—skipped church altogether, finding spiritual nourishment in the doctrine of universal salvation as well as in religious dreams. Reportedly, Joseph Sr. had a history of religious dreams dating back to at least 1811 and continuing through the 1820s, simultaneous with Joseph Jr.'s first visions. But Joseph Sr.'s dreams only confirmed his status as a religious outsider, giving him a satisfying sense of connection to the divine while further alienating him from the institutional religion of his day. Because of his dreams he did not need the churches and they in turn did not look kindly on him.[12]

It was in this context that the fourteen-year-old Joseph Jr. received his First Vision. Neither Smith's culture nor his family gave him any definitive spiritual direction or identity. Confused by the competing claims of his religious marketplace, as well as the differing spiritual practices of his mother and father, Smith asked for clarity and the Lord answered. In 1820, on "a beautiful, clear day, early in the spring," in what Mormons now call the Sacred Grove, God the Father and Jesus Christ revealed themselves to Joseph Jr., who then asked "the Personages who stood above me in the light, which of all the sects was right," and the Lord replied "that I must join none of them, for they were all wrong."[13]

The next step in Smith's spiritual journey did not occur until 1823, but in the meantime his—and his entire family's—identity as outsiders solidified. Sometime after his First Vision, Smith spoke to a Methodist minister about the experience, seeking perhaps encouragement, guidance, or at the very least interest in such a profound encounter. He was "greatly surprised" to find, however, that the clergyman "treated my communication not only lightly, but with great contempt, saying it was all of the devil, that there were no such things as visions or revelations in these days." Afterward, as the story of Smith's vision spread throughout Palmyra, townspeople laughed at the tale, mocking him as a deluded religious quack from a failed and disreputable family.[14]

This was the first of many persecutions Joseph Jr. would suffer throughout his life, and it was arguably a turning point. Having ventured ever so briefly into the world of established religious institutions for validation, he was rewarded for his earnest inquiry by being personally rebuffed and socially humiliated. The context of his family's slowly unfolding financial misfortune, of course, did not help matters. The only silver lining in all of this "great persecution," he later recalled, was that he "had now got my mind satisfied so far as the sectarian world was concerned—that it was not my duty to join with any of them, but to continue as I was until further directed."[15]

Smith received that direction in a series of visits from the angel Moroni beginning in the fall of 1823. On the evening of September 21, the sixteen-year-old "discovered a light appearing in my room, which continued to increase until the room was lighter than at noonday, when immediately a personage appeared." This personage identified himself as the angel Moroni, the son of Mormon, and the last member of a once proud and godly American race, the Nephites. Moroni told Joseph about the existence of a record of this venerable people, inscribed on golden plates and hidden hundreds of years ago for safekeeping. Moroni also told Smith that there were buried along with the plates two seer stones, the Urim and Thummim, with which he could understand and translate the plates' ancient and now lost language.[16]

The next day Smith raced for a hill about three miles south of his home—subsequently named the Hill Cumorah—and found there the plates and seer stones exactly as Moroni had described. But "the messenger" then forbade Smith from extracting the ancient texts, ordering him instead to return to that spot on that date, September 22, each year "until the time should come for obtaining the plates." Four years passed between Smith's initial discovery and that appointed time, with much happening in the interim. His brother Alvin died just two months after Joseph discovered the plates in 1823, the Smiths slipped from landowners to tenant farmers in 1825, and on January 18, 1827, Joseph eloped with Emma Hale, a union that Emma's father bitterly opposed. On September 22 of that year, four years after Moroni's first visitation, that "same messenger delivered them [the plates and seer stones] up to me" and a new revelation was opened.[17]

Enduring intimidation, a lack of funding, and a severe early mishap, Joseph Smith began translating the *Book of Mormon* in 1828. No one knows precisely how it happened, but in June 1828 Martin Harris, Smith's first scribe, lost the first 116 pages of the translation and Smith was disconsolate. Rebuked by the Lord for his carelessness, Smith did not resume translating until the spring of 1829, but then the *Book of Mormon* poured forth. With a new scribe, Oliver Cowdery, recording every word, the two completed the majority of the translation in an astonishing two and a half months between April and June 1829. In March of 1830 the *Book of Mormon* was published for all the world to see. His stories were both thoroughly novel and impressively elaborate, and his overall message was—to some people—convincing. Smith was gaining credibility, although miniscule at first, and it all began with a book.

If the 1820s for Smith started with a vision and ended with a book, the 1830s began with him restoring a church and ended with him building a city. Generally speaking, the first half of the 1830s saw a rush of revelations that solidified the LDS Church as something quite different from the churches around it. That period culminated doctrinally with the publication of the *Doctrine and Covenants* in 1835 and institutionally with the dedication of the Kirtland Temple in 1836. The rest of the 1830s, however, brought many troubles, with Smith having to think much more about the mundane than the heavenly. Pressing issues of money, power, politics, and violence increasingly consumed his time, and the revelations slowed from a flood to a trickle.

Necessity—and brevity—dictates that the history presented here be limited to the essentials, and to what is most relevant to the story of LDS plural marriage. In order to condense this decade down to its most important elements, the rest of this section on Joseph Smith will be organized roughly chronologically according to five themes: revelations, converts, power, persecution, and relocation. The boldness of Smith's revelations attracted a certain kind of convert whose increasing numbers translated in the antebellum democracy into power. Many outsiders feared that power and turned their fear into persecution, to which the LDS community responded by relocating to what they hoped would be a more hospitable environment.

Ongoing religious revelation is where everything started. In four revelations from February 1832 to early 1833, which Mormon theologians call the "exaltation revelations," Smith introduced the Saints to a dramatically different religious universe.[18] "The elements are eternal, and spirit and element, inseparably connected, receive a fulness of joy," one verse proclaimed, destroying the barrier between the spiritual and the material, while vesting and ennobling matter with the property of imperishability. Human beings are likewise eternal, having no beginning or end, and are referred to in the exaltation revelations as "intelligence." With Jesus Christ as an example of perfect earthly obedience resulting in perfect fulness, the exaltation revelations clarified, an individual human intelligence can "act for itself. . . . Behold, here is the agency of man." In other words, ordinary human beings through extraordinary faith and obedience can enjoy the same measure of divine fulness that Christ ultimately enjoyed.[19] "'Fulness' was," Bushman points out, "the critical word in Joseph's exaltation revelations."[20] Smith went on to crystalize this cosmology in the King Follett sermon in 1844, but it is here in embryo in these revelations of 1832–33. What is important to note is that these redefinitions of the afterlife, premortality, spirit, and matter came very soon after the "restoration" of the LDS Church in 1830.[21]

All of these doctrinal innovations were attractive to some and horrifying to others. Those who rejected them were both satisfied by and committed to the various options in their antebellum religious marketplace.

Those who joined the newly restored LDS Church wanted *more* and in Smith's revelations they found it.

By 1832 the LDS Church had close to one thousand members, with some noteworthy converts. Men like Brigham Young and Orson and Parley Pratt were all leaders in the new movement, but by far the most important early convert was Sidney Rigdon. Prior to 1830 Rigdon was a successful preacher in Alexander Campbell's Restoration movement, but when Parley Pratt, whom Rigdon had trained in the ministry, returned from a missionary trip with a copy of the *Book of Mormon,* Rigdon was intrigued. He studied the *Book of Mormon* carefully, concluded that it was indeed a new revelation, and converted to the faith, bringing his congregation along with him and giving the new movement both momentum and credibility. The added members encouraged the faithful in their beliefs, and Rigdon himself was a theologically well-read thinker and a rhetorically compelling speaker. He would contribute much to the LDS Church by spreading the Mormon message and by defending it against outside critics.

From the very beginning, but especially as it grew, the LDS Church needed effective government, which brings up the theme of power in early Mormonism: both the power structures that Smith constructed, and the power that accompanied the Church as its numbers increased. The first was primarily internal and led to institutional stability and communal discipline. The second has to do with how outsiders perceived the growing Mormon community as a threat to both orthodox Christianity and the American republic. In May 1829, while puzzling over matters of religious authority, Smith and Oliver Cowdery asked for guidance and received supernatural assistance when John the Baptist appeared to them and conferred upon them "the Priesthood of Aaron." John the Baptist's presence and the priesthood's ancient lineage vested the institution and its officers with an authority that transcended their time and place. Smith and Cowdery now had divine sanction to oversee the restored Church, ministering to and baptizing others not just as visionaries and translators, but as ordained members of an ancient but long-lost priesthood. John the Baptist also promised them an even greater authority in the future through "the Priesthood of Melchizedek."[22] Smith received this higher priesthood in 1831 and regularly refined its purpose and function until his death in 1844.

What is so special about Mormon polity, and the Melchizedek priesthood in particular, is that it was simultaneously hierarchical and egalitarian. This is obviously a paradox but a highly effective one when it came to governing the Church. While authority ultimately radiated out and down from Smith (and subsequent First Presidents), all male members of the Church, regardless of educational or family background, were empowered through their ordination to the Melchizedek priesthood, conferring upon them a sense of higher status. Being vested with some power by the system, they were therefore invested in the system, a structure and a culture that mutually reinforced one another, and kept the Church together through some very difficult times.[23]

Between 1830 and 1840 Smith and the majority of the Saints had to endure constant persecution. In December 1830, just months after having organized the Church in upstate New York, he received a revelation to "go to the Ohio."[24] Kirtland, Ohio, would be Smith's home for the next seven years, from early 1831 to January 1838. At first all went well in Kirtland. Smith was freed from the distractions of local harassment to hear from God, build his Church, and monitor the advance party that was building Zion on the Missouri frontier. This is where he received the exaltation revelations, translated the Book of Moses and the Book of Abraham, and restored the Priesthood of Melchizedek. This is also where, after the successes of the early 1830s, the Church suffered through a series of challenges—including the first rumors that Smith was a polygamist—that would severely test the faith of its members.

Between 1837 and 1840 the Mormon story is one of almost unremitting hardships. In Kirtland Church leaders established a bank that opened and collapsed all within the month of January 1837, ruining the Church's finances and outside investors alike. People left the Church in droves, while those who remained criticized Smith's leadership and questioned his prophetic authority. Non-Mormon creditors just wanted their money back, and after failing to secure it heaped lawsuit after lawsuit upon him and the other founders of the ill-fated bank. Beset on all sides, in January 1838 Smith fled Kirtland to start over again in the promised land of Missouri.[25]

In Missouri, however, things quickly went from bad to worse. While the Mormons were tolerated at first, when their numbers increased so did the anxiety and opposition of "Gentiles" (the Mormon word for non-Mormons), who eventually forced the LDS community to relocate multiple times within the state.[26] Expecting no legal protection from a potential mob, the Saints decided to defend themselves, which only escalated paranoia on both sides. When the shooting started in August 1838 over a local election, the violence quickly spun out of control.

Depredations occurred on both sides throughout the fall, but the Missourians had the numerical advantage, as well as the backing of the histrionic governor Lilburn W. Boggs, who proclaimed in the middle of the crisis: "The Mormons must be treated as enemies, and must be *exterminated* or driven from the State if necessary for the public peace."[27] The most infamous episode occurred on October 30, when a mob fired upon Mormons at Haun's Mill, killing seventeen in all, including children. Soon known as the Haun's Mill massacre, this slaughter of the innocents left a deep and lasting impression on the Saints. It also brought the Mormon War of 1838 to a close. In early November the terrified Saints laid down their arms, surrendered their property in Missouri at great loss, and agreed to leave the state entirely.[28]

After a year of financial turmoil in 1837, and a year of violence in 1838, Smith spent the first months of 1839 in prison. While being transported to another county for trial, however, Smith and other Mormon prisoners escaped. The likely explanation is that whereas the Missouri authorities were no friends of the Mormons, they were also embarrassed by the recent lawlessness in their state and the recklessness of Governor Boggs. On the night of April 16, 1839, wanting a quick and bloodless resolution to the crisis, the sheriff and guards looked the other way while the prisoners bolted. On April 22 Smith and his fellow fugitives made it across the Mississippi River to Illinois. Chastened by the hardships of the previous years, but not diminished in his ambition to restore the Church of Jesus Christ of Latter-day Saints, Smith soon ordered Mormon leaders to purchase land in Illinois on the banks of the Mississippi. There, the dispersed and dispirited Saints would gather once more, into a city that they would call Nauvoo, which is Hebrew for "beautiful place."[29]

When compared to Mormonism's complex and dramatic first two decades, the origins of John Humphrey Noyes's Perfectionism seem tame. In fact, on the face of it, nothing in Noyes's early life would hint at his later religious, social, and sexual radicalism. Unlike both Ann Lee and Joseph Smith, John Humphrey Noyes was socioeconomically privileged and well educated—in many ways a member of the establishment. On a more invisible and intimate level, however, there are some fascinating parallels between Noyes's, Ann Lee's, and Joseph Smith's formative years. In particular, as with Smith, John Humphrey Noyes's family played an important role in priming him for life as a leader of religious outsiders. And as with Ann Lee, traumatic romantic and sexual experiences primed Noyes to question the goodness of monogamy and conventional sexual relationships.

John Humphrey Noyes was born in Brattleboro, Vermont, on September 3, 1811, to John Noyes and Polly Hayes. Both parents were from reputable and longstanding New England families. Polly's father, Rutherford Hayes, had eleven children in all, and her nephew, Rutherford B. Hayes, would go on to be the nineteenth president of the United States. A teacher for most of his teens and twenties, John Noyes was more of a self-made man and a bit of a late bloomer. He studied theology at Dartmouth, but did not matriculate until he was twenty-seven years old, graduating in 1795 when he was thirty-one, which was rather uncommon for the times. He later launched a mercantile venture that would occupy him for the next twenty years and bring him great success. In 1804, "at the ripe age of forty," he married the twenty-three-year-old Polly and the couple had John Humphrey, their first son, seven years later in 1811, the same year that John Noyes began translating his business success into a political career. He served first in the Vermont legislature, and was later elected to the U.S. House of Representatives, serving in the Fourteenth Congress from 1815 to 1817.[30]

Religiously speaking, John Noyes was a bit like Joseph Smith Sr., close to the orthodoxy of his time, but still on the outside looking in. Unlike Joseph Smith Sr., who was an unschooled religious visionary, John Noyes had trained for the ministry at Dartmouth and had even served as a pastor before going into business; but, as a later account describes it, he "was not in later life a professor of religion."[31] Unsurprisingly, though, the father did not see his heterodox son as a chip off the old block, but as an embarrassment. It was one thing to slip gently into unobservant agnosticism. It was another thing to stride defiantly far outside the bounds of New England orthodoxy and social respectability. Although bequeathing much to his son, John Noyes, the successful businessman and former U.S. congressman, died in 1841 ashamed of him instead, and this was seven years before John Humphrey founded the Oneida Community.

Polly Hayes Noyes, however, was deeply pious her entire life, and insistent on giving her children religious instruction. She took John Humphrey to his first revival when he was only eight years old, and had her children pray and read the Bible daily. She herself regularly prayed for and with them, intent on instilling a fear of the Lord and a life-long devotion to religious matters. Reportedly, she hoped and prayed that John Humphrey would become a minister one day, a desire he doubtlessly internalized.

By all accounts, the young John Humphrey Noyes had a complex constitution. Contemplative to the point of brooding, he was gifted with raw intelligence and burdened with mercurial emotions. Socially speaking, he was yet another walking contradiction: internally confident in his abilities and self-worth, and reportedly a natural leader; but also painfully shy and self-conscious, especially among young women, and as a consequence profoundly frustrated with his own social inadequacy. Before attending Dartmouth College, he was educated alternately at home and in some of Vermont's best boarding schools. The experiences in the boarding schools, when he was only ages nine and eleven, were particularly painful as he suffered often from homesickness and emotional isolation, which he remedied by turning inward and keeping a journal.

Noyes's experience at Dartmouth would be no better. Academically he excelled, graduating Phi Beta Kappa, but he studied so hard in part because he failed so miserably in the college's social life. Unlike his father, who at age twenty-seven was among the oldest in his entering class, John Humphrey at age fifteen was among the youngest, which did not help him get over his social anxieties. With the observational skills of an outsider, he often retreated to his journal to judge his classmates for their pretentions and hypocrisies. In many ways he was jealous of their social confidence, turning his resentment into moralistic rants. But he also engaged in self-flagellation about his struggle to overcome his shyness. "So unreasonable and excessive is my bashfulness," he lamented, "that I fully believe I could face a battery of cannon with less trepidation than I could a room full of ladies with whom I was unacquainted."[32] When he graduated in 1830 these internal tensions and sense of social inadequacy were far from resolved.[33]

In the fall of 1831, when he was twenty years old, a revival changed Noyes's life forever. His religious commitments prior to this time could perhaps be described as nominal or cool. Religion was a part of his life but not an animating force. He therefore resisted the promptings of the spirit throughout the four-day-long protracted meeting, but soon after succumbed. Sick and bedridden after the revival, Noyes had both time and reason to contemplate "the uncertainty of life." While "the house was empty and all was still," he engaged in "some hard thinking, determined to obtain religion, and immediately set about conquering my pride." He then plunged himself into a season of praying, searching the scriptures with his mother, and—most interestingly—"forcing myself into convictions with renewed vigor." The end result of this process was a rather classic evangelical conversion. "The Bible seemed a new treasure of precious thought," he wrote, "Christians seemed kindred spirits; the matters of

God and of eternity seemed alone worth attention." Noyes was indeed a new man, with a new purpose, community, and authority.[34]

Having passed through this spiritual and existential crucible, Noyes's identity was in many ways set, and his future vocation crystal clear: he would become a minister. In his account of this turning point, his nephew George Wallingford Noyes adds a curious and revealing sentence: "Seeing no reason why there should be any diminution in the vividness and ardor of his religious feelings, he vowed with all his inward strength that he would be a 'young convert' forever." This is yet another example of Noyes's indomitable will and self-control, but even more interesting is that he "vowed" to maintain throughout his life a certain emotional state.[35]

From 1831 to 1832, Noyes attended Andover Theological Seminary, the most prestigious school for ministers in antebellum America, and something entirely alien to the formative religious experiences of Ann Lee and Joseph Smith.[36] But perhaps as Lee and Smith would have done had they received a theological education, Noyes was disillusioned. He struggled with the incongruity he perceived between faith as a subject of academic study and faith as a dynamic lived reality, a tension that is revealing of his sectarian priorities and predilections. Though doubtlessly intelligent and capable of impressive academic achievements, Noyes believed religion to be "a matter of the *heart*." "But in a theological seminary," he complained, "religion becomes a *professional* affair, an external business, a prospective means of subsistence. . . . Such a notion is fatal to spirituality."[37] Noyes simply could not stomach the domestication and professionalization of God's spirit that he experienced in America's finest divinity schools. Authentic faith, genuine faith, he insisted, was an internal affair. The heart is ultimately where he would find his spiritual inspiration and authority, although it took him a number of years to reach this conclusion. In the meantime he suffered and struggled to define himself.

Socially speaking, Noyes's "spiritual state naturally threw me into fellowship with those who had the most zeal; and they in many cases were pledged to foreign missions."[38] This cadre of earnest men, a kind of self-styled spiritual elite, would gather for Bible study, prayer, and a communal form of self-examination during which members of the group would collectively tell an individual member "plainly his faults with a view to helping him improve."[39] To maintain equality, each member would both examine his peers and submit to being examined by them. Noyes learned much from this process, and found it so valuable for group cohesiveness that he reinstituted it years later at Oneida, calling it "mutual criticism."

But in spite of these important devotional and theological influences on his life, Noyes nevertheless found "that Andover was a very poor place for one who had vowed to live in the 'revival spirit,' and be a 'young convert' forever."[40] He therefore left for the ostensibly more spirit-filled divinity school at Yale, which he attended for a year and a half, from the fall of 1832 until the winter of 1834, when he publicly declared his Perfectionist beliefs, was expelled from school, and stripped of his license to preach.

Noyes's first year at Yale was uneventful, but the seeds of future heterodoxy were planted. In New Haven, a center of antebellum Congregationalism, Noyes grew to hate the institutional church. He "lost confidence in the religion around me," he wrote, discovering instead "the need there was of a re-conversion of most of those who professed Christianity." Noyes then took his "zeal" and turned it inward once more, hoping that if others imitated him en masse such a movement would effect "an internal reformation of Christendom." Precisely what this amped-up inner zeal would look like, however, either individually or collectively, remained to be seen.[41]

This is where Noyes's radical doctrine of Perfectionism came in, and changed the course of his life. Frustrated that the modern church did not "advance as rapidly as the primitive church did toward the conquest of the world," Noyes prescribed Perfectionism as the remedy for its pathological complacency. Rooting the institutional problem in the tepid faith of nominal believers, Noyes developed a theological taxonomy that placed people in categories according to the fervor of their religious commitments. The first group is simply the unbelievers, while the second group is composed of the kind of nominal Christians Noyes saw around him who are still hindered by sin. The third group is composed of the *real* Christians, undivided in their "affections," consistently zealous for God's kingdom, and—most problematically—sinless. Noyes had converted from the first state to the second in 1831, but came to the conclusion that "the transition from the 'double-minded' state to perfect holiness, requires a radical conversion.... Thus I learned to turn my back on my first conversion, and press toward a second." Noyes wanted *more*. What got him into trouble was his claim that in this third state the believer was sinless and that those in the second state who still sinned were not genuine Christians.[42]

The point of no return came in February 1834. Never one to pull his rhetorical punches after he was convinced of something, Noyes preached unflinchingly on 1 John 3:8: "He that committeth sin is of the devil."[43] One listener was so alarmed that he accosted Noyes the next morning, asking him if he, Noyes, also committed sin. When Noyes tersely answered "No," the controversy captivated much of New Haven. The rumor "Noyes says he is perfect!" raced through the seminary, followed by "Noyes is crazy!"[44] For days students visited him, pressing him on his heretical beliefs and turning his dorm room into what Noyes felt was like a freak-show tent at a carnival. As he recounted, "I was engaged almost every hour, in answering inquirers and disputing with adversaries."[45]

The controversy then escalated beyond the student body to include ministers and professors. Nathaniel William Taylor, one of antebellum America's most influential religious thinkers, visited Noyes's room "to notify me that I was soon to be tried by the Association which licensed me." A pivotal "dispute of some length" between eminent professor and twenty-two-year-old seminarian then ensued. Both wielded the Bible to thrust and parry, but Noyes also brought to the contest his "experience" and his feelings—instruments of theological inquiry that Dr. Taylor dismissed to the point of derision. In the end Noyes was shaken by this fateful encounter with a man for whom "I had great reverence," but he was not moved to renounce either his Perfectionist beliefs or his contentious personal source of authority. In April the Association rescinded Noyes's license to preach, but by this time he could not have cared less. In his sectarian estimation, established religious institutions were as worthless to the kingdom of God as the precious orthodoxies they struggled to preserve.[46]

Like Ann Lee and Joseph Smith, John Humphrey Noyes had both rejected and been rejected by the religious authorities of the day. Like Joseph Smith's interview with the Methodist minister after his First Vision in 1820, Noyes's conversation with Nathaniel William Taylor was formative. Both meetings took place between religiously sensitive young men and established representatives of evangelical orthodoxy. Both neophytes told stories of powerful spiritual experiences and both authority figures chastised them.

Noyes's situation was made even tougher, though, when his father rejected him as well. Unlike Joseph Smith Jr., whose visionary father encouraged him in his unorthodox spiritual path, Noyes's father was estranged from all religion. For a man who was both religiously agnostic and an upstanding member of his community, his son's religious radicalism could not have been a greater disappointment. In between Andover and Yale, he and his father had a row over his alarming but not yet embarrassing theology. If "'you are to be a minister,'" his father warned him, "'you must think and preach as the rest of the ministers do; *if you get out of the traces, they will whip you in.*'" "Never!" John Humphrey replied. "Never will I be compelled by ministers or any one else to accept any doctrine that does not commend itself to my mind and conscience."[47] This was the difference between father and son. John Noyes, the successful businessman, was concerned for his son's future professional life. John Humphrey Noyes was interested solely in intellectual and spiritual integrity, regardless of the consequences.

After his expulsion and loss of his license in April 1834, rather than returning to "*the traces*" as his father commanded, Noyes wandered in the wilderness instead. But unlike the biblical prophets of old, Noyes chose to go to New York City, where he "was to be cut loose from all the moorings of fleshly wisdom, and try the ocean of spiritual experience, with God only for my pilot." Predictably, Noyes's solitary voyage on this "ocean" was a tempestuous one. For three weeks Noyes questioned everything—science, the Bible, Jesus Christ, God, any established wisdom or orthodoxy—"and the darkness of atheism fell upon me." Desperately searching for epistemological solid ground, Noyes once again turned inward. "When the spirit of darkness had done its worst," he wrote, "I said within myself: 'If the universe is a blind chaos without a God, and the destinies of all beings are to be worked out by their own strength, I have as good a right to try what I can do for existence and happiness as anybody.' ... The effect of this mental overturn was permanent."[48] After this dark night of the soul Noyes reached a point of mental clarity. In June he returned to his home in Putney, Vermont, where he received a mixed and awkward welcome. "Father had given up all hope of me," he wrote. "The rest of the family were in great suspense and tribulation" about his sanity.[49]

For two and a half years from summer 1834 to January 1837, Noyes was literally and figuratively all over the place, trying to find a stable spiritual home in which he could be the undisputed leader. His time in New York was in many ways the dramatic crescendo to his spiritual turmoil. That experience taught him that he would have to "'wrestle for victory over evil'" by himself, but he nevertheless looked for companions and especially followers as this uncompromising contrarian sought some kind of community.[50]

Noyes traveled incessantly to meet with fellow Perfectionists scattered throughout the Northeast but sadly the attempts to forge connections almost always ended in conflict. Unsurprisingly, those sectarians simply could not get along. Failing to agree about what Perfectionism even was, each group used its own definition to judge the others. New York Perfectionists, for instance, got a motion passed at the general convention of Perfectionists in 1835 denouncing Noyes as deluded. Given the instability of this period, it is no wonder that a parade of colorful characters marched in and out of Noyes's life, joining forces to promote the Perfectionist cause, but inevitably parting ways after some kind of theological or interpersonal dispute.[51]

The most telling episode in this chapter came in October 1835 when Noyes traveled to Philadelphia to meet Theophilus R. Gates. Gates had famously been expelled from the House of Representatives after he pronounced God's judgment upon it. But rather than sit at the feet of this exemplar of religious dissent, Noyes went there instead to put him in his place. A kind of spiritual anarchist, Gates condemned not only entities like the federal government and established churches, but all organizations, including the emerging Perfectionist movement. In the midst of trying to build his own community, Noyes took umbrage at Gates's anti-institutionalism and wanted to convince him to pipe down. In an inversion of Noyes's earlier dispute with Nathaniel William Taylor, the now twenty-four-year-old spiritual pioneer criticized the theology and authority of an even more radical religious dissident. Gates then kicked Noyes out of his house.[52]

In almost constant motion during this time, Noyes did have a few tenuous sources of stability. The first was his family and their home in Putney, a reliable retreat where Noyes could convalesce when the contumely of the world overwhelmed him. As will be discussed in the next chapter, Putney is also where he established his first communal experiment in 1838. Whereas Joseph Smith and Ann Lee left their homes to launch their communities, Noyes began his at his parents' house.

A second continuity was the *Perfectionist*, the periodical he published for a year and a half from August 1834 to the spring of 1836. Driven by his novel theological ideas, he wanted to share them with the world, hoping that they would find a receptive audience. If it was difficult for him to form community locally, perhaps disseminating his ideas in print could form a virtual community of like-minded believers. Thus he set up a press in New Haven, and issued the first edition of the *Perfectionist* on August 20, 1834, just a few months after he had left the city in disgrace.

The final source of supposed stability in Noyes's life proved to be dangerously fragile: his romantic attachment to Abigail Merwin. Back in the crucible of early 1834, Merwin had stood by Noyes's side as he suffered public and professional humiliation for his beliefs. As he expressed it: "In the darkness of that memorable period you arose like a morning-star to my soul."[53] Abigail Merwin was a fellow member of Noyes's Free Church in New Haven before he professed his controversial beliefs and lost his license to preach. After that profession, when Noyes was all alone, she was his first convert to Perfectionism. At thirty, she was eight years older than Noyes, but a consummate spiritual companion, fully compatible in both the content of her beliefs (his) and the zeal with which she held them. She was also reportedly quite beautiful. When Noyes later wrote that "Religious love is a very near neighbor to sexual love, and they always get mixed in the intimacies and social excitements of revivals," it is likely that he was thinking of Abigail Merwin. "The next thing that a man wants after he has found the salvation of his soul," he continued, "is to find his Eve and his Paradise."[54] In 1834 Noyes had found both: salvation through Perfectionism; and his helpmeet Eve in the form of Abigail Merwin.

It is no wonder that Noyes was devastated when Merwin first renounced her faith in Perfectionism and then announced her engagement to another man. Not only had she supported Noyes in his hour of need, she had also served as a spiritual and romantic anchor in the years after as he sought to win converts to the cause. In some ways she was his only and most intimate community at a time when he was desperately searching for one. As romantic relationships often go, however, there were high risks and high rewards. Add into the already volatile mix Noyes's perfectionistic personality and Perfectionist beliefs, and one has a recipe for an emotionally scarring disaster, which it was. It was also the indisputable reason why Noyes first articulated his radical belief in complex marriage.

5
Sexual

THIS CHAPTER is going to tell the story of how Joseph Smith and John Humphrey Noyes initially departed from monogamous marriage. Both of these stories have their turning points around the middle of the 1830s—the times at which there was no going back for either religious leader. They had committed themselves to a belief and a practice that took them outside of their antebellum mainstream, and for reasons of both theological and personal integrity they chose to maintain their course regardless of the consequences. Because Joseph Smith crossed his own personal Rubicon slightly earlier than John Humphrey Noyes, his story will come first.

Interestingly, the *Book of Mormon,* published in 1830, denounces polygamy in no uncertain terms. In a few episodes, taking more than one wife is actually listed among society's worst sins. In the book of Mosiah, for instance, the Nephite King Noah (not the Noah of the Genesis flood) "had many wives and concubines. And he did cause his people to commit sin, and do that which was abominable in the sight of the Lord." A more comprehensive condemnation is found in the book of Jacob, where the once-righteous people "indulge themselves somewhat in wicked practices, such as like unto David of old desiring many wives and concubines." The passage then goes on to command: "For there shall not any man among you have save it be one wife; and concubines he shall have none."[1]

In the entire *Book of Mormon,* the single exception to its apparent antipolygamy rule comes just a few verses later in the book of Jacob. "For if I will, saith the Lord of Hosts, raise up seed unto me, I will command my people; otherwise they shall hearken unto these things."[2] The general rule is monogamy. This proviso, however, stipulates that in the event that God desires for His people to have more babies (to "raise up seed unto me"), He will set aside the monogamous norm and sanction polygyny. Saints would later point to this verse as scriptural justification for plural marriage, but to the casual reader it would appear that the *Book of Mormon* was an antipolygamous text. At the very least, no one in 1830, including

Joseph Smith, thought that their restored gospel and Church authorized anything but monogamous marriages.

The first hint of the possibility of polygamous relationships, however, came as early as spring 1831. While working on his revision of the Old Testament in Kirtland, Smith reportedly inquired further as to why Israel's greatest patriarchs and kings—Abraham, Isaac, Jacob, Moses, David, and Solomon—had all taken more than one wife. The answer he received, as the official *Comprehensive History* of the LDS Church puts it, was that God allowed polygamous unions "under certain limitations and special conditions," although "it was also made known to the Prophet that the time had not yet come to teach or practice this doctrine in the church, but that time would come later."[3] Also in 1831, while visiting Missouri, Smith first broached the subject with others, although the incident was not recorded until thirty years later. In 1861, W. W. Phelps recalled in a letter to President Brigham Young that on July 17, 1831, Joseph received a revelation guiding him and his fellow missionaries in Missouri: "For it is my will, that in time, ye should take unto you wives of the Lamanites and Nephites [Native Americans], that their posterity may become white, delightsome and just, for even now their females are more virtuous than the gentiles." While explicit in its racism, the instruction here to take more wives was implicit and confusing, so confusing in fact that Phelps had to ask Smith to clarify the revelation's meaning. In the same 1861 letter, Phelps added the following note: "About three years after this was given [approximately 1834], I asked brother Joseph, privately, how 'we,' that were mentioned in the revelation could take wives of the 'natives' as we were all married men? He replied instantly 'In the manner that Abraham took Hagar and Keturah; that Jacob took Rachel, Bilhah, and Zilpah; by revelation—the saints of the Lord are always directed by revelation.'"[4] As usual, belief in God's new revelations to and through Smith was the starting point for changes in Mormon beliefs and practices, including potential deviations from what seemed clear in the *Book of Mormon* itself. The time for raising up a righteous seed was apparently drawing nigh. This 1831 revelation did not initiate plural marriage among the Saints in that same year but it did open the door for it in the future.

These ideas and revelations became reality in early 1833 when Joseph Smith married Fanny Alger. For many reasons this was a turning point, although it, too, is shrouded in obscurity. Despite their best efforts, Mormon historians have not been able to determine precisely when Smith's relationship with Alger began. More importantly, because of Smith's silence during this period, no one can do anything but guess as to his motivations.

Instead, as historian John G. Turner concludes: "Whether Smith was motivated by religious obedience or pursued sexual dalliances with divine sanction cannot be fully resolved through historical analysis."[5]

Scholars agree, however, that Joseph Smith was involved in an intimate relationship with Fanny Alger between 1831 and 1836, and married her sometime in early 1833. Born in 1816, Fanny Alger was only fourteen when her parents, Samuel Alger and Clarissa Hancock, converted to Mormonism in 1830. According to the most reliable source, sometime in the "Spring of 1832" Smith approached Levi Hancock, Fanny Alger's uncle, and proposed "a bargain." Hancock wanted to marry the seventeen-year-old Clarissa Reed, who at the time was a servant in Joseph and Emma's home. The situation was complicated, however, because Hancock was already engaged to another woman. Confused, as well as guilt-ridden about not asking for Smith's consent for the original engagement, Hancock went to the prophet for counsel. Smith told Levi to "Never mind" about his prior engagement, "for the Lord has one prepared for you that will be a Blessing to you forever." Smith then proposed his "bargain . . .—If you will get Fanny Alger for me for a wife you may have Clarissa Reed. I love Fanny." Levi Hancock then brokered the deal first with the parents (his sister and brother-in-law), and then with Fanny Alger herself, all of whom consented to the union. The "bargain" was a success. At age twenty-seven, Smith married sixteen-year-old Fanny Alger in either February or early March 1833, and Levi Hancock married Clarissa Reed a short time later on March 29, 1833.[6]

This first plural marriage lasted for three and a half years, from the ceremony in early 1833 until September 1836, when the Alger family—Fanny included—left Kirtland for Missouri. Two months later, while stopped in Indiana for the winter, the then twenty-year-old Fanny met and married a local non-Mormon named Solomon Custer. The couple lived out the rest of their rather uneventful lives right there in Wayne County, Indiana. Fanny bore nine children and never returned to the LDS Church. She and tragically only three of her children outlived Solomon, who died in 1885. Where and when she died is a mystery, as are her thoughts on her much earlier first marriage to Joseph Smith. When Smith was killed in 1844, one of her brothers reportedly asked her about their relationship, to which she tersely replied: "That is all a matter of my—own. and I have nothing to Communicate."[7]

Although the details of Smith's marriage to Fanny Alger are difficult to piece together, here is an attempt at a rough outline of what happened during those three and a half years. For part of this time, possibly before but definitely after the wedding ceremony in 1833, Fanny lived as a servant in Joseph and Emma Smith's home. One source even reports that Emma, clearly not aware of the true nature of Joseph and Fanny's relationship, was "extremely fond of her." But upon "discovering the fact," Emma "at once took measures to place the girl beyond his reach." Emma's ejection of Fanny from her home—which would be repeated in Nauvoo with other servant-girls-turned-plural-wives—probably happened sometime in mid-1835. The now homeless Fanny Alger was taken in by the Webb family "until she could be sent to her relatives" in Mayfield, Ohio. This is presumably why Fanny Alger accompanied her parents when they left Ohio for Missouri in September 1836.[8]

It is estimated that this story reached an important relational and ecclesiastical turning point in late summer 1835. Mormon historian Richard Van Wagoner "suggests an August 1835 departure date for Fanny." Van Wagoner also tells of Oliver Cowdery "recommending that Joseph leave Kirtland for a time after the flareup with Emma."[9] Smith did leave Ohio for Michigan and on August 17, 1835, in his absence, Church leaders voted to include in the *Doctrine and Covenants* an "Article on Marriage" to publicly combat rumors of polygamy, and to affirm the Church's adherence to monogamy. It reads: "Inasmuch as this Church of Christ has been reproached with the crime of fornication, and polygamy: we declare that we believe, that one man should have one wife; and one woman, but one husband, except in the case of death when either is at liberty to marry again."[10] Smith returned to Kirtland less than a week later on August 23, but the careful timing of his absence is telling. As the controversy reached a boiling point, Smith took Cowdery's advice and left town while the Church's General Assembly cleaned up the mess he had made. Perhaps he did this to help things cool down and because he did not feel he could be present in the meeting to support a promonogamy "Article on Marriage" that he had just violated. In any event, the article was added to the *Doctrine and Covenants* and Joseph did nothing to alter it.[11]

What then followed was a five-to-six-year cessation of plural marriage. As described in the previous chapter, the late 1830s were not easy times for the Church, with Smith having to manage one crisis after another. The added persecution that would have come from practicing plural marriage would have pushed Smith and the Church past the breaking point. Once safely ensconced in Nauvoo, however, the controversial practice resumed and accelerated. Smith married three women in 1841, thirteen women in 1842, and twenty-one more in 1843, the year he received the revelation on plural marriage. He took no additional wives in 1844, the year of his death.[12] He also slowly and secretly began teaching the doctrine to Church leaders, but suffered defection and opposition from those who refused to accompany him on this most arduous part of their collective spiritual pilgrimage.

Oliver Cowdery, who had been at Smith's side from before the Church was restored, broke with him in part over plural marriage before the end of the 1830s. Cowdery had been Smith's scribe while translating the *Book of Mormon,* and he stood by Smith, at first anyway, as his marriage to Fanny Alger spiraled into controversy in 1835. This episode proved to be a turning point in their relationship, however, after which Cowdery lost respect for Smith and was eventually excommunicated from the Church. Using a phrase that would later become famous, Cowdery called the incident "a dirty, nasty, filthy affair of his and Fanny Alger's," and apparently he did not keep his opinions to himself.[13] While in Missouri with Smith in 1837 and 1838, Cowdery spread the news among some leading Saints, and was tried in April 1838 for "seeking to destroy the character of President Joseph Smith jr [sic] by falsely insinuating that he was guilty of adultry [sic] &c."[14]

Much, it turns out, hinged on whether or not Smith had technically committed adultery. At the heart of the matter was a crucial difference of opinion about whether Smith's relationship with Alger was extramarital and thus adulterous, or whether it took place within the institution of marriage, although in this case a plural marriage. For his part, Smith never denied that a relationship existed, but he adamantly insisted that it was not adulterous. Prior to the 1838 excommunication trial, Smith got Cowdery to change his tune, going on record to state that he was not guilty of such a sin. For whatever reasons, Cowdery waffled but in the end maintained that the relationship had in fact been adulterous. On April 12, 1838, he was excommunicated from the Church for slandering the prophet he had once loved.

Smith was preoccupied about having committed the sin of adultery for the remainder of his life. The 1843 revelation on plural marriage speaks to this preoccupation. "If any man espouse a virgin, and desire to espouse another, and the first give her consent, and if he espouse the second, and they are virgins, and have vowed to no other man, then *he is justified; he cannot commit adultery* for they are given unto him; . . . And if he have ten virgins given unto him by this law, *he cannot commit adultery,* for they belong to him, and they are given unto him; *therefore is he justified.*"[15]

The revelation denies adultery and proclaims the polygamous man justified. Joseph Smith and his followers had departed from other orthodoxies fearlessly. Plural marriage, however, was a different story. Rather than boldly proclaiming it, Smith engaged in it secretly in the 1830s with Fanny Alger, and then in the 1840s when he resumed the practice in Nauvoo.

Atypically, Smith seemed conflicted about his plural marriages. This could perhaps be attributed to the fact that he felt guilty about wronging his devoted wife Emma. Although he received a revelation in 1843 sanctioning plural marriage, he had also married numerous women prior to this recorded sanctioning, starting with Fanny Alger. Either these relationships were good and godly, or they were sinful and deserving of punishment. So which one was it?

My interpretation is that Smith felt conflicted about a potential moral infraction that would compromise his own place in the afterlife. Evidence indicates that Smith and Fanny did in fact consummate the relationship.[16] The question then becomes whether or not this sexual activity took place legitimately within the institution of marriage, albeit redefined; or illegitimately as an adulterous, extramarital affair. Without plural marriage the sexual union would be adultery, a sin in the eyes of God and an offense that according to Smith's own revelations about the afterlife would relegate him to the Telestial Kingdom and bar him from the Celestial Kingdom. His revelation of February 16, 1832—and thus prior to his marriage to Fanny Alger—lists among those in the Telestial Kingdom "they who are liars, and sorcerers, and adulterers, and whoremongers."[17] According to Mormon cosmology, Smith would not be damned, but the potential offense nevertheless held out the possibility of dire eternal consequences. Unless his relationship with Fanny Alger was a married one and not an adulterous one, Joseph Smith, the prophet chosen to restore the ancient Church, would himself fail to experience the highest form of exaltation.

Thus technically—and this technicality matters a great deal for Smith's eternal placement—the sexual relationship was not adultery as long as it was within the bounds of plural matrimony. Revelations in the early 1830s had hinted at the possibility of polygamous unions among the Saints, and thus had theologically and ethically prepared the way for such a relationship. But taking such an idea "from Theory to Practice," as historian George D. Smith puts it, was an enormous step.[18] In the early 1830s the theological justification for plural marriage was there in theory, but Smith's embarking on plural marriage with Fanny Alger in the mid 1830s pushed the practice inexorably forward. More elaborate, although secret, revelations and doctrines would have to follow, which they did after Smith resumed plural marriage in Nauvoo in the early 1840s. Similarly, when the Church announced plural marriage in 1852, it followed the announcement with more sophisticated written explications and defenses. There is thus a pattern of theological permissiveness, followed by radical and heterodox actions that require "justification," followed by more systematic theological explanations. And while this book prioritizes the causal importance of ideas, it by no means seeks to reduce this complex process to ideas and ideas alone. Actions and emotions that defy logical or theological explanation are among the most powerful causal forces in human experience. Passions like love, hate, sexual desire, envy, greed, pride, and compassion can drive people to do things that they might only barely understand at the time.

What is fascinating for the historian is when those who commit such actions and experience such emotions then try to express their thoughts about them in words that make sense of them by fitting them into familiar and comfortable mental categories, even if they redefine those categories in the process. That is what I believe to have been the case with Joseph Smith's life-changing relationship with Fanny Alger. And once again, the 1838 trial that resulted in Oliver Cowdery's excommunication is telling. Either Smith's relationship with Alger was adulterous—definitely a familiar category—or it was this nascent category called plural marriage. Smith wanted to make sure that it was the second. Plural marriage would lie dormant until the early 1840s, but a certain point of no return had been crossed, and a new religio-ethical category created, or perhaps restored. When circumstances permitted, Smith would resume plural marriage, and this time he would encourage other men to follow him.

The story of how John Humphrey Noyes experienced his "First Act in Sexual Freedom" is both like and unlike that of Joseph Smith.[19] The two are alike in that they both departed from monogamy—a departure that outsiders considered to be adultery. This chapter will end, in fact, with Noyes being prosecuted for adultery in late 1847 and having to relocate his infant community from Putney, Vermont, to Oneida, New York. There is also a similarity in that their radical religio-sexual ideas came first, followed by their radical sexual experiments. Both men's actions were contrary to the mores of their antebellum culture, but they felt ethically justified to trespass beyond the bounds of monogamous marriage because of what they believed to be prior divine consent. God had sanctioned their actions prior to their acting.

The two men are different in that whereas Joseph Smith had only one major point of no return with his plural marriage to Fanny Alger, Noyes had three turning points, each one involving a different and influential woman in his life. The first was his failed romantic relationship with Abigail Merwin, which led to his condemnation of the exclusivity of monogamous marriage in 1837. The second was his wife's, Harriet Holton Noyes's, many painful and failed pregnancies, which led to his theory of male continence in 1844. The third was his increasingly intimate and ultimately sexual relationship with Mary Cragin, which led to the theory and practice of complex marriage in 1846. Also unlike Joseph Smith, Noyes's journey to "sexual freedom" was slow, methodical, and very well documented.

In November 1836, after two and a half peripatetic years spreading the Perfectionist gospel throughout the Northeast, Noyes was back at his parents' home in Vermont. It was during this time, from 1837 to 1847, that Noyes both developed his heterodox sexual theories and established his undisputed dominance over any and all who joined the community. To say that Noyes grew confident in his leadership during this decade would be a gross understatement. Never one to brook dissent, Noyes would settle for nothing less than total submission to his will and assent to his ideas. Believing he was uniquely gifted and divinely appointed to build God's kingdom, Noyes sought disciples who would follow him unquestioningly.[20]

It is no wonder that when Abigail Merwin, his first convert and the "morning-star to my soul," rejected him for another man, Noyes's universe came crashing down around him. Resorting to what he did best, Noyes then tried to debate her back into love with him. "I came by Providence and her request into the relation of pastor to her, . . . she cannot break it up by a mere change of her feelings and will."[21] Noyes loved Abigail Merwin, but as her "pastor" he also felt a strange entitlement to her devotion, believing that their relationship, rather than being based on voluntary and reciprocal affection, was more like a binding contract from which the unilateral withdrawal of one party was prohibited and even punishable. Disconsolate after her marriage in January 1837 to Merit Platt, Noyes followed the newlyweds—essentially stalking them—to their home in Ithaca, New York. Four years later, in 1841, when his mother asked him what on earth he was thinking in making that trip, Noyes felt as injured as ever. Shifting his metaphorical reference from a church pastor to a military officer, Noyes fired back that he went to Ithaca for the purpose of "confronting Abigail Merwin, who had deserted her post as my helper."²² Whether as her pastor or her commanding officer, Noyes could think of Merwin's actions only in terms of personal betrayal and insubordination to the Perfectionist cause which he led.

On January 15, 1837, Noyes vented spleen in a private letter that would soon become a very public scandal. Even with all of his previous theological provocations, this was the first time he wrote so bluntly about marriage and sex—"one delicate subject" as he called it—but it would prove to be pivotal in setting the trajectory for the rest of his life. Writing to his friend David Harrison, Noyes concluded bitterly: "When the will of God is done on earth as it is in heaven there will be no marriage. Exclusiveness, jealousy, quarreling have no place at the marriage supper of the Lamb." Utilizing his well-honed theological resources to make sense of his emotional anguish, Noyes took out his frustrations on both the deserter Abigail Merwin and on what he considered to be the unfair exclusivity of sexually monogamous marriages. Nothing, of course, was wrong with him. The problem instead was with sinful people and sinful institutions, no matter how hallowed those institutions might be, or how scandalous it might be to question them. If they caused the kind of misery he was currently experiencing, something must be wrong with them.²³

Noyes's private thoughts about sex and marriage became public when his letter was published in August 1837. Fatefully, he had included in his missive a proviso that David Harrison, the addressee, judge for himself "whether it is expedient to show this letter to others."²⁴ Harrison did, and after it worked its way through the ranks of some of the Northeast's most uncompromising Perfectionists, it fell into the hands of Noyes's old "friend," Theophilus R. Gates of Philadelphia, the Christian anarchist whom he had debated in 1835. Serendipitously, Gates too had recently turned his attention to the problematic institution of monogamous marriage, and had just launched in July 1837 *The Battle-Axe and Weapons of War*, a publication through which he sought to lambaste monogamy's many evils and advocate for a different system of conjugal relations. Gates was possibly inspired by Emanuel Swedenborg, the eighteenth-century Swedish mystic who believed that marriage was eternal but only for couples who shared true love. Gates was also possibly motivated by his own apparently less-than-happy marriage. Regardless, he had harsh things to say about a life-long, and potentially eternal monogamous system of "man and wife, so called, living in strife and disagreement."²⁵ When Noyes's letter arrived, Gates thought that the old adversaries now shared a common enemy, and he published it anonymously on the front page of his paper's second edition in August 1837.

Henceforth, Noyes's thoughts about sex and marriage, first expressed in that letter, had a tumultuous life of their own. The following month, as the scandal reached white-hot intensity, Noyes announced in the pages of his own publication, *The Witness,* that he was indeed the author of the letter.[26] But now that the word was out, Noyes considered it God's will, and was more than ready for the next wave of derision he would have to endure from the religious establishment. As with his initial profession of Perfectionism in 1834, Noyes unflinchingly let his radical ideas lead him into intellectual combat, refusing to recant or retreat in any way whatsoever. Even if those controversial thoughts had clearly been born out of his personal pain, and even if they had been expressed unsystematically in what was intended to be private musings only, Noyes displayed his old disputatious stubbornness in all its glory. Having professed it, he was now committed to it. He could work out the details later.

In the wake of "The Battle-Axe Letter" controversy, Noyes's ideas and actions seemed incongruous. He was still in love with Abigail Merwin, and buoyed in his hopes of having her when she separated from her husband in December 1837, less than a year after their marriage. If Merwin had come running back into Noyes's arms, it is uncertain whether he would have stuck to his theories damning the exclusivity of monogamous marriage. As things turned out, however, Merwin had changed her mind irrevocably: she would never marry Noyes. After trying to win her back throughout the winter of 1837–38, Noyes accepted defeat in the spring, but he did not go quietly. Incapable of not expressing his feelings in writing, Noyes fired a parting shot in this final, bitter poem to his lost love.

> I will not give you back your heart,
> I've wooed and fairly won it,
> And sooner with my life I'll part,
> You may depend upon it.
>
> You say your heart is still your own,
> But words will never prove it.
> What God and you and I have done
> Will stand; the world can't move it.[27]

Noyes was clearly both heartbroken and angry, and he blamed his emotional pain on her supposedly inscrutable and sinful decision, and on the evil exclusivity of monogamous marriage itself.

It is therefore highly ironic that just a few months later, after a very brief courtship, Noyes married Harriet Holton on June 28, 1838. To utilize modern terminology, this was clearly a "rebound" relationship, as Noyes was still in love with Abigail Merwin. But Harriet Holton was religiously zealous, financially stable, and emotionally available to support Noyes in another hour of need. In the same way that Abigail Merwin had been Noyes's anchor in the midst of his Perfectionist crisis in 1834, Harriet Holton was now his source of stability during this painful breakup and the "Battle-Axe Letter" controversy of 1837 and 1838.[28]

In many ways, Harriet Holton was a perfect match for Noyes. Like him, she was from Vermont, had devoted her life to God during a revival in 1831, and had similarly become dismayed by her sin after her awakening and sought *more* than what her Congregational Church could offer. When she heard about Noyes's controversial doctrine of Perfectionism she was intrigued. In 1834, just months after Noyes staked his theological claim, Holton declared herself a Perfectionist and later met him on one of his missionary trips to Vermont. Thus like Abigail Merwin, Holton was one of Noyes's first converts. But unlike Merwin, who had captured Noyes's heart while emotionally supporting him in New Haven, Holton was a virtual stranger living hundreds of miles away who could support him only with letters of admiration and financial donations to the cause. Also unlike Merwin, who later abandoned Perfectionism and was guilty of so-called insubordination, Holton was willing to submit unconditionally and indefinitely to Noyes's leadership and to his evolving ideas about the nature of God, man, and marriage. As Noyes himself would later admit, the added financial support was indeed a factor in his decision to marry her, but intellectually and theologically the two were a match made in heaven. Sadly, it seems that the only thing missing was romance.[29]

The couple's so-called "love" letters during their brief courtship are heavy on theological compatibility—along with Holton's unqualified admiration for Noyes—but light on romantic or sexual passion. On June 11, 1838, Noyes wrote Holton a fascinating letter "to propose to you a partnership which I will not call marriage till I have defined it." This single sentence almost says it all. Noyes sought from Holton not romantic fulfillment, but "a partnership" in Perfectionism, and he insisted on literally defining the nature of their relationship. Referencing both Matthew 22:30 ("neither marrying nor giving in marriage"), and the position he had committed himself to in his own "Battle-Axe Letter," he informed her that their partnership must not "limit the range of our affections as they are limited in matrimonial engagements by the fashion of this world." In other words there would be no exclusivity. Such was Noyes's Perfectionist proposal: almost devoid of affection for Holton, and insisting from the very beginning that she be willing to expand their love beyond the bounds of conventional monogamy.[30]

Harriet Holton's responses were rhetorically perfect: assenting to Noyes's demands and boosting his ego with every metaphor. She would happily be the earnest congregant and he the pastor. Quoting Noyes back to himself, which he doubtlessly appreciated, she replied that in "gladly accepting this proposal for an external union I agree with you that it will not 'limit the range of our affections.'"[31] Four days after she wrote those words the two married on June 28, 1838.

What came next for the couple was more incongruity, combined with personal heartache. Even though he had done everything to pave the way for what he would later call "complex marriage," and even though he was not passionately in love with Harriet Holton, Noyes did not act on the idea for the first eight years of their marriage. Whatever later critics would say about his supposedly licentious community at Oneida, this was clearly not a young man in a hurry to have multiple sexual partners. Instead, the early years of his marriage were utterly conventional: monogamous, legal, and with the exception of the radical beliefs that he expressed in the pages of his periodicals, rather bourgeois. Like many other newlyweds, they also seem to have wanted children.

Noyes's shift from ideas into actions, as he put it, was "forced upon me by sorrow"—the couple's heartbreaking experience as they tried to build their family. "Within six years," he recollected about their marriage from 1838 to 1844,

> my wife went through the agonies of five births. Four were premature. Only one child lived. After our last disappointment I pledged my word to my wife that I would never again expose her to such fruitless suffering.... This was in the summer of 1844. At that time the solution came to me as an inspiration, that the social function [of sexual intercourse] could be separated from the procreative. I found that the self-control required was not difficult. This was a great deliverance. We had escaped the horrors and the fear of involuntary propagation, and our married life was happy as never before.[32]

With great empathy for his wife, Noyes put his mind to work on the problem of sex and birth control. The "solution" as he put it was his theory of male continence: intercourse without ejaculation. Thus another component of Noyes's unique sexual order was created—born yet again out of a combination of "sorrow" and his predilection to meet life's troubles with bold innovation, no matter how scandalous that innovation might be.

How and why Noyes began complex marriage in 1846 follows a different pattern. As with the previous two episodes, a woman, Mary Cragin, was at the heart of the story; but this time Noyes's innovation had more to do with his libido than it did with his experience of romantic or emotional trauma. This story also differs in that while clearly about Noyes's intimacy with Cragin, it is less about their one-to-one relationship and more about the community that they shared. Another changed variable was the fact that Mary Cragin, whom Noyes sexually desired, was married when he met her. She and her husband George arrived in Putney together in 1840 to join the community that Noyes was gathering around him.

Back in July 1838, Noyes had a new wife and a new printing press, but still only a handful of "simple-minded, unpretending believers chiefly belonging to my father's family."[33] His earliest followers, in fact, were entirely from his own relations. They included his wife Harriet Holton Noyes, his mother Polly, his two sisters Harriet and Charlotte, and his brother George Washington Noyes. Two of the first additions to this obviously in-house sect only continued the trend: John L. Skinner joined the group in 1839 and married Harriet Noyes in 1841, and John R. Miller joined in 1841 and married Charlotte in 1842. Thus seven members of what one chronicler called "the nucleus of the Putney Corporation" were literally related to John Humphrey Noyes by either blood or marriage. The only exceptions to this rule were George and Mary Cragin, and their outsider status would not last for long.[34]

It is impossible to tell the story of Noyes's first community in Putney without telling the story of the Cragins. The first part of their spiritual biography reads like a description of the quintessential Burned-over-District couple seeking *more*. George Cragin was converted in 1829 at one of Charles Finney's revivals in New York City, and married his soulmate, Mary Johnson, in 1834. That same year George took a job as business manager of the *Advocate of Moral Reform,* one of the era's most established evangelical publications. In fact, in late 1837, in the midst of the "Battle-Axe Letter" controversy, the *Advocate,* acting on its self-appointed "duty as humble conservators of the public morals," took Noyes to task for his "immoral and destructive" ideas.[35] Ironically, George Cragin was still working for the paper at the time. Although he and Mary had been exposed to Perfectionist beliefs before and were actually wrestling with the ideas, George toed the *Advocate*'s party line and kept his thoughts to himself. In late 1839, however, after more reading and discussions with various Perfectionists, the Cragins changed sides and received, as Mary put it, "full salvation from sin."[36] Mary even wrote to Noyes to tell him the joyous development: the Cragins had embraced Perfectionism and were ready to devote their lives to spreading its good news.

Things began to get complicated, however, once the Cragins joined up with the Newark Perfectionists under the leadership of Abram C. Smith. Noyes considered Smith to be a trusted and kindred spirit in the cause, but what happened next would strain their friendship. Sexual license and the rumor of sexual license were becoming problems throughout the Northeast Perfectionist diaspora, but especially for the Newark Perfectionists, with the real "climax of wantonness . . . reached in December 1839," in the Perfectionist snow-bound funeral orgy that included Smith, and George and Mary Cragin.[37]

Just months later, in the spring of 1840, Abram Smith invited the Cragins to live with him and his wife in Rondout, New York, and they accepted. Smith soon manipulated circumstances so that he could have an affair with Mary, which she seems to have been just as interested in as he was. Smith forced his wife to go and live with her relatives, while he loaded down George Cragin "with hard work, self-condemnation and evil thinking." George was so given to pathetic self-reproach in fact that even while in emotional agony at the affair, he "considered himself quite as much in the wrong as they." Thankfully he had an advocate and a champion in John Humphrey Noyes.[38]

Noyes—the future pioneer of religio-sexual experimentation—personally intervened to stop the extramarital affair not once but twice. The first time he "rebuked Smith sharply for his course with his wife," "admonished" the couple to cease their illicit relationship immediately, and took Smith with him to Putney to let things blow over. Not long after Smith returned to Rondout, however, he and Mary Cragin picked up where they had left off, and this time Noyes was less forgiving. He declared the two guilty of adultery, excommunicated Abram Smith from the ranks of the Perfectionists (he was later restored), and invited the now homeless Cragins to join his community in Putney.[39]

In the early 1840s, the Putney Community grew in numbers and matured in its organization. In addition to consolidating incontestable power in himself, Noyes's solution to the problem of governance was what he called "mutual criticism," during which community members took turns both giving and receiving feedback about one's job performance, appearance, interpersonal interactions, and character traits. Noyes had learned this technique from the Brethren during his year at Andover. The idea was that people's comments would build individuals up by praising their strengths, while encouraging them to improve upon their now publicly identified weaknesses. Members were to remain silent while the criticism took place, but then shifted from being the examined to being among the examiners when his or her turn was over. In principle, mutual criticism was a process through which community members would grow in their love for God and neighbor. In practice, mutual criticism provided an intimate system of checks and balances—precisely the kind of internal governing mechanism that Noyes sought. In not submitting himself to the community's criticism, the process also provided Noyes with a powerful and subtle instrument of control, keeping people equal and accountable, and defusing the many conflicts that could have torn the community apart. Thus, by 1846 all the managerial pieces were in place for Noyes to make the final jump from complex marriage as theory to complex marriage as community practice. What pushed Noyes over the edge was Mary Cragin.

It is important to point out, however, that Noyes's "First Act in Sexual Freedom" did not involve just him and Mary Cragin, but both of their spouses as well. Unlike Joseph Smith, who propositioned Fanny Alger without telling his wife Emma about it, all four members of the Noyes-Cragin affair knew about it and assented to it ahead of time. In fact, in addition to John Humphrey Noyes and Mary Cragin's mutual attraction, apparently George Cragin and Harriet Holton Noyes had feelings for one another as well. Mary Cragin's journal recounts a scene in which Harriet revealed that "her heart was drawn out toward" George, "Mr. Cragin confessed a similar feeling toward her," and then after asking Mr. Cragin's permission, John Humphrey Noyes confessed his love for Mary and she returned the sentiment. In many ways this was a nineteenth-century version of "swinging," or spouse-swapping, except that no sex was involved (at least at first) and the interaction was thoroughly religious. "After these avowals," Mary Cragin's journal continues, "we considered ourselves engaged to each other," with "evidence that our love is of God: it is destitute of exclusiveness, each one rejoicing in the happiness of the others."[40] This was hardly an orgy. The whole process was systematic, mutual, transparent, and at first asexual.

The relationships became sexual in the spring of 1846. Because Noyes conveys what happened so clearly, it is worth quoting in full his own recollection:

> One evening in May 1846 Mrs. Cragin and I went for a stroll. Coming to a lonely place we sat on a rock by the roadside and talked. All the circumstances invited advance in freedom, and yielding to the impulse upon me I took some personal liberties. The temptation to go further was tremendous. But at this point came serious thoughts. I stopped and resolved in mind as before God what to do.... After a moment we arose and went toward home. On the way we lingered. But I said, 'No, I am going home to report what we have done.' On reaching Mr. Cragin's house I called a meeting of the four. Mr. Cragin at first was tempted to think that I was following the course of Abram C. Smith, but he finally recognized the difference and gave judgment of approval. My wife promptly expressed her entire sanction. The last part of the interview was as amicable and happy as a wedding, and the consequence was that we gave each other full liberty.[41]

Sexual desire clearly played its part in Noyes's taking "some personal liberties" with Mary Cragin. But after the first "impulse," and in spite of the "tremendous" urge "to go further," Noyes's religious mind took over, he had "serious thoughts" about what was the godly thing to do, and he sought the consent of both his wife and Mary Cragin's husband. Once again, the process was controlled, systematic, and mutual. Now it was also sexual.

It is not clear when John Humphrey Noyes and Mary Cragin consummated what they had started on that "lonely" evening in May 1846. What is evident, however, is that they did, and that he began in the "winter of 1846–7, while Complex Marriage was being extended in strict confidence through the circle of Perfectionists at Putney," to reveal "the facts to a small number of selected Perfectionists abroad." Just as Joseph Smith would introduce plural marriage slowly and secretly at Nauvoo, Noyes insisted upon "Bible secretiveness" among his first initiates into complex marriage.[42] In November 1846, four couples (the Cragins, the Noyeses, and John Humphrey's in-laws, the Millers and the Skinners) pledged in a "Statement of Principles" to surrender "All individual proprietorship either of persons or things," and to "submit ourselves in all things spiritual and temporal,... without disputing" to the leadership of John Humphrey Noyes.[43] As usual, what seemed to matter most to Noyes were his religious ideas and his control of the community. In January 1847, he described himself as the "generalissimo of Perfectionists," and similarly referred to "our undertaking at Putney" as "a military school, a West Point for the training of engineers and officers."[44]

In that year, however, Noyes had to shut down his Perfectionist West Point and leave Putney entirely. And for what it is worth, rather than acting like a brave "generalissimo," Noyes behaved more like a coward and the very kind of deserter he loathed. Over the course of 1847 the number of adults practicing complex marriage at Putney grew from the original eight to thirty-one. Although still a relatively small group, that nearly fourfold increase in the communally married brought with it problems that he could not control. "Bible secretiveness," for instance, diminished to the point of nonexistence. When one would-be initiate, Daniel Hall, could not accept the idea of complex marriage, but feared that his wife might embrace it nonetheless, he tattled on the community to the local authorities and the word was out. On October 26, 1847, the local sheriff arrested Noyes on the charge of adultery. Noyes's brother-in-law John R. Miller posted bail and Noyes was released. A month later, ostensibly to avoid suffering "martyrdom at the hands of a mob, as did Joseph Smith,"[45] Noyes skipped town for Brattleboro, and then left the state, violating his bail. In his absence, outraged Putney citizens demanded "the immediate dissolution of said Association."[46]

Those Putney citizens soon got their way. On the lam in New York City, Noyes finally wrote back to his followers after a two-week silence, instructing them to prepare to liquidate the community's property and relocate, although they would never acknowledge "that we have done wrong, that is out of the question with me."[47] Having encouraged the troops to keep fighting for the cause, Noyes then retreated again into solitary silence, this time for over a month. When he did reconnect with his followers he was even more adamant about the godliness of their struggle. "Our warfare is an assertion of human rights," he proclaimed. "The head and font and whole of our offense is communism of love. . . . If this is the unpardonable sin in the world, we are sure it is the beauty and glory of heaven." Encouraging them with the sectarian perspective in which persecution by "the world" indicates the godliness of the persecuted, Noyes kept his now battle-hardened little group together. Over the course of the winter 1847–48 they sold their property in Putney and relocated to the farm of Jonathan Burt, a sympathetic Perfectionist in Oneida, New York. There, as with the Mormons in Nauvoo, Illinois, in 1839, and the Shakers in America in 1774, they hoped to find a more hospitable environment in which to grow their spiritual, sexual community.

6

Institutional

AT THIS point in their histories, each of the sectarian movements had fled a hostile environment and found a relatively safe one. Ann Lee left England for America in 1774, the Mormons retreated back across the Mississippi River to Illinois in 1839, and John Humphrey Noyes abandoned his hometown of Putney, Vermont, for Oneida, New York, in 1848. And while the stories of each sect thus far have included some institution building, largely they have been the stories of the three charismatic founders. In this chapter, by contrast, I am going to tell how each of the sects, because of their new locations, had an opportunity to establish their communities on a more solid foundation, attract additional followers, and build in relative peace their versions of the kingdom of God.

Developing rules and rituals that reinforced one another was the most important part of this process of institution-building. All three communities had to deal with the serious problems of internal dissent and outside hostility. Without some kind of internal and internalized governing mechanisms, the movements probably would not have survived the challenges that accompanied their first tumultuous years. Part 3 on "Early Crises" will discuss in detail those challenges that put each group's nascent governing structure to the test. This chapter is going to explore how those structures came about in the first place. For the Mormons the story starts in the immensely important Nauvoo period of LDS history, from 1839 to 1846. This is the time when Joseph Smith revealed to the Saints the endowment ceremony, the importance of the temple, baptism for the dead, celestial marriage, and—for his closest associates—plural marriage. He revealed all of these complex ceremonies during the Church's time in Nauvoo. I will also explore the formative years of John Humphrey Noyes's Oneida Community: how he put mutual criticism and male continence into practice and established other governing structures that kept the community together.

But we begin with the Shakers, who existed decades before the Mormons and Perfectionists. If we want to circle back to the real chronological beginning of this story—in America anyway—it would have to be 1774 when Ann Lee and her followers arrived in New York. Another reason to begin with the Shakers is because of their success as institution builders and the comparisons that can be drawn from them. In the half-century after their arrival in 1774, the Shakers perfected their organizational structures.

What transpired between Ann Lee's arrival in America and her death a decade later can be divided into two distinct phases: a period of relative inactivity from 1774 to 1780, followed by a period of hyperactivity from 1781 to 1784. After reaching New York City, the immigrants traveled up the Hudson River to the small town of Niskayuna, near Albany. In those first years in America, the group was in no way evangelistic. Instead, their sectarian desire to separate themselves from the world now finally matched their setting. Enjoying the newfound peace that accompanied seclusion, they kept to themselves and continued their unique religious exhortations and ecstatic worship services. And interestingly, when things did change for the tiny sect it was not because they went out into the world, but because the world started coming to them.

The Niskayuna community's isolation ended in 1780, the year that Shakers say their gospel was "opened" in America. Although Lee and her followers initially sought neither converts nor public notice, word of the eccentric community nevertheless spread throughout the region, inspiring both curiosity and precisely the kind of repression they had hoped to avoid. In 1780, after a local revival stirred up religious sentiments, those who wanted *more* sought them out and began arriving at Niskayuna to learn about their beliefs and possibly to share in them. But rather than stay and join the community, most converts returned to their homes with their newfound faith. Not all of the visitors either believed or persevered in their beliefs, but the sect did grow in numbers with virtually no missionary effort. As pilgrims continued to file into Niskayuna, though, the community inevitably attracted attention. Because the Revolutionary War was still raging, and because the sect was odd, pacifist, and growing, it was deemed a threat. Fearing subversion of the revolutionary cause, the wartime authorities incarcerated Ann Lee and several others for over four months, finally releasing them on December 4, 1780.[1]

Rather than try to regain the splendid isolation that was now clearly a thing of the past, in 1781 the community faced outward and sought to spread the word throughout New England, visiting the new believers in their homes and hoping also to win more converts in the process.

In May of 1781, a small group that included Ann Lee, William Lee, and James Whittaker left Niskayuna for their missionary field, and did not return until September 1783, a full two and a half years later. By all accounts, their first effort at proselytizing was a spectacular success. Like the Apostle Paul, they enjoyed the hospitality of their hosts, encouraged fellow believers in the faith, preached their message in nearby towns, and often suffered physical violence from the angry unconverted. According to sectarian logic, however, such incidents were only more evidence of God's favor, and the missionaries returned to Niskayuna encouraged by both the numbers of those who believed and the persecution of those who did not.[2]

Not everyone these missionaries encountered, however, can be so easily categorized as either friendly believer or hostile unbeliever. A number of people initially embraced the Shaker gospel but for a variety of reasons abandoned it, and they did not keep their opinions to themselves. Because Ann Lee and most of her followers were illiterate, the published views of these apostates are some of the best sources historians have about the early Shaker movement, for good and for ill. Although biased, these polemics nevertheless provide valuable insight into the practices, personalities, and ideas of the young sect.[3] The brothers Valentine and Daniel Rathbun (alternately spelled Rathbone), and Valentine's son Reuben, for instance, all joined the Shakers but eventually lost their faith. All three also published screeds detailing their unpleasant experiences.

Valentine Rathbun published his *Account of the Matter, Form, and Manner of a New and Strange Religion* in 1781, the very year that Ann Lee began her missionary journey. This is an incredibly important and revealing source, explaining and criticizing in detail many of the most fundamental parts of the Shaker metanarrative, including "that they are the only church in the world . . . [that] all the churches now in the world are antichrist, and false churches . . . that the afore-recited woman, about forty years of age [Ann Lee] is the woman spoken of in the xiith chapter of the Revelations of John . . . and that every one that has any thing to do with man or woman, in the work of generation, is acting Adam and Eve's sin over again." In addition to disclosing early Shaker beliefs, the Valentine Rathbun source also documents some of the sect's more alarming practices. It tells of "their manner of worship," which involves "shaking their heads, in a violent manner, . . . singing without words, and some with an unknown tongue." It also records episodes in which "They run about in the woods and elsewhere, hooting and tooting like owls; some of them have stripped naked in the woods, and thought they were angels, and invisible, and could go about among men and not be seen."[4]

But most controversially the *Account* paints a picture of a highly controlling group dynamic. "When any person goes to see them," Rathbun reported, "they all meet him with many smiles, and seeming great gladness." As the neophyte delves deeper, however, the controlling commences. "When he comes again," they tell "him that he must confess his sins to them," but regrettably they inform him that "they [his sins] are not forgiven." And in a passage that for 1781 is an especially insightful observation of psychological manipulation, Rathbun writes: "While they are thus instructing their adherents, they sometimes use great severity, and sometimes great flattery, to frighten on the one hand and allure on the other." As he described it, one of the Shakers' primary goals was reducing people to "absolute dependence on them," and through these means they often achieved it.[5]

The exposés by the other two Rathbuns are even more ad hominem in their arguments, and more scandalous in their disclosures. Daniel Rathbun saved most of his venom for Ann Lee herself, describing her as "very often very angry, and much given to wine and strong drink, and certainly she was a striker, both of me and many others," even "pounding and beating the private parts of both men and women in her discipline." And apparently the rest of the Shakers were no better: "dancing stark naked together," "they will many of them drink hard, sing and dance all night, strip naked and spank one anothers [sic] arses." Reuben Rathbun's *Reasons Offered for Leaving the Shakers* includes more reports of leaders drinking and hitting one another, while describing his fascinating journey from neophyte to apostate. Yet another example of a spiritual seeker after *more*, the young Rathbun "thought I could never get a wife without laying aside my religion," and so he chose the higher path. Intrigued by the Shakers, he soon took up "the cross against the flesh" and labored "to wholly destroy that nature and faculty which is created in men and women for the purpose of propagating the specie [sic]." This cross, however, ultimately proved to be unbearable and their peculiar beliefs unbelievable. Rathbun later renounced his Shaker faith and hoped that his story would serve as a cautionary tale for anyone else who came into contact with the supposedly dangerous and deluded sect.[6]

Far more people, however, joined the Shakers and stayed with the Shakers in the 1780s than left them. Also wanting *more*, seekers like Joseph Meacham and Samuel Johnson journeyed to Niskayuna and kept the faith that they found there for the rest of their lives. When the first missionary journey ended in September 1783, there were so many converts spread out over such a relatively large area that Shaker leaders faced a new and daunting organizational challenge. What could be done to ensure that the many new believers would keep the faith? The answer was to organize them into self-sustaining communities, soon to be called "villages," like Niskayuna.

This organization, however, would not make substantial progress until 1787. Both Ann Lee and her brother William died in 1784, soon after returning from their missionary journey. Fortunately, the third member of their team, James Whittaker, survived to guide the young movement through this perilous time. Both a staunch sectarian and an effective administrator, as well as literate, Whittaker maintained order within the community and vehement separation from the world without. He is the one who wrote in a letter to his non-Shaker "Natural Relations in England," "I hate your fleshly lives, and your fleshly generation, as I hate the smoke of the bottomless pit." He also reminded them that no one except for this "one community that worship God in spirit . . . are in possession of the only hope of eternal life." As for them, he concluded, since "you have forsaken God, so I also forsake you." Clearly severing all ties with these "Natural Relations," Whittaker embraced his new spiritual family with whom he would live in peace, in order, and in light of "God's final visitation." James Whittaker died on July 20, 1787, but over the next forty years, Shakers would build and spread precisely the kind of heavenly families that he had spoken about so passionately.[7]

The period of institution building is largely a story of its foremost institution builders: Joseph Meacham and Lucy Wright. A bit like Brigham Young as we will see, Meacham was more of a manager and a pragmatist than a charismatic mystic. After James Whittaker's death, Shakers recognized that Meacham's abilities perfectly matched the many challenges that confronted their dispersed and disorganized movement, and they willingly submitted to his leadership. To their great satisfaction, Meacham did not disappoint. He turned his considerable administrative abilities to the problems at hand, deemphasized outward-looking missionary activity, and organized the inchoate sect from top to bottom. At the top he "introduced the principle of parallel female authority by choosing as his partner in the ministry Lucy Wright." Reflecting the Shaker belief in the male and female duality within the godhead, the Shaker governing structure would henceforth be a gender-balanced partnership and not a patriarchy. He also found in Lucy Wright a fellow effective administrator and eventual successor.[8]

At the bottom, Meacham and Wright organized Shakers into communities, with rules to govern almost every aspect of their daily lives. Meacham believed that these communities would sustain the Shakers' faith and allow them to be physically as well as spiritually separate from the world. He soon relocated the overall Shaker leadership to New Lebanon, New York, on the east side of the Hudson River, in part to be closer to the communities that were planned for New England. Ann Lee's missionary journey of 1781–83 had spread the seed of the Shaker gospel throughout the region. Now Meacham would "gather" the spiritual harvest into local sheaves.[9]

As these communities coalesced they needed organization and a governing structure, which Meacham was more than willing to provide. Shaker villages would henceforth be internally divided into three or more "courts" or "families," ranked according to religious devotion and physical ability. "An inner circle of adult Shakers constituted the first court," Stephen Stein writes, "younger members of lesser spiritual ability the second, and elderly persons the third."[10] Thus Meacham gave the unformed mass of Shakers a place to live and a clear hierarchy. He also organized the hours of the day, setting rules for when and how they would sleep, eat, work, and worship. Some chafed under the yoke of the elders and their many rules, but others found the clarity and order of communal life liberating rather than oppressing. By the time Joseph Meacham died in 1796, there were eleven Shaker Villages established throughout New York and New England. In nine short years, he had taken a dispersed and fragile movement of enthusiasts, consolidated them into hyper-organized communities, and channeled their zeal into a regularized form of worship.[11]

Because of Meacham's success as an organizer, the next Shaker leader, Lucy Wright, could once again direct the sect's energies outward, sharing their message with a spiritually hungry people, and organizing new converts into even more Shaker villages. In many ways the pattern of sowing and gathering repeated itself. But whereas in the first run of this cycle, Ann Lee had led the outward-focused missionary effort and Joseph Meacham the internal organization, this time everything took place during Lucy Wright's long tenure. As the leader of the Shakers for a quarter of a century from 1796 until her death in 1821, Wright left an indelible stamp on the sect.

With near perfect timing Wright shifted the Shakers' focus outward in 1799. Meacham's attention to internal matters had been necessary earlier in the decade, but now the sect risked insularity. With apostasies continuing and debts mounting, Wright surmised that a renewed missionary campaign would bring more sheep—along with their resources—into the fold, as well as strengthen the faith of the missionaries themselves. Wright also correctly perceived the changing spiritual climate in the new republic. There seemed to be a growing interest in religion throughout the culture, with revivals flaring up more regularly than they had during the revolutionary era. Perhaps they could divert some of this renewed spiritual energy into the proper channel of their Shaker gospel.[12]

When the Cane Ridge Revival happened two years later in 1801, leaders focused their attention on Kentucky and the broader Ohio Valley. There the Shaker proselytes intentionally "sought out camp meetings, where they were assured of large assemblies and a high level of religious excitement."[13] To use a potentially crass market analogy, Shakers used the revivals as a kind of religious trade show. There was a main event in the revivals themselves, but there were also opportunities for other vendors to promote their spiritual goods and services to the self-selected concentration of interested religious consumers. As later recollections indicate, Shaker leaders were thoroughly aware of this environment and how they could use it to their advantage. In two beautiful—if fragmented—sentences in particular, Richard McNemar summed up in his account *The Kentucky Revival* the chaos and competition of the American religious marketplace: "A great Christian empire, divided into a thousand little kingdoms, all inclosed [sic] in the bowels of a great republic, and each contending for the mastery. America exulting in her health, the liberty and equality of her members, and yet full of worms, biting and devouring one another, each pursuing a distinct course to which he presumes all others must finally give way." But McNemar and the Shakers also participated in the very dynamic that he so scathingly critiqued. As he put it elsewhere, with full sectarian condemnation, "the Kentucky Revival . . . we believe it was nothing less than an *introduction* to that work of *final redemption* which God had promised, in the latter days." Unbelievers might have converted at one of the many camp meetings, but "they did not take the last step," which is what the Shakers were there to facilitate, and by all measures their strategy of drafting in the wake of the revivals succeeded masterfully. In 1815, ten years after Lucy Wright sent missionaries into the trans-Appalachian frontier, they had gathered hundreds of believers into five new villages in Ohio, Kentucky, and Indiana.[14]

The now-proven institution of the village organized these western converts, but the sect's expansion into the frontier also brought with it new challenges that could not be solved by simply establishing more villages. Previously, when the movement was small and the leaders illiterate, close contact and oral tradition had been the means of initiating neophytes. But with the Appalachian Mountains in between the more established communities of the East and the newer communities of the West, this close contact and oral tradition became untenable. Lacking wisdom but not zeal, western converts implored Shaker leaders to rethink their aversion to written instruction. When Lucy Wright assented, her "permission simultaneously created a class of Shaker theologians within the society who shed the earlier anti-intellectualism and consciously donned the mantle of intellectual respectability." This was the real "beginnings of sustained systematic theological reflection" for the Shakers. But fascinatingly, instead of the first Shaker systematic theologies flowing from the experienced East to the unrefined West, these western converts did their own writing. What they produced was subject to the approval and revision of the authorities back East, but it was westerners who both identified their need for theological instruction, and then met the need for themselves.[15]

Making up for lost time, Shaker thinkers produced three hefty theological tomes between 1808 and 1823, and one hagiography of *Our Ever Blessed Mother Ann Lee*. In them were laid out as clearly as possible the Shaker metanarrative. They also include long digressions to address the controversies surrounding their beliefs about the evils of sex and the institution of marriage, and the necessity of "a full and final cross against the indulgence of that same fleshly lust." The purpose was to instruct and clarify, but it was also to dispute.[16]

As a growing sect with obviously countercultural beliefs and practices, the Shakers inevitably made enemies who wanted to expose them. Many of those enemies came from the steady stream of apostates, such as the Rathbuns. After 1815 they faced a new challenge from apostate mothers who claimed that the Shakers would not allow them to take their children with them when they left a village. Because these custody cases were multifaceted problems for the Shakers, they will be explored in detail in the next part on "Early Crises." Needless to say, however, it was bad press for the sect. If they were going to set the record straight, they would have to publish in response. Thus these first theological treatises were part catechism written for the instruction of untutored western believers, and part polemic aimed at refuting hostile ex-believers.

But if the Shakers' enemies were growing and publishing, so now were the Shakers themselves, especially under the leadership of Lucy Wright. In her twenty-five years at the helm, the Shakers grew from hundreds of believers to thousands, and from eleven villages in New York and New England to nineteen on both sides of the Appalachian Mountains. Also, when faced with the problems that accompanied this growth, she exercised administrative flexibility, reversing decades of silence and embracing a new culture of printed, systematic instruction. By the time she died in 1821 the Shakers, now called the United Society of Believers, were less of a movement and more of an institution. Even the earlier ecstasy of Shaker worship had been routinized. As the 1823 *Summary View* describes the transformation: "These involuntary operations of singing and dancing were repeated, from time to time . . . till, by Divine Revelations, they became an established exercise in the worship of God."[17]

Indeed, by the mid-1820s much had been "established" among the Shakers. In addition to charisma and a founding metanarrative, they now had effective governing structures, ordered communities, and systematic theologies. They were still definitely a sect, existing in tension with their host culture, but they were now a thoroughly ordered one, with stronger institutional structures that would sustain both individual Believers and the group itself.

Like the Shakers, the Church of Jesus Christ of Latter-day Saints also transitioned from charismatic movement to established institution, attendant with both more elaborate rituals and more substantive theological reflection. The Mormons differed from the Shakers, however, in two key respects. The first is the timeframe. The shift to institution-building occurred soon after the founding of the LDS Church, and once it began it happened quickly. What took the Shakers half a century after 1774, the Mormons experienced in fifteen years from 1830 to 1844. The second difference is that whereas the Shakers had four leaders over the course of their first fifty years in America, the Mormons followed Joseph Smith from the time of the Church's founding until his death. He was both charismatic leader and institution builder, who at Nauvoo had the opportunity to build a city almost from scratch. The result was basically a theocracy, God's kingdom on the Mississippi, and he built it all in five years from 1839 until his assassination in 1844.

Many, many things happened in this crucial Nauvoo period. During this relatively short time, Joseph Smith initiated ordinances that endure down to the present, and he elevated the temple as the exclusive, sacred space in which those ordinances were to be performed. This was also the time when, in addition to being the prophet and president of the Church, Smith became a Freemason, served as mayor of Nauvoo and major-general of the Nauvoo Legion, ran for president of the United States, and was anointed as a king.[18] Obviously he was occupying roles of both spiritual and temporal authority, combining—some might say "amassing"—the powers of both primarily in himself. During this time Smith also reflected deeply on the nature of matter and spirit, marriage and family, in the end fundamentally redefining them as well. In Nauvoo Smith wove what had previously been theological fragments into a more coherent whole that further linked heaven and earth.

At Nauvoo Smith finally had the chance to turn his revelations into realities. He was like an artist in a studio, except that his studio was an entire city. He was inspired, reasonably well funded, and had tremendous natural and human resources at his disposal. All three of the sects investigated here built, but not on this scale and not with these means. Like the Emperor Constantine marking out with his lance the boundaries of Constantinople, Smith got to design and build a miniature kingdom, complete with an economy, justice system, militia, and temple all its own. At Nauvoo he was in charge of it all, exercising fully the godlike power to create and re-create, define and redefine. This was true for the ideas of his highly inventive theology, as well as for his institutions and ordinances. Inspired by God, he would make his patch of the physical earth look like the heavens above.

This kingdom would be both a place and a people. Beautiful buildings such as the temple and meaningful rites such as the endowment ceremony mattered, but so did invisible eternal souls. An unpopulated kingdom would be nothing but a ghost town. Individuals, nuclear families, and soon polygamous families linked together into extended kinship networks all played vital roles in making this "beautiful place" a living, breathing, procreating kingdom of God that would transcend this earth and be eternally perpetuated in heaven.

In terms of the chronology it took Smith a little while to come to these conclusions and muster the audacity to unveil God's radical polygamous plan for a righteous seed. He first arrived in Nauvoo in the spring of 1839 but did not marry his first plural wife there, Louisa Beaman, until two years later in the spring of 1841. But eventually the security of the locale and the exhilaration of building God's city from the ground up gave him the courage he needed to inaugurate plural marriage as a lasting institution for the Church of Jesus Christ of Latter-day Saints.

The main difference in the Church's situation at Nauvoo had to do with demographics and legal protection. Although the Saints did move into a preexisting town and not construct one entirely from scratch, this time they so thoroughly dominated it as the numerical majority that they effectively did not have to share power. Speculators had purchased the land back in 1824 and optimistically named the town "Commerce," but after failing to prosper they were eager to sell when Mormon leaders began arriving in 1839. The land nevertheless cost the Church dearly and saddled it with a worrisome debt. In order to ensure a steady stream of potential land purchasers, Smith canceled plans for other settlements, or "stakes" as Mormons call them, in Illinois, and instructed all the Saints to converge at Nauvoo.[19]

The Saints who built Nauvoo were both veterans from Missouri and brand-new converts from as far away as England. In the spring of 1839, the group called the Quorum of the Twelve Apostles, the Church's most stalwart leaders after the First Presidency, was commanded "to go over the great waters, and there promulgate my gospel, the fulness thereof, and bear record of my name."[20] Orson Hyde went to Israel, but most of the missionaries went to England, where they found a very receptive audience. England is where Brigham Young in particular made a name for himself as a masterful leader, organizer, and winner of souls. Most of the converts were desperately poor religious seekers, who were happy to trade their miserable lives and their indifferent Anglican Church for the opportunities of a fresh Mormon start in America. By 1843 over 2,800 English Saints had made the journey.[21]

Both the British mission and the call to gather at Nauvoo were enormous successes. Precise figures are difficult to determine but census data from 1840 reveals 9,946 people living in Hancock County, Illinois, approximately 3,500 to 5,000 of whom were Mormons at Nauvoo.[22] By the time of Smith's death in 1844, Nauvoo's population had risen to somewhere between 12,000 and 15,000 souls, dwarfing the next largest town in the county, Warsaw, which had a mere 472 residents. In fact—and amazingly—from 1840 to 1846 Nauvoo actually rivaled Chicago as the largest city in Illinois.[23] Per the usual pattern, however, as the number of Mormons grew so did the anxiety and intolerance of neighboring Gentiles. Before the Mormon population reached the tipping point, though, and began to inspire outside persecution, this growth inspired in Joseph Smith and other leaders an almost intoxicating sense of power, possibility, and divine favor. In ten short years the Church had gone from obscurity to becoming an international religion and a force to be reckoned with in state and even national politics. After so many troubles in the latter 1830s, these halcyon days of growth at home and abroad were profoundly encouraging indeed.

The news was just as encouraging on the legal front. In Missouri, the Church had enjoyed no protection. In Illinois things would be different—at first anyway—and they were so because of Nauvoo's city charter. Most importantly, the charter granted the Nauvoo Municipal Court the authority to issue writs of habeas corpus. With such writs Smith and other leaders could avoid extradition to and prosecution in other states.[24]

Joseph Smith had one man, John C. Bennett, to thank for both the details of Nauvoo's charter and its passage through the Illinois legislature. Unfortunately for Smith, Bennett would turn out to be not just another Mormon apostate, but a true a Judas figure, a backstabbing betrayer and outright enemy of the Church. At first, however, Bennett seemed heaven-sent, the perfect man at the perfect time, just as Sidney Rigdon had been in the Church's first year of existence. Like Rigdon, Bennett was an educated and well-spoken man who brought credibility to the Church along with his obvious talents. Significantly unlike Rigdon, Bennett was not a true believer.

John C. Bennett could perhaps best be described as a typical frontier "confidence man." Trained as a doctor but dissatisfied with the profession, in the 1830s he became a Methodist itinerant preacher, the founder of two short-lived colleges, and the brigadier general of an Illinois militia unit. Likely sensing an opportunity in the thousands of Saints who were moving to Nauvoo, in 1840 he began to write Smith, inquiring about the faith and asking if he could be of service to the Church. Equally ecstatic about the possibility of building a city, the two men soon became close friends, so close in fact that Bennett lived in the Smith home for nine months from September 1840 to June 1841. Thus when it came to constructing Nauvoo, Smith brought the Church's growing numbers and Bennett brought the political connections and experience to get things done. On December 16, 1840, the Illinois governor signed the charter, which went into effect on February 1, 1841.[25] With ambitious dreams of creating a world-renowned city, the two men worked as a kind of tag team: Bennett was elected the first mayor of Nauvoo, while Smith continued in his role as revelator, and now a kind of citizen-in-chief.

It was during this season of frenetic activity and boundless opportunities that Joseph Smith resumed thinking about the principle of plural marriage. This is also when things get complicated because Smith had so many plural wives: thirty-seven according to one scholar's count, whom Smith married in two main phases, divided by a crisis.[26] This chapter will treat the first phase, which lasted from April 1841 to August 1842. During this time Smith married sixteen women, introduced a handful of male leaders to "the principle," was initiated into the Masonic Order, and instituted the endowment ceremony. The interruption occurred in the second half of 1842 and was caused by the betrayal of John Bennett. Once the scandal subsided, Smith married twenty-one more women from February to November 1843 and received a revelation on celestial marriage and one on plural marriage. After that, as crises continued to mount, Smith took no more plural wives and received no more revelations of any kind until his death in June 1844.

In response to the question "why?" here is one attempt at an answer. Joseph Smith had grown up dirt poor in a socially marginalized family under the leadership of a failed father. Now this boy-turned-man had the power at his disposal to build his own city on the Mississippi River. Creating heaven on earth, however, involved more than just infrastructure, a legal system, a place of worship, and venerable institutions. A complete kingdom needed families—connected, loving, resource-sharing, procreating families. In Nauvoo in 1840 and 1841, this is what Smith wanted—in spite of the obvious risks—and this is what he got: an extended family. Plural marriage would be another means by which he could construct his kingdom: a materially supportive as well as procreative institution that would link people together in indissoluble family connections.

Focusing on expanded kinship networks also helps answer the related question of "why so many?" With thirty-seven Nauvoo plural wives, clearly Smith was not searching for a romantic soul mate—an Eve to complement his Adam. Some of the marriages were not even sexually consummated, and all of them were more impersonal than intimate, a network of wives rather than a collection of havens in a heartless world. Whom did he choose to make his plural wives and why? Who were they and are there any revealing patterns in Smith's choices?

The historian George D. Smith offers intriguing answers to these questions. In *Nauvoo Polygamy*, the best monograph on the subject that there is, he argues that—with some exceptions—Smith's plural wives had two things in common: they came from trusted Mormon families and Smith met them years earlier, often when they were in their teens or twenties.[27] These women were familiar and safe, and more likely to accept Smith's radical proposition than to turn it down. The situation was like having a longtime family friend marry your daughter. In arranged marriages the families often know one another as peers and agree to pair off their children for the presumed benefit of all. With Smith's plural marriages, the parents of the young women did not arrange a marriage to another family's son (someone approximately their daughter's age), but rather to someone closer to their own age. Smith and the parents were the peers, and polygamy the means by which the two families would interlink. Smith's plural marriages are thus like unions among a traditional society's elite: a way to establish connections, share resources, and gain access to power. In the Mormon subculture, plural marriage enhanced the status of all involved. This was true at the beginning in Nauvoo and became even more so as the nineteenth century proceeded. For men, more wives indicated higher status, while for women it was better to be the plural wife of a leading Mormon man than to be the one and only wife of a Latter-day loser. This topic of forging an elite will be revisited in later chapters, but for now it bears mentioning that status (both earthly and heavenly) did play a role in the initiation of plural marriage at Nauvoo.

Other patterns among Smith's plural wives are nearly impossible to establish. Of the first sixteen from 1841 to 1842, only one was a teenager, five were in their twenties, five were in their thirties, three were in their forties, and two were in their fifties. Joseph married two pairs of sisters, two widows, one mother-daughter pair, and—most shockingly—ten currently married women.[28] There is virtually no consistency among them aside from the fact that they were from trusted Mormon families. It is also remarkable that once Smith initiated plural marriage in Nauvoo he fearlessly expanded it to as many women as he possibly could. While wanting to keep plural marriage a secret, he did not seem to care that taking more wives clearly meant taking on greater risks of the secret being exposed.

According to later affidavits, Smith first broached the topic of plural marriage in the fall of 1840 to Joseph Bates Noble, the brother-in-law of his soon-to-be plural wife Louisa Beaman. A few months later, on April 5, 1841, Smith had Noble officiate their wedding—a ceremony so secretive that Beaman disguised herself as a man so as not to attract attention.[29] This was the first of Smith's Nauvoo plural marriages: Louisa Beaman was twenty-six years old at the time and Joseph Smith thirty-five. *The very next day,* on April 6, 1841, Smith led the cornerstone-laying ceremony for the Nauvoo temple. Everything seemed to be happening simultaneously:

Smith was building his physical city and expanding his earthly and eternal family.

The rest of 1841 was just as eventful. Throughout the year Smith courted, and in October and December married his next plural wives: the sisters Zina and Presendia Huntington. As with Louisa Beaman, the Huntington sisters were from a trusted Mormon family; but unlike Beaman, both were married when they became Smith's brides. After the death of their mother in July 1839, the sisters lived for a few months in the Smith home, a close proximity that gave Joseph the opportunity to introduce them to "the principle." Zina resisted at first, and even went so far as to marry another suitor, Henry Jacobs, but Smith's persistence and the promise of celestial rewards ultimately convinced both her and her husband to change their minds. In a process of inner struggle that would soon be repeated in the lives of hundreds of Saints, Zina found the peace she sought as she contemplated this momentous decision. Ultimately she made the great "sacrifice"—exchanging worldly respectability "as an honerable [sic] woman" for "the privilege of associating in family relationships in the worlds to come."[30] Zina married Smith on October 27, 1841. She was twenty years old and six months pregnant at the time. Six weeks later Smith married her older sister, Presendia Huntington Buell.[31] By making sacrifices in this life, the Huntington siblings secured for themselves the possibility of *more* in the life to come. There were costs to be sure, but the Huntingtons were also at the forefront of the creation of what historian Todd Compton calls "a small, select, spiritual elite, 'separate and apart from all others.'"[32]

Back in July 1841 Joseph had begun sharing the doctrine of plural marriage with only the most trusted Mormon men.[33] He started with members of the Twelve, who were now returning from their foreign missions and who sought the eternal blessings that Smith told them could only be enjoyed if they joined him in practicing plural marriage. It took a while, however, first to convince them, and then for them to convince prospective brides that this was indeed the will of God. The first four men to follow Smith into polygamy were Brigham Young, Heber C. Kimball, Vinson Knight, and Reynolds Cahoon, and they did not marry their first plural wives until the summer of 1842, approximately a year later, with much happening in the interim.[34] The first half of 1842, in fact, is quite likely the apex of Joseph Smith's career as a prophet. As he was shepherding these four men into their first polygamous marriages, he published the Book of Abraham, became a Freemason, instituted the temple endowment ceremony, and took thirteen more wives for himself.[35]

But of this crowd—and it was fast becoming a crowd—two women stand out. The first is Marinda Nancy Johnson Hyde, wife of Orson Hyde, Smith's handpicked missionary to Israel. Traveling so far, Hyde was absent from Marinda for two and a half years, from April 1840 to December 1842, during which time Smith courted and married his wife.[36] When Hyde returned, Smith had two bits of interesting news to share with him: the first was that God had ordained plural marriage to be restored; the second was that he had taken Marinda to be one of his plural wives. Amazingly, although "furious" at first, Orson Hyde submitted to his prophet, perhaps concluding that the benefits of plural marriage outweighed the loss of his exclusive relationship with Marinda, and in 1843 he took two plural wives of his own.[37]

The other young woman who stands out is Nancy Rigdon, the nineteen-year-old daughter of Mormonism's most prominent early convert, Sidney Rigdon. Nancy is noteworthy, however, because she rejected Smith's proposal. On April 9, 1842, at the printing office of the Nauvoo *Times and Seasons,* Smith ushered Nancy into a small room, locked the door, professed his longstanding affection for her, and informed her of God's recent revelation about plural marriage. Repulsed, Nancy demanded that he let her go while Smith promised her personally to put in writing a doctrinal explanation for departing from monogamous marriage. Sometime after the disastrous meeting, Nancy told her father, who summoned Smith to their home on June 28, 1842. In the confrontation that followed, Smith denied making the proposition, but Nancy stood her ground and—fatally for Smith's case—produced the letter he had written her, theologically defending the new order of marriage.

Written sometime in between April 9 and June 28, the letter is an essential source for understanding Smith's rarely expressed thoughts about polygamy. Taking care not to mention plural marriage itself, he nevertheless told Nancy: "That which is wrong under one circumstance, may be and often is, right under another. God said thou shalt not kill,—at another time he said thou shalt utterly destroy. This is the principle on which the government of heaven is conducted—by revelation adapted to the circumstances in which the children of the kingdom are placed. Whatever God requires is right, no matter what it is, although we may not see the reason thereof till long after the events transpire."[38] The argument by analogy was obvious. Just as God generally commanded His people not to kill, so He generally commanded His people not to take more than one wife. But special revelation always trumps any so-called categorical morality. This is the way that God had always interacted with

His people—through "revelation adapted to the circumstances." The implicit message was that circumstances now existed such that God wanted His people to get over their aversion to polygamy and embrace the principle as a new special revelation. Nancy Rigdon, her father Sidney, and the rest of their family, however, would have none of it. Thus rather than strengthening his kinship network, in this case Smith's proposal of plural marriage alienated some of the most trusted allies he had ever had.[39] Smith's fateful meeting with the Rigdons occurred on June 28, 1842, when many other things were starting to go very badly for the prophet.

Before things fell apart, however, Smith indulged his passion for Creation narratives and Old Testament esoterica by joining the Freemasons. As he sought to adorn Nauvoo with venerable institutions it is understandable that he would become interested in the ancient order of the Freemasons.[40] There had been Masons in the Church before this time, including Smith's brother Hyrum, but the most important Freemason by far was John Bennett, his partner in building Nauvoo. In the summer of 1841 Bennett began petitioning nearby lodges to recommend to the state's Grand Lodge that one be organized in Nauvoo. On December 29, 1841, that process was complete and eighteen Mormon Masons organized the Nauvoo Lodge, which in early 1842 admitted Joseph Smith and fifty-seven other Saints.[41]

After the installation of the lodge on March 15, 1842, the history of Freemasonry in Nauvoo was every bit as manic as the rest of Joseph Smith's life. He and Sidney Rigdon (not yet alienated from Smith) raced through the three Masonic degrees in an astonishing two days. "Eleven of the Twelve Apostles became Freemasons," historian Richard Bushman writes, and by "October 1842, the 253 members of the Nauvoo lodge outnumbered the 227 Masons in all the other Illinois lodges combined."[42] In 1843 the throng of Mormon Freemasons had to divide themselves into no fewer than five lodges. So many Saints became Freemasons so quickly, in fact, that other lodges complained that the Mormons were both violating established policy and—to use a modern concept—cheapening Freemasonry's brand by rushing so many initiates so quickly through the three degrees. They were in essence a collection of rogue lodges, whose defiance both reflected the Saints' growing tension with non-Mormon Illinois in 1843–44 and quite likely accelerated it.[43]

Going back to the 1820s and the *Book of Mormon* itself, Smith had always been interested in mysteries, ancient secrets, and Old Testament peoples and practices. In the 1830s those interests manifested themselves in the Aaronic and Melchizedek priesthoods and in his growing fascination with rituals such as washings and anointings, and a suitable Old Testament space in which to perform them: the temple. But coming out of a deeply "non-liturgical background," Mormon scholar Thomas O'Dea writes, "made it necessary to look outside strictly religious practices." Thus, "Joseph went to Masonry to borrow many elements of ceremony," O'Dea continues, and to "find appropriate materials for ritual development."[44]

Joseph Smith indeed took liberally from Masonic rituals in order to put the finishing touches on his own endowment ordinance. This claim—that the endowment ceremony came more from Freemasonry than from God—has been understandably controversial in the Church since the 1840s, but the evidence seems incontrovertible. Both ceremonies have secret signs and passwords that inductees must memorize to continue their journey from darkness into light. Both take place in a temple, and both utilize veils, aprons, and the celestial imagery of sun, moon, and stars.[45]

Smith performed the first endowment ceremony on May 4, 1842, only seven weeks after he had been initiated into the three degrees of the Masonic order. This was when the Mormon metanarrative was literally dramatized in an elaborate ritual. The metanarrative itself had been coalescing for over a decade. It seems, however, that Freemasonry provided the final inspiration Smith needed to give that cosmic story a ceremonial form as a temple ordinance. The purpose of the ceremony was to enable the participants to return one day to God's presence by being progressively endowed with knowledge of the story of existence: where the universe and humankind came from; how things went wrong; and what people must do to experience exaltation. During the ceremony initiates are told this story and endowed with this knowledge as they move through a series of separate rooms decorated to represent the most important chapters—Creation, the Garden of Eden, the world after the Fall, and the celestial paradise.

In June 1842, where this part of the Mormon story will now conclude, plural marriage was also becoming an institution, but just barely so. At this stage in its life, the LDS Church itself was undergoing an important transition from unstable movement to enduring institution. The organization of the endowment ordinance was a pivotal moment in this transition. Mormonism had begun with the translations and revelations of Joseph Smith. Now, as Richard Bushman describes it, the "Mormon temple's sacred story stabilized and perpetuated the original enthusiastic endowment," allowing the growing number of Saints to learn God's story "through ritual rather than a transcendent vision."[46] In the days to come, after more doctrinal development and crisis management, the institutions of the temple, the endowment ordinance, and plural marriage would intertwine all the more. The goal was still the same—exaltation—but the means were becoming more complicated, more controversial, and decidedly more institutional.

The story of institutionalization among the Oneida Perfectionists is both like and unlike that of the Mormons. In both cases a single leader autocratically oversaw the transition from movement to institution during a relatively short period of time. In both cases also, location was key. In Nauvoo, Joseph Smith was free to build as he saw fit. In Oneida, John Humphrey Noyes was similarly free to construct his own community from the ground up.

But more like the Shakers, the Perfectionists' process of institutionalization was gradual rather than frenzied: formulating first as ideas in Noyes's mind and then safely field-tested at his family's home in Putney. When Noyes implemented the controversial practice of complex marriage in 1846, however, the safety did not last. By the end of 1847, the Perfectionists had to flee Vermont for what they hoped would be the more tolerant environment of Oneida, New York. Although they would experience some hostility there, for the most part their hope of finding a safe haven was realized. Now successfully transplanted, they would put down roots in Oneida and grow their community in its hospitable soil for the next thirty years.

The Oneida Community's first three years, from 1848 to 1851—the subject of the rest of this chapter—are when Noyes's ideas matured into enduring institutions as well as more systematic theological reflections. Blessed with a fresh start, he wasted no time, organizing his thoughts into yet another manifesto. As usual in Noyes's life, the ideas came first.

Noyes arrived at Jonathan Burt's farm in January 1848. A Perfectionist since 1834, Burt had fallen on hard times and welcomed the added labor and improvements to his property that would accompany an influx of community members. Noyes accepted Burt's invitation, inspected the farm, and promptly sent word to his followers to join him there. In the meantime, while he was waiting for the others to arrive, he had opportunity to write what would be the community's statement of beliefs, the *Bible Argument; Defining the Relations of the Sexes in the Kingdom of Heaven.*

Called by one scholar "the blueprint for the association about to begin," Noyes's *Bible Argument* systematically lays out in twenty-five propositions the sect's cosmology and its implications for marriage and sex.[47] Fearlessly living out those propositions, Perfectionists would be like "an army sent for the purpose of introducing civil institutions and settling in a foreign territory." "Such," Noyes proclaimed, "is the position of the church which is called to introduce the kingdom of heaven on earth."[48]

Noyes wrote those stirring words in February 1848 but did not publish them until April 1849 as part of the *First Annual Report of the Oneida Association*. Once published, he wanted it to serve as a public declaration of their beliefs and practices. Boldly, he even sent copies to local and state authorities, including the governor of New York as well as the newspaper editor "Horace Greeley, and a half-dozen other prominent persons in New York City."[49] This was more of an act of diplomacy than provocation, intended to build mutual trust with his neighbors and the government through transparency. Unlike both the Mormons and their own communal trial run in Putney, the Perfectionists at Oneida would not engage in their countercultural sexual practices secretly, but openly and unabashedly as a righteous community of kingdom builders.

For the rest of 1848, in between writing the *Bible Argument* and publishing it, Noyes's ideas continued to drive the community. Refugees from Putney began arriving in March, living together in Jonathan Burt's log hut while they built other dwellings, including the "Mansion House." Wanting their architecture to reflect the fact that they had abandoned simple marriage for complex marriage, they would live in one big domicile as one big family rather than in separate homes as discrete and competitive nuclear families. As word spread, Oneida became a kind of magnet, drawing out the scattered community of Perfectionists, previously connected only by shared beliefs and by print, and bringing them to a central location. By the end of 1848, Noyes had attracted eighty-seven people to his daring religio-sexual experiment.[50]

Unsurprisingly perhaps, the institutionalization of complex marriage turned out to be an incredibly difficult process for almost everyone. Most of the newcomers to Oneida were married couples with children, not unmarried men and women looking for sexual adventure. Adjusting to the sacrifices that complex marriage demanded—namely sharing one's spouse with other community members—was often a highly painful transition. Sadly, there are almost no existing records from this important period in the life of the community. If there had been documents, they most likely were among those destroyed in 1947 when executives from the Oneida Company Ltd. burned an enormous collection of manuscripts and archives to avoid public embarrassment about the community's past.[51]

Thankfully, Noyes's *First Annual Report* from 1849 provides some kind of window into the community's tumultuous first year. In addition to the *Bible Argument,* Noyes included a section entitled "Testimony of the Members," as a way of demonstrating "the effects of those institutions and principles" on real, live human beings.[52] Noyes's reason for including them, no doubt, was part public relations campaign: he wanted outsiders to see that they were not hosting some kind of perpetual orgy, but instead an elite cadre of spiritual strivers who took up their cross and died to themselves daily.

Most striking by far in the testimonies is the oft-repeated preoccupation with "selfishness" and "self-will" that the members had struggled to subdue over the course of that year. Testimonies are full of violent verbs like "destroy," "purge," "crucify," "abolish," and "root out." Only after having withstood the fires of this intense internal process, members recorded, will there be "the fulfillment of Christ's prayer for his disciples, that they 'all may be one.'" True to form, Noyes was literally defining the terms of communal life: its common problems, its collective goals, and the process by which they would reach those goals. In addition to the affidavits supporting the public relations campaign that Noyes wanted, they also testify to the fact that Oneidans were internalizing his values and sharing his vocabulary. The many were indeed becoming "*one, even as he and the Father are one.*"[53] A year later, even with numerous deserters and the excommunicated, the Oneida Community had nearly doubled from 87 people at the beginning of 1849, to 172 people at the beginning of 1850.[54]

Two important details, however, are often forgotten in a simple retelling of Oneida's story. The first is that there was more than one community of Noyes-inspired Perfectionists. All told, in 1850 there were six: at Wallingford, Connecticut; Newark, New Jersey; Cambridge and Putney, Vermont; and Brooklyn and Oneida, New York.[55] In 1854, with most of them struggling, Noyes consolidated the six communities down to just two, Oneida and Wallingford, but in the meantime, they tried to establish their unique brand of communal and sexual Perfectionism throughout the Northeast.

The second overlooked detail is that Noyes himself was often an absentee leader. Yes, he had a strong personality—one capable of bending other people's wills into conformity to his own—but he also regularly abandoned those very people when the going got tough. In Putney after being arrested for adultery Noyes violated his bail and fled Vermont, leaving his family and community to fend for themselves. "As to abandoning the testimony that the Kingdom of God has commenced or acknowledging that we have done wrong," Noyes wrote while on the lam, "that is out of the question with me. . . . Yet I shall not brave public opinion unnecessarily."[56] This last sentence is revealing of Noyes's paradoxical character. While clearly a religious rebel against the worldly status quo, Noyes nevertheless cared a great deal about "public opinion" and repeatedly caved in whenever the tide seemed to be turning against him. He was often forthright and adamant in his beliefs, in many ways courting the very outsider status characteristic of a persecuted sect. Other times, however, he retreated from the intellectual battlefield, content instead to fire his published salvos from a safe distance. This latter case was the situation in the middle of 1849.

In the spring of 1849, although the Oneida Community had been in existence for over a year, opposition from their Putney days lingered. In the legal arena, the case for Noyes's violating his bail came to trial on May 5, 1849. In the equally important realm of popular opinion, Hubbard Eastman, a Methodist minister from Putney, was finishing his four-hundred-page exposé of the community, entitled *Noyesism Unveiled*. Knowing that Eastman's book was nearing completion, Noyes raced to get his side of the story out first. He won the contest, publishing the *First Annual Report* in early April, beating Eastman by a month and perhaps influencing the outcome of his trial, which ended with the court reducing his bond from $2,000 to $1,000. Absenting himself once again from the field of conflict, Noyes did not attend the trial but rather left his representation to his brother-in-law, John R. Miller. Having dutifully aided Noyes both in disseminating the *First Annual Report,* and in his trial, Miller returned to Oneida "glad to find sympathy and fellowship," while adding exhaustedly, "I never felt more completely used up."[57]

Noyes weathered these storms well, but then lit out for Brooklyn nonetheless. Biographer Robert Allerton Parker confesses that "Noyes's motive in leaving the Oneida Community for Brooklyn is not altogether clear,"[58] but it would seem that the stresses of the trial combined with the day-to-day challenges of launching a community simply overwhelmed him. Less than two weeks after the resolution of his bail case, Noyes and a handful of trusted associates removed to a new communal home in Brooklyn. There he could literally distance himself from the headaches of community conflict, and devote himself afresh to spreading and ruling through his grand ideas alone. As one community member recorded his parting injunctions: "He concluded by giving the Association some appropriate advice, the substance of which was, that they should be careful not to get into a quarrel with God or with him; then they would never quarrel among themselves."[59] The most tried and true way to avoid conflict within the community was to avoid conflict with Noyes—or "with God." And as community members were learning, those two sources of authority were quickly becoming one and the same.

Lacking the harmony that he sought in Oneida, Noyes surrounded himself in Brooklyn with people who would not challenge him. There he would have the time and the peace to write, as well as the freedom to practice complex marriage in yet another inner circle of elite Perfectionists, including: John Humphrey and Harriet Noyes, George and Mary Cragin, Erastus and Susan Hamilton, and Abram Smith of Newark and 1839 fame.[60] Noyes could thus enjoy once more the intimacy and trust of the original Putney Community, while also directing from afar the progress of his Perfectionist kingdom-builders in Oneida, deputizing the "used up" John R. Miller to oversee the details of that project—a job that ultimately drove him into an early grave in 1854.

When Noyes left Oneida for Brooklyn in May 1849, he left one serious conflict unresolved, however—a conflict that reveals clearly the challenges accompanying the institutionalization of complex marriage. Fascinatingly, problems arose less often from adults, who had chosen to join the community because of its radical doctrines, and more often from the children who accompanied their parents and who were forced to adopt Noyes's beliefs and practices without prior consent. Thus Noyes complained that the "unconverted children are the front rank of the Devil's forces in the Community."[61] Young children—infants, toddlers, and grade-school-age youth—posed problems of their own, but those were more the issues of the parents, who had a difficult time turning over their children to Oneida's communal childcare. This topic will be discussed in chapter 15 on "Children." The problem here was with the children—especially boys—who had reached sexual maturity. As one dispatch to Brooklyn put it, there were "serious difficulties" with this "class of older boys."[62] Both with and without Noyes, the Oneidans had been successful at rooting out the selfishness of adults through religious indoctrination and mutual criticism. The community's teenagers, however, were an entirely different story.

What was going on during these days at Oneida was an ironic inversion of the usual teenage sexual drama. In most cases, parents worry that their sexually maturing children will disgrace the family by becoming promiscuous, getting pregnant, or getting someone pregnant. While the concern about pregnancies was true for parents as well as for children, the concern about promiscuity was decidedly different. Rather than forbidding their children from exercising their sexuality until marriage, parents insisted instead that they participate in Oneida's unique sexual communism. Decades later, the Oneida Community would dissolve in part because a number of younger members, having fallen in love with a single man or woman, wanted the exclusivity of monogamous marriage. During the community's early days, however, the teenagers did not want monogamy so much as they simply wanted to avoid sexual contact with adults. Unsurprisingly, they wanted to have sex with their peers and not with their parents' new friends. John Humphrey Noyes, however, had other ideas.

It took Noyes years to solve the problem of recalcitrant, horny youth, but in the end he gained control of the situation by establishing yet another hierarchy: the rule of ascending and descending fellowship. He conceived the idea in late 1849 while in Brooklyn and had it implemented in Oneida soon thereafter. How "the rule" worked was simple: the young must have their first sexual encounters not with one another, but with older, more experienced members of the community. Those who supposedly lack spiritual wisdom and sexual skill must endeavor to "ascend" in their relationships with the other members of the community in order to learn from them; while the more mature members must "descend" to the neophytes and share with them their knowledge of God, life, and sexuality. As Noyes described it himself: "There is a natural attraction between superiors and inferiors, the old and the young, the spiritual and novices. . . . The time will come when a young person, with no forcing, will naturally be led by the hand of some older person in matters of love; when the idea of persons that are not spiritual embarking on the tempestuous ocean of amativeness without a pilot will be regarded absurd."[63] This last metaphor of an older pilot guiding "novices" into the enticing but treacherous waters of human sexuality is a good one. It took time, but Noyes's reasoning and persistence, as well as the cooperation of the rest of the Community, ultimately succeeded at bringing the youth into line.

While effective, the institution of ascending and descending fellowship created new problems and obvious double standards. The "plan proposed last fall [1849] of introducing the young men to the freedom of the Association through the more spiritual women," Noyes conceded, "has been attended with difficulties. Mrs. Cragin lost her equilibrium in the attempt to carry it out." Mary Cragin was the Community's chief female spiritual-sexual mentor, and even she found the assignment a tough one. Because the community wanted to avoid unwanted pregnancies, the older women were tasked with training the younger men in the practice of male continence. Those men who had not yet mastered the technique—both the young and the old—were branded "leakers" and forbidden sexual access to younger, more fertile women.[64] Until they could control themselves and thus assure Community members that they would not impregnate their partners, they were only allowed to have sex with postmenopausal women. There is no record as to whether or not the young men at the beginning of this arduous journey found their older sexual mentors physically attractive, nor did it seem that anyone cared if they did not. Sex was a spiritual and communal joy, but it was also a spiritual and communal discipline. As Noyes summed up, Oneida's young men "cannot possibly enjoy the freedom of love until they have conquered themselves."[65]

The case with young women was predictably different. An obvious "danger arises from the fact that the young are the most attractive," Noyes opined, and thus young men seek out young women, who "have life and magnetism but lack discretion." This was the heart of the problem at Oneida for years, until into this turmoil strode Noyes himself as the conquering restorer of order. "I felt the responsibility of taking the lead myself," he wrote, "and know that things cannot go right until the most spiritual do take the lead."[66] Armed with the doctrine of ascending and descending fellowship and his own sense of infallibility, Noyes selflessly volunteered to initiate the community's young women. "I went right in among them offering to be their playmate and inviting them up into fellowship with the Association." "I have had to stand in the invidious position of demanding that love should gravitate toward me. . . . I cannot have peace with God unless I keep the ascending fellowship predominant."[67] It is difficult to know whether Noyes's thoughts here are sincere or grotesquely self-deceived. The structure of ascending fellowship, of course, reached its pinnacle in him, "the most spiritual" of all. Although it was difficult to implement, Noyes concluded, "we shall at last establish the principle that the way to induct the young into a true state of amativeness is to have them mate with older persons."[68] Thus the institution of ascending and descending fellowship solved one of Noyes's greatest challenges to date, it cemented his status as the unquestioned leader of the community, and it granted him ultimate control over the community's sexual fellowship.

By the beginning of 1851 Noyes could thus claim some hard-won victories in the struggle to establish a beachhead for the kingdom of God on earth. He and a handful of followers were enjoying the benefits of their intimate communal life in Brooklyn, while at Oneida the tide seemed to be turning against the members' selfishness in favor of the "Community spirit."[69] Those who could relinquish their exclusive claims to spouses and children did so, while those who could not were either mutually criticized into line, or expelled entirely from the ranks. Through these novel institutions, Noyes was forging the army of Perfectionist Christian soldiers he had always wanted, complete with unity, discipline, and an ironclad chain of command.

In 1848, the year Noyes wrote *The Bible Argument* and launched the Oneida Community, he also published his memoir entitled *Confessions of Religious Experience*. He recollected how he had "vowed to live in the 'revival spirit,' and be a 'young convert' forever," and had developed a "theory that Christians might always remain in the 'revival spirit,'" overcoming "the world entirely and perpetually."[70] But as he wrote in 1870, and no doubt learned much earlier, a "church that is capable of genuine revival" could only experience true and lasting community if it "could modulate into daily meetings, criticism, and all the self-denials of Communism." Institutions such as "daily meetings" and mutual criticism, although almost unbearably mundane when compared to the excitement of revivals, were the only means by which believers could expect to "remain in the 'revival spirit.'" "Our hope," he concluded, "is that the churches of all denominations will by and by be quickened by the Pentecostal Spirit, and begin to grow and change, and finally, by a process as natural as the transformation of the chrysalis, burst forth into Communism."[71]

This chapter has described how the Shakers, Mormons, and Oneida Perfectionists did indeed "grow and change" and experience "transformation." To shift the metaphor from that of a butterfly to that of a baby, at this point each sect had survived childhood. Now, however, they would each face even more growing pains. Institutionalization had made them resilient, but they soon confronted challenges—more from without than from within—that again threatened their existence.

PART III
EARLY CRISES

IN PART 3 we will investigate the challenges the sects confronted as they institutionalized. Crises and especially persecution, of course, were nothing new to these religious groups. Because they were sects, they often courted tension with the outside world and they definitely found it, especially in their earliest days. The Shakers had to flee their tormentors in England, the Mormons in New York, Missouri, and Ohio, and the Perfectionists in Vermont.

As they were institutionalizing in America's early republic, however, they faced a different set of challenges. Leaders finalizing the community's rules, systematic theologies, and hierarchies encountered resistance, especially as they enforced their unique beliefs about marriage, sex, and the family. John Humphrey Noyes had run into this problem with the "class of older boys,"[1] but was winning the battle to curb them through the recently invented principle of ascending and descending fellowship. The fact that these problematic community members were minors, however, greatly helped his cause, as they were not entitled to certain legal protections. In the crises described in the following four chapters, the conflicts took place among adults over the status of their individual and familial rights while living in the context of a totalizing religious community.

The environment of antebellum America was hospitable enough to allow the Shakers, Mormons, and Perfectionists a chance to grow, but there were also limits to the control they could exercise over the lives of their members. Part 3 will investigate what those limits were and how these sects bumped up against them. Culturally speaking, limitations existed in an American public that was unwilling to tolerate deviations from monogamy; but structurally speaking limitations also existed in the realm of legal religious toleration. Shaker, Mormon, and Perfectionist communities pushed the boundaries not only of what monogamous Americans could stomach, but also what the American legal system would allow.

These collisions between religious communalism and American liberalism necessarily became conflicts over power. Within each sect the leaders reigned supreme. Within the American republic, however, those leaders were still subject to state and federal laws. Similarly, followers in each sect were willingly subordinate to the community's hierarchy and subject to its disciplinary actions, but they also—as American citizens—enjoyed certain legal rights and protections over and against their religious community, if they chose to exercise them. This is where the leadership of each sect conflicted with the secular powers that surrounded them and that tolerated them up to a certain point, but not beyond it.

In the end each community survived and learned from these early crises, but they were costly. The Shakers lost credibility in the public sphere and were legally chastened in how much they could control the lives of their followers. They were no longer considered harmless oddballs, but controlling and psychologically manipulative tyrants instead. In the legal battle over which family prevailed—the nuclear family of husband, wife, and children or the communal families they were trying to establish—the state ultimately sided with the nuclear families and their rights to their own children and property. For their part, the Oneida Perfectionists were so threatened by both internal and external tensions that they abandoned complex marriage for over half a year. The Mormons, however, being the greatest threat because they had the greatest numbers, suffered the most: in the death of Joseph Smith and in being driven from their home in Nauvoo. Those actions were clearly more extralegal than legal—the work of mobs rather than lawyers—but in this case America's legal system dramatically failed to protect a religious minority. Joseph Smith and the Mormons did not help their cause as they amassed a degree of power that the surrounding society considered threatening, but it was only when that power was exercised in seemingly un-American ways that their days of being peacefully tolerated were numbered.

7
Shaker Family Drama

JUST AS John Humphrey Noyes had problems with unconverted teenagers, so the Shakers had problems with unconverted mothers. What were they to do when a husband and father converted and chose to relocate to a village, and took his worldly wife and children along with him? One of the Shakers' main goals was to abolish family loyalties—"natural affections" as they called them—and replace them with a new community identity. But what if the other members of the family did not believe? How was the community to treat them? In sectarian communities, religious life was all encompassing. One did not merely live out one's faith on Sundays and in private devotions. In a sectarian community, fellow believers were everywhere, with sectarian language and logic saturating every aspect of daily life. Unbelievers in the midst of such a community—such as Noyes's teenagers—did not have the luxury of opting out. Similarly, mixed families could not survive in Shaker villages that were positively determined to destroy them.

The late 1810s were bad years for the Shakers because of two very high profile lawsuits. Significantly, these cases wound their way through the judicial system and leaked out to the public at precisely the same time that the United Society of Believers was strengthening its institutions and systematizing its theology. The crises that these cases precipitated were thus both reactions to this institutionalization and causes for further theological and procedural clarification.

Because of Ann Lee's illiteracy and the early Shakers' aversion to writing, outsiders had long learned about the sect more from its enemies than from its adherents. This pattern dates back to the very first exposés from the apostates Valentine, Daniel, and Reuben Rathbun. Thomas Brown, another apostate, published his *Account of the People Called Shakers* in 1812, but like the Rathbuns he too was a single man when he converted and when he left the community. Thus while still damaging to the Shakers' image, none of these exposers' narratives had the added complications of a wife and children. They wrote as earnest initiates who had slowly but surely discovered the darker side of life among the Shakers.

The sensational cases of Eunice Chapman and Mary Dyer in the late 1810s were much more damaging to the Shaker public image. In both of these incidents, the husband had converted and then forcibly taken the children with him to live in a Shaker village: James Chapman to Watervliet, New York; and Joseph Dyer to Enfield, New Hampshire. Desperate to be close to their young children, the wives followed, even attempting to adopt Shaker ways and become a part of the village.

The published accounts of their experiences, although somewhat melodramatic in tone, are nevertheless harrowing. Eunice Chapman describes her husband James as unstable and abusive for most of their marriage. A negligent and potentially violent alcoholic before (he once threatened Eunice with a razor), Mr. Chapman unfortunately gained from his conversion to Shakerism in 1812 only a new religious vocabulary and rationale with which to assault his family. "He often spit in my face in their [the children's] presence," Eunice recollected, "and said that 'it was the filthyest [sic] place he could find;' (meaning defiled with sin.)" One night, reportedly while drunk, James abducted the three children and took them to Watervliet. When Eunice arrived she pleaded frantically to see them, but was told by one of the leaders: "'If you do not obey the gospel by confessing your sins and putting on a cap [a Shaker head covering for women],'" it was doubtful "'whether you will ever be permitted to see your children again in this world.'" A highly intelligent and reflective woman, Eunice responded that she "was willing to tell them all that ever I did; but I could not acknowledge that they had power to pardon them [her sins]. Neither could I acknowledge that Ann Lee was my Saviour, or the bride of the Lamb's wife; but I could wear one of their caps." In other words, she found it easy to perform the outward functions of Shaker life, but entirely impossible to force herself to believe their foundational doctrines.[1]

Eunice Chapman serves as an excellent example not just of maternal love and determination, but also of the delicate balance of faith and inquiry within a single individual. While obviously biased, she nevertheless observed Shaker life with the detachment of an outsider who could not quite make the final leap of faith. At one point in her narrative, she wrote that she "must pause for a moment, and adore that Allwise and merciful Benefactor, who hath supported me and preserved my reasonable faculties; and not left me to be a wandering idiot, like many other poor women, rendered so by the unkind treatment of the Shakers." Recalling the "frightful and ominous stories" that leaders told to control people through fear, as she put it: "They are taught to believe that, if they go back to the world, they will either sink immediately into hell, or satan will take them and carry them off alive." The effect of this constant and terrifying sectarian message was powerful. Even Eunice had to "confess, that, though established in the firm belief of the fundamental doctrines of the christian religion; still I many times trembled, when I heard them groan and talk in such a manner" about the world, the flesh, the devil, and hell. Eunice remained at Watervliet for as long as the leaders there would tolerate her as an unbeliever, but ultimately they expelled her.[2]

Eunice Chapman, "*a woman alone; a stranger*," then had to resort to political, legal, and extralegal action to regain her children. A judge granted her custody in 1815, but the Shakers at Watervliet hid them and "said they 'knew not where they were.'" Eunice then had to expand her campaign, publishing in 1817 her *Account of the Conduct of the People Called Shakers in the Case of Eunice Chapman and Her Children*, while simultaneously trying to get the state legislature to grant her a divorce, which at the time was the only legal avenue available. The New York legislature granted the divorce in March 1818, but Eunice still had to resort to force to get her children back. Two months after the divorce and with the United Society of Believers still not surrendering the children, she organized a mob to storm the village at Enfield, New Hampshire, where the Shakers had relocated them. Backed by the decision of the New York legislature and the muscle of the New Hampshire mob, the Shakers finally acquiesced.[3] Unfortunately for the Believers, though, another worldly woman was fighting for her children at virtually the same time.

The case of Mary Marshall Dyer is a little different from that of Eunice Chapman. Both women used the legal and political systems to seek custody of their children. Both also dragged not only their husbands but the entire United Society of Believers into the courtroom and the court of public opinion, where they inflicted significant damage to their reputations. The similarities, however, seem to stop there. Unlike Chapman, Dyer's story was much more legally and morally ambiguous, and in some ways Dyer's character less admirable. Also unlike Chapman, Dyer was ultimately unsuccessful in her attempt to win back her children.

Mary Marshall's story began in 1799, when she married Joseph Dyer. The couple had five children and belonged to a Baptist church in Stewartstown, New Hampshire. Sometime after 1810 Joseph converted to Shakerism and informed Mary that he was going to move with the children to the village in nearby Enfield. In response, Mary "strove to gain every favorable idea of the Shakers," ultimately concluding that "they might be right." In 1813, wanting to keep her family together, Mary accompanied Joseph and the children to Enfield, where she "told him I was willing to comply with any thing that was reasonable." Mary eventually found this compliance impossible, however, becoming "completely disgusted with the Society on account of hypocrisy." In 1815 she left the village without her children, which is when her troubles truly began. Unlike the Chapmans' case, in which James had abandoned Eunice and absconded with the children to a village, Mary Dyer initially accompanied her family to the village and agreed to place her children under the Shakers' communal care. Thus when she left after two years' residence at Enfield she is the one who abandoned the family, which proved fatal to her legal case. The New Hampshire legislature denied her petitions for custody in both 1818 and 1819. Joseph Dyer also publicly absolved himself in the local newspaper of any connection with or legal obligation to his deserting wife, which left her alone and without support.[4]

In the midst of the legal wrangling, Mary Dyer followed Eunice Chapman's example and tried to sway public opinion in her favor. The result was a prolonged episode in mutual character assassination involving Mary Dyer, Joseph Dyer, and the United Society of Believers. Mary cast herself as the victim of an abusive husband and an oppressive, family-destroying sect. Joseph responded by painting her as a "loose" and "carnal" woman who flirted with the men of the village, and whose so-called "great concern [for her children] is spurious; for she has not performed the duty of a mother." In their now very public dispute Mary and Joseph Dyer also enlisted the aid of dozens of sworn affidavits. Significantly, two of their children, Betsey Dyer and Caleb M. Dyer, submitted affidavits in support of their father and the Shakers. As the nineteen-year-old Caleb did "depose and say, . . . I am fully satisfied with the agreement of my parents in placing me under the care and providence of the society in which I now reside." He swore that he had experienced only "kind treatment" at Enfield, concluding: "I am under no kind of bondage."[5]

Fed up with the "whole hubbub of Eunice Chapman and Mary Dyer," the Shaker leadership decided to enter the fray, publishing in 1819 their aptly titled counteroffensive, *The Other Side of the Question*. The document is interesting but rhetorically ineffective. By this point they had already lost the legal and public-relations battle with Chapman, but nevertheless wanted to publish a kind of parting shot, making much of her "arrogance and malignity." More substantively, they based their defense of themselves on the free exercise of religion. "To condemn a religious tenet, by legislative authority," they complained about Eunice Chapman's successful case, "is to assume a power hitherto unknown in our statute book," and some outsiders agreed. A writer for the *Albany Gazette* argued that the "constitution of the United States as firmly guarantees to the Shaker the free exercise of his religion, as it does that of the Calvinist or Episcopalian." Religious minorities, he concluded, "are entitled to the respect and protection of the government."[6]

In the case of Mary Dyer there were no winners. Unfortunately for the Shakers, the New Hampshire legislature ultimately sided with her, passing a law in 1824 allowing for divorces when one spouse "joined a religious group that renounced marriage."[7] By that measure, it would seem that Mary had won. After more than a decade of agitating, she finally received her divorce in 1830, but she never got her family back. Two of her children died at Enfield, two others survived but remained Shakers for the rest of their lives, while the one son who did leave the village never reconciled with his mother. Tragically, Mary lived out her days alone, publishing in 1847 yet another exposé of Shakerism, this one decidedly more bitter than the previous two.[8]

Dyer's most damning indictment by far was the alleged tyranny and cruelty of the elders. "The Shakers' *outward* appearances are *all pleasant* and *delightful, all civility*," she seethed, "when within are *task-masters, bondage, and slavery,* and no one is allowed to utter a word of it."[9] This was the "dark side of the picture" that she wanted to expose. Furthermore, the elders took constant and often dramatic steps to ensure their status at the top of the hierarchy. "When we prayed," Dyer wrote, "our devotion must be to the elders."[10] Eunice Chapman similarly complained: "Instead of being taught not to offend God, they are taught not to offend the Elders!"[11]

Accusing Shaker elders of abusing their power, of course, was hardly new. This line of criticism had reached its peak in Thomas Brown's 1812 exposé, *An Account of the People Called Shakers*. Although Chapman's and Dyer's cases would heap notoriety upon the Society, Brown's *Account*, published earlier that decade, in many ways started the wave of outsider hostility. A remarkably balanced—as opposed to sensationalized—document, Brown's exposé took special aim at the elders' hypocrisy. As an initiate, he had been taught "faith in, and obedience to the elders, as the only way to obtain salvation from sin." As he continued in the community, however, he discovered "positive falsehoods in those who make so great a profession of truth," confirming the rumors of Believers dancing naked, and expressing dismay when he learned that the elders told one another the secrets they had heard in supposedly confidential confessions. "Now I began to conclude," he recounted, "that the Elders stood as sole leaders, teachers, and directors; and that acquiescence to them was what in all things was required." He even reported that some members were forced to kneel in repentance before them. All of these "positive falsehoods" led Brown to the conclusion that Shaker elders "are like the Romish church" in their abuses of power and their "doctrine of infallibility."[12]

While these accusations might not have been new, the context in which they were voiced was decidedly different. In between the 1780s and the 1810s lay the Constitution and the all-important First Amendment. Thomas Brown did not dwell much on the topic but he did baldly contrast the tyranny he had experienced with the freedom most Americans enjoyed in their religious and civic lives.[13] Chapman's and Dyer's legal cases, however, focused extensively on the tangled issues of religious freedom and individual rights. In Chapman's original petition to the New York Senate she acknowledged "the importance of preserving to everyone the free and undisturbed exercise of their religious principles, when not inconsistent with the public safety." The Shakers, in short, had a constitutionally protected right to be Shakers: to believe what they believed; to worship as they worshipped; and to live communally in their villages as they saw fit. The question was about the legal status and rights of the unconverted spouse and children when the other spouse had renounced family obligations. In their deliberations, the legislators had to weigh these two competing goods. Even those who were sympathetic to Chapman's plight, in fact, were fearful that they might violate the First Amendment's free exercise clause in granting her a divorce. The majority, however, agreed that the Shakers had ventured beyond the protections of free exercise and acted in a way "inconsistent with the public safety." In 1818 the New York Senate passed Chapman's petition for divorce and custody by the close vote of 51 to 41.[14]

Shaker leaders responded to the Chapman and Dyer cases with what they hoped would be an authoritative pronouncement. They published *The Other Side of the Question* in 1819 to contest the specific charges made against them. Driven now by these crises, Mother Lucy Wright established a commission to set the public record straight about the Society's history, beliefs, and practices. As the authors explained their rationale in the Preface: "in consequence of . . . the false and erroneous statements . . . of those accounts, the Society has been earnestly solicited . . . to publish a plain and correct statement of facts relative to the history of the Society." The result, published in 1823, two years after Wright's death, was *A Summary View of the Millennial Church, or United Society of Believers, (Commonly Called Shakers.) Comprising the Rise, Progress, and Practical Order of the Society; Together with the General Principles of Their Faith and Testimony*. According to both Shakers and Shaker historians, the document lived up to its promise. *A Summary View* was the most systematic, sophisticated, and clear Shaker publication to date. Historian Stephen Stein writes that the over three-hundred-page tome soon "became the official statement of the history of the society," its appearance signaling "the completion of the establishment of the Shakers as a society, now formally called the United Society of Believers."[15] It was, in many ways, the intellectual culmination of the Shakers' forty-year-long era of institution building (1787–1826). It is utterly uncompromising in its condemnation of "fleshly lust," and in the necessity of a "full and final cross against the carnal nature of the flesh" as a prerequisite for salvation.[16]

But in addition to the usual ruminations on the war between the flesh and the spirit, *A Summary View* also focused on the rights of persecuted religious minorities in the American republic. "We live in a country which boasts highly of the freedom of its religious institutions," the preface proclaimed with some sarcasm. Much to their dismay, however, these recent divorce and custody cases had restricted rather than expanded the boundaries of religious freedom. The Shakers therefore cast themselves as the ones entitled to "religious rights and liberty of conscience" over and against the persecutions of the established authorities. They—and not their legal challengers Eunice Chapman and Mary Marshall Dyer—were the victims here. The result was an obvious loss for the Shakers, but according to them it was also a hypocritical violation of the very principles upon which America prided itself. Chapman and Dyer had won when they should have lost. For their part, the Shakers tried to take the defeat in stride. They had been legally chastened as a religious sect, but not destroyed. With the *Summary View of the Millennial Church* now published, they would persist unbowed in their unique beliefs and practices indefinitely.[17]

8

Polygamy and Persecution at Nauvoo

THE MORMONS, 1842-1844

WHEN IT comes to the Mormons, a chapter on "Early Crises" could encompass almost anything, since most of the history of the LDS Church in the nineteenth century was a time of crisis. The Saints were mocked, hounded from state to state, sued, beaten, tarred and feathered, threatened with "extermination," and murdered—and that was all in the Church's first ten years. In 1839 the Saints finally found some security in the "beautiful place" of Nauvoo where they could protect themselves with a robust city charter, bloc voting in local and state elections, and their own militia, the Nauvoo Legion, if need be. In this safe environment, Joseph Smith not only raised a town and a magnificent temple, but also revealed the new ordinances of baptism for the dead and the endowment ceremony through which God would minister to the Saints.

Those good times, however, only lasted for a few years, with May of 1842 as the turning point. That month Smith performed the very first endowment ceremony and endured his most devastating betrayal. John C. Bennett, Smith's partner in constructing Nauvoo, turned on him and initiated a series of crises that would ultimately undo all that they had built together. The period of May 1842 to June 1844 is therefore worthy of special treatment as a time of successive crises that were exceptional even for a Church that had grown somewhat accustomed to them. This story reaches its tragic culmination in Smith's assassination at the Carthage jail on June 27, 1844, but virtually all of these last twenty-six months of his life were particularly trying for the faithful.

The crises unfolded in three escalating phases, each prompted by the controversial practice of plural marriage. In the first phase of these crises, Bennett, bitter at having been stripped of power, sensationally exposed this secret in an attempt to humiliate and destroy his former community. His actions were hypocritical in the extreme and transparently self-serving, but nevertheless irreparably harmful to Smith's and the Church's reputation. In the second crisis Smith confronted an even more intimate foe: his wife, Emma Hale Smith. Joseph had always kept polygamy secret from Emma, but as the practice spread in the early 1840s and the number of his wives grew, she inevitably found out and made their domestic life a living hell. It was in response to this marital crisis that Smith recorded the revelation on plural marriage in writing in July 1843, a revelation that warned Emma in no uncertain terms that "the Lord thy God . . . will destroy her if she abide not in my law."[1] But in addition to Emma, a growing number of Saints refused to submit to this revelation as God's will. They saw plural marriage instead as the corrupt brainchild of a fallen prophet, and they too—like Bennett—published their dissent. This schism and exposure by longstanding Saints was the final crisis, which Smith did not survive.

This dark season began with the betrayal of John C. Bennett. As one of Smith's confidantes, Bennett knew about polygamy. A serial adulterer before he arrived in Nauvoo—his wife had left him for his infidelities—Bennett needed little prompting to continue his extracurricular activities. He soon used plural marriage as a new way to seduce women, telling them that extramarital sexual liaisons were now sanctioned by God and secretly practiced by the Church's leaders. This was not what the adultery-conscious Smith had in mind for his new marital dispensation, and he privately confronted Bennett sometime in the spring of 1842 both to discipline him for his immorality and to prevent his corruption of the idea of plural marriage from spreading. Bennett did not receive Smith's admonitions well, and on May 7 apparently tried to kill the prophet during one of the Nauvoo Legion's military exercises. The details are sketchy, but allegedly Bennett arranged for an "accident" to happen during a mock battle the Legion was staging. Vacillating over what kind of action to take, Smith realized by mid-June that he had to excommunicate his former friend. One by one, Bennett was removed from every position of power: in the Church, in the city, and in the Masonic lodge.[2]

Bennett did not respond kindly to this loss of power and status. After leaving Nauvoo, he retreated to the county seat of Carthage and plotted his literary revenge: a no-holds-barred character assassination of his former friend, entitled *The History of the Saints; or, An Exposé of Joe Smith and Mormonism*. Enemies of the Saints had published before but focused their criticisms primarily on Mormonism's religious claims: the historicity and authority of its texts, and the credibility of Joseph Smith as a revelator. John Bennett's *History of the Saints* took anti-Mormon publications in a new and dangerous direction. Driven by spite and wasting no time,

Bennett originally wrote his *History* as a series of letters, published in local newspapers between July 8, just one week after he had left Nauvoo, and September 2. Describing the LDS Church as a "colossal scheme of rebellion and usurpation," with all of the numbers, military organization, and religious fanaticism necessary to subvert the civil order, Bennett even had the audacity to single out the Nauvoo Legion—the very militia unit that he had recently commanded—as a force to be feared.[3]

Unfortunately for Smith, what Bennett wrote about plural marriage was a mixture of both salacious fiction and verifiable fact. The fictional element could not have been more titillating or more ridiculous: Bennett described a "Mormon Seraglio," not unlike those of "Oriental and African monarchs." In this supposed harem, Smith reportedly lorded over "three distinct orders, or degrees" of female underlings: sex slaves, willing concubines, and *"spiritual wives."*[4] This is the outrageous picture that Bennett painted before moving on to his more substantiated claims. This is also where—sensationalist rhetoric aside—Joseph Smith was in real trouble, as Bennett described in detail several of Smith's "ATTEMPTED SEDUCTIONS," and had evidence to authenticate the women's stories.

One of the more damaging of those stories came from Sarah M. Pratt, the wife of Mormon stalwart Orson Pratt. It is difficult to separate truth from fiction in Bennett's version of Sarah Pratt's story, but something did happen between her and Smith. According to Bennett, in 1841 Smith solicited him "confidentially," while Orson Pratt was away on missionary work in England, to inquire of Sarah whether she would be willing to be "one of his *spiritual wives*." Orson Pratt only learned of the proposition from the letter Bennett published on July 15, 1842, and immediately spiraled into despair and confusion. Caught between the conflicting stories of his wife, who confirmed Bennett's account, and his prophet, who denied it, Orson ultimately sided with Sarah and had an understandably devastating crisis of faith. Having chosen his side—for the moment—he was excommunicated by the Church on August 20. He reconciled with Smith a few months later, but in the meantime Bennett's exposé had begun wreaking havoc within the Mormon community.[5]

Bennett's story of Martha H. Brotherton was more damaging. In 1842 Brotherton was a seventeen-year-old English convert who had recently arrived in Illinois with the rest of her family. She soon became the object of affection not of Joseph Smith but of Brigham Young, whose fumbling first advances resulted in a major scandal for the Church and a major boon for John Bennett. Brotherton not only rejected Young's proposal, but also determined to testify about it in a published affidavit. According to Brotherton's affidavit, only three weeks after she had arrived in Nauvoo in the spring of 1842, Heber C. Kimball and Brigham Young approached her and "requested me to go and spend a few days with them." Kimball and Young, along with Smith, then finagled circumstances such that Brotherton was left alone in a room with Young, who "arose, locked the door, closed the window, and drew the curtain." Young then asked her a series of questions, making sure to ask her first whether she would "'promise not to mention them to any one?'" With her supposed assent, Young then got down to business: "'have you not an affection for me,'" he asked, "'that were it lawful and right, you could accept me for your husband and companion?'" Brotherton's answer to this question, however, was less encouraging. Dumbfounded by the proposition, she asked "for time to think and pray about it."[6]

But rather than grant Brotherton this time, Young and Smith increased the pressure on her, with disastrous results. "'Look here, sis; don't you believe in me?'" Smith reportedly asked her: "'and if there is any sin in it, I will answer for it before God; . . . and if you will accept of Brigham, you shall be blessed.'" When she continued to demur, Smith reminded her of the "'old proverb . . . "Nothing ventured, nothing gained,"'" while Young asked her once more to "'promise me you will never mention it [their conversation] to any one.'" Brotherton did, however, mention this encounter to others. After having shared her story with Bennett, she also determined to "proceed to a justice of the peace, and make oath to the truth of these statements," and to give Bennett full "liberty to make what use of them you may think best." On July 13, 1842, she took this oath before a judge in St. Louis, and on July 16 Bennett published her affidavit in the local newspaper, the *Native American Bulletin*.[7]

Brotherton's story dropped like a bomb in the Mormon community and throughout antebellum America. For the rest of July, newspapers from Illinois to New York reprinted her affidavit and Bennett featured it prominently in his *History of the Saints*. For Smith and the handful of Mormon polygamists, the word was now officially out. Church leaders had been trying to squelch the story for months but failed miserably in the attempt. As far back as April 7, 1842, Hyrum Smith, Joseph's brother, addressed at a Church conference what were then merely rumors "that a sister had been shut in a room for several days, and that they [elders] had endeavored to induce her to believe in having two wives."[8] That July, the Church went into full damage-control mode, publishing in August their own *Affidavits and Certificates Disproving the Statements and Affidavits Contained in John C. Bennett's Letters*. Their counterarguments, however, convinced few and did nothing to make Bennett's stories go away. That October, when Bennett published his original eight letters as *The History of the Saints,* the book was so popular that it went through three printings to meet the demand. Thus by the fall of 1842 the ranks of disaffected Mormons were growing, with even more threatening forces amassing outside Nauvoo.[9]

Back in May 1842 someone shot former Missouri governor Lilburn Boggs in the head. Boggs was no longer governor, but he was still active in politics and he had issued the infamous Mormon "extermination order" in 1838. In the wake of the assassination attempt—Boggs somehow survived the blast—people initially suspected political rivals, but Bennett helped shift the blame to Smith and his supposed henchman, Orin Porter Rockwell. In this episode Bennett had what he believed to be a clear example of the Mormon penchant for violence and political usurpation, and unfortunately for the Saints, it was highly likely that Rockwell had done it. Although he was later acquitted for the shooting due to lack of evidence, there were no other real suspects.[10]

In the second half of 1842, at the same time that newspapers throughout America were publishing Bennett's inflammatory letters, Missouri authorities were trying to extradite Smith and Rockwell on the charge of attempted murder. Smith thus fought two battles simultaneously: a public relations campaign against Bennett's charge of a "Mormon Seraglio"; and a legal campaign against the Missourians he knew would lynch him if he ever set foot in the state. Fearing for his life, Smith went on the lam. From August until basically the end of 1842 he was a fugitive, staying in various friends' and relatives' homes around Nauvoo, while at the same time trying to mount his legal defense. In January 1843 Smith won decisively when a federal judge ruled that Missouri's attempt to extradite him was unconstitutional. Extradition, the judge declared, allowed a state to claim a fugitive who had committed a crime in that same state. Since Smith was in Illinois when Governor Boggs was shot on May 6, the state of Missouri had no right to extradite him. Rockwell, who *was* in Missouri that night, was still on the hook, and indeed languished in a Missouri jail for months until he was acquitted, but Smith was now cleared of the charges.[11]

But while Smith enjoyed victory over the Missourians, Bennett had still done lasting damage to the prophet. Already prejudiced against Mormons, local Gentiles just needed a demagogue to bring those prejudices to the surface. After Bennett's *History of the Saints* Smith was no longer considered a person but a beast leading a mindless horde of religious fanatics. Given Smith's megalomania and the average Mormon's obedience to him, Bennett claimed, he could easily lead women into sexual immorality and men into subversive violence. The only solution, supposedly, was to meet potential Mormon violence with preemptive violence of their own. "Retributive justice must put forth the arm of power, and pass from the FORUM to the FIELD," he declared.[12] In doing so, virtuous American citizens would restore order and remove from their good land an alien menace. Bennett's words had an immediate and powerful effect, although not yet a lethal one. In 1842, he primed local anti-Mormons for mob violence, one might say, but did not spur them to it.

Most importantly, after Bennett's betrayal Joseph Smith was never the same. The evidence to substantiate this claim is not found in a single place but rather in a comparison of Smith's language and style from before and after the crisis. After mid-1842 Smith became more egocentric, angry, and at times seemingly desperate. "I have the whole plan of the kingdom before me," he wrote on August 29, 1842, "and no other person has." He did not so much claim authority as he had to proclaim it. He did not have a bunker mentality before, but he did now, and it was understandable that he developed one as he fought a dangerous throng of outside enemies.

After Bennett's exposé he also had good reason to fear inside sabotage as well. As Smith bitterly protested: "And as to all that Orson Pratt, Sidney Rigdon, and George W. Robinson can do to prevent me, I can kick them off my heels, as many as you can name; I know what will become of them."[13] In this bona fide crisis, Smith retreated into suspicion and controlling behavior, seeking power as a means of self-preservation and utilizing every resource at his disposal: legal systems, theology, institutions, and people. Smith originally established institutions such as the Masonic Lodge and the endowment ordinance to bless and exalt his fellow Saints. Now he would use these and other institutions to serve the understandable but less-than-noble purpose of self-aggrandizement and self-protection. This pattern reached its crescendo in 1844 when Smith ran for president (a very American thing to do) and had himself anointed as a king (a very un-American one). Increasingly autocratic, he would also tolerate no further internal dissent, which is what ultimately got him arrested and killed.

During this time Joseph Smith's story took a dark turn and plural marriage took a dark turn along with it. Some might judge the institution of polygamy to be irredeemably rotten, or at the very least morally problematic. The fact that Joseph did not tell Emma about his plural marriages is indefensible. And then there are the controversial acts of marrying teenagers and propositioning other men's wives without the husband's knowledge. As mentioned, Smith and other leaders also used emotionally manipulative, high-pressure tactics to try to force some women into plural marriages: holding them in locked rooms, questioning the sincerity of their faith, and trying to muzzle them with vows of secrecy. In 1843 and 1844 all of these morally questionable elements of Mormon polygamy continued, while unfortunately the coercion got decidedly worse. Soon men would threaten prospective brides with everlasting punishments if they rejected them. In the context of suspicion and fear that permeated Nauvoo after 1842, this is how Smith and other polygamists treated some of the female Saints.

After Bennett's betrayal Smith also treated male polygamists differently, using plural marriage as a test of their loyalty. Clearly this was a risky plan that ultimately backfired. Introducing more men and women to plural marriage would expand the community of loyal secret-keepers. But what was supposed to be another layer of protection soon became a catalyst for outside hostility and internal dissent. In 1844 those internal and external forces combined with lethal results. In the meantime, between the summers of 1842 and 1844, Smith believed that expanding plural marriage would somehow provide protection from those who sought to destroy him.

At the height of the Bennett and Boggs crises of late 1842, however, it was simply too risky to expand plural marriage. When Smith had to go into hiding he ceased taking additional wives for six months. He married Martha Knight on August 5, 1842, and did not marry his next bride, Ruth Sayers, until February 1843, a month after the attempted murder case had been dismissed.[14] Upon winning his extradition battle against the Missourians, however, Smith's spirits lifted and he resumed taking plural wives more manically than before. Between February and November 1843, he married twenty-one more women.[15] After his last plural sealing on November 2, crises again consumed him and, as in the latter half of 1842, he ceased marrying. From the end of 1843 until the end of his life on June 27, 1844, Smith took no more wives.

But throughout the frenetic marrying days of 1843, polygamy resumed full force with a new emphasis on secrecy, loyalty, and outright defiance of the world. Binding scores of men and women in the secret covenant of plural marriage would be a means by which Smith could protect himself from hostile outside forces. Plural marriage would also be a dramatic means by which the Saints could further differentiate themselves from the Gentiles around them. Sex, in other words, would reinforce sectarian identity. In the ultimate inversion, polygamy would go from being an act of moral turpitude and marital failure in the eyes of the community, a crime in US law, and a sin before God, to being an indication of high status in the community, a way of setting Mormons apart from the godless American republic, and an outright command from the Lord to establish His restored kingdom on earth.

For Smith during this time, keeping secrets became of paramount importance, both from the outside world, but also, sadly, from Emma. At precisely the time that Smith needed intimacy and trust, he destroyed both with Emma by pressing ahead with plural marriage. When he finally had to deal with the devastation she felt, he responded with more control, this time in the form of an official revelation.

This next crisis in Joseph's life supposedly started with a bang. In February 1843, Emma expelled Eliza Roxcy Snow from her house. It is known from Eliza's diary that she left on February 11. It is also known that Smith had married Eliza back in June 1842, and that in August, clearly unaware that she and Eliza now shared a husband, Emma asked her to live in the Smith home. Precisely what happened before Eliza's departure has been the subject of much speculation ever since. The two most colorful versions of the story have Emma pulling Eliza down the stairs by her hair, or assaulting her with a broomstick. Another version asserts that Emma shoved Eliza down the stairs and that the fall caused her to have a miscarriage, presumably of her child by Joseph.[16] Melodramatic rumors aside, something had gone wrong in their friendship and it is most plausible that Emma had discovered Eliza and Joseph's secret relationship.

Emma had lived through this nightmare before. In 1835 in Kirtland, she had invited Fanny Alger into their home, only to expel her after discovering she was also married to Joseph. Clearly Emma did not approve of this new understanding of marriage. As her biographers put it, she bore the humiliation with "a quiet reserve, but her anxiety showed through."[17] Since Joseph did not practice plural marriage for the rest of the 1830s, Emma had no reason to be anxious about this particular affront. The couple worried instead about finances, persecution, and imprisonment. The move to Nauvoo brought stability to the Church and to the Smith home, but it also provided Joseph with the safe context in which he resumed plural marriage. When he did, beginning with his marriage to Louisa Beaman on April 5, 1841, he did not tell Emma or ask her permission. Apparently, Emma did not know about any of Joseph's plural wives until this fateful encounter with Eliza R. Snow in February 1843.

Now that he faced once again the wrath of his wife, Smith had a momentous decision to make: either continue plural marriage as a revealed institution of God, or discontinue the principle as he had after Emma expelled Fanny Alger in 1835. This time, however, Joseph chose differently. Emma, the loving and dutiful wife, would simply have to make her peace with this new order of things.

But if Smith was now committed to polygamy, regardless of the consequences, Emma vacillated in her opinions. From March to May 1843 the couple spoke openly about the principle, Joseph laboring to convince her of its truth and necessity for exaltation, and Emma struggling to come to terms with it. In May she relented, with the important stipulation that she be able to choose Joseph's plural wives. Diving headlong into polygamy's deep waters, Emma chose not one but four young women for Joseph to marry before the end of the month: two pair of sisters, Emily and Eliza Partridge, and Sarah and Maria Lawrence. Both pairs had lost their fathers in 1840 and both subsequently lived in the Smith home as domestic servants. The Partridge sisters moved in in 1840, years before they became plural wives. Unbeknownst to Emma, however, Joseph had courted and married them *before* she gave her consent. According to Emily Partridge's diary, Joseph approached her as far back as the spring of 1842, ceased his advances for the rest of the year after she protested and while he dealt with the Bennett and Boggs crises, and resumed the courtship on "the 28th of Feb, 1843 (my nineteenth birth day)."[18] This time Emily was receptive and the two wed less than a week later on March 4. Courting her sister simultaneously, Joseph married Emily on March 8. Thus when Emma chose the Partridge sisters to be Joseph's next plural wives, they already were his plural wives. In a situation that was saturated with irony, Emma then took it upon herself to help them with the transition, teaching them about the new marital dispensation and attending the official wedding ceremony on May 23, 1843. Earlier that month, Emma had also given her permission for Joseph to marry Sarah and Maria Lawrence, who moved into the Smith home at approximately the same time.[19]

After these ceremonies, Emma's opinion of plural marriage and these young plural wives changed almost instantly. Perhaps she had come to stomach polygamy as an idea, but found it intolerable as a lived reality.

Unwilling to share her husband, Emma became suspicious of every prolonged absence and every closed door, and soon took out her resentment on both the wives and Joseph. Not long after the marriages she summoned the Partridge sisters to a meeting of the four of them and insisted that "Joseph should give us up or blood should flow." Apparently Emma had worked Joseph over rather severely before they arrived, for he, "looking like a martyr," said little, and then simply "shook hands with us, and the understanding was that all was ended between us."[20] This unbelievable divorce-by-handshake concluded the Partridge sisters' plural marriages, as well as their residence in the Smith home. Emma kicked them out just as she had expelled Fanny Alger and Eliza Snow. Joseph's attempt to persuade Emma had failed.[21]

In spite of this setback Smith continued undaunted in his other plural marriages. He had married women secretly before and he would continue to do so after Emma's change of heart. "By late summer 1843," Emma's biographers write without hyperbole, "most of Emma's friends had either married Joseph or had given their daughters to him."[22]

Each of Smith's thirty-seven plural wives has a story to tell about how he courted her and why she accepted his proposal, but two in particular—Lucy Walker and Helen Mar Kimball—stand out. Like the Partridge and Lawrence sisters, Lucy Walker moved into the Smith home after the death of a parent. In this case it was her mother who died in January 1842 when Lucy was fifteen years old. Lucy's father was still alive but Smith sent him away on a mission trip to the eastern United States. Sometime in that year, as Lucy records it, Smith "sought an interview with me" and informed her that "'I have been commanded of God to take another wife, and you are that woman.'" Like many of Smith's prospective brides, Lucy was gob-smacked: "My astonishment knew no bounds. This announcement was indeed a thunderbolt to me." Smith then proceeded to explain "the principle" to Lucy and that "it would prove an everlasting blessing to my father's house, and form a chain that could never be broken, worlds without end."[23]

When Lucy continued to equivocate, Smith asked her to "pray sincerely for light and understanding in relation thereto," while increasing the pressure on her. The two met again sometime after their initial "interview" and this time Smith was less patient. "'I have no flattering words to offer,'" he told her: "'It is a command of God to you. I will give you until to-morrow to decide this matter. If you reject this message the gate will be closed forever against you.'" Smith issued this ultimatum in the spring of 1843, in the wake of the Bennett crisis, when he was less placating and more willing to manipulate and threaten people into doing his will. In 1842 after Nancy Rigdon had rejected his proposition, Smith wrote a theological rationale for plural marriage in an attempt to persuade her. In 1843 Smith touted his authority as a prophet and informed prospective plural wives of the eternal rewards that could be theirs if they accepted polygamy, and the eternal missed opportunities if they rejected it. Lucy's prayers in between these two meetings had clearly not brought her peace. Faced with this ultimatum, however, she experienced an epiphany, during which "Supreme happiness took possession of me, and I received a powerful and irresistible testimony of the truth of plural marriage."[24]

In 1843 Smith also courted the fourteen-year-old Helen Mar Kimball, but approached her through the ministrations of her father, Heber Kimball, who in June 1842 was one of the first four men to join Smith in polygamy. There are some obvious similarities and differences between Helen's and Lucy's experiences in the spring of 1843. The most obvious difference is the two girls' family situation. Pitifully, Lucy was on her own, lamenting: "I am only a child in years and experience. No mother to counsel; no father near to tell me what to do in this trying hour."[25] Perhaps the Walker family would have rejected Smith's proposal as Nancy Rigdon had, with the support of her father Sidney Ridgon. As it was, though, Lucy had to make this momentous decision by herself. In contrast, Helen Mar Kimball's obedient and ambitious father, Heber Kimball, "having a great desire to be connected with the Prophet, Joseph, he offered me to him."[26] This arranged plural marriage can clearly be described as "dynastic," to use historian Todd Compton's word, "an example of male bonding through polygamy."[27] First Heber came to believe that his heavenly status would be enhanced by the union, and then he successfully convinced Helen of "so glorious a reward."[28]

In terms of similarities, both were in their mid-teens and both went through a crucible of profound tension and ethical confusion followed by spiritual clarity and release. Lucy wanted to die. "Oh that the grave would kindly receive me," she exclaimed. She also feared the social ostracism she would endure as a plural wife, but in the end "felt at this moment that I was called to place myself upon the altar a living sacrifice." Helen likewise submitted to the sacrificial role her father had chosen for her. With only one daughter, her "father had but one Ewe Lamb but willingly laid her upon the alter [sic]."[29] This was the main commonality between the two women's experiences: an emphasis on personal earthly sacrifices to obtain familial heavenly rewards.

Sadly for Joseph, he could not persuade Emma to make the same personal sacrifice to ensure their own family's exaltation. And as the reality of her intransigence sank in, Joseph likewise chose earthly sacrifice to obtain celestial glory. He undoubtedly sacrificed domestic peace with his beloved first wife, but he also sacrificed Emma herself, and without her consent. Helen Mar Kimball had consented to be her father's "Ewe Lamb." Emma would agree to no such role. In the end Joseph would have to command her and even threaten her with eternal punishment.

In spite of problems with Emma, in the first half of 1843 Smith built momentum for plural marriage, with eight more men following him into the principle.[30] Many of these men also resisted at first, but "as Joseph applied intense pressure to act," historian George D. Smith explains, "and they risked being marginalized or even banished from the community as heretics, those chosen to accept their celestial privileges eventually consented."[31] One of those people was Joseph's brother Hyrum. When Hyrum first learned of plural marriage, he feared the effects it would have on the community and actually wanted to end the practice, even if it meant opposing Joseph. But not long thereafter Hyrum changed his mind and sought out Brigham Young to teach him this new doctrine. As Young remembers Hyrum saying, "I want to know the truth to be saved."[32] Apparently Hyrum was also thinking about earthly costs and eternal rewards.

What prepared Hyrum and several other Saints to accept plural marriage were Joseph's revelations in the winter and spring of 1843. Revelations had ceased during the crises of late 1842, but after his case was dismissed in January the revelations resumed and are in many ways the culmination of Smith's meditations on the mysteries of heaven and earth, spirit and matter, marriage and family. They began by revisiting the question of spiritual beings having physical bodies. "The Father has a body of flesh and bones as tangible as man's," he revealed on April 2, 1843.

Smith's revelation on celestial marriage on May 16 and 17, 1843, was equally revolutionary. "In the celestial glory there are three heavens or degrees," it reads:

> 2 And in order to obtain the highest, a man must enter into this order of the priesthood [meaning the new and everlasting covenant of marriage];
>
> 3 And if he does not, he cannot obtain it.
>
> 4 He may enter into the other, but that is the end of his kingdom; he cannot have an increase. . . .

7 There is no such thing as immaterial matter. All spirit is matter, but it is more fine or pure, and can only be discerned by purer eyes;

8 We cannot see it; but when our bodies are purified we shall see that it is all matter.[33]

With these few verses Joseph Smith redefined the cosmos and humankind's purpose within it. Both mortal life on earth and the afterlife are material, the revelation declares. And perhaps more importantly, this afterlife is not egalitarian. There are ranks, and if one wants to enjoy eternity at the top of the spiritual heap, one has to be sealed to a partner in celestial wedlock. This ordinance, however, could only be performed on earth between either the couple in the flesh, or with one of the partners by proxy.

This revelation made Hyrum Smith a believer in plural marriage. On Sunday May 14, 1843, Hyrum had actually preached *against* "having many wives & Concubines" as "an abomination in the Sight of God."[34] Days later, Joseph recorded the revelation about celestial marriage and Hyrum, who had intensely personal reasons for wanting to be sealed in an eternal marriage, was converted by the end of the month. Significantly, Hyrum's beloved first wife, Jerusha, had died in 1837, years before this revelation about celestial marriage. Now Hyrum wanted to be sealed to her for eternity, even though he was remarried. His second wife, Mary Fielding Smith, consented to the eternal sealing, but also told Hyrum, "I love you and I do not want to be separated from you nor be forever alone in the resurrection."[35] In the sealing ceremony on May 29, 1843, Mary stood as proxy for Jerusha before being eternally sealed to Hyrum herself. Celestially speaking, Hyrum was now a polygamist. On August 11 Hyrum began practicing polygamy in real time when he married his sister-in-law, Mercy Rachel Fielding, and three more women before the end of September.[36]

Perhaps because a revelation had helped convert him, and perhaps because as the prophet's brother he was concerned about Joseph's marriage to Emma, Hyrum urged Joseph to sanctify plural marriage with an official revelation. "If you will write the revelation," Hyrum is recorded telling Joseph on the morning of July 12, 1843, "I will take and read it to Emma, and I believe I can convince her of its truth, and you will hereafter have peace." Joseph consented, but also pessimistically cautioned his well-meaning brother, "You do not know Emma as well as I do." Due to the obvious importance of this revelation, Hyrum suggested that Joseph use the Urim and Thummin for guidance, but Joseph, brimming with full prophetic confidence, said that he knew it "perfectly from beginning to end."[37]

Smith's July 12, 1843, revelation on plural marriage can be found in the contemporary *Doctrine and Covenants,* section 132. Sixty-six verses in all, the revelation raised the eternal stakes for all Latter-day Saints—especially Emma—while greatly reinforcing the power of the prophet Joseph Smith. As the revelation clearly explains, those not sealed in eternal marriage on earth "are not gods." Conversely, the obedient ones who are sealed according to "the new and everlasting covenant" can anticipate literally no limitations whatsoever to their celestial rewards. The revelation further "anointed and appointed" one person and one person only "to hold this power in the last days" and perform those eternal sealings: "my servant Joseph."[38]

The revelation then addressed the lingering and anxiety-inducing question of adultery. As it turns out, there was a crucial difference between adulterers and those practicing the God-ordained new dispensation of plural marriage: namely, the sealing power vested in the prophet Joseph Smith. Extramarital relationships were adulterous and illegitimate unless they were sanctioned through "the power of my Holy Priesthood" to "take" and to "give" women to men in order that they "be made ruler over many." Covered with the sealing power of the priesthood, all polygamists were "justified." In fact, rather than being guilty of adultery, those who practiced plural marriage were engaged in the great procreative "work of my Father continued"—the creation of material bodies to "bear the souls of men." This was precisely what had occurred in the Old Testament, when King "David also received many wives and concubines, and also Solomon and Moses . . . and in nothing did they sin save in those things which they received not of me." The biblical precedent was irrefutable: one did not have to be a monogamist in order to serve the Lord. In fact, if God commanded it, as He apparently was in this latest revelation, one might sin in *not* practicing polygamy. Latter-day Saints could thus rest assured. While obviously jarring and controversial, plural marriage was once again ordained by God and duly administered through "the power of my Holy Priesthood" and "my servant Joseph" in particular. Even with all that had happened, Smith apparently still enjoyed the Lord's favor.[39]

This was not the case, however, for "mine handmaid, Emma Smith." For her, the Lord had only commands and threats. "I am the Lord thy

God," the revelation boomed, "and ye shall obey my voice." Whereas Joseph would "be made ruler over many things; for he hath been faithful over a few things," Emma was ordered "to abide and cleave unto my servant Joseph, and to none else." And "if she will not abide this commandment she shall be destroyed, saith the Lord." The only way forward for Emma, the revelation stipulated, was to "forgive my servant Joseph his trespasses; and then she shall be forgiven her trespasses."[40]

While both clear and frightening, the revelation failed to convince Emma. Hyrum Smith attempted to establish peace in his brother's home by reading it to her. Upon returning from this diplomatic mission, however, Hyrum is reported to have said: "I have never received a more severe talking to in my life."[41] A few days later she reportedly destroyed the manuscript in a fire. As had happened previously, Emma waffled but ultimately opposed plural marriage categorically. She seemed to wrestle in particular with whether or not the revelation was in fact a revelation. If it truly was the word of the Lord, she had no choice as a devout Saint but to obey it with fear and trembling, especially since she was mentioned in it by name and threatened with destruction. Emma, however, could never reconcile herself to this latest manifestation of God's restored order and the unhappy couple continued to fight: Emma venting her rage on Joseph and her jealousy on his suspected plural wives, while Joseph wept, pleaded, and lied in his efforts to placate her.[42]

Toward the end of summer 1843, Joseph and Emma reached a kind of uneasy non-aggression pact that would last for the rest of their marriage. According to the recollection of William Clayton, Joseph's secretary, on August 16, after Emma threatened to divorce him, Joseph told "her he would relinquish all for her sake." Joseph did keep part of the bargain—he sullenly allowed Emma to expel the Partridge and Lawrence sisters, and in November he took his last plural wife—but he hardly relinquished "all." He even told William Clayton that "he should not relinquish anything." The ruse seemed to work, however, and brought some measure of peace to their home.[43]

Meanwhile, other Saints also wrestled with whether or not to accept the revelation on plural marriage as the word of the Lord. Smith had been teaching trusted associates about plural marriage since July 1841. By the end of June 1843 a dozen men had taken at least one plural wife, and a dozen more would follow by the end of the year.[44] Thus when the revelation came on July 12 it added both momentum and legitimacy to what Smith had already been teaching. But the official revelation also amplified the dilemma that Latter-day Saints faced. When first told about polygamy, virtually everyone—from Emma Smith and Lucy Walker to Orson Pratt and Brigham Young—recoiled in horror and disbelief. Orson Pratt, historian Martha Bradley-Evans writes, "fell into a dark, perhaps suicidal, despair," while Brigham Young reportedly said that "it was the first time in my life that I desired the grave."[45] The idea was simply too radical and the emotional costs too painful. As believers in ongoing revelation through Joseph Smith, however, Saints confronted a real theological, ethical, and existential conundrum: either their deeply rooted understanding of marriage was flawed, or their deeply held faith in the authority of their prophet was misguided. Although not made public until 1852, a full nine years later, Smith's revelation on plural marriage did circulate among Church leaders in Nauvoo for the rest of 1843, with decidedly mixed results. At this point in the life of the Church, plural marriage indeed became the ultimate loyalty test: either one stood with the prophet or stood against him. Steadfast spiritual adventurers such as Brigham Young passed with flying colors, while many other Saints would soon fail the exam.

Chief among Smith's critics was William Law. Originally from Northern Ireland, the Law family—William, his wife, Jane, and his brother, Wilson—were reportedly people of manners and means. Joining the Saints in Nauvoo in 1839, William was just as impressed with Joseph as Joseph was with William. William helped build Nauvoo, and Joseph admitted him to his inner circle, including him among the first nine men to experience the endowment ceremony in May 1842. William also served with Joseph as a member of the First Presidency, the highest position possible in the Church's hierarchy.[46]

When William Law defected, it must have reminded Smith of John Bennett's betrayal, although the two were quite different. While both men were trusted and talented insiders, Bennett was a charlatan and a rake who used the opportunities afforded by plural marriage to seduce women. William Law was a bona fide convert to the LDS Church who, along with his wife, Jane, chose monogamous marriage over the new teachings of their Church. Also unlike Lucy Walker or Orson Pratt, whose spiritual struggles to accept polygamy were followed by cathartic releases once they did, William and Jane Law ultimately rejected polygamy as immoral and Smith as a fallen, although not a false prophet. The couple did not reach these conclusions quickly or impetuously, but after much anguish and prayerful reflection. William Law had first heard about plural marriage from Hyrum Smith sometime after Smith's own acceptance of the doctrine in the spring of 1843. Joseph Smith's revelation that summer, however, failed to convince the Laws that plural marriage was from the Lord, and they soon began to oppose their prophet, privately at first and then quite publicly. On January 1, 1844, William Law recorded his negative opinion of plural marriage in his diary, writing that the idea "paralyzes the nerves, chills the currents of the heart, and drives the brain almost to madness," and Joseph Smith celebrated his last New Year's Day.[47]

In addition to William Law and other Saints who were repulsed by polygamy, Smith had made powerful enemies in Illinois state politics. Reflecting their understandable lack of trust in the powers that be, Smith and the Church never warmed to the antebellum two-party system. Rather than playing by the rules that expected and rewarded loyalty, Smith regularly switched allegiances according to what he thought at the time was in the best interest of the Church. This made the Mormons frustratingly unreliable political allies. With so many like-minded people gathered into one place, Mormon bloc voting could make or break political careers and whole partisan agendas. Fatefully, back in August 1843, two days before a congressional election, Smith reneged on an earlier promise to back the Whigs, and Mormon votes sent the Democratic candidate to Washington instead. Illinois Whigs were furious and vented spleen in the press for months.[48] Coming just a year after Bennett's *History of the Saints*, Smith's political blunder reinvigorated anti-Mormon sentiment throughout the region. He had long feared and loathed Missourians, but now he and the Church were wearing out their welcome in Illinois as well. Once again, they were becoming strangers in a strange land.

In 1844, as the environment became increasingly hostile, Smith's responses became even riskier and more irrational. It would be entirely understandable for someone in Smith's position to feel defensive and besieged. He was besieged. But rather than retreat into a bunker and wait it out, Smith went on the offensive and sought even more power, esteem, and national exposure. Although he had incurred the wrath of the political parties in Illinois through his own actions, he was nevertheless frustrated at the Church's long history of mistreatment and inadequate legal protection from state and local governments. The only real help had come when the Mormons helped themselves through the Nauvoo city charter. In 1844, with even that safeguard faltering, Smith reached beyond the city and the state into federal politics and theocratic fantasy. On

January 29, Smith had the Quorum of the Twelve Apostles nominate him for president of the United States. More than a lark, Smith actually developed a platform, organized a campaign, and sent missionaries around the country to stump for him. A few months later, on April 11, Smith had the Council of the Fifty "elect" him a king. This was the opposite of keeping a low profile during a time of crisis.[49]

Grand aspirations and grander titles, however, could not protect Smith from the storm that was building inside and outside his kingdom, and neither could more draconian measures. On January 8, 1844, one week after William Law had confided to his diary his rejection of polygamy, Smith had him removed from the First Presidency. On April 18, Smith had him, his wife, Jane, and his brother, Wilson excommunicated without allowing them to speak in their own defense or even attend the proceedings. This ecclesiastical kangaroo court was the last straw for the already alienated Law family, who retaliated three days later by organizing their own church.[50]

William Law and the other founders of this alternate body did not consider themselves to be apostates, but rather true believers who wanted to restore the LDS Church's original purity. Thus they still believed that the *Book of Mormon* and the restoration of the Church of Jesus Christ of Latter-day Saints "is verily true."[51] Recently, however, Smith had corrupted the Church by teaching heterodox doctrines, spreading immoral practices, and despotically concentrating power in himself. In response, they wanted to reform the Church, not destroy it outright. As they put it: "*we* are constrained to denounce *them* as apostates from the pure and holy doctrines of Jesus Christ."[52] In May, encouraged by the addition of three hundred like-minded supporters in less than a month, William Law formally charged Smith with adultery and purchased a printing press to spread the reform agenda further.[53]

On June 7, 1844, in a broadside that they aptly titled the *Nauvoo Expositor,* the reformers sought to "explode the vicious principles of Joseph Smith, and those who practice the same abominations and whoredoms." They condemned as "false and damnable" Smith's new teaching about "a plurality of Gods above the God of this universe," and they similarly wanted to expose the "notorious fact" that Church leaders were taking advantage of recently arrived single women. "Lo!" they warned, "The wolf is in the fold, arrayed in sheep's clothing" and preying upon the innocent. Having converted in Europe, these "many females in foreign climes" had bravely journeyed to Nauvoo, only to be taught when they arrived that they must become a "Spiritual wife" to one of the Church's leaders. And if those stories struck readers as sensationalized, the *Expositor* also published signed affidavits from William and Jane Law, testifying that Smith's latest "revelation (so called) authorized certain men to have more wives than one at a time, in this world and in the world to come."[54]

Plural gods and plural wives might have led their list of grievances, but the writers of the *Expositor* also took aim at Smith's "attempt at political power and influence, which we verily believe to be preposterous and absurd." No doubt thinking of his current presidential campaign and his recent election as a monarch, they resolved "*not* [to] acknowledge any man as king or law-giver to the church," and determined instead to "disapprobate and discountenance every attempt to unite church and state."[55]

In exposing "all manner of abominations... practiced under the cloak of religion," these reformers appealed unabashedly to deeply held American values. The US Constitution separated church and state, and guaranteed its citizens the right to a fair trial. "Are the people forgetting at once the elements of Republicanism," the *Expositor* pleaded, "viz: tolerance of opinion, freedom of thought and action, and obedience to the laws?" In publishing their "full, candid, and succinct statement of *facts, as they exist in the city of Nauvoo*," the writers "confidently look to an enlightened public for aid in this great and independent effort." And their appeal to shared civic values struck a chord among their equally frustrated non-Mormon neighbors, who unfortunately responded to their plea in an unenlightened way.[56]

Joseph Smith did not help his case when he violated yet another cherished American value: the freedom of the press. On June 10 he had the Nauvoo city council condemn the *Expositor* for libel and he directed the city's marshal and Nauvoo Legion to destroy the press. Later that day he heard the report that the press office had been ransacked—its type and paper thrown into the street—an action that stirred a hornet's nest throughout the region. A judge issued warrants for the arrest of Smith and his accomplices, while local papers screamed for blood. In the ensuing paranoia, the Saints feared a full-scale invasion by an anti-Mormon mob, while Gentiles feared that the Nauvoo Legion would violently defend their prophet. In the end Smith sought protection in the due process of the law and on June 25 turned himself in to the authorities in the county seat of Carthage, fifteen miles away.[57]

Illinois governor Thomas Ford arrived to help ease tensions but his presence could not avert the inevitable violence. While in Nauvoo trying to persuade the Saints that armed resistance would only provoke the mob action that all wanted to avoid, he left in charge of Smith's protection a militia unit called the Carthage Greys. Around five o'clock in the afternoon on June 27, members of the Greys, their faces blackened for disguise, stormed the jailhouse. At the time, Joseph and Hyrum Smith, along with John Taylor and Willard Richards, were in the jailer's private quarters on the second floor. The four men attempted to block the door when someone shot through it, striking Hyrum in the face. The bullet hole in the door exists to this day, a tiny grim reminder of how one man lost his life. Smith ran to the window and gave the Masonic sign of distress while musket balls poured into the room from both the hallway and the ground below. Struck four times, Smith tumbled from the window. Prostrate at the feet of his enemies, Joseph Smith propped himself up on the curb of the jailhouse well and passed through the final veil.[58]

9

"A Scatteration at Oneida"

WHILE NOT nearly as violent as what the Mormons suffered, John Humphrey Noyes's Perfectionists also weathered serious threats to their existence. For over a year, from mid-1851 to mid-1852, the community at Oneida passed through the refining fires of untimely deaths, "a newspaper mob," and persistent lawsuits.[1] As their leader, Noyes initially caved in to the pressure, discontinuing complex marriage for over six months, and considered disbanding the community altogether, what one Perfectionist referred to as the potential "scatteration at Oneida."[2]

A number of factors converged, however, to make the outcome for the Perfectionists different from that of the Latter-day Saints in Nauvoo. The Oneidans had powerful friends as well as enemies in the local community, and Noyes ultimately showed himself to be a shrewd strategist. Both Joseph Smith and John Humphrey Noyes had autocratic leadership styles, but the two men differed markedly when it came to dealing with outsiders. Rather than Smith's secrecy and militancy, Noyes opted for transparency and diplomacy instead, to nearly everyone's satisfaction. Thus this season of crises ended not with murder but with a picnic of strawberries and cream. Before this episode in the Perfectionists' life reached its happy denouement, however, it was indeed a very trying time.

The Perfectionists' trial by fire began with a literal fire. On July 5, 1851, the printing office and store at Oneida burned, a loss that Noyes interpreted "as a criticism from God." Feeling "that inspiration was lacking in the editorial department" of *The Circular,* he believed that God was chastising said editors and directing him personally to resume leadership of their publishing ventures.[3] Responding to God's not-so-subtle hint, Noyes soon reestablished their press not in Oneida but at his smaller community in Brooklyn with him as chief editor.[4] Thus, Noyes turned the accident into an opportunity. What happened next, however, nearly derailed him. He could neither benefit from it personally, nor discern any clear meaning in it spiritually.

Less than two weeks later the Perfectionist community suffered a devastating loss in the death of Mary Cragin. A fearless spiritual and sexual pioneer, in some ways she had led Noyes into complex marriage back in 1846. On July 16, 1851, Mary Cragin decided to accompany other community members on the sloop *Rebecca Ford* as it transported a load of limestone to New York City. A storm blew up in the afternoon that caused the heavy cargo to shift and the boat to dip into the Hudson River and fill with water. The four men onboard were able to swim to safety, but the two women, Eliza A. Allen and Mary Cragin, were in the cabin dining when the accident happened and were unable to escape.[5]

Noyes and the Perfectionists grieved for months and groped desperately to find meaning in the deaths. The Lord "chastens those whom he loves," Noyes told the mourners, and this was yet another "'fiery trial,'" one of the "fire tokens of God's love."[6] Noyes even posthumously elevated Mary Cragin to a position of co-leadership alongside him in establishing complex marriage and ushering in the kingdom of God. "It is well understood that God has raised me up to take the lead," he reminded his followers, but Cragin was obviously his "female correspondent," or "the female head."[7] And if it was not clear already from Noyes's deeply pained musings, he stated explicitly "that there was no other woman whom I loved as I did her."[8] Ironically, this was the kind of selfish, exclusive love that the Perfectionists were trying to stamp out. And yet Noyes repeated on another occasion: "I loved her more than any other being on earth."[9]

In the middle of this season of mourning, the Perfectionists at Oneida faced their most threatening external crisis to date. Just as the Shakers had found out with the legal cases of Eunice Chapman and Mary Dyer, the Oneidans encountered profound resistance from family members who opposed their loved ones' joining a religious community. In those cases it was the unconverted wives who wanted to regain custody of their children. For the Oneidans, it was a local father, Noahdiah Hubbard, who wanted to protect his daughter, Tryphena, from her abusive husband, and remove her from the clutches of the heterodox community. Henry Seymour, his son-in-law, had converted to Perfectionism and joined the Oneida Community as a single man in 1848. Soon thereafter he met Tryphena Hubbard, who lived nearby and was not at the time a Perfectionist. By the time they wed, however, Tryphena had embraced her husband's faith and was apparently willing to join him in the community.[10]

Serious trouble began for the young couple when they attempted to expand their marriage from simple to complex. Documents from as early as

1850 report that Tryphena "has been in a desponding, unthankful state," as she tried to adjust to the community's demands, while also fending off her father. In September of that year she had a very public argument with her father "in which she denounced and renounced him for his enmity to us [the Oneida Community] and abuse of Mr. Noyes." Noahdiah Hubbard responded by confronting Oneidans first with "a sneering and contemptuous spirit," and later with "a company of eight or ten rowdies, all ready for a quarrel." Cooler heads prevailed and violence was averted, but the conflict between Noahdiah Hubbard and the Oneida Community was far from over. In December, in response to Tryphena's rebelliousness, leaders at Oneida unanimously decided that she "be placed under the special charge of Henry Seymour [her husband], and required to submit herself to him as her head and the representative of the church." Apparently, when community discipline failed, they were more than willing to revert back to the patriarchal discipline of Victorian monogamous marriages.[11]

The crisis reached its crescendo when Henry Seymour tried to flog Tryphena into submission and Noahadiah Hubbard took legal action against the Community. As the *Oneida Journal* described it, Henry "Seymour had confessed . . . that he had whipped Tryphena with a rawhide every day for three weeks, that her back was in consequence as black as his pantaloons."[12] On September 27, 1851, Noahadiah Hubbard formally charged the community with assault and battery. Fortunately for the Perfectionists, Hubbard agreed to settle the case out of court just two months later. On November 26, 1851, the Oneida Community agreed to pay for Tryphena's treatment at an asylum and provide her an annuity after she was released. This seemed to satisfy the Hubbard family, but as had happened in the Shakers' dealings with Chapman and Dyer, this trial in the legal system turned into a longer-lasting trial in the court of public opinion as well.[13]

On January 22, 1852, the *New York Observer* published a scathing editorial entitled "Perfectionism and Polygamy." Using the reviled Latter-day Saints for comparison, the piece was sensationalized, salacious, and intended to generate moral outrage against the Oneidans. This "disgusting order of united adulterers . . . are living in a state of vile concubinage . . . such as is not even thought among the Mormons." According to the editorialist, at least the polygamists sanctioned their many unions as some kind of marital bond and covenant. Among the Perfectionists, by contrast, one finds only "the freest licentiousness practised as the highest development of holiness"—veritable "orgies of the heathen" taking place in their own beloved state. Conservative in every sense of the word, the editors concluded that the "only safety is in steadfast adherence to the good old-fashioned morality of our fathers and mothers, on whose principles the first half of the nineteenth century has made no improvement." Unlike John Bennett's *History of the Saints*—and fortunately for John Humphrey Noyes—the piece did not call for mob action. The unfriendly press, however, did revive local hostility against the Perfectionists just as they thought they had settled their conflicts.[14] Emboldened by the apparent shift in public opinion, Noahdiah Hubbard renewed his legal cases against the Oneida Community, and the Perfectionists were forced to play defense, which in general was not when Noyes was at his best.

As mentioned previously, Noyes was an odd mix of bold contrariness and sensitivity to criticism. He obviously enjoyed being an intellectual gadfly and was often happy to debate his detractors publicly. Noyes also seemed to care a great deal about what outsiders thought of him and his ideas—what he referred to as "public opinion"—and whenever the host culture shifted from hospitable to hostile he would sound the retreat. In the current crisis Noyes believed that sensationalists had misinformed the public. We "have all been more Shakers than Bacchanalians," he argued. "Still it is true that we have abandoned the fashion of the world, and there has been among us what the world would call transgression." As a result, he told his followers at the end of February 1852, "it is not at all likely that we shall resume our operations [complex marriage] until public opinion allows it."[15] On March 7 *The Circular* announced "a somewhat interesting change of position . . . in regard to marriage." Because "our liberty on this subject is looked upon with jealousy and offense by surrounding society . . . we have decided to forego it, . . . *and formally resumed the marriage morality of the world.*"[16] To the Oneidans' dismay, their enemies took this retreat as the sign of weakness that it was and attacked the community with renewed vigor. On April 18, and in spite of their previous settlement, "the Hubbards were attempting to prove seduction in the case of Tryphena."[17]

What happened next was a fascinating conflict that expanded beyond the Hubbards versus the Perfectionists to engross virtually every citizen of Oneida County, and enlist every competing value and corresponding power structure in upstate New York: religious, legal, political, and popular. The brouhaha lasted from April to August 1852, forged some very unlikely partnerships, and took some very unexpected twists and turns. At first the Oneidans confronted a seemingly invincible alliance: Noahdiah Hubbard; his sons Dexter and Lucius, who happened to be the local constable; Utica Judge O. P. Root; and Samuel Garvin, the district attorney for Oneida County. Even though the Hubbards did not have the most powerful legal case, as it turns out, they obviously had powerful legal contacts, and they were all determined to drive the Perfectionists out of their fair county. In response, Noyes flinched. "The law is not our chosen field of battle," he reminded his subordinates. The Perfectionists had lost before back in Vermont. "We are dealing with the enemy on the field of public opinion," he told them, and a trial would only turn "a local difficulty into a general scandal."[18] Thus with both popular opinion and such well-connected enemies arrayed against them, it is no wonder why Noyes was willing to surrender so quickly.

Before the end of April, Noyes had not only decided to suspend complex marriage at Oneida, but also "decided to break up our Association, if that is what you want." Even though these words are those of Noyes's loyal and overworked manager at Oneida, John R. Miller, they convey Noyes's decision, which he had made earlier that day. For his part, Noyes was strangely serene about the decision, maybe even a little relieved. Fellow Perfectionists were surprised by his "appearance," describing him as "remarkably well and bright, and not at all cast down or disturbed by the prospect of a scatteration at Oneida." Perfectionism had started out as a dispersed movement of like-minded believers. Perhaps it would and indeed should be once more. Noyes speculated that ending their communal life, in fact, "might be God's design to scatter [Perfectionists] as missionaries all over New England and New York." Disbanding the community seemed like the only way to end the legal wrangling and satisfy the prosecutors. District Attorney Garvin was reportedly pleased with the initial offer and even happier in mid-May when Miller "told him that we had begun to disperse, that one or two had already left, and others would go soon." Garvin had not destroyed the Perfectionists' faith, but he was successfully destroying the Perfectionist community.[19]

A few weeks later, however, everything changed when an unexpected hero entered the fray on the Perfectionists' behalf. On May 24, 1852, the Honorable Timothy Jenkins, US congressman for Oneida and one-time district attorney for the county, wrote to Miller with "kind regards to yourself and the Community," and with his legal advice. Encouraging the Oneidans to stay, he believed that the Hubbards' latest round of lawsuits had no merit. Instead, he conjectured, it "may be that persons opposed to you are desirous to coerce you to sacrifice your property at Oneida, perhaps with a view of benefiting themselves." In his search for powerful allies, Noahdiah Hubbard had previously contacted Representative Jenkins to help argue his case. Reportedly, after Jenkins turned him down, Hubbard told him that the Oneidans "dread the law, and I will make them believe I am going to bring them to trial, and then at last get what I can."

Hubbard had rightly estimated John Humphrey Noyes's fear of the law, but he fatefully underestimated Congressman Jenkins, who sided decisively with the Perfectionists and turned the tide in their favor. As a long-time legal defender of the Oneida Indians, perhaps Jenkins naturally allied himself with the underdog. Perhaps he also simply saw the Hubbards' suit as the opportunistic farce that it was and did not want it to succeed. But no matter the reason, with Representative Jenkins on their side the Perfectionists had thoroughly one-upped their legal antagonists. The Hubbards had a judge and the district attorney on their team, but now the Oneidans had a US congressman and favorite son of the region on theirs.[20]

Greatly cheered by Jenkins's endorsement, the Perfectionists were inspired to launch a counterattack through—of all things—a strawberries and cream party. "An idea has just occurred and been talked over with enthusiasm," George Washington Noyes wrote. Just as there "is policy in war, . . . why would it not be a grand stroke of policy to devote all your strawberries this season as a peace offering to the neighborhood?" The idea caught on and a month later, on June 24, 1852, the Oneidans opened up the mansion to visitors, set out tables and chairs throughout the grounds, and ultimately served "about three hundred" of their neighbors "an abundance of strawberries, cream and sugar." "The attendance and singing of the Community children added to the pleasure of the occasion." By all accounts the party was a total diplomatic success. John Humphrey Noyes was not present but he was thrilled to hear that the public opinion that so preoccupied him had shifted. As Miller informed him, the neighbors' "good report of us now is as much exaggerated as their evil report was three months ago." District Attorney Garvin and Judge Root were livid but powerless to stem the tide now that it had turned against them. Even the Hubbards attended the party and reportedly called again the next "morning to eat strawberries," Miller reported. "How can they fight after this?"[21]

To put teeth in their diplomatic coup, the Perfectionists followed up their party with a petition to be "signed by the most influential men" in the region recommending that the current prosecution "be discontinued."

In the end twenty-two "of the very first men in the neighborhood" signed it, including Judge O. P. Root, and even Dexter and Noahdiah Hubbard. In securing these signatures, they also secured a legally binding guarantee that their antagonists would not bring other charges against the Oneida Community in the future. With this document, as well as a $350 settlement to the Hubbards, the crisis was resolved. After her stint in the asylum, Tryphena Seymour lived out her days at Oneida and her father never again sued the Perfectionists. As John R. Miller summed up the affair: "we have not only got out of the clutches of the law, but ... there has been a great change in the public mind toward us." This is precisely the outcome that the publicity-sensitive Noyes wanted. In his own providential interpretation of things, "He [God] has vindicated us, and brought us out white as snow before the surrounding public." A month later, on August 29, *The Circular* boldly reasserted the Perfectionists' "Platform of our new state of Society," including the "CULTIVATION OF FREE LOVE."[22]

In conclusion, the experience of the Oneida Perfectionists in 1852 was clearly different from that of the Mormons in 1844. Both sects had autocratic leaders and both engaged in countercultural sexual behavior, but the Perfectionists avoided violence and got to stay in Oneida. The Mormons, by contrast, suffered the assassination of their prophet and—not long after, as the next chapter makes clear—were forced to abandon Nauvoo for the uncertainty of the wilderness. Several factors can help explain the dissimilarity.

At perhaps the most foundational level, whereas Joseph Smith and the Mormons were increasingly secretive, John Humphrey Noyes and the Perfectionists were transparent. In Nauvoo Joseph Smith first enthusiastically developed and then retreated into the comforts of secret societies, mysterious rituals, fantastic titles, and undisclosed conjugal relationships. In part it was the very mystery of those institutions that made them so fascinating and so frightening to outsiders. It is also what made their exposure, whether from the scamp John Bennett or the true believer William Law, so explosive. People simply wanted to know what was going on behind all of those closed doors in Nauvoo, and if they should be worried about these increasingly odd strangers in their midst. Once that group of strangers had amassed power in the form of the Nauvoo Legion and significant numbers to outvote their rivals in local elections, the mood shifted from curious concern to real fear with every intention to strike first. Anti-Mormons' most acute anxieties were only confirmed when Joseph Smith violated the cherished American value of freedom of the press, and they soon turned their paranoia into vigilante action.

None of this was the case with John Humphrey Noyes and his Perfectionists in 1852. They had their own enemies in the form of Noahdiah Hubbard and sons, and they thought that the legal authorities were uniformly arrayed against them, but things turned out quite differently. Their smaller size—hundreds of Perfectionists in Oneida versus thousands of Mormons in Nauvoo—did not make them a threat either militarily or politically. Neither was John Humphrey Noyes particularly threatening as a leader. He kept a low rather than a high profile during conflicts—he did not run for president for instance—and he seemed to know the rules of the legal system and antebellum politics more generally. Perhaps that is why he opted to be as transparent as possible with the surrounding community. As soon as it was published in 1849, Noyes "placed a copy of the First Annual Report, containing a full disclosure of our Social Theory, in the hands of the Governor of the State, and various high functionaries, including the distinguished Representative of our district in the national Congress," Timothy Jenkins. In other words, everyone in the surrounding area and state knew what was going on behind the Oneida Community's closed doors and yet "for four years we lived undisturbed."[23]

It also bears repeating, however, that the Oneidans had friends in high places whereas the Mormons did not. In the final analysis this too might be a testimony simply to the difference in numbers between the two groups. The Perfectionists could be tolerated as a nonthreatening religious minority in the same way that Native American communities, if small enough, could be tolerated. This might have been the comparison Representative Jenkins made when he first defended the Oneida Indians and later defended the Oneida Community. Regardless of the motive, he intervened magnanimously on behalf of the Perfectionists and prevented them from disbanding. The Mormons never had such a champion in the halls of government. Missouri governor Lilburn Boggs had threatened the Saints with "extermination" in 1838, while in 1844 Illinois governor Thomas Ford, although friendlier to the Church, was nevertheless incapable of preventing the violence that claimed Joseph and Hyrum Smith's lives. Smith's assassination is an even greater injustice when we consider the fact that it was members of a local militia ordered to protect him who killed him.

Both sects, as sects, had renounced the world, but for various reasons the Perfectionists discovered that they still had friends in it: neighbors who would attend their strawberries and cream party, and politicians who would defend their right to exist. The Mormons had neither. This is one reason why Joseph Smith ran for president in 1844. The only way to provide governmental protection for his Church and his people was for him to do it himself. After his death, anti-Mormon violence only continued and so did the authorities' unwillingness to protect the Saints. As the new leaders of the Church found out, the only way to ensure that Americans would tolerate them as a religious minority would be to leave America altogether.

10
Succession, Relocation, and Proclamation

THE MORMONS, 1844-1852

Now THINGS get really complicated. Joseph Smith had done virtually nothing to prepare his people for the possibility of his death. Emotionally the Saints were devastated, while institutionally the Church had no protocol whatsoever for how to determine succession. What was going to happen to the more than twelve thousand Saints in Nauvoo, and the twenty-six thousand Saints worldwide?[1] Who was going to lead them and defend them from a clearly hostile world? And perhaps most importantly, who was going to hear from and prophesy for the Lord? Through revelations from God, Smith had restored the ancient Church and been entrusted with the authoritative keys of the kingdom. When he died did those keys go with him? In his absence, what authority could the LDS Church claim, and in whom or which institutions was that authority vested?

The Saints were tremendously confused and anxious in the face of these vast uncertainties, and admirably resolute. Very few Mormons abandoned the faith or their fellow believers in this ultimate crisis. To be sure, the Saints in Nauvoo suffered multiple divisions in the succession crisis and over the question of polygamy, but the shock of Joseph's and Hyrum's deaths hardly destroyed the Church of Jesus Christ of Latter-day Saints. On the contrary, as one Mormon historian writes, the martyrdoms "actually unified the Saints."[2]

Building on this insight, I argue in this chapter that this extended time of crisis from 1844 to 1852 was the foremost identity-forming crucible of the Mormon people. Tertullian's observation that "the blood of martyrs is the seed of the church"[3] was just as true for Latter-day Saints in the nineteenth century as it was for Christians in the first and second centuries. The Mormon community, in other words, was born out of persecution and strife, and this eight-year period was arguably the most strife-filled of all.

Fortunately for the Saints during this time, an indomitable leader emerged who positively thrived on crises. A highly imperfect man, Brigham Young was nevertheless perfect for the times. Throughout his long life (1801–1877) Young always seemed most alive during an emergency, while the Church never seemed to have any shortage of emergencies to animate him. The sincerest of sincere believers, in 1844 Young adamantly refused to watch his beloved community disintegrate, but rather quickly and effectively took charge. Whether he ascended to leadership more by seizing power or by claiming authority will be debated forever. What is certain, however, is that very soon after Joseph's death, he became the Saints' "indispensable protector" and problem-solver-in-chief, a position he held for the next thirty-three years.[4]

In 1844 Young's official title was president of the Quorum of the Twelve Apostles. Joseph Smith had formed the Quorum in 1835 to be an evangelistic body, facing outward to the mission field rather than inward to the Church's day-to-day affairs. This distinction between external and internal jurisdictions is an important one for understanding both LDS polity in general and the succession crisis of 1844 in particular. Once Mormon missionaries had reaped a harvest of one thousand or more converts, they would organize them into a "stake"—the LDS equivalent of a diocese. Smith called them "stakes" after the pegs that anchor a tent to the ground, reinforcing the image of an outside wilderness, and an inside orderly shelter. Thus the Twelve had authority—for instance to "ordain evangelical ministers"—but only in the mission field and not inside an organized stake. That responsibility fell within the jurisdiction of an individual stake's governing body, the high council.[5]

After Smith's death there were three main contenders for leadership of the Church: Brigham Young, president of the Quorum of the Twelve; Sidney Ridgon, the only surviving member of the First Presidency (Joseph and Hyrum Smith were the other two); and William Marks, president of the high council of the stake of Nauvoo. So how exactly did Young, the leader of the outsiders, become the leader of the entire LDS Church? In an abstract weighing of the claims of these three groups, which Mormons call "quorums," the Twelve would most likely not come out on top. Thus, as the president of the Twelve, Young was at a significant disadvantage in the succession crisis of 1844.

Brigham Young had tremendous advantages in pressing his claim to leadership, however, because he was Brigham Young and the others were not. Although only a little over five and a half feet tall, Young was, as one biographer puts it perfectly, "a quarry-stone of a man" with an equally "square face ... always fixed in an expression just between a scowl and a smirk." He had an iron will, expert organizational skills, limitless stamina, and was seemingly incapable of self-doubt. He was charismatic, autocratic, and unabashedly patriarchal. Like a general, he "moved with deliberate economy and presented himself at rest as immovable."[6] Also like a general, he reveled in the ability to command, while expecting his subordinates—basically everyone else—to obey without question. All in all, he was simply not a man to be trifled with.

Fiercely protective of his independence, Brigham Young had nevertheless submitted body and soul to Joseph Smith and his revelations. Like Smith, Young had been born into poverty in turn-of-the-century Vermont, and moved frequently throughout the Burned-over District as his struggling family searched for opportunities that never seemed to materialize. In 1830 he read the just-published *Book of Mormon*, and carefully assessed the claims of the new religion for over a year. He was baptized on April 14, 1832, and later that year set out for Kirtland to meet the prophet for himself. Utterly satisfied with the encounter, Young found the flesh-and-blood revelator to be even more impressive than his printed revelations. He said often during his life that he "loved" Joseph Smith. According to his daughter's biography, he died calling Joseph's name.[7]

In the tumultuous time between his conversion and Smith's murder in 1844, as apostates fell by the wayside and naysayers criticized, Young never betrayed or even second-guessed his prophet. In 1839, with most of the Church's leaders in Missouri prisons, responsibility fell to him to organize the Saints' exodus to Illinois. Although initially thrust into leadership, Brigham strode into the position with confidence and omni-competence—the first of many crises in which he proved himself "indispensable." Later that year he led the mission to England, where he reaped a harvest of converts beyond anyone's wildest imagination. He was just as effective abroad as he was at home.

When Young returned to Nauvoo in mid-1841, much had changed in the Church and much was about to change even further for the Quorum of the Twelve. Smith and John Bennett were building the city as quickly as they could, while in secret Smith had resumed polygamy when he married Louisa Beaman on April 5. With all of this activity, Smith needed capable leaders and he found them in the Twelve, many of whom, like Young, were then returning to Nauvoo at the conclusion of their missions. The Church's high council in the stake of Nauvoo was simply not enough for the tasks at hand. As a result Smith expanded the Twelve's responsibilities to include internal matters, a change that he initiated and not one that the Twelve ambitiously grabbed for themselves.[8] Smith also secretly shared the principle of plural marriage with some of the Twelve, which only strengthened the bond between them and further enhanced the quorum's status in the Mormon hierarchy.

For his part Young stewarded this secret—and all others—arguably better than any man in Mormonism, a quality Smith prized even more after Bennett's betrayal. In early 1842 Young officiated at two of Smith's plural marriages.[9] In June, even after being rejected and publicly exposed when Bennett published Martha Brotherton's scandalous affidavit, Young forged ahead and took his own first plural wife, Lucy Ann Decker, a married twenty-year-old woman and mother of two children. By the time of Smith's death, he had taken three more wives, making him one of the foremost polygamists in Nauvoo. He trusted his prophet's revelations completely no matter how inexplicable they may seem, and he committed himself to them no matter the cost to himself.[10]

Young's unimpeachable loyalty to Smith positioned him well in the leadership struggle. Young also had an unshakable confidence that he and he alone should be the Church's next leader: a drive that pushed other contenders aside and a certainty that was attractive to the Saints in confusing and dangerous times. Young was in Massachusetts when he learned of Smith's death on July 16. "The first thing which I thought of," he recollected, "was, whether Joseph had taken the keys of the kingdom with him from the earth," a terrifying prospect in that it would mean that the LDS Church no longer had divine authority. "My head felt so distressed [I] thought it would crack." Then, with typical resolve, he reportedly slapped his knee and proclaimed with assurance: "The keys of the kingdom are right here with the Church."[11] At first Young was not sure who, or which quorum had the keys, but on his journey back to Nauvoo he received a "vision of the Spirit" telling him that it was the Quorum of the Twelve, and he arrived in Nauvoo just in time to press his claim.[12]

The secret practice of Mormon polygamy also played a decisive role in how the succession crisis unfolded. Both William Marks and Sidney Rigdon opposed plural marriage, whereas Brigham Young clearly supported it. The widowed Emma Smith also figured into the deliberations about the future leadership of the Church. Only a week after Joseph's death Emma began to back Marks for president. Publicly, she argued that as the president of the Nauvoo high council, Marks was the most legitimate successor, while privately and silently she hoped that the Church's next leader would share her antipathy for plural marriage.[13] To her and others' great disappointment, however, William Marks demurred and threw his support to Sidney Rigdon, who was not the right man for such challenging times.

Sidney Rigdon was much that Brigham Young was not: well-read and well-spoken as opposed to folksy and brusque; sickly as opposed to indefatigable; and thoughtful and vacillating as opposed to obedient and resolute. As the sole surviving member of the First Presidency, Rigdon had the strongest claim to succeed Joseph Smith as president of the Church. As things turned out, however, Rigdon failed miserably.

The seeds of Rigdon's failure had been planted years before when Smith propositioned his daughter Nancy to be a plural wife and the entire Rigdon family confronted him in return. Rebuilding trust took over a year, but in early 1844 Smith reconciled with his old friend. In April he reappointed Rigdon to the First Presidency, replacing the recently excommunicated William Law, and on May 6 Smith named him his vice-presidential running mate. Thus Smith had restored Rigdon to a place of high status in the Church, but this restoration took place only a few months before Smith's death. Brigham Young by contrast had never fallen out with the prophet and never needed restoring, a point that he did not fail to make when the two men squared off.

On August 8, Sidney Rigdon and Brigham Young presented their cases for succession in front of thousands of Saints. Rigdon spoke first, basing his claim on his long record of service, his position in the First Presidency, and a revelation he had recently received instructing him to be the Church's "guardian." Young took the stage in the afternoon and masterfully dismantled his opponent, playing to his audience's hopes and fears, and—most importantly—promising them continuity with their beloved slain prophet and assurance of their celestial exaltation. Referring to the endowment ordinance, which most of the Saints had not yet experienced, Young informed the crowd that only the Twelve had "the signs and the tokens to give to the Porter [of heaven] and he will let us in." The ensuing vote was a landslide. At most only twenty people chose Rigdon to lead the Church. The vast majority of Saints put their earthly trust and their eternal hopes in Brigham Young.[14]

This meeting and this decision have been controversial ever since. Was it "the reorganization of the Church," as Wilford Woodruff later described it?[15] Was it a coup—a populist usurpation of the First Presidency by the Twelve? Ironically, in the way that politics and political rhetoric often work, it is perhaps best to think of it as promising continuity through discontinuity.

In this context of existential crisis and jarring change, Mormon leaders and rank-and-file Saints alike desperately sought continuity with the life and legacy of Joseph Smith. They found that continuity primarily in the institutions—both the known ones and the secret ones—that he had established at Nauvoo: the temple, the endowment, and plural marriage. They therefore chose in overwhelming numbers to submit to the man who could most assure them of a viable connection with those institutions and that legacy. Brigham Young promised the Saints the possibility of exaltation through the Church's ordinances, and soon delivered on his promise in the form of a completed Mormon temple in which priests properly endowed thousands of Saints and sealed thousands of marriages, including hundreds of plural marriages. In the Church's sea of troubles, those were the Saints' most secure connections to a familiar past and a hopeful, celestial future.

Behind the scenes, historian D. Michael Quinn adds, most Mormon leaders also wanted continuity with Joseph's "secret practices," including plural marriage. At the time of Smith's death, thirty-two men and eighty-six women had become polygamists. If an antipolygamy leader such as Sidney Rigdon or William Marks were to become president and discontinue the practice, Quinn observes, it "would brand polygamous wives as whores," a status that none of the practitioners could tolerate. They were committed to the secret institution, while those who opposed it would simply have to lose out, which is exactly what happened. After his defeat, an understandably bitter Rigdon sniped at the Twelve as corrupt usurpers, but truly crossed the line when he threatened to expose "the secrits [sic] of the Church." On September 8, exactly one month after the fateful meeting, Young had Rigdon excommunicated, and soon had William Marks removed as president of the Nauvoo high council. For the time being, Emma Smith remained quiet, mourning the loss of her husband and tending to the needs of her children. Thus, those who hated plural marriage and were in positions to challenge it were effectively marginalized.[16]

Young demonstrated his commitment to plural marriage by first tending to the needs of Smith's thirty-seven widows. Starting as early as September 1844, he married eight of Smith's widows himself, Heber Kimball married nine of them, and eight other Church leaders married eight more.[17] In doing so these Saints honored their prophet, provided some security for these women, and declared boldly to the Church's inner circle that plural marriage as a Latter-day institution was here to stay. Mormon opponents of plural marriage simply had no place in Young's Church and were forced either to find a new religious home, or live the rest of their lives in the spiritual wilderness.

While risking hyperbole, it is nevertheless worth considering the crises in Nauvoo from 1844 to 1846 to be *the* crucible of Mormon identity. There were arguably more possible destinies for the Church at this time than any other, with Brigham Young and plural marriage determining that destiny. This was a time of community formation through hardship, when the Saints embraced their sectarian status, enhanced their solidarity with one another, and defied a hostile outside world. Publicly they would express their defiance by completing their temple, a place of great religious significance and a highly visible reminder to outsiders that Mormonism endured. Privately, Saints could express their defiance by continuing another one of Joseph Smith's institutions—plural marriage.

In mid-1844 the Mormons in Nauvoo were indeed a people besieged. Although numbering over ten thousand, the surrounding countryside teemed with even more anti-Mormons: driven by hate, obviously inclined to violence, and seemingly immune to the rule of law. The gears of the Illinois legal system moved slowly after the assassinations of June 27 and ultimately convicted no one for the crimes. The message this sent was loud and clear, and unfortunately familiar to the Saints: anti-Mormons could literally get away with murder. In the general context of paranoia that had built up over the years, however, local Gentiles feared that Mormons would seek to avenge Smith's death. Immediately after the murders, bands of armed citizens marched on Nauvoo in a kind of preemptive strike, only reversing course after Governor Thomas Ford intervened personally and pleaded for calm. In October they marched again and were again only stopped when the governor ordered a state militia to intercept them. This was the context in which Brigham Young took control of the Church, and in which most of the Saints willingly granted him that control.[18]

Although it was not at all inevitable that Mormons would abandon Nauvoo, the situation deteriorated so much over the course of 1845 that in October Young had to promise his enemies that he would lead the Saints to a new home. As usual, local politics—and not polygamy—fueled the hostility, with elections serving as provocative actions that anti-Mormons believed warranted even greater, and increasingly violent reactions. On August 6, 1844, a mere forty days after the assassinations and just two days before the Church's fateful meeting to determine succession, Mormon-backed candidates dominated elections in Hancock County. In their grief and disgust with the authorities, the Saints had considered boycotting the vote, but ultimately decided to participate, sending a strong message to their neighbors that they were not going to retreat from civic life. In response, anti-Mormons lobbied the Illinois state legislature to repeal the Nauvoo charter, which it did on January 29, 1845. That was how the year began for the Saints. Stripped of their legal and military defenses (repealing the charter also ended the Nauvoo Legion) and with no faith in the state to protect them, Mormons determined to fend for themselves. Things were starting to look like Missouri all over again. In August 1845 Mormons won another landslide victory in local elections, but it would be their last. Anti-Mormons now determined that if they could not beat the Saints at the polls, they would be more than happy to drive them bodily from the polity.[19]

The turning point occurred in September, when someone fired shots into a meeting of anti-Mormons. No one was ever apprehended for the incident, and the whole affair might have been staged; but no matter who the shooters were, anti-Mormons now had the so-called aggression they needed to justify violence of their own. Over the course of the following week they burned several Mormon homes and buildings. During the same time someone shot and killed the commander of the guard at the Carthage Jail at the time of the murders, doubtlessly a Mormon act of vengeance. Acting more out of fear of bloodshed than anti-Mormon hatred, concerned citizens from neighboring Adams County asked the Church to leave Illinois and to put their commitment in a written response. On October 1, 1845, the Quorum of the Twelve wrote back and acquiesced. With winter soon upon them, they famously promised that the Saints would leave Nauvoo "when grass grows and water runs" the following spring.[20]

Amazingly, as leaders made plans to move the Church they also continued constructing the Nauvoo temple at a frenetic pace. Outsiders might consider such a project a monument to futility. Why would people work so hard building something that they knew they would abandon in just a few months? From the perspective of the faithful, however, that structure and all of the sacrifices of time, money, and muscle that went into it made perfect sense. In a revelation in early 1841 God commanded:

"let this house be built unto my name, that I may reveal mine ordinances therein unto my people."[21] This would be the special place where they would receive their endowments, baptize their dead, and eternally seal their marriages.

The Saints were determined to receive those blessings properly, in the completed temple, before they faced the uncertainties of the future. That, and not a lasting handsome building, would be the real fruit of their labor. Young even suspended missionary work to get the project done in time, calling missionaries back to Nauvoo and using their added resources to construct a physical building rather than reap a spiritual harvest. In December 1845 the work paid off and the temple was ready for the sacred ordinances. In two short months, between the temple's completion on December 10 and the beginning of the exodus from Nauvoo in early February 1846, 5,634 Saints received their endowment. As biographer John G. Turner puts it: "Church members practically stampeded the temple to get what Young offered them," forging a shared identity—or peoplehood—and enhancing Young's "standing as Smith's rightful successor and the church's chief priest." Young's public commitment to continuing Joseph Smith's institutions and legacy was a resounding success.[22]

Privately at first but with increasing insouciance, Young also honored Smith's legacy by spreading the institution of plural marriage. Setting the example for the rest of the Church, he personally took thirty-nine plural wives before leaving Nauvoo, eighteen of them in the first six weeks of 1846.[23] Many Saints were more than happy to follow suit. At the time of Smith's death there were an estimated thirty-two polygamous men married to a total of eighty-six polygamous women. During the rest of 1844 and all of 1845, forty-nine men and seventy-seven women joined the expanding polygamous tribe. In the first six weeks of 1846, when the temple was in full operation, the list explodes: 102 more men married a total of 169 women in what can only be considered a frenzy of polygamous unions. All told, when the Saints abandoned Nauvoo, 834 people, knowledgeably or not, were practicing polygamy: 183 men were married to 468 plural wives. That sum of 651 plus the 183 first wives of the polygamous husbands gives us the total of 834. Scholars will continue to contest the precise figures but agree that the overall trajectory was the same: Mormon plural marriage grew by leaps and bounds in the Church's last eighteen months at Nauvoo.[24]

Without a doubt, this was a pivotal moment in the history of Mormon polygamy. As the situation in Nauvoo became increasingly uncertain,

Saints reached for the certainties of their faith, no matter how unorthodox and shocking they might be to outsiders. This explains the frenetic building of the temple, as well as the equally frenetic "stampede" of Saints to receive their endowment and eternally seal their marriages, plural or not, before they had to face the privations of the wilderness. Theologically speaking, marriage and family were all-important means of celestial exaltation. In the perilous journey West, family would be the Saints' traveling fortress.[25]

The Saints' epic exodus from Nauvoo to the Salt Lake Basin deserves its central place in Mormon history and identity. Although exact figures are difficult to calculate, from 1846 to 1849, between ten and fifteen thousand men, women, and children braved the 1,300-mile trek.[26] They crossed frozen rivers, plodded across the seemingly endless plains of Iowa, Nebraska, and eastern Wyoming, and then had to confront the 11,000-foot-high Wasatch Range of the Rocky Mountains before finally descending into their promised land. Much like the ancient Israelites, with whom they justifiably compared themselves, the Saints fled an oppressive power and struggled across a wilderness to worship their God as revelation commanded them. In the process they became a people. Unlike their Old Testament forebears, however, whose pioneer generation passed away before crossing over Jordan, most Mormons completed their journey, although hundreds of Saints would die along the way.

Fortunately, the Saints had Brigham Young, who was boldly, autocratically, and undeniably in charge of it all. In 1845 Young prepared his people by organizing them into emigration companies of hundreds, fifties, and tens, each under the leadership of a captain. In early 1846, Young put this organization in motion. The first wagons left on February 4. On February 8 Church leaders ceased performing ordinances and packed up the temple's records, altar, veil, and accompanying adornments. The Saints would not be able to experience the ordinances in a proper temple for decades. The very next day, as if to put an exclamation point on the fact that an era had ended, the roof of the temple caught fire. Thus as some Saints crossed the frozen Mississippi River, they looked over their shoulders to see both their Illinois homes for the last time and their physical connection to God in flames. Brigham Young left Nauvoo on February 15, while the exodus of Saints continued in waves over the next seven months.[27]

As the Saints moved farther from the reach of US law, they became bolder and more open about their plural marriages. At Sugar Creek, Iowa, a mere nine miles from Nauvoo, people began to talk. As historian

Richard S. Van Wagoner describes it: "Eliza R. Snow, now one of Brigham Young's plural wives, noted in a February 1846 diary entry that 'we felt as tho' we could breath [sic] more freely and speak one with another upon those things where in God had made us free with less carefulness than we had hitherto done.'"[28] At Mount Pisgah, a Mormon way station halfway across Iowa, Emily Partridge, another of Smith's plural widows, had to endure a steady stream of onlookers who wanted to inspect her and Young's infant son—born of their polygamous union—like some kind of exotic animal in a zoo.[29] In the relative isolation and security of Winter Quarters, however, in Indian Territory on the western side of the Missouri River, Mary Woodward, another one of Young's plural wives, spoke too freely about their plural sealing ceremony in the Nauvoo temple, and he terminated the marriage—the first of many divorces over the course of his life. She pleaded to be readmitted to the family, but Young remained unmoved. There would be no second chances for those who could not keep their mouths shut. Meanwhile at Winter Quarters, some of his wives broke with the more clandestine practice of polygamy at Nauvoo by choosing to live with one another in "an intimate and intensely spiritual *'female family.'*"[30] While this was hardly announcing plural marriage as the indiscreet Mary Woodward had done, these kinds of living arrangements did contribute to a new climate in which the practice was basically, in one scholar's words, "the Mormons' worst-kept secret."[31] Distance had spread confidence among the Saints—a trend that would intensify once the wagons finally stopped in the Great Basin.

The first of those wagons resumed the journey from Winter Quarters under Young's leadership in April 1847. He intended for this vanguard party to blaze the trail for the thousands that would follow and in typical fashion he succeeded at his goals entirely, entering the Great Basin a little over three months later. From 1847 to 1869 when the continental railroad opened up, an estimated fifty-six thousand Saints had made the harrowing overland journey to Salt Lake City, some of them dragging their possessions in handcarts.[32]

Young and other city planners had a great deal of real estate with which to work. The Salt Lake Valley is simply enormous. Nauvoo was roughly five square miles—a small, walkable river town. The Salt Lake Valley is approximately five hundred square miles, bounded in the east by the Wasatch Range (part of the Rocky Mountains), and the Oquirrh (rhymes with "joker") Mountains in the west. It was there that Mormons would plant their city, centered on the lot designated for a future, magnificent temple. But unlike in the East, where Mormons purposefully concentrated, or "gathered," in a single city, in their new home Young had the Saints spread out, establishing colonies and various industries up and down the Wasatch Front from Ogden forty miles north of Salt Lake City, to Provo forty miles to the south. Constructing this Mormon civilization from scratch took years and immense amounts of labor, but the Church now had plentiful land, a steady stream of believers who wanted to do their part, and an undisputed leader who was more than willing to put them to work.

The inexhaustible Brigham Young and the indomitable Saints ultimately succeeded, but their first dozen years in the Salt Lake Valley were ones of great expectations and almost unremitting challenges and disappointments. In the fall of 1847, just a few months after first reaching Utah, Young actually traveled back east to Winter Quarters to consolidate his power and legitimize his authority. To that end, on December 27, 1847, he reorganized the First Presidency, stepping into the position that only Joseph Smith had held before him, and relegating the Quorum of the Twelve to its original limited jurisdiction over missionary activity.[33]

But at the exact time that Young became the unassailable sovereign over a people beyond the reach of any organized state, the American people and their government invaded his kingdom-in-the-making and threatened his omnipotence. On January 24, 1848, less than a month after Young was named Church president, James Marshall found gold near Sutter's Fort in the Sierra Nevada Mountains, initiating what would become the largest overland migration in the history of the United States. Although the hordes of Argonauts were bound for California and not Salt Lake, the Mormons' dream of isolation in the American West was ruined before it could begin. Numerically and culturally, they could still dominate their extensive territory, but they would nevertheless soon have to deal with thousands upon thousands of strangers in their midst.

The Saints' more pressing problems, as usual, were political. In the winter of 1847–48, in the town of Guadeloupe Hidalgo, over a thousand miles away from both Winter Quarters and Sutter's Fort, diplomats wrangled over just how much land the United States was going to wrest from Mexico after defeating that nation in war. The Mexican-American War had been the constant backdrop for the Mormons' exodus, but its conclusion brought even greater consequences. The conflict lasted for a year and a half, from the spring of 1846 (the exact time that Saints were leaving Nauvoo) to September 1847 (precisely the time that the first migrants were struggling into the Salt Lake Valley). In the Treaty of Guadeloupe Hidalgo that followed, the United States acquired over five hundred thousand square miles, including all of modern-day California, Nevada, and Utah. Diplomats signed the treaty on February 2, 1848, less than two weeks after James Marshall had discovered gold in California. For First President Brigham Young, while he had secured his leadership over the Church, he was no longer leading his people out of the hated United States. Instead, he was merely moving them from one part of the country to another; and thanks to the Gold Rush he would soon have to share the road and his scarce resources with thousands of greedy and transient Gentiles.

In 1849 Young responded brilliantly to both of these challenges. On the political front, he organized the Mormon state of Deseret and petitioned Congress for admittance to the Union. Reflecting an "if you can't beat 'em, join 'em" strategy, he wanted to at least be incorporated into the United States on his own terms. As a state the Mormons would still have to be in partnership with the federal government, but they could write their own constitution and enjoy a good measure of self-government. Given the escalating conflict between North and South over America's new western possessions, however, Congress refused to create another state, and the Mormons had to settle for territorial status. This was a disappointment to the sovereignty-seeking Young because in a territory the federal government appointed the officials and judges, whereas in a state they were popularly elected, but he was greatly relieved and perhaps surprised in late 1850 when President Millard Fillmore named him the territorial governor. The Saints would conflict early and often with the federally appointed judges, but for the time being Young had secured both legal recognition for the extensive Mormon territory, and a good deal of personal political control over its affairs.[34]

Meanwhile, the horde of Argonauts that Young feared would taint the purity of the intermountain Saints turned out instead to be their economic salvation. In securing territorial status, Young had won a kind of legal and political victory, but in building his autonomous kingdom, he desperately—almost obsessively—wanted to found it on a stable and self-sufficient economy. In 1849 it was difficult to envision a dynamic and diversified economy in Utah considering the fact that for the previous two years the Saints had nearly starved to death. As usual, however, Young was entirely undeterred. He had an abundance of productive land, more than enough labor, and plenty of time with which to bring forth a Mormon economic empire. What he initially lacked was capital, but after 1849, thanks to the steady stream of California-bound Argonauts with whom the Saints traded, he and the Church began to accumulate wealth. Leonard Arrington, the great economic historian of nineteenth-century Mormonism, estimates that between 1849 and 1852, the economy of Utah might "have been enhanced $250,000 as the result of the Gold Rush trade."[35]

Young was especially sanguine about the human resources at his disposal. Whereas in the trying times of 1846 to 1849 when more migrants only meant more mouths to feed, with the Gold Rush (and adequate harvests after 1849) more settlers meant greater opportunity to build the kingdom. They could settle more territory and they could engage in increasingly diversified commercial exchanges with the Argonauts. Thus the Deseret government formed the Perpetual Emigrating Fund for the Poor in 1849, and the Perpetual Emigrating Company in 1850 to facilitate an even greater influx of settlers. Thanks to the Perpetual Emigrating Company, Arrington writes, "the Mormon population in the Great Basin had soared from some 6,000 persons in the spring of 1849 to approximately 20,000 persons in 1852."[36] There were now thousands more Saints in the intermountain West than there had been in Nauvoo. The company reached out first to the migrants spread out between Illinois and Utah, and then reached all the way across the Atlantic to begin bringing the approximately thirty thousand English Saints to their new American home. Brigham Young could now happily reap what he had sown. Having planted the Mormon Church in England a decade earlier, in the early 1850s he started relocating those Saints to his expansive and expanding kingdom.

So what about the equally expansive principle of plural marriage? After the flurry of polygamous unions that took place as the Saints abandoned Nauvoo in 1846, and the steady leaking of the secret on the trail, how fared the institution in the Great Basin kingdom? Unsurprisingly, given the raft of challenges Mormons faced in their first years there, Church leaders did not consider spreading and enforcing plural marriage to be a high priority. They also did not consider announcing the principle to the rest of the world to be a prudent move politically. Feeling secure in the intermountain West, Mormon polygamists started living the principle more openly, but there was no need to invite unnecessarily the censure and potential repression of Americans and their government.

The Gold Rush and the arrival of federally appointed officers and judges, however, forced the issue. The territorial judges arrived in mid-1851 and immediately butted heads with Brigham Young. Their private disagreements soon became a very public row, during which Young, using thinly veiled terms, threatened the life of one of the judges. With no real power to enforce their rulings, and surrounded by over ten thousand Mormons in their isolated kingdom, the judges decided to flee the territory before the end of the year and take their story back to Washington, DC. There these "runaway judges" as they were then called, told of Young's recalcitrance, the Church's theocratic ambitions, and of the open practice of plural marriage. By this time, though, the Saints had representatives of their own in the capital to lobby for their cause and counter the judges' claims. To many people's surprise, the government decided in the Mormons' favor: Brigham Young retained his position as governor of the territory, while the judges lost their jobs. This was an unprecedented political victory for the Church, although news of Mormon polygamy was once again a matter of national discourse.[37]

Word of plural marriage in Utah spread further with the 1852 publication of Lieutenant John W. Gunnison's book, *The Mormons, or Latter-Day Saints, in the Valley of the Great Salt Lake*. Like the "runaway judges," Gunnison worked for the federal government and quickly told others what he had observed in Utah. Unlike them, he was admirably fair and even charitable in his depiction of the Saints. In 1849, with the Salt Lake Valley filling permanently with thousands of Mormons and seasonally with thousands more California-bound migrants, the US Army decided it was time to survey the land. As a member of the Topographical Corp of Engineers, Lieutenant Gunnison assisted in this task, wintering with the Saints in 1849–50 and turning his observations into a book a few years later. He did not convert to Mormonism while there, but neither did he seek in his publication to denigrate the faith. As he put it, "I have endeavoured to give their true teaching, and do not intend to criticise or explain any apparent contradiction." There is little doubt that he thought that some Mormon beliefs were "folly," but he felt it to be his task to observe and record these people and their faith in the same thorough and dispassionate way that he surveyed a landscape. With an almost religious faith in the power of science, he hoped that such an approach would "let folly tire on its own pinions, and reason regain its sway over erratic feelings." Then and only then, he believed, would "the mists of prejudice on one side, and of fanaticism on the other, [be] dispelled by the light of knowledge."[38]

Given his general trustworthiness—as opposed to the usual malice of non-Mormon writers on Mormonism—Gunnison's observations provide a valuable window into the world of plural marriage at this time. "That many have a large number of wives in Deseret," he wrote of the poorly kept secret, "is perfectly manifest to any one residing long among them." While the Church's official position was to deny the existence of plural marriage, clearly the Saints had grown bolder in the practice of it—to the point that they were not afraid to let even a member of the armed forces know about it. Furthermore, as Gunnison reported: "it is announced that a treatise is in preparation, to prove by the scriptures the right of plurality."[39] This is a remarkable and revealing statement. By 1850 Church leaders had decided to announce polygamy publicly and defend it scripturally. When Gunnison wrote these words, they had not yet made the proclamation, but they were clearly preparing both their fellow Saints and their potential antagonists for a bold new era in the life of the Church.

The Church of Jesus Christ of Latter-day Saints publicly announced the principle of plural marriage on August 29, 1852, mere months after Gunnison had published his book. Brigham Young had reportedly proclaimed to the Saints as early as February 1851 that he was a polygamist.[40] By the time the territorial judges and Lieutenant Gunnison had exposed the practice to larger and more influential audiences, he had decided that the Church should end its policy of denying publicly what thousands were practicing privately. The incongruity was both confusing and stressful for the Saints, and Young might have considered the secrecy to be craven. Thus for reasons of integrity, simplicity, and identity, he decided it was time for the Church to reverse course. It is also possible that he was emboldened by the recent victory over the "runaway judges." Although he and the Saints remained a part of, rather than outside of the United States, they were going to declare to the world what they believed and practiced about marriage, and hope that their relative isolation would continue to provide them safe haven.

Brigham Young gave Apostle Orson Pratt the unenviable task of making this bold proclamation. Highly literate and already the author of several works of Mormon apologetics, Pratt's job was to validate plural marriage in language and logic that Saints could understand. Church leaders had decided that the entire body of believers must now embrace and promote a custom that would likely entail even more personal sacrifice and collective persecution. It would be best if the Saints understood why they were embarking on such a perilous course.

Orson Pratt's announcement in 1852 is a masterly exercise in persuasive argumentation. In order to prepare his fellow Mormons for the journey ahead—what he euphemistically called "rather new ground to the inhabitants of the United States"—he started with what they believed already, appealing to well-known and shared religious priorities, beliefs, and commitments. He did not have to teach them these. He could rightly assume that they had internalized them already. Then, having affirmed their common faith, he could assure them that plural marriage, while profoundly countercultural, was a logical and theological extension of their revealed religion.[41]

Pratt constructed his argument along the lines of *more, metanarrative,* and *marriage*—and in almost precisely that order. He both started and concluded with an appeal to his listeners' celestial self-interest, and desire for *more* "in the world to come." Plural marriage, he straightforwardly informed them, is "necessary for our exaltation to the fullness of the Lord's glory." As Pratt explained throughout the discourse, if one wanted to experience that glory one simply had to embrace this doctrine. Those who reject it outright "will be damned," while those who fail to abide by the Church's rules for celestial and plural marriage will not become gods in the afterlife. Rather, they will become mere angels, who "though they are saved, they are to be servants to those who are in a higher condition." Why was this the case? Why did the Church emphasize marriage so much that it expanded the boundaries of the institution beyond monogamy and into "a plurality of wives"?[42]

The answer, Pratt explained, had to do with the Mormon's "peculiar doctrine in regard to our pre-existence." In other words, the answer was imbedded in the Saints' metanarrative, and in particular in their beliefs about the nature of matter and spirit. As physical creatures, "We are of the earth earthy . . . with bones, and flesh, and sinews, and skin." But "how was the spirit formed?" and "where do you suppose all these tabernacles [bodies] got their spirits?" As Pratt reminded them, these spirits were not created, but were preexistent. In the beginning, God organized matter into a planet and then organized "from the dust" the bodies of Adam and Eve to serve as tabernacles, commanding them in no uncertain terms "to multiply and replenish the earth." Procreation, Pratt emphasized, is God's design for marriage: for both the very first married couple and for all married couples since.[43]

When it came to plural marriage in particular, Pratt argued that it was God's desire to re-establish His people amongst the evil nations of the world that necessitated the peculiar marital dispensation. Just as it was in the days of polygamous Abraham, through whom God established ancient

Israel among the pagans, so it would be in the Saints' latter days in the midst of "Gentile Christendom." Sarah was willing to share her husband with Hagar because she knew that "unless seed was raised up to Abraham, he would come short of his glory." Mormons were now commanded to do the same. No matter how taboo plural marriage might seem, the times demanded and justified it. "Whoredoms, adultery, and fornication, have cursed the nations of the earth for many generations," and doomed them "to destruction." In the midst of this rampant wickedness, "God is gathering out from among these nations those who will hearken to his voice ... to establish them as a people alone by themselves."[44]

And then Pratt connected the dots. "One thing is certain—that that people [Mormons] are better calculated to bring up children in the right way, than any other under the whole heavens. . . . Among the Saints is the most likely place for these spirits to take their tabernacles, through a just and righteous parentage." Think of all the poor spirits stuck in pre-existence. Of course they long for physical bodies and a chance to experience the second estate, but mortal life can also turn out to be a curse rather than a blessing, especially if they are born "among the Hottentots, the African negroes, the idolatrous Hindoos, or any other of the fallen nations that dwell upon the face of this earth." No, "this would be their highest pleasure and joy, to know that they could have the privilege of being born of such noble [Mormon] parentage." As odd as it may seem both to outsiders and to themselves, it was both "reasonable, and consistent that the Lord should say unto His faithful and chosen servants . . . take unto yourselves more wives." The "noble spirits, that have been waiting for thousands of years, to come forth in the fulness of times" cried out to the Utah Saints impatiently from their premortal purgatory, and God sought to make them an everlasting "kingdom of Kings and Priests, a kingdom unto Himself."[45]

Nearly two thousand miles away, John Humphrey Noyes had his periodical, *The Circular*, publish a similar declaration of the Oneida Community's "Theocratic Platform." The Hubbards' lawsuits had been resolved a month earlier and he wanted the rest of the world "to comprehend the main features of the Revolution which we believe in as the kingdom of God," including the "CULTIVATION OF FREE LOVE." Serendipitously, his public reannouncement of complex marriage coincided with the LDS Church's announcement of plural marriage. Both took place on the exact same day: August 29, 1852.[46]

PART IV

PRACTICES AND ENFORCEMENTS

IN PART 4 I explore what life was like during the heyday of Mormon plural marriage, Perfectionist complex marriage, and Shaker communal celibacy. Each group emerged from its early crises determined to defy the monogamous norm of American Christendom and embrace its radical sexual practice and corresponding sectarian identity more confidently than ever. There were still problems to manage, such as the "Selfishness and Status" that will be explained in the next chapter, but these were largely internal matters that were dealt with effectively—at least during this time of maturity—through the groups' internal mechanisms of "Control" and "Revival," the subjects of chapters 12 and 13.

There are several reasons why the Mormons, Shakers, and Oneida Perfectionists experienced periods of stability when they did. For starters, they had purged the lukewarm and the most vocal dissenters from their ranks, and each had found a safe space, or spaces, in which to flourish. This was especially true for the Mormons under Brigham Young. The Saints in Nauvoo who knew about plural marriage and opposed it—Sidney Rigdon, Emma Hale Smith, William Law, among others—all stayed behind. Those who were willing to endure the 1,300-mile trek to the Great Basin were either committed to the institution or willing to accept it.

Perhaps more importantly, each sect also enjoyed a measure of economic stability and material security. As sects all three sought a separation from the world that ideally would include financial self-sufficiency. When the movements were young and more carefree, pecuniary matters did not concern the leaders. As they institutionalized, however, and thought about the stability of their communities and the perpetuation of their beliefs into the future, money became a more serious preoccupation. Thus all three were forced to trade with the same American society that they had renounced. The Mormons, Shakers, and Oneidans did this with varying degrees of success, but all three shared a common paradox: economically, their continued existence as a sect depended on a material connection with the very world that they shunned.

Shaker villages were highly productive economic communities that reflected both their values and their times. Prizing manual labor and hard work, Shaker leaders developed diverse communal economies that focused on farming and small-scale manufacturing, trading their surpluses in local markets and branching out into other ventures such as commerce in seeds, herbs, and livestock. They also operated mills and of course built and marketed their famous furniture. This diverse array of enterprises brought prosperity to Shaker villages before the Civil War, but as the American economy industrialized they could not keep pace, a development that contributed to the Society's decline.[1]

By contrast, the Perfectionists profited immensely from heavier industry. After moving to Oneida in 1848, the community struggled to find an adequate financial foundation. Searching for a niche in the diversifying antebellum economy, Noyes experimented with an array of entrepreneurial ventures: building a gristmill and a sawmill, cultivating silkworms and honeybees, and manufacturing brooms, shoes, and animal traps. After about four years of unprofitability, it was the animal traps that finally brought the Oneidans out of debt and into abundance, thanks to innovative genius, mechanized mass production, and an expanding market.

The story of how the Oneida traps were manufactured and distributed reads like the development of the antebellum northern economy in microcosm. The men responsible for the enterprise were William Inslee, a machinist, and Sewell Newhouse, a long-time trapper and citizen of Oneida. Newhouse's devices are precisely what one thinks of when one imagines a nineteenth-century trap: opened steel jaws that slam shut on an animal's leg when it steps on the circular triggering plate. Previously Newhouse had forged the traps by hand, but in early 1852 Inslee "made a machine for bending the jaws," John R. Miller informed Noyes: "They are bent in an instant and are all exactly alike." Manual labor was still involved in the traps' production, but mechanization had streamlined and standardized the manufacturing process. Thus while the Community was fighting lawsuits and debating whether or not to disband, it had found its economic deliverance. "I think we shall make this a very profitable business," Miller concluded with excitement.[2] For years the Community sold their product locally and in New York City, but with the completion of a railroad between Toledo and Chicago, they expanded in the spring of 1852 into the lucrative Midwest, where there were far more trappers plying their trade. At the end of that year, Miller enthusiastically announced: "this is the first time we have been free from debt since the commencement of this community."³ Then the business simply boomed, permanently changing the structure and culture of Oneida. "Before long," one chronicler sums up, "the whole Community, men, women, and children were making traps." Production expanded exponentially from a few thousand units a year in the early 1850s "to 11,150 in 1856, 25,000 in 1857, and 275,000 in 1864." George Wallingford Noyes insists that this newfound material abundance did not make his uncle, John Humphrey Noyes, any less spiritual, but it nevertheless did make "constantly clearer" his "conception of the kingdom of God as a practical, mundane institution," an extraordinary shift for such a passionate sectarian.⁴

In the intermountain West, Brigham Young was likewise preoccupied with the "practical, mundane" side of building the kingdom of God. From its inception, Mormonism had a tradition of intermingling the spiritual and the material. In the Great Basin, the historian Leonard Arrington comments, economic activity "came to occupy a position of honor alongside evangelization. While some looked upon this adaptation as a materialization of religion, the Mormons were proud to regard it as the spiritualization of temporal activity."⁵ As long as it was demonstrably building the kingdom, all kinds of activity could be considered holy: both preaching and farming; both serving as a missionary and trading sharply with Gentile migrants. It was therefore no accident that Young named his nascent kingdom Deseret, a word taken from the *Book of Mormon* meaning "honeybee." The Saints' home in the Great Basin was a hive of activity—productive and with everyone performing a specialized responsibility for the good of the whole and under the undisputed leadership of the First President.

When compared to the Shakers and Oneida Perfectionists, the Mormons under Young sought economic independence the most energetically and initially failed at it the most miserably. He dispatched thousands of colonists to scores of specialized colonies in an attempt to create a diversified, mutually supportive regional economy. In one location settlers would grow sugar beets, while in another they would herd sheep, or mine and refine iron. By the late 1850s, however, almost all of these attempts at self-sufficiency had foundered, usually due to a lack of expertise.

Ironically and repeatedly, the Saints' financial rescue came from the very people and government they were trying to escape. After two years of near-starvation, the migrants finally enjoyed some degree of abundance in 1849 once they began trading with California-bound Argonauts.

Then, from 1858 to 1861, the Saints profited massively from an even more hated enemy, the US Army. After the abortive Mormon War of 1857–58, which will be discussed in chapter 18, the federal government kept an occupying force in the Salt Lake Valley to keep an eye on the Saints, and once again commerce between Mormons and the outsiders made a blessing out of what could have been a curse. In 1861, when the Civil War broke out and the much-needed troops were recalled to the East, the army shut down Camp Floyd, leading to what Arrington calls "probably the largest government surplus property sale yet held in the history of the nation." Rather than transport the material back across the Rocky Mountains, the army sold the Mormons approximately $4 million worth of equipment, livestock, foodstuffs, and other valuable resources for the cut-rate price of only $100,000.[6]

After the war, the completion of the transcontinental railroad then changed the Utah Saints forever. The famed golden spike was driven on May 10, 1869, just north of the Great Salt Lake, ending whatever isolation they still enjoyed. The kingdom would now be permanently linked to the rest of the United States and have to deal with the outside people, goods, ideas, and government that were inevitably going to encroach on their unique community and practices.

Economically speaking, the railroad was both a boon and a calamity: a boon because it could bring converts to Utah more efficiently; a calamity because it threatened the dream of Mormon autonomy. Rather than a diversified, self-sufficient economy of farmers, manufacturers, and merchants each contributing to the kingdom in his own way, Utah might now fall into colonial status, specializing in mining to serve the broader national economy of which it was now a part. Brigham Young, however, met these challenges head on and turned them to the Church's benefit. Eschewing mining due to its boom-and-bust instability, as well as the greed and immorality it engendered among miners, Young was nevertheless happy to grow the kingdom's economy by outfitting the miners. To that end, Utah Saints were perfectly situated to support this capital-rich, heavy industry when it arrived, supplying them with produce, livestock, and manufactured goods.[7] Young also joined in on the railroad bonanza, contracting out teams of Saints to work for the Union Pacific Railroad, and constructing several interior lines that connected every valuable corner of the kingdom into an integrated network. The Church often clashed with the railroad and mining magnates, but it immensely profited from them as well.[8]

The railroad also brought tens of thousands of converts to Utah. In 1849 Young had established the Perpetual Emigrating Fund to gather as many Saints as possible in Deseret. In the 1850s and 1860s these migrants struggled across the plains in wagons or dragging handcarts. After 1869 they could ride the rails. In 1850, with thousands of Saints strung out along the trail, Utah's population was only 11,380. By 1860 it had nearly quadrupled to 40,273, and then more than doubled again by 1870 to 86,786. After the railroad, Utah's population continued to surge: in 1880 it was 143,963 and in 1890 had reached 210,779.[9] Scholars estimate that during this first forty years "European emigration to Utah totaled over 85,000" people, mostly from England and Scandinavia.[10] This influx of foreign converts, plus natural population increase through childbearing, accounts for the staggering growth among the Saints. As Young had wanted, they were indeed building up the kingdom, one way or another.

Given the enormous number of Mormons practicing plural marriage after 1850, the way of telling its story also has to change. When plural marriage was the belief and practice of a single man and his wives, the narrative both could and should be detailed and intimate, delving into their biographies and analyzing as much as possible their complex motivations and emotions. As the institution spread and became public, however, the focus of the story inevitably changes: from an individual, to a small and clandestine subculture, to a massive intermountain kingdom with tens of thousands of people unabashedly living the principle, although not every Mormon in nineteenth-century Utah was a polygamist. Precise figures are difficult to calculate because of the Church's understandable unwillingness to record plural marriages for fear of prosecution, but the classic and still accepted figure of polygamists is 15 to 20 percent of Mormon families.[11] While this means that the majority of Mormon marriages were not plural ones, thousands of Saints did practice polygamy and it is simply impossible to tell all their stories in detail. Instead, for good and for ill, scholars of Mormon polygamy in Utah make use of statistics and quantitative methods. Thus while many individual stories have to go untold—or remain intentionally hidden from the prying eyes of outsiders—the aggregate of them remains both informative and moving nonetheless.

The story of all three sects is still a profoundly human one: full of longings, love, belief, sacrifice, heartbreak, and joy. As such, the exploration in this penultimate part seeks to remain as qualitative as possible, employing numbers when necessary and illuminating, but focusing even more on the complex emotions and interactions that accompany religiously inspired sexuality. In particular, it aims to explore the problems that emerged in Mormon polygamy, Shaker celibacy, and Oneida complex marriage—even in this most mature and stable phase—and how the problems in those "practices" were effectively countered by the community's "enforcements."

11
Selfishness and Status

JEALOUSY AND the desire for exclusivity are two of the most powerful emotions that sexualized human love can engender. According to Shakers, Oneida Perfectionists, and polygamous Mormons, those emotions were also deeply sinful—hindrances to creating a more inclusive love for the community of believers. As described in chapter 3, "Marriage," both John Humphrey Noyes and the Shakers waged a relentless war against selfishness, and especially the selfishness that was nurtured within monogamous marriage. Noyes famously called marriage "Egotism for Two," and considered the "selfish family spirit" to be "the enemy of communism."[1] In his Perfectionist communities, by contrast, people would be stripped of their worldly "*I-spirit*," and have it replaced with the godlier "*we-spirit*" of genuine Christian fellowship.[2] Only with this kind of radical reorientation could believers experience community, family, and marriage in the way that God intended them.

Shakers similarly loathed the institutions of marriage and family for the sinful "natural affections" that accompanied them. Shaker villages were to be the Believers' new family, complete with spiritual mothers, fathers, sisters, and brothers all living together in harmony: worshipping the Lord, working hard for their bread, and waging a communal war against the flesh. The cases of Mary Dyer and Eunice Chapman make clear just how much Shakers considered even the love between a mother and her children to be selfish and sinful, while the horrifying story of Steven Sutton reveals the extreme measures Shakers employed in their war against "natural affections." Sutton's wife prior to joining the community "was an amiable woman, and I loved her," he wrote.

> But now I must hate her as much more as I had been fond of her, or I could not be saved. The leaders said, "She was my god." . . . After I neglected my wife, and took the children from her care, she appeared in constant trouble, and weeping, and being of a delicate constitution, her trouble threw her into a decline. . . . When she was buried, I was ordered

to cover the earth over her coffin, to show that I had no natural affections; this I did, when at the same time, I felt as though I should pitch into the grave with her.[3]

These are the kinds of sacrifices Believers were forced to make. Such was "the only way to save my soul."

The history of the Oneida Perfectionists is filled with similar episodes in that community's campaign to extirpate selfishness. In 1851, when the Community was still young and Noyes still living in Brooklyn, there was a flare-up of "philoprogenitiveness" (love for one's children) among the young girls at Oneida. These prepubescent girls obviously did not have children of their own, but were—according to the reports between Oneida and Brooklyn—directing undue affection toward their dolls. As both surrogate children and private property, dolls threatened to instill in these girls the wrong kind of values. A specially appointed investigatory panel was formed, which concluded: "We think that this doll-spirit . . . seduces us from a Community spirit in regard for helping the family." In the end, after some coaching from the adults, the children voted to immolate their cherished toys. Unsurprisingly, "the little boys were loud in their clamors for the great massacre, and the little girls, after a few struggles, were ready to make the sacrifices of their idols." Then, one by one, in a solemn procession accompanied by song, the girls cast their dollies on the coals, where they "burned up with a merry blaze, and all hands rejoiced in their condemnation." Thus was the "doll-spirit" slain, "and we opine they [the children] are all the better for it."[4]

Noyes also took strong measures to deal with jealousy and selfishness among Oneida's adults. As people who valued pleasure and leisure as gifts from God, the Oneidans enjoyed their recreations. In addition to work, religious instruction, and study, community life was full of parties, theatrical productions, games, and music. In none of these activities, however, were individuals encouraged to outshine their fellow Perfectionists. Competition, Noyes declared, or any activity in which one might be exalted over others, was anathema to the spirit of community. Thus while individuals could use their musical talents for the edification of the whole, there were instances when "music has evidently become a selfish, personal thing," with performers taking pride in their abilities and provoking envy among the less talented. In 1874 Noyes observed such a spirit among some of the Community's female singers. By this time Oneida had enough money to send young adults to college. These young women "have gone to New York for musical education," Noyes complained, "They have been brought up on the stage, and have got the *prima donna fever*." Back in Oneida they would have to exorcise this spirit of selfishness, and if they could not, he concluded, "I should go for giving up music."[5] Apparently the threat of these drastic measures—accompanied by the mutual criticism of the singers—worked, and music remained a part of the Community.

But the Perfectionists had the most trouble combating jealousy when it came to sharing sexual partners. "By the mid-1850s," the historian Spencer Klaw writes, "many of the rough edges of complex marriage had been smoothed away. If jealousy had not been abolished, it had at least been contained."[6] Noyes accomplished this containment primarily through the institutions of mutual criticism and the law of ascending and descending fellowship. How Noyes continued to utilize these and other governing mechanisms during the heyday of Oneida complex marriage from 1852 to 1879 will be discussed in the following chapter on "Control." One final point bears mentioning, however, before moving on to discuss similar challenges among Mormon polygamists.

Oddly perhaps, the Perfectionists' campaign against jealousy and exclusivity lost rhetorical steam over the course of the 1850s, 1860s, and 1870s. The theme is still present, but it steadily recedes from their publications during the thirty years when complex marriage was practiced at Oneida. During this time, Noyes's main periodical was *The Circular*, which ran from 1851 to 1876, and was then followed by the *American Socialist* from 1876 to 1879. Through these publications, Noyes communicated to both the outside world and to his fellow Bible communists, seeking converts to the cause on the one hand while nourishing the faith of Perfectionists on the other.

During the 1850s, when Oneida was struggling to find its equilibrium, Noyes steadily beat the anti-selfishness, antifamily drums. He filled the pages of *The Circular* with articles on "Egotism—Its Character and Cure" (Jul. 2, 1853), "The Family and Its Foil" (Nov. 16, 1854), "Self-love and Communism" (Sept. 13, 1855), and "Christ and the Family Spirit" (Oct. 13, 1859). In these he pitted the *"undue . . . attention to self"* against the true love of God and neighbor.[7] In God's rightly ordered society, individuals must sacrifice their self-love and equally selfish love of family for the good of the whole.

In the 1860s these themes waned as Noyes and the Perfectionists became interested in other, potentially worldlier subjects. *The Circular* did publish revised articles on "Egotism for Two" (July 3, 1862) and "Christ and the Family Spirit" (Nov. 12, 1863), but then the subjects virtually disappear for the rest of the decade. Perhaps Noyes simply got tired of saying the same thing over and over again. Perhaps also it was because pressing national issues were so distracting. In the 1860s *The Circular* ran more stories on current events such as secession, the Civil War, and emancipation.

The topics of the articles during this decade also reveal Noyes's growing preoccupation with business. No doubt he became more interested in the national economic climate because of Oneida's flourishing trap manufacturing operation and improved financial outlook. With more money at his disposal—up from $1,763 in net profits in 1858 to over $13,000 in 1866—Noyes had much to be thankful for, but also new ethical questions to ponder.[8] As a result he became more concerned with things like balance sheets and business ethics than with what marriage and sex were like in the kingdom of heaven. In fact, in 1869, on the twentieth anniversary of the publication of "The Bible Argument: Defining the Relations of the Sexes in the Kingdom of Heaven," *The Circular*—quite strangely—acknowledged the commemoration and then announced that it was *not* going to reprint the piece. "The only reason why we have not been forward to publish new editions of this work," the editors explained, is that "it does not seem adapted to the times. The world has gone so far away from the Bible in the last twenty years, that a Bible argument on any subject now-a-days goes for nothing. When the public mind shall swing back (as we believe it will) to respect for Bible ideas, we shall be happy to republish our Bible Argument."[9] The "times," the "world," and "the public mind" had indeed all changed, and the Oneida Community had changed along with them.

Relatedly, articles from the 1860s reveal Noyes's growing fascination with science and technology. He had always been a man of ideas, reading voraciously about new philosophies and current affairs, but in his youth his mind focused largely on theology. In the 1860s Noyes branched out into other, potentially faith-threatening realms of human understanding. In 1861, he addressed head-on "the difficulties and objections which for the past thirty years have been raised against the Bible from various points of verbal, historical, and scientific criticism." Advances in the fields of geology, textual criticism, philology, and biology were challenging religious beliefs, and Noyes had taken notice. "Suppose," he wrote, "Mr. Darwin should succeed in establishing his theory of the gradual development of species in the animal kingdom by a law of force—Would that affect our faith in Christ as the Savior of men?"[10] Noyes answered with a resounding "no," but it was clear that even his faith was shaken. A few weeks later, in an article tellingly entitled "The Value of Certainty," he wrote: "I find it very important and profitable to me, to withdraw my mind, from time to time, from speculations, reasonings, doubtful disputations, and all such unhealthy food, and fix my attention on some certainty—one of God's eternal facts—and hug it—separate it from these everlasting doubts and speculations and abandon my life to it."[11] Sometimes Noyes was simply exhausted after combatting so many opposing ideas and needed to take refuge in a bit of pietistic fideism.

Like many other believers of this era, Noyes welcomed and marveled at technological innovations, but was troubled by how new scientific theories problematized traditional religious metanarratives. Thus in the 1860s *The Circular* published enthusiastic announcements of things like "A New Microscope of Astonishing Power" (Apr. 17, 1865), "The Atlantic Telegraph" (Apr. 24, 1865), "Nitro-Glyerine or Blasting Oil" (Apr. 30, 1866), "The Suez Ship-Canal" (Oct. 28, 1867), and "The Age of Steam" (Oct. 11, 1869). It also published Noyes's first fumbling attempts—often humorous to modern readers—to harmonize science and faith: "Is the Earth Fireproof?" (June 6, 1864), "Jesus Christ. The Scientific Aspect of His Claims" (Mar. 20, 1865), "Geologic Account of the Devil" (Apr. 8, 1867), and "Spiritual Geography" (May 31, 1869).

In the 1870s, the last and troubled decade of the Oneida Community's existence, Noyes returned to his first principles and renewed his attack on the selfishness of monogamy. There are a number of reasons for this. Internally speaking, as his social experiment began to falter, he wanted to remind the disaffected of what they stood for—their sectarian distinctiveness and collective identity. In 1869, after years of theorizing about it, the Oneidans had launched their program of "stirpiculture," or selective breeding, in which carefully chosen men and women were allowed to have children. This obviously reversed the longtime practice of birth control through male continence and it permanently changed the Community's culture and dynamics—changes that will be discussed in chapter 15 "Children," and part 5, "End Times." "Philoprogenerativeness," or the love of one's children, soon became a very real problem at Oneida; but Noyes's Perfectionists could still find common cause in their ongoing war against "amativeness," the selfish love for a monogamous spouse. *The Circular* and later the *American Socialist* regularly published pieces in the 1870s denouncing the nuclear family and praising the virtues of community life. Articles like "The Genesis of Marriage: Its Origins Traced to Captivity in War" (Nov. 14, 1870), "Why Wives Fade" (Jan. 9, 1871), and "Decadence of Marriage" (Jan. 27, 1876) clearly pulled no punches.

Noyes also had pressing external reasons to reemphasize Oneida's understanding of marriage and sexuality. In the 1870s, as similar moralistic campaigns were being launched against Mormon polygamists, the Community came under attack and had to defend its beliefs and practices. The climate in the United States was becoming hostile to alternative religio-sexual communities, and Noyes paid close attention to the changes. In order to protect his Perfectionists, Noyes wanted to highlight the distinctions between them and Mormon polygamists. In 1870 he published an article aptly titled "A Difference," and in 1879 one with the more urgent heading "Wide Apart," in which he declared "that there is no good reason for associating Oneida Communism with Mormonism and sentencing them together."[12] Throughout the decade *The Circular* regularly updated readers on the crusade against the Mormons with stories like "Polygamic Discussion in Utah" (Sept. 5, 1870), "A National Law of Marriage" (May 20, 1872), and "Anti-Mormon Legislation" (June 22, 1874). Noyes also took the opportunity to contrast complex marriage with plural marriage. "We reject polygamy because it multiplies the radical evil of monogamy, viz., property in women."[13] As he reminded readers, "Marriage is an institution rendered necessary by the selfishness of mankind, . . . not adapted to the unselfish spirit of heaven" that characterized his version of the kingdom of God on earth.[14]

In some ways the rhetoric of the Mormons was like that of the Shakers and Perfectionists. They shared a common enemy but referred to it differently. What the Shakers called "natural affections" and Oneidans called "amativeness" and "philoprogenerativeness," Mormons simply called "selfishness." But regardless of the moniker, the message was the same: religious duty and the effort to establish a more inclusive love for the sectarian community required individuals to sacrifice their exclusive love for their family. And it bears repeating that these sacrifices were often truly painful for the adherents, which is why leaders needed mechanisms of control to enforce the communities' practices whenever individual discipline wavered. Shakers, Oneidans, and Mormons all struggled profoundly to root out the special love they had for others—a love that they were told was selfish and sinful.

Unsurprisingly, Mormon leaders especially targeted women in their campaign against selfishness. Elder George Q. Cannon, for instance, pleaded with his female listeners for self-sacrifice. Plural marriage is God's revelation to His chosen people to forge them into a "purer community," he reminded them, and if you resist it because it is a difficult "trial," then you are selfish and will be judged for it on the "day of reckoning." The words of Helen Mar Kimball Whitney, plural widow of Joseph Smith and later apologist for Mormon polygamy, indicate that she had internalized this logic. "When lived up to as the Lord designed it should be, it [plural marriage] will exalt the human family, . . . in the place of selfishness, patience and charity will find place in their [plural wives'] hearts, driving therefrom all feelings of strife and discord."[15] As with the Shakers and Oneida Perfectionists, selfishness was the real enemy—an impediment to godliness and unity. For Mormon women in particular it could only be slain through the painful sacrifice of one's exclusive claim to one's husband.

Mormonism, as revealed and practiced by Joseph Smith, was originally an optimistic, expansive, and joyful faith. Rather than threaten listeners with hellfire and damnation, Smith attracted followers with promises of "fulness," exaltation, and an eternal destiny in the telestial, terrestrial, or celestial kingdoms. He also empowered the Saints through institutions like the Aaronic and Melchizedek priesthoods, and ministered to them with stirring ordinances such as the endowment ceremony. Life was still serious—a test in which mortals could perform either well or poorly—but it was also a blessing to be appreciated and lived to the full. As the *Book of Mormon* famously summarizes the LDS metanarrative: "Adam fell that men might be; and men are, that they might have joy."[16]

In Utah from the 1850s through the 1880s, it is often difficult to find much joy. The mood instead is rather dour, and the dominant religious outlook one that emphasizes earthly sacrifice as a means of achieving heavenly rewards. As one antipolygamist observed: "The question has often been asked what induces women to go into 'plurality' when they are acquainted with its horrors. It is to them a duty to be performed, no matter what the sacrifice may cost them—in short, it is their religion."[17] This is one understanding of the religious life: stoic resignation to suffering in this world in the hopes of a better everlasting experience in the world to come. As one man recollected about his first wife's decision-making process: "She was willing to sacrifice her own feelings in order to be able to inherit a place in his Celestial Kingdom. She then consented to let me have her sister Caroline for my second wife, this she did in full faith that it was a commandment of God, and that she would be rewarded for doing so."[18]

But whereas for women the payoff for being a plural wife was purely otherworldly, men benefitted in this life as well, which is where status plays an important role. As another ex-Mormon wrote in an exposé: "Mormonism teaches that all salvation is material; that men's positions here determine their stations hereafter, . . . desire for glory is the only incentive of Mormon action, so, therefore, he tries to get as many wives as he can."[19] For men there was an important continuity between their earthly status and their eternal status. Whereas women were told to crucify their selfishness in this life so that they would reap the fruit of their suffering in the afterlife, men were encouraged to almost selfishly pursue status in both.

At this point it is important to remember that only a minority of Utah Saints practiced polygamy, somewhere between 15 percent and 20 percent.[20] This constituted an elite—the top of the socioeconomic pyramid. Male Saints gained admittance to this exclusive echelon through a mutually reinforcing process of accumulating both leadership positions and wives. As Mormon scholars Leonard J. Arrington and Davis Bitton describe the beginning of this process: "The privilege of polygamy was granted to the pure in heart and hence was a clear sign of worthiness for promotion in the Mormon hierarchy." As they add, "all the central church leaders were polygamists. From the president down through the apostles and the Presiding Bishopric during the period [1850s–1880s], no general authority was a monogamist."[21]

Other scholars of Mormon plural marriage agree that the institution played a powerful role in forging both an elite and a stronger collective identity for the Saints. "Joseph Smith initiated a social system that appealed to deeply held human concerns," writes historian George D. Smith. "People want to be counted among the elite, the initiated few, the chosen of God or, as Joseph promised, to be given the unheard-of opportunity to become as gods themselves."[22] These were the optimistic and eternally expansive promises that Smith claimed would accompany plural marriage in the afterlife, but only for the obedient few. In this life, however, and for all of the intermountain Saints after 1852, plural marriage had different effects. "Though polygamy reduced the exclusivity of marital relationships, it greatly improved the cohesiveness of the larger Mormon community," writes Richard S. Van Wagoner. "Group violation of what had been conventional behavioral norms served to weld the Saints into a new fraternity of people—a 'peculiar people,' as they were fond of calling themselves—united in their opposition to government interference in marriage practices."[23]

This is sex and sectarianism encapsulated. Religiously inspired alternative sexual practices, freely chosen, created a sense of separateness and identity among the choosers. Plural marriage distinguished them from "the world" as a special and godly people. And whenever hostile forces threatened this people and their unique beliefs, it only enhanced their sense of specialness. In other words, defying culturally acceptable sexual/marital practices—even when it was only a minority doing so—reinforced the sectarian identity of the whole. As Arrington and Bitton add, the persecution that followed this defiance "was not pleasant, but social psychologists have recognized that there is nothing so effective as outside pressure to create a sense of group identity and cohesiveness."[24] This book, whose title is the not-so-subtle "Sex and Sects," obviously agrees with this claim.

12
Control

IN THIS chapter I am going to investigate the darker side of life in community. As I hope the previous chapter made clear, communal living requires individuals to sacrifice themselves and their self-interest for the good of the whole. There is something undeniably beautiful about this—about people living for something larger than themselves in a way that puts others before themselves. Both joys and sorrows accompany this kind of shared religious life. Individuals experience a sense of purpose as well as rich companionship with like-minded believers, but they also have to submit to the group's leaders and disciplinary practices. What happens when people did not follow the rules? What were the range of options—from subtle social pressure to public humiliation to excommunication—the Mormons, Shakers, and Oneida Perfectionists had at their disposal to bring them back into line?

We are going to start with the Shakers, who seem to be the most overtly, as opposed to covertly, controlling of the three sects. After their move to America, the Shakers oscillated between seasons of expansion and consolidation. During the seasons of gathering, leaders organized virtually every aspect of life in a Shaker village. In the 1790s Joseph Meacham regulated the hours of the day, dedicating roughly six hours for sleeping and then precise times for meals, work, and worship.[1] A Shaker village was therefore less like a free-flowing civil society and more like a monastery, complete with established rules, leaders, and a fixed schedule.

Unsurprisingly, apostates were the first to expose the Shaker rage for order, condemning the tyranny of the elders in particular. Valentine, Daniel, and Reuben Rathbun all criticized the Shakers for their corporal punishment and psychological manipulation. Mary Marshall Dyer and Eunice Chapman were equally unsparing in their criticisms, describing how elders twisted community members into fearing and revering them as surrogate gods. Ordinary Believers in Shaker villages, Chapman complained, "are kept in more slavish fear, than though they were under the power of the Court of Inquisition."[2]

No one, however, decried the power dynamics of a Shaker village more than the apostate David R. Lamson in 1848. Like Eunice Chapman in the 1810s, Lamson walked the thin existential line between faith and inquiry. Unlike Chapman, who could adopt the outward trappings of Shaker life but never force herself to believe, Lamson was once an enthusiastic convert. Typical for an antebellum sectarian, Lamson "was greatly disgusted with the empty professions and formalities of the members of the nominal church," and wanted *more*. He found it among the Believers, whose village and lifestyle he described as "to all human appearance, neat, plentiful, orderly, peaceful, devout and beautiful." He also "found some things which dampened my hopes a little," as he put it: "they thought too much learning a dangerous and hurtful thing," while he was also uneasy about the fact that the "only door of entrance was the confession of sins." He converted to Shakerism nonetheless, but soon found the hypocritical actions of the elders intolerable. "*They are above the laws,*" he wrote with disdain.[3]

Lamson had an especially harsh assessment of Shaker confession. "This is the secret lever by which the Shaker despotism has been wielded so long and so successfully," he wrote. "The elders are intimately acquainted with the thoughts and feelings, purposes and propensities, character and condition of the several members of the several families of the denomination. And consequently know exactly what influences to exert to keep them in subjection."[4] Knowledge, in other words, was power—a power that the elders held monopolistically. People revealed their weaknesses to them in confession and then awaited their punishment, but the elders did not subject themselves to the same.

Other apostates from the 1780s to the 1840s likewise complained that Shaker leaders used confession as their chief means of control. "The reason of their success may be attributed," Amos Taylor reported as early as 1782, "to a very extraordinary skill which these people have acquired in hearing confessions."[5] It was, William J. Haskett wrote in 1828, "the initiating ceremony in Shakerism, and being a tenet, is strenuously observed."[6] In particular, confession was a means by which the elders could monitor and stamp out dissent, "or conspiracy" as they sometimes called it, and all ideas or behaviors "that are not congenial to the system of Shakerism." It was also the means by which the elders militantly policed the separation of the sexes.

David Lamson's conclusion was that Shakerism was "a most crafty game played by the few at the expense of the many," and "a very curious anomaly, that a despotism should exist in the midst of a republic." As he went on to describe life in a Shaker village: "Every waking hour has its duties, and the sleeping hours are limited," while "'*book larnin*" as they call it, is very scarce.... Knowledge is the bane of Shakerism." Lamson explained how the elders exercised a tight control on information: "No brother or sister is allowed to read any books or papers, but those printed by 'believers,' or recommended by the elders." As for the sermons, Lamson added, "'Simplicity and obedience,' is the stereotyped text of all preaching and exhortation among this people.... Obedience to them is obedience to God." "It is *management*," Lamson contemptuously concluded: "Shakerism is (principally at least) a game which the Lead perpetuate upon the common members.... Their government is a tyranny, its subjects are in bondage."[7]

Lamson's scathing critique of Shaker power dynamics could possibly be dismissed as the rantings of a disaffected former member, were it not for the fact that they are substantiated by the writings of the Shakers themselves. "ORDER is the first law of heaven," Richard McNemar wrote in 1831, "and the ensign of every deliberative assembly on earth," while Frederick W. Evans echoed in 1853: "No truth can be more certain, than that God is a *God of order*, and not of confusion."[8] Prior to the 1820s Shakers prioritized order but were committed to oral rather than written instruction, which Mother Lucy Wright forbade. A mere six months after Wright's death in 1821, however, her successors published the "Millennial Laws" that were to govern all nineteen villages in existence at the time. They were, as Stephen Stein describes them, "the first systematic codification of regulations within Shakerism."[9]

The "Millennial Laws" of 1821 strongly reinforce the old Shaker emphasis on order with a new emphasis on unity—or uniformity—across the now broad Shaker diaspora. They also confirm David Lamson's image of a Shaker village. On the one hand, they paint a picture of the "neat, plentiful, orderly, peaceful, devout and beautiful" community that originally attracted him.[10] The laws instructed Believers to keep themselves and their community as meticulously clean as possible: fencing in fields; properly disposing any "filthy substance" near a shop or kitchen; promptly repairing or destroying worn-down buildings; and even making sure to replace a broken window "before the Sabbath." They also encouraged piety through their rules for worship, Sabbath-keeping, and daily times for prayer and silence.[11]

On the other hand, however, the laws paint a picture of an ideal community that is not only ordered but also tightly controlled. The first chapter is devoted to "*the confession of sin,*" a placement that indicates its priority for the leaders who authorized the laws. In addition there are the equally unsurprising restrictions on "*intercourse between the sexes.*" The gist of these rules is that a man and woman "must not be together alone," which precluded working or performing errands together, and even passing "each other on the stairs."

The laws also prescribed strict rules to control Believers' speech and bodies. Speech violations were deemed particularly disorderly. People guilty of "tattling, talebearing & backbiting," tellers of "filthy stories," and users of "*nick-names*" were all required to confess their sins to the elders. Perhaps most tellingly, these speech restrictions also forbade members "to make any enquiry or take any pains to find out who it was that opened the matter to the Elders." This prohibition protected the informer and created a climate in which Believers were encouraged to report on one another, with the accused having no opportunity to refute the accuser directly. And finally, the Millennial Laws had some very unique prescriptions for how Believers should move, pray, sit, and sleep. Prioritizing the right over the left side of the body for some reason, members were instructed to kneel and rise first on the right leg and then the left, and "clasp our hands together our right thumb and fingers . . . above our left." At bedtime, members were instructed to "kneel down together, either in ranks or facing each other, and go to bed at the same time."[12] In sum, all of Shaker life—from the village grounds to the conversations between Believers to how one folded one's hands—was to be ordered and enforced.

The spirit of the Millennial Laws of 1821 endured in Shakerism for decades. In 1828 the apostate William J. Haskett published as a part of his exposé, *Shakerism Unmasked,* a copy of the rules as they were expressed in his village. The emphasis on order, government, and obedience is the same, with some slightly peculiar specifics. The very first rule, for instance, was that it was "'Contrary to order for any one to write the orders.'" This was basically a clarification that the elders and the elders alone had the monopoly on rule-making. In addition, when it came to controlling one's passions and one's body, Haskett's version of the rules was even stricter. As usual, men and women could not "'be in a room together without company,'" but it was also considered "'contrary to order for brethren and sisters to milk together,'" as well as "'Contrary to order to look at beasts when they copulate,'" because it "excites a sympathy of feeling in the beholder." And just as watching animals copulate could lead Believers into lust, so could playing "'with dogs and cats'" produce "a feeling different from that which should always fill the believer's mind"—presumably the universal love for God and humankind rather than the special love for another creature, human or not.[13]

The severity of Shaker rules peaked in 1845 with a new version of the Millennial Laws. At the time, the United Society of Believers was in the middle of its "Era of Manifestations"—the season of spiritual fervor from 1837 until the late-1840s, which will be discussed in the next chapter, "Revival." During this period, more outpourings of the Spirit necessitated more numerous, more detailed, and more severe rules. As they believed, God spoke through special people, called "instruments," who admonished members of the community to return to ascetic purity in every aspect of life. In 1840 Shaker mystic Philemon Stewart received via inspiration the new and more demanding rules, which continued the emphasis on personal purity and devotion but took it to a new extreme. Believers were instructed to enter worship meetings on their tip-toes, be at least five feet from members of the opposite sex at all times, and not whisper or wink at one another. These are the rules in effect that David Lamson described in his *Two Years' Experience among the Shakers*. It is no wonder that they inspired such cynicism in him. The "whole concern is under the entire control of the ministry," he concluded: "Who can possess absolute power and not abuse it?"[14]

As the fervor of the Era of Manifestations inevitably waned, however, so too did the Millennial Laws of 1845. In 1860 the United Society of Believers revised them, removing their "more exotic features," as Theodore E. Johnson puts it, and in 1887 they revised them once more. Those rules, Johnson adds, were "wholly free from the strangeness of the laws of 1845," and "have remained in effect in the several communities down to the present day."[15] Order still mattered to the Society—as one Shaker wrote as late as 1893: "We believe in the practice of industry, order, economy, cleanliness"[16]—but apparently the desire to control had diminished some over time.

In contrast, both Brigham Young in Utah and John Humphrey Noyes at Oneida never relaxed control. Young was not able to wield power autocratically until assuming leadership in 1844, but then he never relinquished it. Noyes exercised dominion continually: first over himself; then over his "simple-minded, unpretending believers" in Putney; and finally over his gathered Perfectionist communities at Brooklyn and Oneida.[17] He often thought of himself as a general in charge of the Lord's Perfectionist army, tolerating no dissent while harshly condemning so-called deserters. As he wrote in 1849, shifting the metaphor, "The kingdom of God is an absolute monarchy," with little doubt as to who was the monarch.[18]

Mutual criticism at Oneida played the same regulatory role as confession in a Shaker village. As one observer described it: "Criticism was to the Community what ballast is to a ship. To the individuals it was as fire is to gold."[19] And as Noyes himself put it, mutual criticism "held a very prominent place" in "the machinery of religious and moral discipline."[20] Depending on the metaphor, it either steadied the ship, refined the gold, or kept the communal machine running. In a Shaker village the Believers confessed privately to elders, whereas at Oneida they took turns both giving and receiving criticism publicly. The result, however, was nearly identical—instilling shame in the confessor or the criticized, and self-righteousness in the elders or the critics.

Mutual criticism also hid Noyes's subtle control over the group. Noyes did not subject himself to mutual criticism and somehow never had to defend the hypocrisy. Like the Shaker elders, he simply established himself above it all and never had his own flaws discussed publicly. Except for the very end of the Oneida Community's existence, when disgruntled members effectively challenged him, most simply accepted this double standard as a fact of Perfectionist life. In particular they accepted it as part of the doctrine of "ascending fellowship." Since they had agreed to stamp out selfishness and subject themselves to the will of the community, they had no real grounds to complain. And when their own self-control failed, mutual criticism kicked in to enforce discipline from the community for the good of the community. Individuals endured this discipline as individuals, and only enjoyed the power of an enforcer as part of the larger group. The exception of course was John Humphrey Noyes, who as the pinnacle of the ascending fellowship pyramid could swoop in during emergencies as Criticizer-in-Chief and either drive errant members back into line or out of the community entirely.

Noyes controlled the Perfectionists through sex just as much as he controlled them through mutual criticism. In 1849, as he struggled to impose complex marriage on unenthusiastic teenage boys, he developed his rule of ascending and descending fellowship, which solved multiple problems simultaneously and brought multiple benefits to Noyes personally. Most importantly, compelling young men to have their first sexual experiences with postmenopausal women prevented unwanted pregnancies.

The rule of ascending fellowship also allowed the older men in the community—Noyes in particular—to have privileged access to young women, an access that simply *was* power. As his son Theodore Noyes astutely observed: "you must realize that the government of the Community was *by* complex marriage. Much has been said about mutual criticism and in itself it certainly was a very powerful force in favor of law and order, but all moral government, no matter how benign, in the end has to look to penalties for its enforcement. The power of regulating the sexual relations of the members, inherent in the family at large and by common consent delegated to Father and his subordinates, constituted by far the most effectual means of government."[21] Displaying a sophisticated understanding of political philosophy, Theodore Noyes argued that real power exists in the ability to penalize. Through mutual criticism, the Community could chastise errant individuals, but through complex marriage and ascending fellowship Noyes could truly control them.

At Oneida, ascending fellowship allowed Noyes to govern every demographic within the Community. Older women did his bidding as the sexual mentors of young men, while younger women were obliged to be the sexual partners of older men, and especially Noyes himself when he so wished. As for the males, teenagers had to sacrifice their desires for younger women, while older men had to make sure to stay in Noyes's good graces in order to have access to the Community's younger women. As Theodore Noyes also made clear, "the young and attractive women form the focus toward which all the social rays converge; and the arbiter to be truly one, must . . . exercise his power by genuine sexual attraction to a large extent." For a long time, because of his own "extraordinary attractiveness to women," John Humphrey Noyes was this one and only "arbiter," controlling both the Community's young women and the men who had to seek sexual access to them through him.[22] As we will see in part 5, "End Times," once his sexual magnetism began to wane, the Oneida Community's days were numbered. Until that time, however, Noyes was in solid command. For more than a quarter century, from August 1852 until August 1879, Perfectionists lived complex marriage as a mature alternative conjugal institution.

Although the Oneida Community would change over the years—especially when it reversed its policy on having children and began the eugenic experiment called "stirpiculture"—this was a period of stability and growth. Structurally speaking the governing mechanisms were in place with enough time since their establishment to work out the kinks, while financially the trap business and other ventures continued to bring in enough money to keep the Community in the black. With these resources Noyes added a second Mansion House to the property in 1862, the impressive brick structure that greets visitors today and that is connected to the original 1849 Mansion House. Membership also remained steady at between two hundred and three hundred people. The only real setback came in 1854, when John R. Miller, the Community's chronically overworked manager, died, and Noyes decided to consolidate his Perfectionist communities from six to two. He closed down Newark, Putney, Cambridge, and even his recent home of Brooklyn, and kept Oneida and Wallingford in operation. Noyes's days of absentee leadership of Oneida had lasted from 1849 to 1854 but were now over. Thus until his departure in 1879 Noyes lent not just his powerful ideas but also his powerful presence to the everyday management and culture of the Oneida Community.

During this time Noyes's sexual governance of his fellow Perfectionists extended beyond his ability to match the young and the old through the rule of ascending fellowship. In fact, it is safe to say that Noyes controlled every aspect of the Community's sex life: from how the bedrooms in the Mansion House were shaped; to how long a sexual encounter should last; to the position lovers should use. On September 22, 1852, Noyes issued his "Practical Suggestions for Regulating Intercourse of the Sexes." This Home-Talk, which he wrote while still in Brooklyn and sent to John R. Miller to implement, came less than a month after the Community had resumed complex marriage following the successful resolution of the Hubbard lawsuits.

Noyes's "Practical Suggestions" in 1852 further clarified how the institution of complex marriage would work. Prospective lovers first had to run their request for a sexual encounter "through a third party." This person would then either broker the deal or let the initiator down gently if the object of his or her affection refused. "This method excludes selfish privacy," Noyes argued, "and makes love a Community affair." If the three parties agreed, however, a rendezvous would take place, and another set of rules would go into effect to guide the lovers. Rule number one stated bluntly that "The sexes should sleep apart." Sexual encounters, or "interviews" as they were also called, were obviously social in nature, whereas "sleeping is essentially an individual function." Therefore Noyes recommended "Short interviews will be found the best. Lovers should come together for an hour or two, and should separate to sleep," a rule that was reinforced by and literally built into the Mansion House's architecture. Most bedrooms are small, with single beds, reminiscent of a college dorm-room for one.[23] Partners would enjoy the physical fellowship for the recommended "hour or two," but then, after retiring to his or her own room, could get enough rest to perform the next day's work.[24] Also to ensure sexually satisfied but well-rested workers, historian Louis Kern writes: "Intercourse was . . . limited to the period between ten and twelve P.M."[25]

During the "interview" itself Noyes encouraged less talk and more action. "The tongue has its field to itself all day," he reasoned. "Why should not the other members have their turn?" He also encouraged lovers in "the midst of passion [to] watch for improvement. So shall the spirit of truth go with you and perfect you in the heavenly art." Male continence prevented the men from experiencing ejaculation, but they reportedly were proud of their ability to please their lovers. This was not officially a part of Noyes's 1852 "Suggestions," but allegedly the Oneidans had a favorite sexual position to help women climax. The partners both lay on their sides—what is referred to today as "spooning"—the man behind the woman, which allowed him to manually stimulate her during intercourse. That is how an ideal sexual encounter at Oneida was supposed to be: efficient, laconic, and—for the woman anyway—satisfying.[26] Community members obviously enjoyed freedom in the variety of their sexual partners, but this freedom took place entirely within a mechanism that Noyes invented and closely monitored.

Ultimately, John Humphrey Noyes's real genius for controlling people was his ability to hide the fact that he was controlling people. "His keen intellect and strong will make themselves visible in every department," John B. Ellis wrote in 1870. "Yet he rules without appearing to do so, and is such a master of this art, that his followers, while blindly carrying out his wishes, think that they are performing their own will. He is a born ruler of men with all his faults. . . . He loves power dearly, and, as long as he lives, will never relinquish it."[27] Although Ellis was an enemy of the Oneida Community, his reflections here are more accurate character sketch than unsubstantiated character assassination. John Humphrey Noyes was indeed "a born ruler of men," a lover of power, and "a master of this art" of ruling "without appearing to do so."

The same could be said about Brigham Young, and it was. All students of his complex personality—from nineteenth-century friends and enemies to twenty-first-century historians—agree that he was a force to be reckoned with. Ann Eliza Young, for instance, who later wrote a sensationalist exposé of her experience as one of his plural wives, described how he would sometimes flash "a sinister smile, which every Saint who had had dealings with him knew well, and whose meaning they also knew. It meant, 'Do as I command you, or suffer the weight of my displeasure.'"[28] "Even his enemies have to acknowledge a great charm in the influence he throws around him," another ex-Mormon wrote. Young simply had a "magnetism that attracts and infatuates, that makes men feel its weight and yet love its presence."[29] These polemical sources have to be read carefully, but they can also say in more unflinching language what others also observed but were afraid to express.

Young's critics also shed light on how he subtly exercised control, both in personal interactions and throughout the Mormon kingdom. As one visitor to Salt Lake City reflected in 1874: "I noticed that he never seemed uninterested, but gave an unforced attention to the person addressing him which suggested a mind free from care. I used to fancy that he wasted a great deal of power in this way; but I soon saw that he was accumulating it. Power, I mean, at least as the driving-wheel of his people's industry."[30] And as one ex-Mormon wrote in 1857, echoing the above comments about John Humphrey Noyes almost exactly: "So universally is this unseen power felt, although very seldom traced, that it has become a very common saying among the faithful Mormons at Salt Lake, 'When I obey counsel, every thing prospers with me; when I neglect it, I prosper in nothing.'"[31] As with Noyes, Young's real genius for controlling people was his ability to hide the fact that he was controlling people.

So how did Brigham Young maintain control? He and John Humphrey Noyes had strong personalities but they presided over profoundly different circumstances. Noyes had only three hundred followers at most, who after 1854 were gathered primarily into his community at Oneida. Young had tens of thousands of Mormons spread out over hundreds of square miles of intermountain territory. How did he rule? The quick and facile answer is that the Saints wanted to be controlled. "The strength of Mormonism consists in the 'blind obedience' of its disciples," one apostate complained.[32] But as the rest of this chapter seeks to make clear, a far more accurate, although complicated, answer can be found in the unique culture and structure of Mormonism at the time.

It takes both care and charity to explain the populist dynamics at work in Mormonism. Nineteenth-century anti-Mormons of course had neither. "The whole secret lies in that one world, fanaticism," apostate John Hyde seethed in 1857: "The engine of Mormon power is not brute force; not attempted or threatened violence, but the lever of a skillfully-combined and ably handled system of religious machinery, operating on duped and bewildered fanatics. They feel its force, are not able to explain or investigate and discern its reality, but supinely obey its impulses."[33] Another outsider described the Saints as being "divided into the leaders and the led; ... unprincipled men of talents ... [and] the credulous, wondering part of men."[34] Such statements are highly unfair, depicting the whole faith community as a sham in which the wily few manipulate and swindle the gullible, fanatical many. The biggest problem is with terms like "unprincipled," "credulous," "duped and bewildered"; but not necessarily with the division of Saints "into the leaders and the led." The structure of the LDS Church is undeniably hierarchical. The First President presides over a massive bureaucracy and expects deference to his initiatives. There is, in other words, no system of checks and balances. Unsurprisingly, a personality like Brigham Young's would only exacerbate the autocratic features of this structure, "the several quorums being the mere instruments of his will," one outsider observed.[35]

The culture of Mormonism, however, is simultaneously hierarchical and egalitarian. Excepting the First President, all Latter-day Saints are equal as brothers and sisters in Christ. They are also both "the leaders and the led," invested with power over others within the hierarchy but also subservient to those above them. The tradeoff was that in order to be empowered *by* the institution and advance within it, one has to submit *to* the institution. A person (exclusively men) could not have the former without the latter. Thus Lieutenant Gunnison, although an outsider, was much closer to the truth when he wrote: "Nor must we look upon all as ignorant and blindfolded, guided along the ditch of enthusiasm by self-deluded leaders. Indeed almost every man is a priest, or eligible to the office, and ready armed for the controversial warfare; ... And among that people, so submissive to counsel, are those who watch with eagle eye that first principles are adhered to, and stand ready to proclaim apostacy [sic] in chief or in layman."[36] Gunnison did not deny that many Saints were "so submissive to counsel," but he accurately identified the reason for their obedience. Rather than the "ignorant" tools of "self-deluded leaders," rank-and-file Saints were empowered: "every man is a priest," Gunnison wrote, a holy warrior, and a doctrinal policeman. As the Mormon historians Leonard Arrington and Davis Bitton perceptively describe it: "very real power ... became increasingly available to Latter-day Saints through Mormonism's nearly universal male priesthood.... Those powers filtered down in varying degrees to the mass of the priesthood." Rather than being concentrated into a few hands, power was liberally shared—although closely monitored—from the top of the hierarchy to the bottom. Average Saints therefore felt empowered rather than powerless, while leaders' real control existed in their ability to dispense that power to others.[37]

Mormons' ongoing sense of empowerment, however, required ongoing submission within the Church's hierarchy. As biographer John G. Turner brilliantly describes it, the phrase "'Mind Your Own Business'" became the "'Mormon Creed'" in the 1850s, the Church's "'eleventh commandment,'" and "Young's golden rule."[38] If Saints trusted their leaders and sacrificed for the good of the whole, the entire Church—themselves included—would benefit. If they did not, they could jeopardize the kingdom-building project and would inevitably suffer the wrath of that project's director, Brigham Young.

When exhortations to sacrifice for the common good were not enough, however, Young often used fear to keep people in line. "Brigham was our spiritual guide," one famous apostate wrote; "it might be that in refusing him I should lose all hopes of future salvation. That was my mother's plea. My father's was, that Brigham was able to hurt him pecuniarily. And then came my brother, who added . . . that Brigham had it in his power to ruin him, and was very angry with him, and had threatened to 'cut him off from the church.'"[39] In this case, the whole family risked earthly and eternal ruin if the daughter refused Young's marriage proposal. And in plenty of other instances, critical but nervous Saints ultimately toed the line. As another apostate reported: "I clearly saw that many of the most devoted brethren around Brigham Young did not approve of much that he said and did; but their observations were always tempered with a fear of 'meddling with the servant of the Lord.' There is, indeed, a dread in the soul of every good Mormon of entertaining any doubts about their leaders, or criticizing in any way whatever they might think proper to do or say."[40] In the nineteenth century, the Saints' obedience came out of a complex combination of piety, self-interest, and fear.

The institution of plural marriage was yet another means by which Young controlled the Saints. For starters, all marriages, plural or not, had to receive their ultimate approval from him. The Quorum of the Twelve had granted Young the power to seal celestial marriages in 1846 as the Saints were leaving Nauvoo, and he guarded it jealously for the rest of his life.[41]

Young also used the institution of plural marriage to create a Mormon elite. In many ways, polygamy became a kind of sectarian status symbol, indicating one's devotion to Latter-day beliefs, leaders, and collective projects. Those hoping to climb Utah's intertwined ecclesiastical and social ladders first had to be admitted to the club of polygamists. As historian Davis Bitton summed up: "Between 1852 and 1890 it is clear that if one was not a polygamist at the time of being elevated to the hierarchy, he almost inevitably soon succumbed to the pressure to take plural wives."[42]

It turns out that appealing to people's ambition—both worldly and otherworldly—was an effective and subtle means of control. "Mormonism teaches that all salvation is *material*," John Hyde wrote, reinforcing a major theme of this book: "That men's positions here determine their stations hereafter."[43] All "good Mormon brethren," Ann Eliza Young clarified, "intended to build up a 'celestial kingdom' after the 'divinely ordained plan,'" but "if he could not rule his earthly kingdom, he never would be fit to be a king in the world to come."[44] As for women, another ex-Mormon explained: "One of the most popular axioms of the elders at the time was, 'It is better to be the mate of a ship of war than the captain of a schooner.' This was well understood by the sisters to mean that it was better to be *one* of the wives of a *great* man in 'the kingdom,' than to be the *only* wife of a little man."[45] Worldly and heavenly status were indissolubly linked. If one were either "a little man" or married to one while on earth, so would it be for eternity. Both men and women therefore had a self-interested motivation to achieve as much in this world as they possibly could so it would transfer into everlasting rewards in the afterlife. For men this meant accumulating property, church offices, and wives; for women it meant being sealed to "a *great* man in 'the kingdom.'"

Brigham Young unabashedly promoted this kind of celestial-marital social climbing. In 1861 he even made clear that it was permissible for a married woman to divorce and "upgrad[e]" her status by remarrying a man better positioned in the Church's hierarchy. "If a woman can find a man holding the keys of the priesthood with higher power and authority than her [current] husband," he wrote, "and he is disposed to take her[,] he can do so, otherwise she has got to remain where she is." Similarly, for unmarried women, Young encouraged the "young sisters" to dream big, and "go into the hands of a man, that will lead you into the kingdom of heaven, and exalt you there to become an Eve—a queen of heaven—the wife of a god."[46] To say the least, the social, religious, and psychological pressures on Utah Saints must have been extreme. What comes next is an exploration of the time when those pressures were at their most extreme, the Mormon Reformation of 1856–57.

13
Revival

EVANGELICAL REVIVALISM has a long and controversial history in America. It stretches back to the Great Awakening of the mid-eighteenth century and reached white-hot intensity during the Second Great Awakening of the early nineteenth century. Since then, revivals have been a constant if episodic feature of the American cultural milieu, and are routinely disparaged for their emotionalism and anti-institutionalism. Advocates for revivalism are typically Janus-faced: calling believers to return to a tradition's first principles, and willing to endure short-term disruptions in order to restore that tradition to a purer version of itself. As this chapter will illustrate, some of these patterns hold true for revivals among the Mormons, Shakers, and Oneida Perfectionists, while others do not.

The phenomenon of revivalism is different for sectarians than it is for evangelicals. For the sake of simplicity, I would like to define revivals as identifiable periods during which religious authorities more earnestly call people to adopt and live out their particular beliefs about God and God's kingdom.[1] This begs some important questions, however, about who constitutes the "called" and who is doing the calling, and reveals some of the differences between evangelical and sectarian revivalism more clearly. For evangelicals, the "called" are both outside and inside of the church, with revivals serving the dual purpose of proselytizing the unconverted and rejuvenating the faith of lukewarm believers—thus the term *revival*. In contrast, revivals among Mormons and Shakers were focused exclusively inwardly. (As will be explained shortly, the Oneida Perfectionists are a different story.) Mormons and Shakers definitely engaged in missionary activity in an effort to win converts, but that was a separate endeavor. During their periods of revival, Mormon and Shaker authorities admonished fellow sectarians to make their latent and nominal faith more active and central to their identities.

The internally focused nature of Mormon and Shaker revivals brings up some other salient differences with evangelical revivalism. Evangelicals often intend for their revivals to have two interrelated goals: win individual souls for Christ and positively impact the broader culture. They are therefore both intensely personal and wildly ambitious, often hoping to alter the destiny of entire nations by changing the hearts and consciences of their humble listeners.

The sectarian revivalists investigated here had no such grand ambitions. While they could control what went on within the confines of their own faith communities, they knew that changing the corrupt world they had abandoned was beyond their power. Alienated from and at odds with American culture, they focused instead on getting their sectarian houses in order, hoping to purify the larger community one believer at a time. Thus in many ways revivalism among Mormons and Shakers looked the same as revivalism among evangelicals, complete with heightened emotions, earnest preaching, and intensely personal appeals. But if they had similar techniques or means, they had very different—sectarian rather than culturally transformative—ends.

Also unlike evangelicals, Mormons and Shakers had powerful internal governing structures through which they could officially channel and encourage their sect's revivalistic energies. Evangelicals' impact on American culture comes from the fact that they would regularly leave the insular confines of their particular churches, set aside their denominational rivalries, and engage the public sphere directly as a mobilized and semi-united front. The crucial difference with sectarian revivals comes from the fact that these new evangelical converts were far freer to choose their affiliations and move around than was the average Mormon Saint or Shaker Believer. With so many options in the evangelical religious marketplace and with no real disciplinary power in individual denominations to bind them, spiritual consumers could easily leave one church for another when the one they initially joined displeased them. Thus when it comes to power, evangelical churches experienced a paradoxical tradeoff: individually they were weak; collectively, however, they exerted profound cultural influence.

The opposite was the case for the Mormons and the Shakers. On the one hand, they had almost no ability to influence American culture, while on the other hand they did have powerful institutional means to control the movements and the actions of their members. People of course did leave, sometimes writing damning exposés of their experiences after they had done so, but most of those who were in, were in, and would wholeheartedly subject themselves to the sect's leadership and discipline. Revivalism within any religious community, however, is an incredibly powerful force—one that can either fortify an existing power structure or challenge it. As we will see, revivalism for the Mormons bolstered the hierarchy's control. For the Shakers revivalism threatened the control of the leadership at first but was effectively managed in the end. In both cases, however, these periods of revival ultimately succeeded at reinforcing sectarian identity and distinctiveness by forcing members to re-encounter the group's founding principles. These principles put Mormon Saints and Shaker Believers at odds with the outside world and made them turn more intently inward, reaffirming not only their commitment to their unique sexual beliefs and practices, but also to their equally unique sectarian communities.

Interestingly, John Humphrey Noyes, who back in 1831 had "vowed to live in the 'revival spirit,' and be a 'young convert' forever,"[2] did not encourage revivalism at Oneida until the very end of the Community's existence. That exception to the general antirevival rule was led by two members from evangelical backgrounds and came in late 1876, at a time when the Community was deteriorating and collective spiritual energies were waning. Although Noyes first encouraged the revivalists, they quickly overstepped their bounds, judging the unrevived "for infidelity and worldliness," including Noyes himself. Noyes took this to be the assault on his leadership that it was, "'became convinced that the revival was being conducted in a disorganizing spirit and that the time had come to call a halt. Accordingly, on April 3,'" 1877, he had them shut down.[3]

This dalliance with revivalism at Oneida, although brief, late, and somewhat inconsequential, nevertheless reinforces two points about the phenomenon that will be illustrated in greater detail in the cases of the Shakers and Mormons. The first is that revivalism is a convenient means of addressing a community's spiritual demoralization. Both the Mormons and the Shakers used revivals as a way to boost the flagging spiritual interests of rank-and-file sectarians. The second point is that revivals are often unwieldy forces, slipping out of the grasp of their original handlers and potentially threatening the institutions they were intended to reinforce.

As for why the Oneidans did not experience a revival until 1876, the best answer is that prior to that time they had neither the external promptings to motivate them nor the internal resources to carry one out. After 1852 things were going relatively well for the Perfectionists, both materially and spiritually. The trap manufacturing business was expanding, the lawsuits were behind them, John Humphrey Noyes had moved back to Oneida in 1854 to lead the community, and the mechanism of mutual criticism effectively kept selfishness and interpersonal conflict in check. Perfectionism was also an ideas-driven rather than an emotions-driven faith. Although his ideas were radical, Noyes had always led with his mind, and apparently so did the people he attracted to Oneida. The possibility of a Perfectionist revival was therefore about as unlikely as that of a revival among Unitarians or Episcopalians. Those flames simply could not climb high enough up the American socio-religious ladder, and apparently Noyes did not need them to.

In contrast, the Utah Saints, who were also driven more by ideas than by emotion, did experience a period of revival. Called the "Mormon Reformation" by both contemporaries and later historians, this chapter of LDS history lasted for approximately ten months in 1856 and 1857, and was initiated by Brigham Young, who had become concerned about the Saints' lack of spiritual fervor. He wanted migrants to continue streaming into the territory to boost its numbers, but he also insisted that they be proper Saints: ardent in their devotion to the Church and obedient to its leaders. If spiritually immature newcomers and lukewarm old-timers became the majority, the kingdom would disintegrate from within. Thus in the spring of 1856 he planted the seeds of revival—instructing Church leaders to prepare the Saints for repentance—and that autumn began to reap a harvest that is unique in early LDS history.[4]

Young had admonished and berated the Saints plenty of times before, but this season was different, thanks in large part to the work of Jedediah Grant. By all accounts Grant was a severe, no-nonsense alpha male. Tall and a gifted speaker, he replaced the slain Joseph Smith as the president of the Quorum of the Seventy, he unwaveringly supported Young against his challengers, and once in Utah he served as the mayor of Salt Lake City. On April 7, 1854, Young elevated him as far up the Church hierarchy as possible, making him a counselor in the First Presidency, and in 1856 he entrusted Grant with the reins of the Mormon Reformation. That spring Young initiated what John G. Turner describes as "a 'home missionary' program to monitor and improve the morals and spirituality of the people."[5] That summer, Utah Saints increasingly sensed that some kind of spiritual momentum was building and that it was coming, as usual, from the top.

The dam broke at a meeting of home missionaries and other Church leaders in mid-September 1856. Brigham Young was not present, but what Jedidiah Grant said and accomplished there had his full support.

Basically, Grant excoriated the attendees for their lack of faith and admonished them, using Young's words, to "live your religion." As leaders, Grant enjoined, they should repent of their spiritual laxity, be rebaptized, renew their commitments to personal purity and kingdom work, and then go forth into their various communities to preach the same. Those present got the message loud and clear, and did exactly what Grant asked them to do. For the next several months these home missionaries and Jedidiah Grant himself spread the spirit of renewal throughout the kingdom. When calls to repent and recommit did not yield enough fruit, speakers sometimes used shame, singling out individuals and their sins for special attention. In early November Grant codified his understanding of virtuous Mormon living into a catechism of probing personal questions. Among other things, respondents were asked whether they had lied, coveted, committed adultery, gotten drunk, paid their tithes, and bathed regularly. Taking on an almost inquisitorial air, home missionaries would read this now standardized list of questions to individuals, families, and wards throughout the realm, imposing if not a renewed zeal among the Saints then at least a heightened expectation of moral conformity.[6]

The fires of the Mormon Reformation burned intensely but briefly. In early December 1856, just two-and-a-half months after having begun in earnest, it literally suffered a mortal blow. Jedidiah Grant died, worn out from the ardor of his own preaching, and possibly from pneumonia that he contracted while performing so many rebaptisms in increasingly cold streams. The program that he championed continued on without him, especially in the form of the catechism he authored, but its days were numbered. Without its most powerful animating force, the Mormon Reformation gradually lost steam, and in the summer of 1857 was eclipsed by potential war with the United States. Its effects upon the Utah Saints, however, were powerful, long lasting, and impossible for some to expunge from their memories. In other words, for many people the Mormon Reformation was actually traumatic.[7]

The doctrine of blood atonement was foremost among those traumatizing developments. While the idea had originated with Brigham Young years earlier, during the Mormon Reformation it received new life and widespread attention. On October 1 Jedidiah Grant proclaimed the doctrine in the pages of the *Deseret News,* opining that for some sinners rebaptism would not be enough. Instead, they "need to have their blood shed where water will not do, their sins are of too deep a dye."[8] Heinous offenders such as murderers, adulterers, and—most frighteningly—apostates were considered beyond the reach of Christ's atonement and could hope for reconciliation with God only through the shedding of their own blood. To say the least, this kind of rhetoric bolstered the omnipotence of the Mormon hierarchy and terrified many of the Saints. The personal process of introspection, conviction, repentance, and rebaptism was one thing. The possibility of state-sponsored executions for religious infractions or disbelief was another. Thankfully, the Church did not turn this possibility into any kind of organized practice, but the doctrine of blood atonement undeniably created a culture that sanctioned violence. On October 29, a bishop in Manti had a criminal castrated and left for dead while he was being transported to prison. Rather than removing the bishop from his position, Young sustained him, clearly condoning the action. That winter Young also authorized vigilantism whenever the wheels of justice turned too slowly, leading to one case of attempted murder and another instance in which assassins killed three men trying to flee the territory. The Mormon Reformation's rhetoric of blood atonement dramatically shifted the boundary of what was acceptable behavior. Good Mormons could now kill in the name of the Lord.[9]

Given this context of heightened emotions and sectarian pride, it is not at all surprising that Mormon leaders pushed plural marriage as a way for Saints to "live their religion" and separate themselves further from the world. Infused with the spirit of the Reformation, Young, Grant, and their cadre of home missionaries rebuked ordinary Saints for not living the principle, considering it a sin of omission that prevented an untold number of unborn spirits from inhabiting their earthly tabernacles. As one apostate recollected: "'Build up the kingdom! Build up the kingdom!' has been drummed into their ears till all good sense and propriety were driven out of their heads."[10] But most importantly, emphasizing duty and sacrifice, these leaders told their listeners that plural marriage was the most obvious way to demonstrate a renewed faith and distinguish themselves from lukewarm believers. A real Saint, in other words, would be a polygamous Saint. Once again, sex and sectarianism were interlinked.

By all accounts, the pressure, the guilt, and the appeals to ambition worked; but it was incredibly traumatic for many Utah men, women, and children. "The 'Reformation' was productive of nothing but evil," apostate Ann Eliza Young wrote. It was, as she and another former plural wife put it, "A Reign of Terror."[11] While histrionic, these statements are not outright falsehoods. A kind of polygamous mania seized people throughout the territory. Mormon scholar Stanley S. Ivins famously wrote that during the Reformation "plural marriages skyrocketed to a height not before approached and never again to be reached . . . [resulting in] sixty-five per cent more of such marriages during 1856 and 1857 than in any other two years of this experiment."[12] "Nearly all are trying to get wives," Wilford Woodruff wrote, "until there is hardly a girl 14 years old in Utah, but what is married, or just going to be."[13] Unmarried women and girls became precious commodities, with eager polygamous men expanding their search for wives far down into the ranks of Utah's teenagers. In one case, Brigham Young authorized a man to marry a thirteen-year-old, but horrifyingly had to counsel him to "preserve her intact until she is fully developed into Womanhood."[14] For those Saints who found such practices morally reprehensible, the Mormon Reformation was indeed "productive of nothing but evil."

For those who entered polygamy as reluctant but dutiful Saints, the effects of the Mormon Reformation were equally problematic. In the midst of the enthusiasm one such unenthusiastic woman wrote to another: "if the reformation has taken as much effect where you are, . . . and [if] your husband is a true Saint, I might possibly be obliged to send the comforting words of 'grin and bear it' to you. . . . Indeed this is the greatest time for marrying I ever knew."[15] This is a brilliantly revealing couple of sentences. Although anecdotal it nevertheless corroborates Ivins's claim about the Mormon Reformation's being the high point of polygamous unions in LDS history. It also clearly illustrates two of the most important preconditions for a man to become a polygamist at this time: the zeal of the Reformation, and whether or not the man considered himself to be "a true Saint." Finally, and most depressingly, it shows the stoicism with which some Mormon women faced the possibility of becoming a plural wife: "'grin and bear it.'"

From start to finish and from top to bottom the concept of duty was central to the Mormon Reformation. The fires of revivalism did not break out spontaneously among rank-and-file Saints in some obscure corner of Zion. The program of renewal that became known as the Reformation originated first in the mind of the Church's president and was then systematically implemented through the Church's hierarchy. It took a while to assemble all the necessary ingredients to initiate combustion—from spring to September 1856—but once the fire started it spread quickly, thanks to the meticulous preparation of the home missionaries. These functionaries obeyed their leaders out of a sense of religious duty and their listeners obeyed them for precisely the same reason.

Jedidiah Grant, who earned for himself the nickname "Brigham's sledgehammer," let his driving sense of duty drive him into an early grave. Likewise, some renewed and rededicated Saints let their sense of duty drive them into polygamy.

One final point needs to be made before turning to the Shakers: the difference between Brigham Young's plural marriage of 1857 and Joseph Smith's plural marriage of 1842. Both the LDS Church and this institution had changed significantly over those fifteen years. The Utah Saints practiced plural marriage openly and had since 1852. But while revealing the secret had liberated them from having to hide their marital arrangements, it does not seem to have brought them much joy. Living the principle was a sacrifice and a religious duty, plain and simple. It was such a sacrifice, in fact, that average Mormons needed prodding from their leaders to enter into it. As Ivins aptly concluded: "It is evident that, far from looking upon plural marriage as a privilege to be made the most of, the rank and file Mormons accepted it as one of the onerous obligations of church membership. Left alone, they were prone to neglect it, and it always took some form of pressure to stir them to renewed zeal."[16] Mormonism had changed greatly since 1842 and plural marriage was both an indication and a cause of that change. Gone were the predominantly optimistic, expansive days of Joseph Smith. The predominant authoritative voice of Mormonism during the Reformation—Jedidiah Grant—was almost Smith's opposite: a stern, humorless enforcer of discipline and author of catechisms, who dutifully passed down the chain of command the order from his superior: "Live your religion."

The Shakers' revival, in contrast, was decidedly more bottom-up than top down, and was at least somewhat more joyful. This "Era of Manifestations," as it was later called, lasted from 1837 into the late 1840s, and is arguably the most well known chapter in the history of the United Society of Believers. Its dramatic inauguration is especially well known. "On the 16th of August, 1837," at the village at Watervliet, one Shaker source recollects, "a new era commenced in the society.... Some of the little children, who were learning to sing and to read, were suddenly entranced." These girls, ages ten to fourteen, experienced "visions, trances, revelations and communications from the spirit world."[17] Historian Stephen Stein points out that the "fundamental concept of gift had never disappeared from the Shaker religious consciousness," and that "experiential spirituality," such as visions and dreams, had always been a part of Shaker praxis.[18] The manifestations of 1837 were therefore nothing new. What made this chapter different was the frequency and the intensity of the visions, and—more importantly—the attention they received. Word spread of the outpourings of the spirit, and the girls' ecstatic worship quickly became a spectacle, first for the other families at Watervliet and then for Believers from neighboring villages. Taken in trances they would then describe for those assembled their unique experiences of the spirit world, including visions of heaven or hell. Other times their visions took them to a parallel spiritual universe, a kind of mirror image of their familiar worldly environment, complete with the usual buildings, but populated with angels and deceased Believers with whom they interacted. As one Shaker put it: "Our trance goers would sometimes be absent for hours together, and on their return, relate their travels on the 'other side,' which to us were intensely interesting. They visited beautiful mansions and saw the angel inmates."[19]

One girl in particular, Anna Mariah Goff, claimed to be in contact with Mother Ann Lee herself. In a succession of visions Goff had in November 1837, Lee led her on a tour of spiritual Watervliet and told her that Believers should repent and humble themselves, for a day of judgment loomed. The Lord would allow the evil world to have its way with those lacking faith, while Mother would deliver the faithful through the refining fires. One's measure of repentance and devotion, the vision warned, would determine one's fate. As word of Goff's visions spread, crowds of Believers from other villages traveled to Watervliet to participate in the increasingly ecstatic and lengthy worship meetings, hoping that the spirit would touch them too. Sometimes they would take that spark back to their home villages, and sometimes villages would spontaneously combust with visions and gifts of their own. But regardless of the source, by 1838 the Shaker revival known as the Era of Manifestations was on, with whole villages in the East and the West partaking of its energies.[20]

During worship, Believers experienced various manifestations of the spirit. They convulsed, spoke in tongues, and communicated with the dead, all of which are among the more "conventional" practices of charismatic worship. Over time, however, some of the manifestations became rather unique and even more dramatic. In keeping with the Shaker tradition of gift, Believers began receiving not only messages from the spirit world, but things as well. Operating through a medium, or "instrument" as they were known, spirits would bestow precious—although invisible—objects to worthy beneficiaries. "Many beautiful presents were given by spirit friends," Henry Clay Blinn described, "robes, wreaths, satin slippers, handkerchiefs," for example.[21] Some worship services thus became a kind of exercise in make-believe, or "elaborate mime" to use Stephen Stein's term, with the instrument acting as the principal giver and the rest of those assembled the eager recipients.[22]

Outsiders and apostates unsurprisingly lampooned these practices as folly. David R. Lamson, the bitter former Believer, described "what they call a real free and lively meeting" as "the consummation of all silly actions and speeches." Sometimes Mother Ann Lee would be present, dispensing "'bright balls'" to the worshippers. "The inspired one receives these balls of Mother's love, and tosses them out to the brethren, and sisters, who hold out their hands and catch them. Sometimes St. Paul is present, Peter, and others of the apostles."[23] Stranger still, these deceased visitors also included prominent historical figures. Revolutionary-era generals George Washington and Lafayette made semi-regular appearances, as did the Indian princess Pocahontas. "We were visited by all the different nations," Blinn wrote. "Kings and Queens came—some to be instructed, and others to administer for our benefit." It is unclear why these "worldly" people entered into the collective imagination of an otherworldly sect, but the Believers nevertheless appreciated their presence. "Under the influence of the Indian spirits they would shout and dance, and then give their war-whoop," Blinn wrote. "Some acted precisely the peculiar traits of the negro, the Arab, the Chinese or even the politeness of the French. They conversed, and each class seemed to understand their own company, but to the spectators it was peculiarly amusing."[24]

The Shakers' revivalistic energies peaked in the early 1840s. In 1841 "Holy Mother Wisdom, the female aspect of the deity," began to visit the Believers in worship.[25] In early 1842, because of the solemnity of Holy Mother Wisdom's presence, Shaker leaders decided to restrict meetings to Believers only. They wanted to protect the privacy of the worshippers and eliminate the possibility of scornful onlookers. Their worship was meant to be serious and not a spectacle for the curious.

By the late-1840s, those energies were burning themselves out, "which left us," Blinn nostalgically reminisced, "in a barren, and almost despondent condition of mind."[26] The Era of Manifestations was coming to a close, but its termination is not as easy to identify as its commencement. In some villages, Shakers tired of the manifestations early or suffered the devastating apostasies of some of their most active instruments. Believers did not know how to respond when such prominent guides to the spirit world stopped guiding them, left the village, or lost the faith. In these cases they had become sheep without any revivalistic shepherds.

This brings us back to the concept of "callers" and "called" in revivals generally, and brings up some of the most important comparisons between the Mormon Reformation and the Shaker Era of Manifestations. In both, the "called" were exclusively members of the group. As such they were being asked to revitalize their lukewarm sectarian faith, reaffirm their sectarian identity, and recommit themselves to their sectarian community. The fact that the Saints referred to the main functionaries of the Reformation as "home missionaries" and the fact that in 1842 the Shaker leadership restricted access to worship meetings to Believers testifies to the inward-focused nature of these revivals.

The main difference between the two has to do with the "callers." The Mormon Reformation was top-down from start to finish whereas the Era of Manifestations was, for the most part, bottom up. The Reformation began with Brigham Young's dissatisfaction with his Saints' lukewarm faith, was executed through the ministrations of his loyal lieutenant Jedidiah Grant and a cadre of deputized "home missionaries," and ended not long after Grant died. The Era of Manifestations began with the trances and visions of a handful of pubescent girls—hardly the most powerful members of the United Society of Believers.

The original "callers," therefore, were not members of the established hierarchy, which put Shaker leaders in a bind. As Henry Clay Blinn reminded readers: "Mother Ann Lee, the founder of Shakerism, enjoyed visions in her childhood, and right along through her life."[27] Thus when the girls at Watervliet began having visions of their own in August 1837, they were participating in a venerable Shaker family tradition. Those visions, however, created problems for the Shaker leadership by potentially challenging their authority in the name of an even higher authority. In this time of religious enthusiasm, spiritual gifts bestowed upon the relatively powerless could undermine the control of those at the top. Soon after the girls' visions attracted attention, Shaker leader Rufus Bishop observed them and concluded that they were in fact from the Lord, although he also warned the instruments that their gifts "must be used to support union and order within the society."[28]

If the Shaker hierarchy gave free rein to the charismatic instruments they would risk diminishing their own authority. If they silenced or clamped down on the visionaries they would be undermining some of the most fundamental aspects of their sectarian faith: visions, gifts, and ongoing revelations. Their only option was to try to control the revival's energies, a task that they ultimately accomplished through a variety of mechanisms. They began by requiring the instruments to relay their trance experiences to elders and eldresses before sharing them with the rest of the village, thereby vetting them. They also encouraged village leaders to counsel young instruments regularly, and they actively promoted more mature Believers into positions of leadership to balance out their enthusiasm with some wisdom.

Unlike the evangelical revivals of the mid-eighteenth and early nineteenth centuries, which splintered Protestants into competing denominations, in this revival the United Society of Believers remained united. As with the Mormons who controlled their Reformation entirely, the Shakers were able to maintain control during theirs, and even use it to their advantage. In both cases sectarian identity, community, and power were key—elements that were entirely absent from the Awakenings. Evangelicalism also had no overarching hierarchy to counteract their revivals' rampant energies, resulting in institutional chaos. Brigham Young could order Saints through his chain of command to "Live your religion," and they obeyed. Similarly, Shaker leaders could exert pressure on the Era of Manifestation's instruments and keep their energies in check. The visionaries and the hierarchy coexisted awkwardly, but they coexisted nonetheless. For a while, one group was the Society's driving force, while the other succeeded in steering it.

One crucial tension that intensified in both sectarian revivals was the tension between men and women. Although Shakers believed in the equality of the sexes, this belief was imperfectly lived during the Era of Manifestations. In the revivals male leaders worked especially hard to control the enthusiasm of their predominantly female visionaries: they promoted more men into leadership positions, and they even reasserted the theological importance of the male divinity. Holy Mother Wisdom appeared in 1841 to visit and bless the Believers. Later that year Almighty Father also appeared, restoring gender balance to the cosmos and to their Society.[29]

Ironically, it is possible that Brigham Young was more egalitarian during his revival than the Shakers were during theirs. In his case, however, he was an equal-opportunity castigator. It was during this time that Young famously chastised plural wives to "round up their shoulders to endure the afflictions of this world, and live their religion, or they may leave."[30] The next chapter will explore whether this was the exception in Mormon plural marriage or the rule, and will explore more generally what gender roles were like in Mormon polygamy, Shaker celibacy, and Perfectionist complex marriage.

14
Gender

THE PREVIOUS chapter on "Revival" concluded by asking whether Brigham Young's admonition that women "round up their shoulders" and accept their lot in life was the exception for Mormon gender relations or the rule.[1] In other words, was this harsh language just another extreme expression fitting the extreme times of the Mormon Reformation, or was its content indicative of broader and more enduring patterns within nineteenth-century Mormonism? As this chapter will show, Young's chastisement of Utah's unhappy plural wives was far more the rule than it was the exception.

The reason for Mormon women's nearly powerless status has to do with the particularities of the Mormon metanarrative and the institutional structures that were built to perpetuate it. According to this story, all human beings on earth are in their probationary state, suspended between premortality and a hierarchical afterlife in which they will, if worthy, spend eternity as exalted royalty in the celestial kingdom. The problem with this eternal prospect—or its beauty depending on how one looks at it—is that no one can experience exaltation alone. One has to be eternally sealed to a partner in the ordinance of celestial marriage. Thus men and women need one another to progress to this highest eternal status, a theology that holds out the prospect of egalitarianism between husband and wife, man and woman.

In practice, however, Mormonism in the nineteenth century was profoundly disempowering for women, especially if they were plural wives—a point outsiders and apostates stressed constantly. "In my opinion, Mormonism is not a religion for women," wrote William Hepworth Dixon, a Briton who traveled to Utah in the 1860s. "I will not say that it degrades her, . . . but it certainly lowers her, according to our Gentile ideas, in the social scale. In fact, woman is not in society here at all."[2] "The dominant principle of Mormonism is marriage," ex-Saint Fanny Stenhouse wrote, and the sole purpose of women in marriage was to bear children—"to encourage an increase of 'the kingdom,'" rather than "to seek the personal happiness of the married pair." Thus "the younger the girl is, the better," Stenhouse continued. "An unmarried girl in Utah is old at twenty, and it is rarely the case that any attractive girl passes out of her teens before she is wedded." "To bestow these tabernacles is the highest glory of woman," another outsider observed, "and her exaltation in eternity will be in exact proportion to the number she has furnished."[3]

Latter-day authorities taught these principles unapologetically. Orson Pratt warned women: "you can never obtain a fulness of glory without being married to a righteous man for time and for all eternity."[4] From the pulpit, Brigham Young similarly rained duty, guilt, and fear down on his female listeners, and not just during the Mormon Reformation. "The Tabernacle in winter, and the Bowery in summer, were to resound with the arguments in favour of Polygamy," one ex-Mormon reported.[5]

The cumulative effect of this unremitting message was disempowering and psychologically crippling for many women. "Seeing polygamy constantly practiced, and hearing submission constantly preached," ex-Mormon John Hyde wrote in 1857, "she sinks, and to sink is to be lost." "They have been previously made to believe that woman can not obtain any kind of salvation but through the man," Hyde added, "and that these men are God's vicegerents; they swallow the gilded bait, marry, and when they wake up to the temporal miseries of their position, console themselves in more dogmatically believing their fanaticism and their creed.... To marry this old, well-proven, and sealed man, would not only secure her own salvation but that of her children."[6] As another anti-Mormon put it, polygamy "robs married life of all its sweet sentiment and companionship; and while it degrades woman, it brutalizes man, teaching him to despise and domineer over his wives, over all women."[7] Like slavery, many critics were quick to point out, plural marriage's interpersonal dynamics made tyrants out of the powerful and wretches out of the powerless.

When plural wives complained, they were met with a combination of ridicule, smug patriarchy, and the threat of abuse. "Wife-whipping is not uncommon in Utah," one exposé reported.[8] Another anti-Mormon polemic told the story of a wife who knew her husband was going to beat her as soon as they got home. "Bishop Scott had just said in his sermon, 'If your wives do not obey you, beat them till they do; they will soon give in.' I was so unfortunate as to disobey my husband this morning and he is very angry with me. I saw him looking significantly at me when the bishop made that remark; I shall get a cruel beating—and I suppose I had better hurry along and take it—it will be the sooner over."[9] While occasionally exaggerated or sensationalized, these outsiders' accusations were not imaginary. Things like Mormon "harems" were made up by deceitful writers for salacious consumption. Women's relative powerlessness within Mormon society and the emotional trauma they experienced as plural wives, however, is historically substantiated and not the product of a polemicist's bias.

Ann Eliza Young, the plural wife of Brigham Young who divorced him and published her story, broadcast a number of vivid and disturbing images. In addition to her brilliant description of Brigham's "sinister smile, which . . . meant, 'Do as I command you, or suffer the weight of my displeasure,'" she likewise described her ex-husband's "indifferent, matter-of-fact manner, tinged with a 'help-it-if-you-can' air, which most Mormon men assume towards their helpless wives." Men simply had all the power in the Great Basin kingdom, and women had virtually none. "When women go to Brigham Young," she wrote in yet another perfectly described and revealing scene, "and tell him of their unhappiness, and ask his advice, he whines, and pretends to cry, and mimics them, until they are fairly outraged by his heartless treatment. . . . They may consider themselves fortunate, indeed, if he does not refer to the interview in his next Sunday sermon, and tell the names of the unhappy women, with coarse jests and unfeeling comments."[10] It is hard to imagine a less pastoral interaction, but then again Brigham Young was not exactly known for his pastoral tenderness. One gets the picture instead of a barrel-chested patriarch at the height of his influence, shifting into a sardonic, high-pitched "girlie" voice as he mocks the hapless woman into submission. The fact that in some instances he continued his mockery publicly from the pulpit only adds further insult. An unhappy woman in Utah had neither power nor recourse. If she wanted a different kind of life, she would have to do what Ann Eliza Young did—leave the territory. As William Hepworth Dixon had put it so well: "woman is not in society here at all."[11]

Aside from the obvious power discrepancy between men and women, it is difficult to generalize about life in plural marriage because there were so few social norms—even in isolated Utah, and even at the height of the Church's practice of polygamy. As historian Richard S. Van Wagoner perceptibly notes, "Mormon polygamy, unlike plural marriage in other cultures, developed rapidly and without long-term cultural shaping. . . . Courtship manners were not well established, . . . rules of wooing depended on the individuals involved," and "no set patterns of living arrangements evolved."[12] Jessie L. Embry, another historian of Mormon plural marriage, reinforces Van Wagoner's point with exactly the same language, using the term "no set patterns" regularly throughout her study. "As in all aspects of Mormon polygamy," she writes, "no set patterns developed as to where wives lived and how often husbands visited." Similarly, she adds, "with no pattern of how they should treat a co-wife, the wives used relationships from their Euro-American background to define their activities, including mother-daughter (if there was an age difference), friends, and most commonly, sisters."[13] The Saints had religious sanction to implement their unique marital system, but they had absolutely no authoritative guide for how to live it out, from tradition, historical example, or scriptural admonitions.

Polygamous Saints literally had to make it up as they went along—the leaders and followers alike. Seeking whatever wisdom they could for how to live out "the principle," they had to turn to their decidedly antipolygamous "Euro-American background" for cultural support and guidance. Unsurprisingly it was not a good match, leaving many of them all the more baffled as to how to proceed. Even the LDS Church, with all of its mechanisms of control, could not impose uniformity over the thousands of polygamous unions in the Utah territory. Brigham Young could thunder religious duty from the pulpit, and mock unhappy polygamists when he met with them privately, but he could not give definitive shape to this ultimately unwieldy institution. The result was confusion among both the Saints who were earnestly trying to "live their religion," and among historians who hope to make generalizations and identify patterns where they are difficult if not impossible to find.

Some things about Mormon plural marriage, however, are clearer than others. For starters, polygamists were *never* the majority in Utah. Even at plural marriage's peak the vast majority of Mormon marriages—80 to 85 percent—were monogamous. Neither was there ever a time when polygamous individuals outnumbered monogamists. Federal census data from 1860 reports that 43.6 percent of the territory's individuals (not families) that year were in plural marriages, leaving the other 56.4 percent of Utahans monogamists or unmarried. The fact of the matter is that plural marriage peaked "in the decade after its announcement in 1852," cresting dramatically during the Mormon Reformation of 1856–57. This accounts for the high number of polygamists found in the 1860 census. "After that," historian Richard Bushman writes, "the number of plural marriages declined until only 25 percent of the population [of individuals] was in polygamous families in 1880 and 7.1 percent in 1900."[14]

Researchers have also tabulated revealing demographic information about these plural marriages. Stanley S. Ivins concluded that in 66.3 percent of the cases husbands took only one extra wife. This technically made them polygamists, but it was also the minimum required commitment. Having checked the polygamous box, those men demonstrated their devotion to the Mormon faith, ensured their chance for full exaltation, and likely opened up doors for advancement within the Church's hierarchy. They also might not have had either the financial or emotional resources to provide for more wives. Of those who did, Ivins reports, "21.2 per cent were three-wife men, and 6.7 per cent went as far as to take four wives. This left a small group of less than six per cent who married five or more women."[15] Plural marriages in Utah were hardly the oversexed harems that outsiders imagined.

Enemies of polygamy, however, were on firmer ground when they criticized the age differences between husbands and plural wives. One apostate recalled seeing "old withered white-haired men, walking the streets with young brides hanging on their arms, while at the same time an aged female, their true and lawful wife, is bewailing their absence at home."[16] Such scenes made for good propaganda and regrettably they are substantiated. Because of the theological emphasis on procreation, men wanted plural wives of childbearing age. Their probable sexual attraction to younger women, no doubt, also must have played a role. Almost 90 percent of Mormon men were married before they turned twenty-five, with their first wives (almost 100 percent) coming from the same age range. Jessie Embry demonstrates that as polygamous men advanced into their thirties, forties, and even fifties, however, they consistently chose teenagers to be their brides. The vast majority of second, third, and fourth wives (over 82%) were between the ages of fifteen and twenty-five. Embry's most salient data is the following:

Wife's age at time of marriage	15–20	21–25	Total for age 15–25
First wife	74.3%	25.0%	99.3%
Second wife	56.5%	28.3%	84.8%
Third wife	58.9%	25.0%	83.9%
Fourth wife	65.2%	17.4%	82.6%

The conclusion is indisputable: while polygamous men grew older, their brides stayed roughly the same age. The uptick in teenagers as third and fourth wives (from 56.5% to 58.9% to 65.2%) is especially alarming.

Apparently as polygamous men aged, even more of them preferred younger women.[17]

These age differences reinforced other power discrepancies within polygamous households. In order to take additional wives, men usually had to have above-average financial resources, and most likely a corresponding above-average social status. Plural wives, on the other hand, were often among Utah's most vulnerable citizens, recent immigrants and other young women without strong family support. "It is not our city girls who maintain so much the plural marriages," Fanny Stenhouse wrote in 1872, "but it is chiefly the newly arrived English and country girls who supply the Patriarch. The American Elders have derived a rich harvest from Britain for many years past."[18] And as historian Kathryn Daynes summarizes one of her more melancholy findings: "Fatherless women were disproportionately in polygamous marriages. Moreover, about 30 percent of plural wives had been previously widowed or divorced." Conversely, Daynes adds, the "women least likely to enter plural marriage were those whose parents were monogamous and both living." In this sense, monogamy was somewhat of a hereditary phenomenon. The large majority of women who came from monogamous and intact families (83.4%) remained monogamous themselves. Those who had suffered the trauma of losing a parent or husband, or were virtually alone as European converts in an American wilderness, disproportionately became plural wives.[19]

While life in polygamy did indeed follow "no set patterns," there does seem to be a somewhat uniform process by which men and women became polygamists. In almost all cases, a heightened sense of religious obligation spurred on a Saint—usually male—to take this step. Fanny Stenhouse brilliantly describes what she considered to be "several never-failing signs by which one might know when a man wished to take another wife." "He would suddenly awaken to a sense of his duties, and would have great fears that 'the Lord' would not pardon him for any neglect. He would become very religious, attend to his 'meetings'—testimony meetings—singing meetings, and various *other* meetings!"

Fear of being judged a lukewarm Mormon—by either God or fellow Saints—seemed to play a pivotal role for men, followed by their increased involvement in Church activities, followed usually by their broaching the topic with their first wives. Then, Stenhouse scathingly adds, the man would almost always choose a second wife who was "very pretty, and very *youthful.*"[20]

In some instances, however, women initiated becoming a polygamous family. Jessie Embry tells the story of Sadie Adams, a young wife who after hearing a sermon on plural marriage "felt deeply convinced of it," and soon told her husband, Edmund: "'You know that you should be entering into this principle,'" and not "'deprive that good woman of having a family.'"[21] A few months later he married Sarah Matilda Rogers, who at thirty-one years old was supposedly approaching the end of her childbearing years. This case was atypical in that Sadie initiated plural marriage and Edmund married an "older" woman, but it was not atypical at all in that the decision to enter plural marriage sprang from an amplified sense of religious duty.

Of course, many women—both first wives and prospective second ones—did not respond enthusiastically to the idea of becoming polygamists, but religious conviction usually swayed them. Even female apologists for polygamy recounted their initial disgust when confronted with the possibility. "The thought was very repugnant to my feelings," Eliza R. Snow wrote, "and in direct opposition to my educational prepossessions." Phoebe W. Carter Woodruff likewise testified that she thought it "the most wicked thing I ever heard of; consequently I opposed it to the best of my ability, until I became sick and wretched"; and Mary A. Freeze added that "it tried my spirit to its utmost endurance, but I always believed the principle to be true." All of them—just as Lucy Walker had back in Nauvoo in 1842—struggled intensely with the decision and then experienced a welcome cathartic release. "But when I reflected that this was the dispensation of the fullness of times," Snow continued, "it was plain that plural marriage must be included." "I wrestled with my Heavenly Father in fervent prayer," Woodruff similarly wrote. "The answer came. Peace was given to my mind. I knew it was the will of God." As some went on to explain, plural marriage was indeed a trial, but one that they ultimately welcomed because it was a powerful instrument by which the Lord could strip them, as Freeze described it, of "the selfishness and jealousy of my nature."[22]

Once everyone agreed to the union, the three could then proceed to the utterly unique plural marriage ceremony. During this ordinance, Ann Eliza Young reported, the first "wife stands on the left of her husband, the bride at her left hand." Rather than the parents of the bride giving away their daughter, the man's first wife performs the duty, joining the right hands of her husband and new wife, while taking "her husband by the left arm, . . . and the ceremony then proceeds."[23] The first wife thus gives ecclesiastical public assent to the union and remains a part of the service. Jennie Anderson Froiseth, a bitter ex-plural wife, described this rite of passage as the "most cruel sacrifice which this barbarous faith demands of woman,—that of placing the hand of the new bride in that of her husband."[24] In many cases a plural wife's religious convictions simply could not overcome "the selfishness and jealousy" of which Mary Freeze spoke.

Life in plural marriage was not easy for either women or men. While there are examples of happiness and concord in polygamous families, the vast majority of the historical record paints the opposite picture. This does not mean that every day in every polygamous household was a living hell, but the consistent image one gets is of an environment full of suspicion, jealousy, pettiness, and rivalry—in short of almost total mistrust. Trust is one of the most pleasant attributes of family life—when it is a functional family. Individuals can let down their guard, be themselves, and believe (trust) that the other members of the family have their best interests in mind. This is what Christopher Lasch meant when he referred to the modern family as a "haven in a heartless world."[25] This is sadly not what most men and women seemed to have experienced, however, in plural marriage. In some ways the plural marriages themselves could be heartless, leaving polygamous husbands and wives to seek emotional refuge elsewhere. Although there are examples of a sense of sisterhood among some plural wives, they frequently thought of one another as rivals. Often lonely, most women found the intimacy they desired in the only human beings whom they could truly call their own—their children—a dynamic that will be explored further in the next chapter.

The emotional lives of polygamous men are harder to discern as they did not often bare their souls in writing. In part this was because they feared that federal prosecutors could use the writings against them. As historian Lawrence Foster points out, there was also the chance that the other wives might read a husband's feelings for one wife in particular, "and it would not do to show any trace of favoritism."[26] But the men's plural marriages also seemed to have been more pragmatic, duty-driven, and patriarchal rather than the romantic, companionate marriages of their monogamous Victorian peers.[27] Mormon polygamous men also seem to have found emotional intimacy and a sense of belonging in the homosocial bonds of the Church's all-male priesthood and hierarchy, rather than within the confines of their home or homes.

The lack of physical closeness of many polygamous households only reinforced their lack of emotional closeness. Jessie Embry rightly points out that "no set patterns developed as to where wives lived and how often husbands visited," although she does say that "often the wives shared a home just after the second marriage, but as soon as it was financially possible, the husband provided a separate one for each wife." Some of those homes could be close to one another, while other times they could be in entirely different towns, or one in town and another "on a farm, usually several miles away." No matter the distance between houses, however, they were still separate. Thus rather than one, big, (un)happy family all living under a single roof, these nineteenth-century plural marriages were more like discrete, woman-anchored homes with a roaming, providing patriarch dividing his time, attention, and resources among them. "While it is impossible to define a typical schedule," Embry writes, often "the husband lived in each home for a week or a night at a time."[28] Ex-plural wife Fanny Stenhouse confirmed this point, writing: "When a man has more than one wife, his affections must certainly be divided; and he really has no particular home, for his homes are simply boarding houses."[29] And as Harriett Hutchings recollected about her childhood in a polygamous home: "It was just like two different families. We did not try to live together as a family. But we got along."[30]

It is questionable, however, just how often and how well plural wives "got along" with one another. Even Jessie Embry, who makes it a priority in her study to debunk the stereotypes of the "oppressed plural wife, [and] the first wife who was dropped for a younger bride," admits that polygamous husbands "had unique problems helping their wives get along, and plural wives had unique periods of loneliness." She also admits that the "stereotype of a favored younger wife and a resentful older one also had some basis in fact."[31]

But by far the most important stereotype of Mormon polygamy that Embry confirms rather than debunks is the heartache that many plural wives suffered. "Even if the wives felt equally loved," she writes, "they encountered feelings of loneliness—especially when the husband was at another home."[32] "Ladies," Fanny Stenhouse implored, "how do you think you would feel if *you* were kept waiting long after the hour of midnight, far away into the morning, until your husband had got through with their dancing and flirting, while your own hearts were breaking?"[33] In spite of all the admonitions that living the principle would help crucify their selfishness, plural wives in Utah wrestled mightily with jealousy, rivalry, and anxiety. No wife could ever assume that her exclusive relationship with her husband was permanent. As Ann Eliza Young put it: "Wives did not know when their husbands would bring home another woman to share their home and their husband."[34] And as one visitor to Utah observed as early as 1854: "In families where polygamy has not been introduced, she [the wife] suffers an agony of apprehension on the subject."[35] Given the power disparity between husbands and wives, the threat of becoming a polygamous household hung constantly over the marriage like a sword of Damocles.

Polygamy also affected social engagements throughout the kingdom. Plural husbands "had to determine which wife to take to church and to social events," Embry writes, although in some towns it was acceptable to "be seen with more than one wife at a time at a public gathering."[36] Occasions when the husband could choose only one wife to accompany him to an event inspired resentment in the hearts of the unchosen; but even the chosen wives had to endure their husband's divided attention. A man is "always in the market," Fanny Stenhouse wrote. At parties, she adds, no "matter how old and homely a man is, he thinks that he has as much right to flirt and dance with the girls as the youngest boy." Every unmarried woman was "fair game," so to speak, while absolutely every man—married or not—could vie for their attention. Although unpleasant for virtually all the women involved, this dynamic also must have been discouraging for Utah's unmarried men who were simply hoping to find a first wife. They had to compete with both their unmarried peers and with the kingdom's established patriarchs. In polygamous Utah, life was often as socially unstable as it was emotionally unstable.

In polygamous families, the majority of plural wives simply did not get along. As Ann Eliza Young puts it bluntly: "Polygamy does not tend to make one woman just towards another." There were exceptions to this rule, she explained, such as her own experience growing up in a polygamous household. Her father had two wives, "and our two families have been more united than polygamous families usually are." But she attributes this harmony to "the common-sense of the two mothers, who, . . . knew each that the other was not to blame for the mutual suffering." In most plural marriages, however, "there was no end to the muddles." Although potentially exaggerated for effect, she told stories in which "women died of broken hearts," and one harrowing tale in which a plural wife "grew nearly insane under this trouble, and was wrought up to such a frenzy by jealousy and despair that she committed the most flagrant acts of violence." As Young described herself as a plural wife: "I no longer took pleasure in their society [other women], for I saw in each one a probable rival, and a possible addition to our household."[37] "How I watched their looks and noted their every word," Fanny Stenhouse wrote of her husband and his new wife. "To me, their tender tones were like daggers, piercing me to the heart." "Everything is noticed. Nothing is overlooked. When a woman's heart is anxious her eye is never weary.... Women in Utah have a perfect dread of growing old."[38] Far from a relaxing "haven in a heartless world," these exposés describe marriages of constant vigilance, suspicion, and outright hatred.

Sometimes the only joy plural wives could experience in polygamy—in addition to their children—was in spreading their misery throughout the household. Jennie Anderson Froiseth, who lamented that polygamy had twisted her into "a cold, calculating, heartless woman," exacted her pound of flesh upon her husband and his second wife by facilitating his marriage to a third woman. The whole experience, she confessed, "made me the meanest kind of deceiver in carrying out a plan of revenge, and caused me to glory in the sufferings of another woman."[39] The more even-tempered Fanny Stenhouse likewise sought comfort through vengeance against her husband's second wife. "One thing consoled me," she wrote: "I felt that my husband's intended [second wife] would some day learn that *she* was *not* his *first and only love* after myself."[40] Neither woman was proud of her actions, but neither did they blame themselves for them. Life as a plural wife could be incredibly hard. Even in some of the best cases—those in which the "'wives were friendly and kind to each other,'" someone reared in a plural household recollected—"'there was an undercurrent of feelings between them that I as a child of twelve could detect.'"[41] Rarely those undercurrents reached the surface and burst forth in dramatic and malicious manifestations, but they were almost always present.

Two concluding points bear mentioning. The first is that there was often a dramatic difference between the public image Mormon women projected and their private experiences as plural wives. As Lieutenant Gunnison observed in 1852: "That the wives find the relation often a lonesome and burdensome one, is certain; though usually the surface of society wears a smiling countenance."[42] This discrepancy only increased throughout the 1860s, 1870s and 1880s, as the institution was subjected to greater outside pressure. The second point is that over the course of those same decades, fewer women chose to become plural wives. "Increasingly," Daynes writes, "young women rejected plural marriage in favor of romantic love." Exercising the only power they had, single women delayed marriage or chose "as husbands men unqualified to participate in the sealing ceremony." Those women's attitudes toward plural marriage are difficult to discern from the thin historical record, but as Daynes concludes, "it is certain that fewer women, both absolutely and relatively, entered plural marriage in the last twenty years it was sanctioned by the church."[43] The collective private miseries of plural wives were starting to have a more public, demographic impact on the institution.

Those women who were already in the institution, however, continued to suffer in silence while keeping up appearances. As another visitor observed in 1870: "The most noticeable fact to a Gentile travelling through Mormon settlements is the strangely quiet way in which women discharge their household duties. They stand behind the guest at the way-side hotel, replenish the table and attend upon his wants, but never enter into the conversation, venture not the slightest observation or inquiry, and very rarely answer his questions in anything more than monosyllables."[44] This paints a rather stark image of female inequality in nineteenth-century Utah, but then again, as William Hepworth Dixon had observed, "woman is not in society here at all."[45]

The Shakers, in contrast, were radically committed to equality between women and men. They lived out this egalitarian ideal imperfectly, but they nevertheless institutionalized their theological commitments in their governing structure as well as in the everyday lives of average Believers.

The Shaker metanarrative posits a gender-balanced cosmos. For them, the division of humankind into male and female reflected the heavenly reality that the Creator was likewise divided into Almighty Father and Holy Mother Wisdom. This is why, Shakers believe, God uses plural pronouns in Genesis 1: "And God said, Let *us* make man in *our* image, after *our* likeness: . . . male and female created he them."[46] Similarly, the gendered nature of the Fall necessitated a dual Savior—divine beings who condescended to share in humanity. Just "as there was a *natural Adam and Eve*," one early Shaker apologist explained, "so there is also a *spiritual Adam and Eve*." "The woman was the first in the transgression," the logic went, "and therefore must be the last out of it."[47] For the Believers, Mother Ann Lee was that female Savior, finishing the new creation that the male Jesus Christ had begun centuries earlier.

The fact that a woman inaugurated and led the Shakers in their first years reinforced the movement's commitment to gender equality for at least four decades. From the 1770s until 1821, when Mother Lucy Wright died, women either led equally alongside men or led the Shakers outright. After Wright's death, however, the United Society of Believers developed a new governing structure that maintained gender equality in the leadership numerically, but that also sadly produced, in Stephen Stein's words, a "gradual but real subordination of women in the upper ranks of the society." After 1821 a team of four constituted the central ministry: a first and second eldress and a first and second elder. Given the Society's rapid expansion into the trans-Appalachian West, this leadership team continued to wrestle with numerous spiritual and temporal challenges. Governing a far-flung, problem-filled organization now required less charisma and more bureaucracy. It also brought along with it a more traditional, gendered division of labor. As mentioned in the previous chapter, during the Era of Manifestations the central ministry promoted more men into leadership positions and had them spiritually counsel the largely female instruments to prevent them from getting out of control. Men also gradually became the public face of the Society, engaging with "the world" on economic, political, and civic matters, while women increasingly tended to domestic duties. Gender equality had characterized the central leadership during the more radical earlier generations and would characterize it again in the twentieth century. During the heart of the nineteenth century, however, the power dynamics of the central leadership reflected rather than challenged the gender norms of the broader American and Victorian culture that the Shakers had renounced.[48]

When it came to daily work—and the Shakers valued work—men typically performed the more physically demanding labor in the village and women the more domestic tasks. Men and boys plowed fields, tended livestock, sheared the sheep, and were the chief manufacturers and blacksmiths. Women and girls "prepared meals, cleaned the dwelling, washed and mended clothing," spun and wove, knitted and sewed.[49] This kind of gendered division of labor had almost always characterized life in Shaker villages, but it was motivated more by practicality than it was by a desire to restrict women's opportunities. As Lawrence Foster rightly explains, "they did not view either men's or women's work as inherently 'superior' but felt instead that all occupations were of equal importance in God's sight."[50]

In other words, men and women did different jobs but their Shaker faith compelled them to consider one another as equals. In "the completed order of my new creation," one Believer put it succinctly, "male and female dwell together as brethren and sisters, not as husband and wife."[51] This Shaker "family," which could range from a dozen to over a hundred Believers, was the basic unit in which an individual Believer lived, worked, and worshiped. Apostates obviously found this ordered and regulated communal life intolerable. But others—the majority—welcomed the discipline, and found acceptance and love within their new Shaker "family." They had to fit somehow into the village mold, but the collective order and rules did not stamp all the individuality out of them.

The same tension between uniformity and particularity could be said for the Shakers' beliefs about gender and the way they lived out those beliefs. When comparing the Mormons, Shakers, and Oneida Perfectionists, the United Society of Believers was by far the most egalitarian of the three. It is a shame that for half of the nineteenth century Shaker leaders followed the pattern of the world by relegating women to a supporting role in the central ministry, but this is an exception to their general belief in the inherent equality of the sexes. Likewise, in a village women and men did different, gender-divided work, but women still had more access to positions of religious authority than in virtually any other religious institution of the time. While far from perfectly lived out, it is nevertheless noteworthy that Shakers shared so much power between the sisters and the brothers, the eldresses and the elders.

When it comes to his thoughts about gender roles, John Humphrey Noyes occupies an odd and paradoxical place somewhere between Mormon patriarchy and Shaker egalitarianism. Believing to some extent in women's liberation, he also unabashedly believed in male superiority and in women's subordination to men in general. Although his reinterpretation of the Christian metanarrative led to radical sexual experimentation in his communities, it did not lead to a similarly radical reconceptualization of women's roles and their capabilities.

Both Shakers and Perfectionists believed that marriage was ungodly, locking individuals in life-long bonds that encouraged their sinful tendency to love a single person exclusively. As Noyes and others argued, the institution of marriage turned women into property in the exact way that chattel slavery did. "Now this property in persons we utterly disown and repudiate on religious grounds," he wrote in the aptly-titled article "Decadence of Marriage." "We look upon marriage as upon slavery. We regard them both as institutions adapted to a state of bondage to selfishness and sin, and not to a state of holiness and liberty."[52] In abolishing marriage as both Perfectionists and Shakers had, they were not only campaigning against sinful exclusivity, but also striking a blow for women's liberation.

Fascinatingly, Noyes used this line of argument against Mormon polygamists. He did this in part because he genuinely disliked the idea of women-as-property that he believed both monogamous and plural marriages perpetuated, but he also wanted to distance himself as much as possible from the Latter-day "principle." Critics regularly linked complex marriage and polygamy, a connection that Noyes believed was unfair and potentially threatening to his community's existence. Thus he did his best to differentiate the two. "The opinion is held," he complained, "that what is called complex marriage, is really nothing but a combination of polygamy and polyandry." As he made clear, however: "We reject polygamy because it multiplies the radical evil of monogamy, viz., property in woman."[53] In another article, simply titled "The Difference," he called polygamy "a system of female slavery, and of unregulated propagation," doubly condemning it for restricting women's freedom, and for treating women as little more than the bearers of children.[54]

But in spite of Noyes's apparent desire to liberate women, he still had a traditional understanding of their role in both society generally and his own Perfectionist communities in particular. In the article "Man and Woman—Their True Relation," Noyes criticized contemporary women's rights activists. Wrongly considering the Apostle Paul an "'old fogey,'" they dismissed his division of men and women into "superior and subordinate," and misguidedly advocated instead for "entire equality."[55] Noyes considered such an outlook to be contrary to both scriptural and natural revelation. As historian Spencer Klaw describes it, in his understanding of "the spiritual hierarchy of the universe, God stood above Christ, Christ stood above man, and man stood above woman."[56] Given Noyes's obsession with being in charge, it is not at all surprising that he would put so much emphasis on hierarchy. Thus unlike the Shakers, who largely split leadership positions between men and women, Noyes concentrated power in himself alone: a man, authorized by the law of ascending fellowship to occupy the top of the community's social and religious heap. *Everyone* had to subordinate themselves to him, both women and men.

In their system of complex marriage, women could take the lead and initiate sexual encounters with men, but this did not make them men's equals. In fact, and greatly to the contrary, Noyes insisted that women should embrace their subordinate status and their femininity by being beautiful and sexually attractive to the Community's men. Far from being androgynous or "unsexed" as Noyes called it, men should be men and women should be women, whatever that means.[57] With himself as the model of such masculinity and Mary Cragin the model of femininity, Klaw explains, "Noyes taught his followers that women owed their male masters more than just respect and loving receptivity. They had a further obligation to make men love them—if possible, to love them wildly."[58] These were the proper relations of men and women in the kingdom of God. In their corrupt American Christendom, however, the selfish institution of monogamous marriage made these relations impossible to realize. Only in Perfectionist communities that embraced complex marriage could people come close to living out this ideal. But as always, such an effort involved reinforcing the differences between men and women rather than negating them, and in subordinating women to men rather than equalizing the sexes.

In order to clarify Perfectionist beliefs and defend them from misguided calumny, starting in 1870 Noyes had *The Circular* regularly print a manifesto called "Our Social Position." "Free Love with us does not mean freedom to love to-day and leave to-morrow," it insisted. Nor, it continued, striking a progressive note, did it mean "freedom to take a woman's person and keep our property to ourselves; nor freedom to freight a woman with our offspring and send her down stream without care or help; nor freedom to beget children and leave them to the poor-house." Such were the world's sinful practices that had unfairly taxed women in the past. In Perfectionism, even if women did not experience full equality, at least they would not be burdened with the responsibility of rearing children by themselves, or at all if they so chose; and they would absolutely not be considered property. "Our Communities are families," the manifesto concluded, "as distinctly bounded and separated from promiscuous society as ordinary households."[59] Family clearly mattered to Perfectionists, just as it did to Mormons and Shakers.

At precisely the time that *The Circular* started printing this manifesto in 1870, the Oneidans had started becoming even more familylike by purposely having children. This change was a reversal of the decades-old policy of birth control through male continence, and it was to have serious effects on the community. The next chapter will describe this change in detail, as well as the clearly important role of children in Mormonism. The celibate Shakers were obviously a different story, although their thoughts about procreation will be explored as well. For the Mormons and the Perfectionists, however, children were both a blessing and a challenge. This is true for virtually every parent in the world, but for these sectarians children posed not just a challenge to their way of life but also to their religious beliefs.

15
Children

CHILDREN OFTEN create problems for communitarian life. In an intentional community the individual's loyalty, identity, and resources are supposed to be oriented toward the group. Like a spouse but arguably more so, children can divide those loyalties and resources, anchoring the individual's identity in the sinful exclusive love for one's family rather than in the godly and inclusive sectarian community.

Because of their different religious metanarratives, the Mormons, Shakers, and Oneida Perfectionists navigated the challenge of children in different ways. Eschewing the natural affections as worldly, the Shakers wanted to sever individuals from their familial ties and resituate them within a new "family" of Believers in Shaker villages. As the custody cases of Mary Dyer and Eunice Chapman illustrate, the children of converts—especially reluctant converts—could severely disrupt community life. The Mormons, by contrast, were the least communitarian and the most profamily and pronatal. As Mormons believe, once properly sealed, the procreative unit of the family is eternal, and in many ways more valued than either the individual Saint or the Latter-day community.

In contrast to both of these sects, whose theology and praxis regarding children remained consistent over time, Noyes's Perfectionists went through a transformation. They started out in the 1840s opposed to unwanted pregnancies, and indeed to almost all pregnancies. By the late 1860s, however, Noyes had changed his mind, turning his version of Perfectionism from antinatal to pronatal. As always, Noyes theorized intensely about this change first and then thoroughly controlled its implementation. In the end, however, this reversal proved to erode his control. Children fundamentally altered life at Oneida and were arguably the beginning of the Community's end. This chapter will explain the Shakers' and the Mormons' thoughts about children, as well as tell the story of this fateful transition at Oneida.

Of the three groups investigated, the Shakers are obviously going to have the least to say about children. Considering sex the most sinful of sins, Believers did not have to deal very often with the problems that pregnancy and childrearing posed. When impoverished parents or guardians surrendered their dependents to one of their villages, however, Shakers did all that they could to set those children on the path of righteousness. Unsurprisingly, the young had to put their hands to work and hearts to God just as much as the adults did, performing their share of chores. "Children were called up by a bell, at half past four in the winter, and half past three in the summer," Mary Dyer wrote. The elders "do not make allowance for children, they think they must be as men and women."[1]

In addition to cleaning, performing agricultural tasks, and learning the specialized trades of their particular villages, children were also taught Shaker doctrines and included in religious worship—a requirement that, to outsiders, smacked of sectarian brainwashing. "The Shakers weaken and intimidate their minds by telling them frightful stories, and by reading 'Mother Ann's sayings,'" Eunice Chapman protested, "and make them fear to go to the world lest they should become monsters!" As a result, she claimed: "Those who are brought up among the Shakers, seldom leave them.... They are taught to believe that if they go back to the world, they will either sink immediately into hell, or satan [sic] will take them and carry them off alive."[2] Apostate David R. Lamson was less sensationalistic in his description of the Believers' sectarian educational objectives, but no less critical. He claimed that the elders' desire to retain young Shakers stemmed from both spiritual and worldly interests. In addition to saving the children's souls, Lamson wrote, there "was a fear expressed in our society, that enough young people would not remain to take care of and make the aged comfortable through life." Thus he quoted one elder as stating rather candidly: "'We don't educate our children for the world; we educate them to stay here.' And so it is in fact."[3]

The reality of childhood retention in Shaker villages, however, was not so simple. Young adults regularly apostatized and left the villages, a phenomenon that contradicts anti-Shakers' image of a spiritually captive audience, indoctrinated and disciplined into submission. Having not originally chosen to live among the Shakers, these young people voted with their feet as soon as possible. Of course, not everyone did—two of Mary Dyer's children converted and elected to remain in the village—but the trend of leaving accelerated over the course of the nineteenth century, causing the United Society of Believers tremendous concern. In short, it seems that the Shakers were both uncomfortable with children and ultimately unsuccessful at keeping them. They did not have much of a place for them in either their theology or their villages. While they needed them to keep the faith alive, over time they simply could not stop the exodus of those who chose the world over their "full and final cross."[4] As the chapter on the Shakers in "End Times" will illustrate, in the second half of the nineteenth century children continued to leave, elders inevitably died, and the proselyted failed to convert—a process of spiritual and communal enervation that became impossible to reverse.[5]

Given the Mormons' preoccupation with children and procreation in general, it is shocking how little they wrote on the subject. The vast majority of both Mormon and anti-Mormon commentary on children merely repeats the theological party line—that offspring are the chief end of marriage and the means to a couple's celestial glory. This understanding of children also reinforces an understanding of the afterlife that is unabashedly patriarchal. After death, a married man becomes a god, who "in connection with his sons, organizes a new world," in which all "are required to reverence, adore, and worship their own personal father."[6] Neither women nor children play little more than supporting roles in creating this patriarchal paradise. Thus when asked the supposedly preposterous question "Can a woman have more than one husband at the same time?" Mormon authorities replied emphatically: "No. . . . The object of marriage is to multiply the species, according to the command of God."[7] A man with multiple wives can theoretically procreate more often and more rapidly. A woman with multiple husbands cannot. According to Mormon beliefs, children and procreation were the sole reason why there could be polygyny (one man and several wives) but not polyandry (one woman and several husbands).

So how did this theology work in practice, and what was childrearing like in Utah's polygamous society from roughly 1850 to 1890? Again, and unfortunately, the primary sources do not tell us very much. No doubt as a result of this thin evidentiary base, most scholarship on Mormon polygamy devotes a good bit of attention to women, but relatively little to the children of plural families. An exception is Jessie L. Embry's study, *Mormon Polygamous Families: Life in the Principle,* but even that contains only one chapter on the subject.

For the most part, Embry's work confirms two expectations about plural marriage and discredits another. As discussed previously, Embry actually reinforces the stereotype of the lonely and emotionally deprived plural wife. Given that they had to share with other women their husband's time, affections, resources, and body, plural wives often turned to their children for intimacy. As she quotes one plural wife: "A woman in polygamy is compelled by her lone position to make a confidant of her children." And as another recorded succinctly and sadly: "her comfort must be wholly in her children."[8] The other expectation about plural families that Embry confirms has to do with the lack of emotional closeness between children and their fathers. From her survey data, only 35 percent of children from plural homes responded that they felt "Close to father" as opposed to 83.7 percent of children from monogamous homes. The majority of children from plural homes (52.3%) instead responded that they felt "Little attention from father," while the remaining 12.7 percent felt "No attention from father." In contrast, 0.0 percent of the children from monogamous families felt "No attention from father."[9] As Embry sums up, the prevalence of children feeling neglected by their polygamous fathers was "because their [the father's] interests were spread between several families."[10] Or to quote Brigham Young: "I pay no attention to the children, but leave that to their mothers, according to the law of nature. The bull pays no attention to his calves."[11]

Evidence about birthrates in plural marriage, however, discredits the principal theological justification for the institution. Church authorities encouraged Saints into polygamy to raise up a righteous generation more rapidly. Although plural marriage increased the number of children for the husbands, "plural wives had fewer children than their monogamous counterparts," Embry writes. It is therefore simply "not clear," she concludes, "whether plural marriage actually increased the Mormon population" overall.[12] Stanley S. Ivins agrees. Based on his calculations, plural wives had an estimated 5.9 children per person, whereas monogamous wives had 8.0, leading him to suggest "the possibility that the overall production of children in Utah may have been less than it would have been without benefit of plurality of wives."[13] Scholars have recalculated these figures with the benefit of hindsight and statistical data and confirmed Ivins's insight. Mormons at the time would most likely not have realized the irony that practicing plural marriage was actually undermining the very theological reasons for it, namely "of raising up to His name a royal Priesthood, a peculiar people."[14]

John Humphrey Noyes also wanted his Perfectionists to create a "peculiar people"—but not at first. From 1838 to 1844, after the fateful "Battle Axe Letter" but before instituting complex marriage, Noyes watched helplessly as his wife, Harriet Holton Noyes, endured the "fruitless suffering" of four miscarriages out of five pregnancies.[15] As a result, in the summer of 1844 he developed his theory of male continence as a means of birth control. Thus after originally trying for children—or at least not attempting to prevent pregnancies with Harriet—he turned against the idea.

Noyes remained generally antinatal for the next quarter of a century. Opposed to exclusivity in all its forms, in 1844 he published an article criticizing the "Love of Children"—or "philoprogenitiveness" as he called it—for being "one of the strongest passions . . . against the claims of Christ."[16] Two years later he likewise condemned "Woman's Slavery to Children," arguing that mothers' "almost exclusive devotedness to waiting on their children . . . robs them of much that they owe to God and to themselves."[17] The Perfectionists and the Mormons were thus miles apart on both the purpose of sex and the role of women. For Mormons, sex was first and foremost for procreation and women were primarily breeders. For John Humphrey Noyes, sex was for physical pleasure and spiritual fellowship; and women, while still subordinate to men, were valued partners in that fellowship—"made for God and herself" and liberated by male continence from the life sentence that accompanied an unwanted pregnancy.[18]

While clearly not desiring children during their first decades at Oneida, the members of the Community nevertheless had them and provided adequately and lovingly for them. Women still got pregnant accidentally, although not nearly as often as one might expect. In the first twenty years at Oneida, the historian Spencer Klaw writes, unplanned "pregnancies occurred at a rate of fewer than one a year," a remarkable testimony to the Perfectionists' success at practicing male continence.[19] During this time Noyes also permitted some women—usually those who did not have children and were in their mid-thirties—to get pregnant intentionally. The resulting birthrate at Oneida, however, is still astonishingly low: only thirty-five children in the twenty-one years between 1848 and 1869.[20]

For the first twelve to fifteen months of her child's life, biological mothers at Oneida were relieved of their usual community work to nurse and care for their newborns. But after that stretch of time, and to discourage "philoprogenitiveness," she had to hand over her baby to the care of the Children's House. This transition, of course, did not always go well. In the *First Annual Report* in 1849, Noyes noted "the temporary distress of the mothers in giving up their little ones to the care of others, which made occasion for some melo-dramatic scenes." He criticized these women for their "sickly maternal tenderness" and in the end successfully implemented his system of communal childrearing. According to him, it not only helped cure women of their exclusive love for their children, it also taught them "to value their own freedom and opportunity of education," and it reportedly resulted in "the improved condition" of the children themselves.[21]

Youth from age two to twelve were reared communally in the Children's House by a rotating staff of volunteers. Noyes established the first of such houses as early as 1848, in one of the separate buildings of Jonathan Burt's farm. By the next year they had constructed a new Children's House, and in 1869 they added an entire wing to their second brick Mansion House, also dedicated to childrearing.[22] In these separate spaces, the Community's children slept, ate, bathed, were educated, and received religious instruction as a group. Parents were allowed to visit their children but not too often or for too long lest it stoke their "philoprogenitiveness." According to Noyes, children reared in community were like wildflowers flourishing freely in the abundance of God's good Creation. While the exclusive nuclear family might initially be a nurturing environment for little ones, he admitted, it ultimately stunts their growth by not exposing them to the glories of the outside world and the expanded resources of a larger body of adult caretakers. The Oneida Community, after all, was an enormous extended family: full of literal aunts, uncles, cousins, and grandparents. In time, they found that they wanted to grow that happy family even further. As Noyes indelicately put it: "We have recovered that old Jewish eagerness for offspring."[23]

For years Community members, including Noyes, had been slowly changing their minds from antinatal to pronatal. In 1859, for instance, *The Circular* reported that there "is a keen appetite rising among us for having children." As always, however, Noyes insisted that acting on that "appetite" must "wait on the improvement of our accommodations."[24] In the early days—1848 to the mid-1860s—his Perfectionist communal experiments were both fragile and poor. The mechanization of animal trap manufacturing and the expansion of their market into the Midwest, however, set the Community on a solid financial foundation, and as their material situation changed so did Noyes's opinion about procreation. With greater resources at his disposal came the possibility of providing adequately for the Community's children.

But concerned with control as usual, Noyes was not about to expose his Community to the chaos of "*random* procreation."[25] Few things are less controllable than children, and Noyes feared that shifting to a laissez-faire kind of attitude toward couples' pairing off would threaten everything. The biological parents would likely succumb to "philoprogenitiveness," while their offspring ran the risk of being genetically inferior and thus another burden on the Community. Noyes was prepared to loosen the Community's restrictions on pregnancy because of their improving financial circumstances, but he would not loosen them entirely. Who would procreate with whom would be strictly regulated—subject to Noyes's discretion as to what was best for the Community religiously, and to what couples he deemed would produce the best children scientifically. He called the resulting program—yet another product of long study and careful implementation—"stirpiculture." "*Stirpes*" is the Latin word for "race," while "culture" is to be thought of as a verb, meaning "to cultivate or improve."[26] Noyes had imposed his will on community members' sex lives through male continence and the rule of ascending fellowship. With stirpiculture (pronounced "*stur*-pi-culture") he would satisfy their—and his—desire for children, while also ensuring that those children would be genetically superior human specimens.

Noyes had been thinking about the possibility of "*scientific* propagation" for decades. In Oneida's very *First Annual Report* in 1849, when having children was decidedly not a community goal, Noyes esteemed "propagation, rightly conducted, . . . [as] the next blessing to sexual love," but enjoined against "*involuntary*" and "*random* procreation." In the case of unwanted pregnancies, unborn children "lie nine months in their mother's womb under their mother's curse," he explained: "Such children cannot be well organized." But "the time will come," he prophesied, "when scientific combination will be applied to human generation as freely and successfully as it is to that of other animals." This "*intelligent, well-ordered* procreation" would reverse the curse of worldly procreation and prove instead to be a blessing to both mother and child, as well as to father and community.[27]

Noyes had to wait two decades to implement his program of scientific breeding, during which time he read extensively in Darwin and genetics. Noyes's mind had always ranged beyond the fields of theology and biblical studies, with his periodicals filled with articles on current affairs and scientific and technological discoveries. In the 1850s he began reading in geology. In the early 1860s he added the work of Charles Darwin to his studies. He wrestled for the rest of his life with the questions that science posed for faith, but he was also enamored with the way science could explain the laws of nature, and he was exhilarated by the way human beings could apply scientific insights to solve ancient riddles and master the physical world. Thanks to science and technology, humankind could now peer into the recesses of outer space, observe microscopic phenomena, move mountains, conquer continents, and win wars. Thanks also to science and technology, Noyes concluded, human beings could control as never before the process of passing on only their best traits to the next generation.

In the mid-1860s Noyes began preparing Oneidans for their collective experiment in eugenics, moving cautiously and deliberately as always. In the spring of 1865, precisely as the Civil War was ending, he published three articles on "Improved Breeding by Selection," "Scientific Propagation," and his own program, "Stirpiculture." Darwin had both excited and disturbed him. "It startles one at first," he confessed, "to conceive that mankind have been developed under the pressure of a struggle for existence . . . and are in fact related in their origin to the monkey and even to the oyster." The process of "*selection in breeding*" was also a double-edged sword: religiously troubling in that the apparent randomness of "*Natural Selection*" could have been responsible for the evolution of noble human beings from such ignoble origins; but also capable of now being controlled by those same human beings to produce a better species. People had been breeding "sheep, cattle, and horses" for millennia, improving their stock with each generation. "What is man," Noyes asked, "that he is not applying the same principles . . . to the improvements of his own race?"[28] Noyes's answer, of course, was that he should.

His article on "Stirpiculture" was so long and involved that it had to be divided into two parts in two separate issues of *The Circular*. As always, Noyes was drawn to perfection—in theology, in community, and now in people. Like his earlier controversial ideas, stirpiculture would be another divinely inspired, although radical, means of bringing the kingdom of God to earth. The world had seen "'born geniuses'" before, he argued, people who "illuminate and delight with the splendor of their endowments, the generation in which they live." But such human gems were produced only "at rare intervals, and by wholly unknown laws." Now, Noyes concluded excitedly, the Community could participate in the production of such people "by the definite laws of breeding. It will be the business of Communistic societies to find out those laws and apply them."[29]

Noyes waited another three and a half years to "apply" those laws, and then did so with characteristic rigor. In early 1869 he and the chosen Oneidans were ready, but only after Noyes had secured signatures from the breeders on a pledge promising him their obedience. Fifty-three women agreed to devote themselves "first to *God,* and second to Mr. Noyes as God's true representative." They likewise surrendered "all envy, childishness, and self-seeking" in the upcoming project, and offered to "become martyrs to science" and "'living sacrifices' to God and true Communism." Thirty-eight men signed a similar self-renouncing contract, pledging: "We claim no rights. We ask no privileges. . . . We are your true soldiers."[30] With yet another chain of command and these willing volunteers, Noyes ordered his troops forward in a new godly offensive against the world's sinful institutions.

The stirpiculture campaign started out fast and then settled into a slower, steadier pace. Just one year after it had begun, Oneida could boast that three children had been born and five more women were expecting. Noyes gloated especially that such a rapid "expansion . . . casts to the winds" his critics' prediction that Oneida's twenty years of male continence must have rendered the men impotent and the women infertile.[31] Clearly that was not the case. In the decade from 1869 to 1879 one hundred Perfectionists participated in the stirpicultural experiment, having fifty-eight children in all. John Humphrey Noyes sired at least nine of them.[32] He also strictly controlled who could have children with whom. Sometimes he or other leaders would suggest that a particular man and woman pair off. Most times, however (estimated by one historian to be 75% of the cases), prospective partners came to him for permission to breed. Once approved, the woman would have sex exclusively with that man until either a pregnancy occurred or the two gave up trying. During this time the man was free to have sex with other women but had to continue practicing male continence with them.[33]

For most of the 1870s Noyes made these decisions alone or in informal consultation with other Community leaders. In 1875 he created a Stirpicultural Committee to vet the applications, but dissolved it after only fifteen months of operation and resumed the responsibility personally. There are no documents to explain this back-and-forth although one historian speculates that it was "perhaps because the selection of parents was too important in the politics of the Community to be delegated to a committee." Understandably, those not approved to have children could be very resentful. At least one such couple, Mary Jones and Victor Hawley, ended up leaving Oneida in order to marry monogamously and start a family—a small but troubling sign of things to come. During its fifteen months of operation, the Stirpicultural Committee rejected only nine out of fifty-one applications, and was decidedly more restrictive with the men than with the women. Reflecting their belief in the inequality of the sexes, Oneidans assumed that the man's genetic material would overpower that of the woman. They therefore rejected male applicants more often, prohibiting the supposedly unfit ones from passing on their genes. As for the initially rejected women, Community leaders would often attempt to find for them more suitable partners according to the rule of ascending fellowship. Unsurprisingly, Noyes still occupied the top of this spiritual hierarchy, which is why, to quote one scholar, at least nine female participants "felt honored at the privilege of having the patriarch as the father of her child." It is equally unsurprising that the selected fathers were 12.2 years older on average than the selected mothers.[34]

As stirpiculture proceeded at Oneida, Noyes championed it in print. Continuing to study genetics over the 1870s, Noyes fashioned himself an expert on the subject in both theory and practice. "Marriage," he declared, was "dying, and scientific propagation coming to the birth," a radical change that the established sinful traditions of the world were naturally going to resist. "In ordinary society," as he put it, "experiment is forbidden. Mating is left to the same irresponsible, careless guidance that prevails among the buffaloes and antelopes of the prairie." This kind of procreation "by promiscuous scrambling," he added, "is the very nature of marriage."[35] As an enemy of monogamy, Noyes renewed his war on this old order in the name of a new, godlier reproductive regime. For generations to come, Noyes dreamed, Oneida would be a modern "city on a hill," an example to the rest of the world of authentic New Testament faith in action, and a living genetic validation of everything he stood for and everything he was.

Studying natural selection gave Noyes yet another outlet for his ego—a new category in which he could judge himself superlative. Previously, intellect and religious devotion had been the chief metrics in the rule of ascending fellowship. But these traits, he reasoned, must also be a part of a person's inherited material as well, and therefore capable of being transmitted to future generations. That is why he and his Perfectionists paid such "careful attention to pedigree, . . . favoring the production of pure-blood races of men."[36] That is also why, Noyes added, no doubt thinking of himself, that "Providence frequently allows very superior men to be also very attractive to women."[37] Those women want to mingle the "superior" man's genetic material with their own and transmit it to the next generation. That was also why Noyes privileged his own blood-related male relatives in the stirpicultural selection process. He allowed his son Theodore Noyes to father no fewer than four children.[38] Under the strict controls of "scientific propagation," Noyes's Perfectionists would also breed exclusively "from the best," producing a clutch of children who were as genetically superior as they were religiously devout.[39]

So how did the experiment turn out? Did the children—called "stirpicults"—live up to the expectations of their parents and engineers? The results are doubly surprising, both for Father Noyes and for modern inquirers. In 1891, a dozen years after the Oneidans had abandoned complex marriage and stirpiculture, a physician from Johns Hopkins University, Dr. Anita Newcomb McGee, interviewed twenty-two stirpicults. By the metrics of health and material success, she found them to be superior indeed: "The boys are tall—several over six feet—broad-shouldered, and finely proportioned; the girls are robust and well built." All of the young men were either in college or working in business at "white-collar jobs," while the young women were likewise either in college, married, or employed as teachers. But the children did not appear to have inherited their parents' religious genes as Noyes had predicted. "It is a surprise," Dr. McGee wrote, "that in spite of their early doctrinal training only a very few are church members and but one is a Perfectionist."[40] Noyes's dream of a "self-perpetuating institution" of spiritually superior kingdom-builders had died less than a decade after its inception.[41] His "unlimited advance" of "science and the Higher Law" had failed, and ironically these children were partly responsible for it.[42] As the final section on "Sectarian End Times" will explain, in launching his stirpicultural experiment, Noyes had also planted the seeds of the Oneida Community's dissolution.

PART V

SECTARIAN END TIMES

THIS BOOK began with a look at historical context and an analogy from nature. The context was the hyperactive religious environment of antebellum America: a time and place in which plentiful land, mobile people, burgeoning but tenuous religious institutions, and flexible notions of religious authority made conditions perfect for populist religious renewal and experimentation. In this wide-open world of shifting cosmologies, millions of people were "awakened" at evangelical revivals, joined various churches, or left them unsatisfied and dared to start their own. The analogy from the natural world was that of a typical life cycle: childhood, adolescence, maturity, and decline. Part 1 described the radical theological and sexual ideas of the Mormons, Shakers, and Oneida Perfectionists, while the next three parts traced their origins, early struggles, and prime of life. This final section explores how those ideas, as lived institutions, fell apart.

Mormon polygamy, Shaker celibacy, and Oneida complex marriage succumbed to a combination of natural causes and an increasingly toxic environment. Intolerant of so-called obscenity, moralists on the local and national levels renewed their crusades against the supposedly aberrant sexual behavior of the Mormons and Oneida Perfectionists and would not stop until they were victorious. No one bothered to go after the Shakers because celibacy was not morally threatening and because the United Society of Believers had been declining since before the Civil War. The story of the Shakers' slow decay is therefore decidedly less dramatic, but like the Mormons and Oneidans it also had its internal and external causes.

Postbellum America was very different from antebellum America, and proved to be much less hospitable to radical sectarian experimenters. For starters, unsettled land—and the freedom from government intrusion that accompanied it—was starting to run out. This was most relevant to the Mormons. With the advent of the transcontinental railroad in 1869, Mormon polygamists were more threatened than before. In the antebellum era the federal government had been relatively weak, incapable of projecting its power and thus controlling its millions of people. With the transcontinental railroad and other lines that began to lattice the former Wild West, the federal government could now stretch the long arm of the law into every corner of the republic to enforce national legislation. Along with this gradual and inexorable increase in federal power came the confidence to finally gain control over the American continent and any remaining "un-American" peoples and practices. After much bloodshed, a kind of final victory was achieved in 1890 with the closing of the frontier, the last lopsided "battle" with Native Americans at Wounded Knee, and with the Church of Jesus Christ of Latter-day Saints officially abandoning plural marriage.

Just as innovations in science and technology enhanced the power of the federal government, they profoundly threatened the existence of these sectarian communities. Railroads and mining enterprises encroached upon Mormon territories, peoples, and institutions. Similarly and ironically as we will see, laborsaving machines began to endanger the simpler manufacturing techniques and lifestyle of Shaker villages. These new machines were actually good news for the already mechanized Oneida Community, but other discoveries in science shook the foundations of this people who so earnestly sought harmony between the spiritual and the material. The theories of Charles Darwin offered an alternative and potentially irreligious metanarrative. It was now possible to explain humankind's origin and nature materialistically. John Humphrey Noyes was fascinated by these new theories but they also troubled him; and they troubled his son, Theodore Noyes, even more. Perhaps reflecting his father's interest in the human body, Theodore had become a doctor, but he also—very much unlike his father—became a positivist and an agnostic. Noyes's inability to pass on his faith to his son but his strange insistence on naming him Oneida's next leader was a recipe for disaster and one of the principal internal causes of the community's collapse.

In many ways the spiritual hunger for *more* that had characterized the antebellum era abated as the nineteenth century progressed. Science did not completely replace religion, of course, but it did problematize faith, with the new social milieu creating far more people like Theodore Noyes than John Humphrey Noyes. The father, in other words, was becoming antiquated, while the son fit the times almost perfectly. These changes in the spiritual climate boded poorly not just for the Oneida Community but for the Mormon polygamous empire and the celibate United Society of Believers as well.

16

The Shakers, from Revolution to Refuge

THE STORY of Shaker declension is highly instructive but literally anticlimactic. Unlike the Oneidans there was no epic power struggle that eroded the sect from within; while unlike the Mormons there was no massive political crusade to repress them from without. There was instead a slow but constant ebbing away of sectarian vitality as Believers lost the faith and left the villages.

It is perhaps best to view Shaker struggles in the second half of the nineteenth century through the historical uber-categories of change and continuity. Unfortunately for the United Society of Believers, both what changed and what endured destined them to decline. What remained remarkably the same, for the most part, were Shaker doctrines. Treatises, testimonies, and other proselytizing literature from the 1850s to the 1890s largely just repeat and repackage the old fundamentals of the Shaker faith. In fact, rather than modify their beliefs and practices to better fit the times, apologists doubled down on their unique theology and the demanding "full cross" of authentic Christian discipleship.[1] Most foundationally, Believers continued to insist that "there is a natural and a spiritual world, and a natural and a spiritual body," and that "*true* Christians" in "the *true* Church of Christ" must eschew the first and earnestly pursue the second.[2] Ascetic values and a dualistic, Manichean worldview, in other words, were as strong as ever. "Bodies are only fictitious, fleeting, fading tenements or present coverings for the real Shaker," one Believer railed in 1879.[3] In terms of their theological pronouncements, the Shakers did not let up on their sectarian war against the flesh, the world, and worldly Christians one bit.

They also did not back down from their beliefs in Mother Ann Lee's divinity, their denial of the physical resurrection of Christ, or their insistence that sex was the root of all sin. "The Fountain whence all things originally flowed," Shaker theologian Frederick W. Evans explained in

1853, "is dual—Male and Female—*God*"; while the "first *man* redeemed from the earth was *Jesus*," and the "first *woman* redeemed in like manner was *Ann Lee*." In 1869 Evans published the story of his conversion from atheistic "Materialist" to Shaker Believer. The only hope of salvation for "the so-called Christian world," he prescribed, lay in doing what he had done: embracing Shaker beliefs, renouncing sex and marriage, and sharing in the earnest spiritual purity of a Shaker village. "Marriage," he explained, "is *not a Christian institution*," but a carnal one and one that Jesus renounced. From the 1850s to the 1890s, the message was the same: Jesus "was a Shaker; he lived a celibate life," and "has left us the example of total abstinence from sexual intercourse." If one truly wanted to follow Christ, one had to separate oneself from the world entirely, crucify the desires of the flesh daily, and as Evans misquoted Jesus as saying: "'Agonize to enter in at the straight gate.'"[4]

As the nineteenth century wore on, though, converts and potential converts simply found the Shakers' special brand of lifelong agony too much to bear. The United Society of Believers refused to compromise with the world, and as American society changed around them they began hemorrhaging members. Like John Humphrey Noyes with his son Theodore, as we will see next, they had a difficult time transmitting their unchanged faith to succeeding generations. Profound transformations in American demographics, economics, and culture were all turning Shaker villages into living relics of a bygone era. The Believers' obvious inability to replenish their ranks through procreation forced them to rely on converts for sustained communal life, but the demands of celibacy were less and less attractive to outside spiritual consumers. All in all, this was not a winning strategy for long-term sectarian vitality. Thus while the Shakers clung faithfully to their unique beliefs and practices, they were increasingly unable to sell them in a rapidly changing religious marketplace. The faithful enjoyed doctrinal continuity with earlier generations, but it cost them dearly. Sadly, whenever they embraced change, it also cost them dearly.

Shakers always valued manual labor and hard work. "Hands to work and hearts to God," is arguably the Believers' most famous axiom. Attributed to Mother Ann Lee herself, the saying shows up in print as early as 1816, and was a veritable mantra for Believers from some of the earliest days to the present.[5] This adage and the strong work ethic that it promoted are therefore further examples of continuity within Shakerism.

What changed as the nineteenth century progressed was the nature of work itself. Shakers paradoxically valued both hard work and laborsaving innovation. They were therefore not like the Amish who cling to both their religious tradition and to a certain, horse-and-buggy kind of lifestyle. The Amish insist on performing most of their labor by hand, in the same way their forebears did, in part to prevent modernity's encroachment. The Shakers had no such prohibitions and in fact welcomed technological innovation both from the outside world and of their own making. Most famously, they improved upon household items such as the flat broom and the clothespin, and more industrial-sized equipment such as the circular saw and other "power tools."[6]

In terms of the impact of new technologies on traditional religious communities, however, the Amish were right and the Shakers were wrong: welcoming modern conveniences exposed the Believers to modern systems and values that slowly eroded both their way of life and their cosmology. Celibacy and their faith in Mother Ann Lee had separated them from the world, but their economic life increasingly conformed them to it. As mentioned earlier, all three sects ironically depended on trade with the world in order to maintain a measure of separation from it. They all needed outside consumers to infuse their communities with cash or credit. The problem for the Shakers was that for a variety of reasons the outside economic world slowly crept into their villages and changed them. Believers welcomed the railroad, for instance, as an efficient means of distributing their products, but over time they increasingly had to live according to its schedule, which forced them to change their traditional routines of work, rest, and worship.[7]

The real insurmountable challenge for the Shakers, however, lay in economic production and not in distribution or consumption. Villages were supposed to be semi-autonomous communities of specialized and hard-working laborers, with tasks divvied out according to skill, gender, and age. Aiming to instill in children the community's strong work ethic, elders made sure to give them copious chores according to their strength and abilities, and apprenticed them in the more skilled trades. Similarly, able-bodied seniors never enjoyed the relaxed life of a retiree, but kept working in less physically demanding but still productive enterprises. Every Believer had a job to do that would contribute to the good of the whole. The trouble came when one of the most vital demographics of this structure weakened to the point of collapse.

Census data from 1840 lists 3,627 members of the United Society of Believers. Right in the middle of the Era of Manifestations, Shakers hoped that the spiritual intensity and numerical growth would continue ever upward. But rather than a launching pad, the 1840s turned out to be more like a plateau before the long and irreversible decline. The 1860 Census reveals that the Society had shrunk to 3,489 members—a relatively small loss—but then the trickle turned into a flood. In 1880, membership had declined almost 50 percent to 1,849, and then by 1900 had dropped more than 50 percent again to a mere 855 Shakers. But unfortunately a closer look at who was leaving and why paints an even more ominous picture.[8]

Devastatingly, most Shaker apostates were young men—precisely the people who performed the more physically demanding kinds of labor. While every Believer did his or her share of the community's work, the rapidly shrinking population of adult males disrupted beyond repair the economic life of village after village. As organic, multigenerational productive entities, Shaker villages functioned like little societies unto themselves, with healthy adults taking care of the children and the elderly who could not entirely take care of themselves. Ideally the children would grow up, take over the jobs of older members as they aged, and then work productively for decades until they too were replaced by the next generation. After the middle of the nineteenth century, however, the departure of so many young men upon reaching the age of maturity destroyed this system. The problem, in other words, came from the fact that a village's harmonious functioning depended on young recruits from the outside world who would not only grow up in a Shaker village but also remain committed to it for the rest of their lives.

In addition to being places of work and worship, Shaker villages had also long served as sanctuaries for children whose parents were either deceased or destitute. Believers had rejected the world and took good care of their own, but they also cared for the world's neediest whenever they arrived at their doorstep. Knowing that the villages could provide the stability and support that they could not, parents and guardians regularly turned children over to be raised by Shakers until they came of age. In this mutually beneficial arrangement, the young received physical care, education, and instruction in Shakerism, while the Believers gained potential converts and productive lifelong members. Some village leaders even sought out children when they feared that their numbers were in decline. The problem came when more residents accepted the benefits of communal life as dependent youngsters but then refused to shoulder their responsibilities as independent adult members. Financially, they cost the community dearly and gave little in return. As one Believer sardonically noted in 1865: "A real money making scheme for Shakers to raise them up[,] give them a good education[,] board[,] and clothe them till they get to be old enough to be of some benefit and then have them up and kick the bucket."[9] Apostate young adults did not physically die, but from the Shakers' perspective they might as well have. And unlike elderly members, who presumably passed away after a lifetime of productive contribution to the village, these apostates were primarily liabilities rather than assets.[10]

Demographic data reveals that in the second half of the nineteenth century these former wards left the villages in droves. Working with the Censuses of 1860, 1880, and 1900, scholar William Sims Bainbridge highlights this alarming and ultimately unsustainable trend. Members aged ten to nineteen years old were anywhere from 21.5 percent to 28.4 percent of the total population of the Society during these years, while members aged twenty–twenty-nine years old account for only 9.7 percent to 12.3 percent. The first set of figures demonstrates the Shakers' willingness to take in orphaned and poor children, while the second exposes their inability to retain them. More than half of village minors apostatized once they became adults. Former lively villages were turning into lonely ghost towns, or retirement communities for the shrinking, aging, and predominantly female Shaker remnant. "By 1900," Bainbridge writes, "the Shakers were 72 percent female." In that same year 43.5 percent of the United Society of Believers were over the age of fifty and only 26.5 percent in the prime working years between the ages of twenty and forty-nine. The other 30 percent were nineteen years old or younger, but the by-now familiar pattern of young adult apostasies gave Shaker leaders little hope of retaining them.[11]

As villages lost their able-bodied men and women, they inevitably reached a point of economic unsustainability and existential crisis. Local elders and eldresses had to hire outside laborers to keep their villages minimally functional—a practice that allowed "the world" and its values to infiltrate the sectarian communities all the more—and the central ministry at New Lebanon increasingly had to take the drastic step of shutting down and consolidating anemic villages. In 1875 they shuttered the village at Tyringham, Massachusetts, relocating its seventeen-member skeleton crew to the nearby village at Enfield, Connecticut. This was the first village the Shakers had to close in over fifty years and it was far from the last.[12] The central ministry closed four more villages before the turn of the century: North Union, Ohio, in 1889; Groveland, New York, in 1892; Canaan, New York, in 1897; and Poland Hill, Maine, in 1899.[13] Between 1900 and 1950 they closed twelve more, consolidating what remained of the United Society of Believers (fewer than 100 members) into one of the three villages at either Hancock, Massachusetts; Canterbury, New Hampshire; or Sabbathday Lake, Maine. Hancock closed in 1960 and Canterbury in 1992. At the time this book went to press in 2021, Sabbathday Lake is the only active village left, housing the world's last two living Shakers: Brother Arnold Hadd, age sixty; and Sister Jane Carpenter, age seventy-eight.[14]

I wrote at the beginning of this chapter that the story of Shaker decline was literally anticlimactic. Unlike the Oneida Community, which effectively died in 1881, Shakerism is still alive but clearly not well. As we will see in these final two chapters, Oneidans and Mormon polygamists fought and lost their battles against internal dissent and external hostility. The Shakers, in contrast, degraded slowly and undramatically by half-lives, from thousands of members, to hundreds, to dozens; but never quite reaching zero. As a historical interpreter and storyteller, it is difficult to find clear and illuminating turning points in an asymptotic demographic slope. Historian Stephen Stein chooses as one of his turning points the closing of the Tyringham village in 1875. He also rightly cautions against trying to graft the timeline of Shaker history onto the timeline of the rest of American history, warning in particular about the "searing, knifelike effect of the Civil War," and "the typical dividing line at 1860." He argues instead that "the Shakers require a different historical timetable to reflect the distinctive rhythms of their communal experience."[15]

If still searching for a meaningful turning point in Shaker history, however, I would nevertheless choose 1860. In that year Shaker leaders fundamentally revised their *Millennial Laws*. The 1845 version had been written during the Era of Manifestations and reveals the fervent asceticism of the time. The revised *Rules and Orders for the Church of Christ's Second Appearing* of 1860 retains the traditional Shaker emphasis on order, obedience, and separation from the world, but are decidedly less stringent. They are also far more concerned with mundane affairs. Rather than being preoccupied with lust, orderly worship, or the necessity of confession, the first section deals with "money," "business," and "purchases." The very first rule, in fact, is that "Believers must not run in debt to the world." Only then do the rules move on to more spiritual subjects like keeping the Sabbath holy and the importance of edifying as opposed to "filthy" language.[16]

Also, whereas earlier versions of the *Millennial Laws* had aimed—and failed—to impose uniformity throughout the Society, the 1860 version shows a shift to more local autonomy. The authors, for instance, divided the *Rules* into three broad classifications of "Orders," "Conditional Orders," and "Supplementary Orders," which can perhaps be thought of as a gradation from inflexible to more flexible to most flexible. Dealing with separation and sin, the first group was considered non-negotiable for all Believers in all villages. The second and third were more like lists of guidelines.[17]

The particulars of the 1860 *Rules,* however, are less important than the overall tone that they struck—one that was both new and apparently lasting. With their new flexibility, worldliness inevitably crept in. Believers were ordered to remain separate from the world, but they interacted with that world more frequently, going out into it to conduct village business and bringing back with them its values, distractions, and baubles. For instance the *Rules* explicitly forbade "superfluously marbled, or gilt books" and "Fancy articles of any kind." They also warned Believers not "to go into Museums, Theatres, or to attend Caravans or shows, to gratify curiosity." After 1860, however, curiosity apparently got the best of many Believers, luring them out of their villages permanently.[18] As William Sims Bainbridge writes: "After 1860, the census records show clear evidence that Shakerism had become a refuge rather than a revolution."[19]

This date of 1860—chosen by Bainbridge because it was a census year and not the beginning of the secession crisis—is not nearly as important as his beautiful description of Shakerism having become "a refuge rather than a revolution." Sectarian communities such as the Shakers, Mormons, and Oneida Perfectionists had always been refuges from the world; but in their earlier days they had also been radical beachheads for the invading, impending kingdom of God. Thus rather than a bunch of cowards retreating into defensible compounds, these sectarians were expectant revolutionaries, hoping to change their world by providing a religious, communal, and sexual alternative to it. Over time, however, the revolution failed to materialize and their communities took on new, more mundane functions and meanings. As Perry Miller famously wrote of the Puritan experiment in New England: "Having failed to rivet the eyes of the world upon their city on the hill, they were left alone with America." As American society became less religiously fervent after the Civil War, these groups became less relevant, popular, and ironically less sectarian and distinct. Rather than change the world, the world was changing them. As Miller describes the collective letdown of a fading, failed revolution: "This sense of the meaning having gone out of life, that all adventures are over, that no great days and no heroism lie ahead, is particularly galling when it falls upon a son whose father once was the public hero or the great lover. He has to put up with the daily routine without ever having known at first hand the thrill of danger or the ecstasy of passion."[20] The same was true for the later generations of Mormons, Shakers, and Perfectionists. The fires that had burned so intensely now only smoldered. Rather than the "thrill" of launching a movement or constructing a community, the spiritual descendants of Joseph Smith, Ann Lee, and John Humphrey Noyes had to "put up with the daily routine" of merely managing what remained.

The Shakers seem to have turned this invisible corner around the year 1860. They had begun to lose their revolutionary optimism as early as the 1840s. When the Era of Manifestations fizzled out, so did the growth of the United Society of Believers. In between 1840 and 1860 their numbers dipped slightly from 3,627 to 3,489; but more importantly so did their confidence and their outlook. Rather than an offensive campaign, they began to adopt more of a defensive strategy. In the first half of the nineteenth century, a Shaker village was both a refuge and a revolution—a revolution for all Believers and a caring refuge for the elderly among them, as well as for "the world's" unwanted children. The elderly and destitute youngsters they had always with them, but with the passage of time they simply could not retain a critical mass of committed adult members who would keep the revolution going.

17
The Triumph of Bread and Butter at Oneida

ON JANUARY 1, 1881, Oneida officially dissolved as a community and reorganized itself as a joint-stock corporation. Ironically, John Humphrey Noyes knew what made communities succeed and fail, and could have predicted Oneida's collapse. In 1870 he published his *History of American Socialisms,* a truly impressive intellectual achievement. Coming in at almost seven hundred pages, this tome is Noyes's encyclopedic description and assessment of many of America's communitarian experiments. It is also, in its own way, a valedictory and a lament. Sensing that the era of such communities was drawing to a close, Noyes wanted to catalog them for posterity and pass on the hard-won wisdom that could be gleaned from both the long-lasting successes and the short-lived failures. Without the "*afflatus,*" as he called it, of a shared religious belief system to unify people, secular communities inevitably attracted a heterogeneous bunch of members and inevitably fell apart when the going got tough. The second sine qua non of communal success was "to decompose the old family unit and make Communism the home-center." As always, the sinful institutions of marriage and family militated against the collective selflessness of religious disciples and had to be abolished. The third "general conclusion" Noyes reached was that "the *afflatus* must also be strong enough to prevail over personal leadership in its medium, and be able, when one leader dies, to find and use another."[1] As we will see, over the course of the 1870s, Noyes failed to take his own advice.

Like the Shakers, Oneida's most serious threat came from the younger generation, but Noyes made matters much worse by not following his own prescriptions for long-term communal viability. He continued to make Oneida more about himself and his projections of self (his son) than about his original, religious metanarrative. Most fatally, he violated the very Perfectionist doctrines that he authored. He had long campaigned against the sinful exclusivity of "philoprogenitiveness." But as Noyes aged and he thought about who would lead Oneida after his death, he brazenly privileged his own biological son, Theodore Richards Noyes, and began grooming him for the role of Community leader. Theodore, however, turned out to be a terrible choice. In Oneida's internal politics, Noyes's hypocrisy and nepotism angered community members, while Theodore's poor management only amplified their resentment.

Born in 1841, Theodore Richards Noyes was the only surviving son of John Humphrey Noyes and his legal wife Harriet Holton Noyes. As it turns out, he had inherited his father's keen mind, but not his resolute constitution. Whereas John Humphrey Noyes, like Brigham Young, was seemingly incapable of self-doubt, Theodore was prone to waffling and had a somewhat nervous disposition. In the 1860s he attended Yale for both his bachelor's degree and his training as a medical doctor. When he returned to Oneida in 1867 at twenty-six years old his father had big plans for him, placing him in charge of the community's business affairs as a kind of proving ground for more responsibility to come. To his father's great satisfaction, Theodore excelled in the position but displayed an inflexible leadership style that alienated some community members and boded poorly for the future. Theodore's rapidly changing and often-unclear religious convictions, however, troubled Noyes much more.[2]

In the 1860s and 1870s, the Oneida Community had proudly sent a dozen of its finest young men, including Theodore, to Yale and Columbia for college, hoping that they would return as accomplished and cultured, but still sectarian community members. The youngsters' time in college, however, changed them and they soon changed Oneida. What they learned was quite different from what Noyes had learned forty years earlier. Whereas his education had been primarily in the liberal arts and theology, this generation studied science, and as a result, Theodore Noyes explained, "tended to what is now called Agnosticism or Scientific Materialism."[3] John Humphrey Noyes had been troubled by these new theories in geology, biblical higher criticism, and evolutionary biology, but he ultimately reconciled them with his faith. Members of this younger generation often did not, with his son Theodore by far the most devastating apostate of all.

In 1873 the Community had to take tough measures against two of their Yale graduates: Theodore Noyes, and his cousin, Joseph Skinner, the son of Harriet Noyes Skinner. In college both had drunk deeply from the wells of positivism and German higher criticism, and both had become scientists: Theodore a doctor and Joseph Skinner a civil engineer.

Unable to keep their skepticism to themselves, both were disciplined through mutual criticism in hopes of restoring them, but both soon departed the Community: Joseph Skinner left permanently; Theodore could live apart from Oneida for only a little over a week. Caught between his insistence on religious uniformity at Oneida and his own "philoprogenitiveness," John Humphrey Noyes bent the community's rules and allowed his prodigal son to return, on the condition that Theodore not spread irreligious ideas and undermine unity. In this compromise—a kind of Puritan "Half-Way Covenant" of their own—Noyes explicitly stated that he allowed Theodore to return only because of "my hope that you will be converted."[4]

As another concession to rehabilitate his son, Noyes gave him a unique assignment—to investigate the popular religious phenomenon called spiritualism. Originating in the late 1840s in a nearby town in upstate New York, spiritualism was a means of communicating with the dead through mediums or spirit guides. Noyes had long pooh-poohed these séances as farcical and these so-called mediums as religious hucksters, but he thought that investigating spiritualism would loosen positivism's grip on his son and ideally be the first step in a return from darkness into light.[5]

By 1875 Noyes was so encouraged by Theodore's spiritual progress that he again lobbied to make him Oneida's heir apparent. In January John Humphrey Noyes moved to the other remaining Perfectionist community in Wallingford, Connecticut. At sixty-three years old, his metabolism was slowing, his hearing was diminishing, and he struggled increasingly with a throat condition that made speaking difficult. By December, after months of factionalism, business mismanagement, and generational tension at Oneida due to Noyes's absence, even those who had opposed Theodore previously now supported him. For the next year and a half Theodore oversaw Oneida's daily operations while his father in Wallingford remained Perfectionism's titular leader and ultimate authority. This new and clear governing structure worked reasonably well from December 1875 to May 1877, but it neither resolved the question of succession, nor did it effectively counterbalance the centrifugal forces that were continuing to threaten the Community.

Hoping to reinvigorate the Community's religious life, in late 1876 Noyes approved of a revival that was beginning to stir at Oneida. Led by two members from evangelical backgrounds, this season of renewal did indeed bring welcome spiritual energy to the community before it inevitably spun out of control. Enjoying an enhanced status, the revival's leaders threatened both Theodore's management at Oneida and Noyes's overall leadership from Wallingford when they insisted that those who did not participate in the enthusiasm—including Theodore, John Humphrey Noyes, and the entire community at Wallingford—were spiritually inferior. Noyes feared the rift that the revivals created between the communities, and so he ordered the revivalists to cease in the spring of 1877, after only a few months of activity.

In order to heal the division that the revival had created between Oneida and Wallingford, Theodore proposed that the communities be combined. Oneidans greeted the proposal enthusiastically and soon welcomed their Wallingford brothers and sisters with open arms as members of their one big happy family. On May 17, 1877, John Humphrey Noyes and company made a kind of triumphal reentry at Oneida, his fellow Perfectionists cheering his return as a sign of hope for their collective future. Taking advantage of this momentary spirit of solidarity, Noyes named Theodore as his successor and the majority of Oneidans accepted the proclamation. Theodore had mended his positivist ways and proven himself a capable manager. All hoped he would now fill his father's big shoes and carry his Perfectionist legacy into the future.[6]

Theodore Noyes's administration, however, only lasted until January 1878. Theodore had neither his father's religious authority nor his political dexterity, and Oneidans soon came to regard him instead as a divinely uninspired bureaucratic killjoy. Most unpopular of all, Theodore implemented new rules and regulations to crack down on what he perceived to be inefficiency in the community's business affairs and liberality in its sexual affairs. Reflecting perhaps the growing fascination with statistics and recordkeeping, he ordered Oneidans to keep a log of their daily work, and to submit in writing their proposals for sexual "fellowship." The first was designed to track people's productivity and rebuke them when necessary for any demonstrable laziness. The second was to reverse, as he saw it, an alarming trend toward sexual disorder. For years, he protested, members had been flouting the rule of ascending fellowship by arranging liaisons without first gaining permission from community leaders. Theodore insisted that the community return to the time-honored system of elder-approved sexual encounters, with the addition of a written application. Rank-and-file members naturally resented both of these novelties as managerial intrusions into what had become their more relaxed rhythms of work and sex.[7]

Even more problematic than the new rules was the person Theodore appointed to help enforce them: his female co-leader, Ann Hobart. Attractive, intelligent, and—by her own admission—more than a little manipulative, Ann had long been a special interest of Theodore's and a special concern to the rest of the Oneidans.[8] Back in 1863 Theodore had helped lead Ann through a dramatic religious conversion. Family history seemed to be repeating itself with tragic consequences. His father's unrequited love for his first convert, Abigail Merwin, had launched complex marriage. Now Theodore's love for his first convert would soon help end it. Theodore was smitten with Ann and succumbed to precisely the kind of exclusive love that the Perfectionists anathematized. Adding fuel to their romantic fire, in 1873 when Theodore started investigating spiritualism, Ann followed his lead and soon proved to be a talented spirit guide. Theodore and Ann enjoyed the usual sexual intimacy at Oneida, but during séances the two experienced a spiritual intimacy that they did not share with anyone else, exploring and making discoveries in the invisible world together.

Ann soon wanted to parlay her spiritual powers into temporal leadership. In 1875, when Theodore was appointed community superintendent, she rode his coattails as he took on more responsibilities. In 1877 when Theodore became the official "Father" of the community, he elevated Ann to the role of Oneida's "Mother," a decision that concerned many members. Ann had not stewarded power charitably before and some felt—rightly it turns out—that in this new role she would be even more self-serving. As the counselor to young women in 1874, for example, Ann had often denied them sexual access to men whom she wanted for herself.[9]

At first John Humphrey Noyes did not want to meddle in his son's new administration but he soon changed his mind. Throughout 1877 he watched nervously as the two implemented their unpopular bureaucratic regulations of the community's economic and sexual affairs. Ann had also started to turn against Theodore, talking "very disrespectfully of him," one community member testified, adding that she could "scarcely remember an instance of his beating her in their discussions."[10]

In January 1878 the crisis reached its crescendo. Shocking his father, the henpecked Theodore defended Ann, refused to dismiss her as his co-leader, and tendered his own resignation instead. Both were removed from their posts and soon left Oneida. Ann then contacted Joseph Skinner, the father of her child and Theodore's cousin and fellow Yale graduate who had left Oneida permanently back in 1873. Breaking Theodore's heart, the two soon married and restarted a monogamous life together in New Haven. As with his previous sojourn, Theodore could not stay away from Oneida for long, soon returning to the Community on the condition that he would never again be its leader. Thus the crisis was passed, but there was still little direction or enthusiasm for the future.[11]

Starting in 1878 the Oneida Community entered a kind of "end-game" phase. The Perfectionists had been animated during the disastrous reign of Theodore and Ann, but after they abdicated, the Community "fell into a rather melancholy anticlimactic humdrum," as one historian puts it.[12] John Humphrey Noyes was back in charge but irreparably weakened by the fracas; and as he physically declined further, long-suppressed resentments turned into outright opposition—a previously unthinkable revolution. Sensing his vulnerability and their own opportunity, some Oneidans started to challenge his monopoly on power. Noyes had carefully constructed his religious metanarrative and ecclesiastical governing mechanisms over more than forty years. His rivals dismantled them in less than three.

John Humphrey Noyes finally met his match in the remarkable figure of James William Towner. Born in upstate New York in 1823, Towner grew up—much like Joseph Smith—a poor religious seeker. He soon found his spiritual home in Universalism and his calling as a reformer, championing such radical causes as socialism, abolitionism, and—most relevantly—free love. Displaying the spiritual restlessness of the time, he was ordained a Universalist minister in 1849, joined the secular free-love community at Berlin Heights, Ohio, soon after its founding in 1856, and was admitted to the bar in Iowa in 1859. A man of action as well as conviction, when the Civil War broke out he joined the Union Army, was promoted to captain, and lost his left eye at the Battle of Pea Ridge in 1862. After the war he returned to Berlin Heights and became a judge in nearby Cleveland. In 1866 Towner petitioned Noyes to admit him and his wife to the Oneida Community, claiming that, in addition to their interest in sexual freedom, they were also now more deeply religious and would find Oneida more to their liking than the irreligious Berlin Heights. Noyes rejected their application, perhaps sensing that the Towners would bring their former community's secularism and libertinism along with them. Undaunted, the Towners reapplied several times, finally gaining admission after Noyes deemed their religious convictions genuine. In 1873 James William Towner brought to Oneida his wife, children, several other friends and relatives, and a dowry of $14,000. Towner also brought, however, his unbridled ambition and a coterie of followers who would soon coalesce into a rival faction: the Townerites.[13]

From 1873 to 1878 Towner watched Oneida falter under Noyes's declining influence and Theodore's inept leadership. In 1878 and the first half of 1879, after Theodore was permanently removed from power, the Townerites clamored increasingly for change. While admiring complex marriage and Perfectionist faith, they wanted to replace Noyes's theocracy with a democratic governing structure and replace his system of elder-mediated sexual liaisons with the kind of unsupervised sexual freedom they had enjoyed at Berlin Heights. Noyes, of course, would entertain neither, claiming a commission from God as the inspired author of Perfectionism and the original pioneer of complex marriage.[14] As such he believed he could appoint a successor, as he had with Theodore, but he would not tolerate a usurper.

Undaunted, Towner built his coalition carefully, identifying other disgruntled Oneidans and conducting secret meetings before launching any concerted public attack. But as his confederacy grew so did his impudence, eventually crystalizing into overt calls for reform. When Noyes ignored these, the opposition devolved into shouting matches in the Community's once hallowed evening meetings, precisely where Noyes had long held his audience captive to his ideas and his person. Now he had to feebly deflect the Townerites' jeers and cries raining down on him from their seats in the meeting hall's balcony. He had dealt with opposition before, but not like this. Hindered by hearing loss and a weak voice, the former champion debater could not mount an effective defense, and after eighteen months of nearly incessant agitation, Noyes conceded defeat. He left Oneida on June 23, 1879, never to return. There were other factors involved in Noyes's sad abdication, but none of them as important as the Townerites' irksome hostility.[15]

Inside the Community, this unprecedented discord soon had a toxic effect. The Townerites never constituted a majority and their brazen attacks made everyone fear for the future. John Humphrey Noyes *was* the Oneida Community. For thirty years he had been the unifying center of their spiritual, sexual, and mundane-material life. Now he was entering his dotage, his son Theodore had proven incompetent as a successor, and approximately one third of the Oneidans were screaming for a revolution. For those who had devoted their lives to the causes of Perfectionism and complex marriage, what did the future hold, both for them and—more importantly—for their children?

This uncertainty affected the Community's women the most, especially if they were mothers. "Every woman wants to lean on some man to protect her and provide for her," one Oneidan opined: "At present the Community as an organization does this, but if the Community is not positively certain to last, she wants to know what man is to take its place as a guardian and provider and husband to her." Frank Wayland-Smith, a friend of Theodore Noyes and a loyal Perfectionist, confided these words to his diary on February 5, 1879, and although clearly sexist, what he said about the predicament Oneida's women faced was understandable given the limited resources and opportunities available to them in the nineteenth century. "Women are more helpless than men," he added, "and greater odium attaches to any sexual irregularities they may have engaged in. After having borne children to several men, their chances in the outside world would therefore be very bad unless some man stood ready to claim them and take care of them." In other words, Oneida's women would have to endure both Victorian America's limited economic opportunities and its sexual double standard.

This unease about the future, Wayland-Smith explained, soon constituted a powerful undercurrent at Oneida. As he described the dread: "great suffering would inevitably result if we should make shipwreck." As biblical communists, they had shared everything. Now their sectarian Eden was ending and they were about to be cast out into an uncertain and unforgiving world. To employ Wayland-Smith's metaphor, their happy but now wrecked ship was sinking and the only lifeboat they could reach for was monogamy. Although still a true believer, Wayland-Smith did not fault these women for their "temptation to exclusiveness." He knew that it was born out of self-preservation and not selfishness or disloyalty to Perfectionism; and he reasoned that their growing dissatisfaction with complex marriage came not from any inherent flaw in the practice, but from changes that the Community was now powerless to arrest.[16]

The national mood outside Oneida—in "the world"—gave Perfectionists only more reason to fear for the future. Back in 1873 Congress passed the Comstock Law, which made it illegal to distribute so-called "obscene" material—including information relating to birth control or human anatomy—through the US Postal Service. This governmental crackdown on supposed immorality was the brainchild of twenty-eight-year-old Anthony Comstock, the recent founder of the New York Society for the Suppression of Vice. Working with the Young Men's Christian Association (YMCA), Comstock declared war on the lewd and the lascivious, and was more than willing to use the power of the federal government to help him advance his campaign. As the next chapter will illustrate, these crusaders likewise sought to cleanse the national stain of Mormon polygamy in faraway Utah, but they had a convenient target closer to home in the Oneida Community. Emboldened by the new national tone, moralists in upstate New York began to clamor once more to extirpate the sexual sinners in their midst.

The leader of this renewed crusade was John W. Mears, a Presbyterian minister and professor at Hamilton College, ten miles from Oneida. In early 1873 he denounced the "impure and shocking practices" "here in the heart of the Empire State," and actually praised the citizens of Illinois, who "could not endure the immorality of the Mormons, but drove them from Nauvoo in 1846." Noyes and company had good reason to be concerned as Mears's call for repression soon won the support of ministers throughout the region. Methodists, Congregationalists, and Baptists all joined with the Presbyterians, adopting condemnatory resolutions in their effort to stir people to action.[17]

In 1873 and 1874 Mears's campaign gained some support but went nowhere. Concerned as ever with popular perception, Noyes had *The Circular* publish ripostes such as "What the Papers Say About Us," "What the Presbyterians Say," and "What We Say About Ourselves," in an effort to get out the Oneidan side of the story.[18] In October 1874 Mears's Presbyterian Synod of central New York published what they hoped would be a devastating exposé on Oneida, but there was literally nothing new to report. Everyone in the region already knew about complex marriage and stirpiculture, and apparently had made their peace with those practices. As *The Circular* exulted: "There is room for all of us."[19] That might have been the end of Mears's abortive crusade, until news of Theodore Noyes's failure and abdication in 1878 revealed the community's internal problems and revived the hopes of its external foes.

Seeing an opportunity to strike while the Perfectionists struggled, Mears renewed his offensive at the beginning of 1879. On February 14 he convened a meeting of fifty local ministers to denounce Oneida's immoralities and discuss what action could be taken to end them. Fatefully, he excluded members of the press from attending the meeting, which annoyed them and turned their skepticism about the crusade into outright hostility. In the months that followed, many local and even national newspapers sided decisively with the Oneidans, reminding readers of their longstanding contributions to the region and of the weakness of any potential legal case against them. Some even turned their pens against Mears and his co-conspirators, mocking them for their self-righteous hypocrisy. Most famously, the satirical magazine *Puck* published a scathing cartoon in which a gaggle of sourpuss ministers point menacingly at Oneida and exclaim: "Oh, dreadful! They dwell in peace and harmony, and have no church scandals. They must be wiped out."[20] Noyes was ecstatic about these allies coming to Oneida's defense.[21] Mears's campaign had backfired. Even in the context created by the Comstock Law and the crusade against Mormon polygamy in the 1870s, it was impossible to marshal public sentiment against complex marriage when the Perfectionists had been transparent about it for decades. Thus rather than turning Noyes into a pariah, Mears became one instead; "the butt of stinging rebukes," one historian writes, "met with glacial courtesy by most of the sound pillars of business and industry between Syracuse and Utica."[22]

With public support trending in his favor, it was somewhat of a fluke that prompted Noyes to leave Oneida in June 1879, and end complex marriage two months later. Not every local newspaper had come to his defense. On June 21 the *Syracuse Standard*, perhaps desperate to rescue the losing cause that it had joined, brazenly lied to the reading public. In sensationalistic capitals, their headline read: "NOYES, TO BE ARRESTED. LEGAL PROCEEDINGS TO BE COMMENCED. TESTIMONY BEING TAKEN WHICH STAMPS THE ONEIDA COMMUNITY AS FAR WORSE IN THEIR PRACTICES THAN THE POLYGAMISTS OF UTAH."[23] The story was a total fabrication. The headline, however, profoundly affected Noyes, landing a lucky punch precisely where he was most vulnerable—his fear of public odium, prosecution, and incarceration. The next day and without explaining why, he put some of his legal affairs in order, including who was to govern Oneida in the event of his death or absence, explicitly excluding from the list his son Theodore as well as James W. Towner and his cronies. Sometime in the middle of that night, June 22–23, he left Oneida without making a sound—supposedly creeping, one historian writes, "downstairs in his stocking feet."[24] Once outside he and one of his most loyal supporters, Myron Kinsley, rode to the nearest train station and departed for the Canadian border, safely beyond the reach of American authorities.

Exhausted and demoralized by the Townerites' opposition, Noyes could not rely on a united home front to protect him. As more neutral Oneidans—both men but especially women—started losing faith in him to guarantee their future, they undermined his defenses all the more. With only a precious few to safeguard him, Noyes sensed that he was running out of options. When the *Syracuse Standard* reported on his imminent arrest—false and deceitful though the story was—both he and Myron Kinsley feared that the Townerites might find common cause with the outside agitators and conspire to ruin Noyes. Both groups wanted him gone, and legal prosecution and possible imprisonment would remove him permanently. The fact that James Towner was a lawyer and could possibly contribute to any legal case against Noyes only fueled the loyalists' paranoia. In truth, though, there was no conspiratorial alliance of internal and external foes, just as there was no real threat of prosecution in the first place. But in Noyes's and Kinsley's minds, they were all out to get him and there was a very real fear that they might succeed.[25] Noyes thus took Kinsley's advice and left the country. What would happen to Oneida next was anyone's guess.

Unsurprisingly, rather than solve any of the Community's problems, Noyes's departure only magnified them. Without their longtime shepherd, the Oneidans divided into three bickering sub-flocks. Encouraged by the abdication, the Townerites pushed their reform agenda with renewed energy, but they sought illogical goals. They wanted to replace Noyes's autocracy with a more democratic governing structure, but they themselves were a numerical minority, roughly one third of the Perfectionists. They therefore stood to lose—and did lose—in any community-wide election. They likewise sought to replace Noyes's restrictive law of ascending fellowship with a more laissez-faire communal sexual order, but many Oneidans were now losing their faith in complex marriage altogether and gravitating increasingly toward monogamy.

Against the Townerites stood the loyalists: older, longstanding members who continued to revere Noyes and hope for his return. They had been supportive but relatively quiet during the first half of 1879, perhaps assuming that their omnicompetent leader could manage things one more time. When he abandoned them they were both shocked and angry and soon took out their resentment on the Townerites, blaming them for Noyes's departure and obstructing their agenda at every turn as a highly motivated voting bloc. But, like Noyes, they were part of an older generation, speaking for him and nostalgically longing to return to the community's good old days, but lacking any real vision for a future without him.

The third group was comprised of Oneida's younger generation, people like Theodore Noyes and Frank Wayland-Smith who were more scientifically and pragmatically oriented than religious and idealistic. Adding to the confusion, they opposed the changes that both the loyalists and the

Townerites wanted most. Whereas the Townerites sought sexual freedom, they were content to embrace the world's institution of monogamous marriage; and whereas the loyalists wanted Noyes back, they were at peace with the likelihood that he would never return. Obviously, no matter which faction would prevail in this contest, the way Oneida had been operating for over thirty years was clearly ending. John Humphrey Noyes had woven himself so deeply into the community's social fabric that it simply could not exist long without him.[26]

Complex marriage died first. On July 19, 1879, Frank Wayland-Smith wrote to Noyes about the emergency situation and included a radical proposal for the future. As he aptly surmised: "Now I see clearly that unless the young of both sexes are trained and controlled substantially as you have trained and controlled them in the past, our social system must eventually go down." Wayland-Smith was right to stress the importance of control. Without a controller, he feared that the Community would "run into the looseness such as is generally understood as attaching to the term 'Free Love,'" a prospect that he and any real Perfectionist—Noyes especially—could not tolerate. "What then are we to do?" he asked plaintively. There seemed to be no other path before them than the obvious nuclear option: complex marriage would have to be abolished and the Community would temporarily embrace sexual abstinence. The beginning of the end for Oneida complex marriage quite possibly came with the following sentences: "I am more than half convinced that it will be better for the record of our experiment if you close it up in a round and handsome way during your lifetime, leaving us all in good and safe position and then withdrawing your sanction from all [future] sexual irregularities. You would then have conducted the experiment of a lifetime and brought it to a safe conclusion, instead of leaving it to decay or fall into worse disaster, as so many other leaders have done. It would astonish the world to see such an example of continence." Noyes was convinced. Long had he defended complex marriage against the accusation of "free love," establishing his sexual "experiment" on a religious and a personal foundation. Now that he was not there in person to administer it, and the Townerites were threatening to "establish a new code of morality—I might almost say, a religion—different from that you have taught," Noyes chose to terminate his prized creation rather than see it hijacked and bastardized by a group of religiously suspect libertines.[27]

As the factions at Oneida debated the future, Noyes proclaimed authoritatively one last time. On August 20, 1879, less than two months after his departure, the remnants at Oneida received Noyes's proposal "that we give up the practice of Complex Marriage." With characteristic organization and intellectual rigor, he made his case. Life, he pontificated, could be divided into two "great motives . . . the religious motive which looks to heaven, and the worldly motive which looks to 'bread and butter.'" He had spent the majority of his life looking "to heaven" and trying to bring it down to earth, but he also recognized the importance of "worldly . . . 'bread and butter'" concerns. Confessing "supreme anxiety" about the community's future, he feared especially for those who had lived most of their lives in Oneida's sheltered paradise and were now about to "be thrown out into the world and compelled to get their living by hard work." With genuine pastoral tenderness, he put those people's needs ahead of his own religio-sexual innovations, announcing that the community should sacrifice its unpopular sexual arrangement in order to "keep that great machine—the business organization which shelters and feeds them—going with unfailing momentum."[28]

Regarding the future of sex and marriage at Oneida, Noyes suggested that the community be "put on Paul's plan, which *allows* marriage, but prefers singleness."[29] He still considered monogamy to be a selfish and exclusive compromise with the world, but he no longer recommended complex marriage as an alternative, and the majority of Oneidans agreed. Complex marriage, they declared, would officially terminate at 10 A.M. on August 28, 1879. In the days and hours leading up to the deadline there was a flurry of horizontal fellowships, as members said their "sexual 'good-byes'" to their favorite partners.[30] The many wedding ceremonies soon after the deadline indicate that most Oneidans were ready to settle down into a monogamous, monotonous life, but they also wanted to partake one last time of the variety that complex marriage had allowed them to enjoy.

Without the presence of John Humphrey Noyes and the practice of complex marriage to unite them, Oneida soon collapsed as an alternative religious community. In his 1870 *History of American Socialisms,* Noyes had been prophetic. There he had argued that successful communities distinguished themselves from the many unsuccessful ones by having a religious "*afflatus*"; by reorienting followers away from family and toward community; and by effectively passing their unique *afflatus* from one generation to the next.[31] Noyes had definitely developed an *afflatus,* but unlike both Joseph Smith and Ann Lee, he could not make it outlast him. Theodore's failure as a leader, major generational differences among the Perfectionists, internal dissention, and external hostility all combined to bring his experiment to a close. Ending complex marriage, it turns out, was like removing the community's cornerstone: without it, the rest of the building soon came crashing down. As community structures and values started to dissolve around them, anxious members started to fend for themselves, either as individuals or as newly married couples. The selfish individualism that Noyes had long kept outside Oneida's borders now infiltrated the Community and ended it. By 1880 many of the Perfectionists had paired off into monogamous marriages. No longer would they share sexual partners in common.

By 1881 they had decided to end common property as well. It was simply impossible to have the one without the other. Over the course of 1880 they debated how to divide up the community's assets fairly among the individual members; "to unscramble the eggs of communal living and industry," as one historian memorably puts it.[32] The details of the plan were complicated but fair, and not nearly as important as the spirit of individualism behind them. The former communists wanted what was theirs so that they could provide for themselves and their families in the future. In the end they voted almost unanimously to divide and reorganize as a joint-stock, limited-liability corporation, with the former members receiving cash or stock, or both, according to how much they had contributed to the community and for how long. Legally speaking, the transition was scheduled to go into effect at midnight, December 31, 1880. On New Year's Day 1881 there was no more communal property and no more Oneida Community.

18
The War on Polygamy and the Temporal Salvation of the Mormon Church

THIS FINAL chapter is about power. In particular it is about the conflict between two powers: the US government and the Church of Jesus Christ of Latter-day Saints. As the Civil War faded into memory and Reconstruction failed to revolutionize the South as its architects had hoped, government forces trained their guns on Mormon plural marriage. In Brigham Young's LDS Church, however, they encountered a formidable foe with impressive resources of its own. The polygamous Great Basin kingdom was not as daunting as the slave-owning Confederacy had been, but it still represented an affront to the credibility of the state and a stain on America's reputation as a so-called Christian nation. In order to claim mastery over its territory, its people, and its culture, the US government had to end the institution.

This particular story begins in the decade before the Civil War, when the Church announced plural marriage and the American people and government responded with predictable disapprobation. In 1856 the brand-new Republican Party included in its platform a resolution as to "the right and the imperative duty of Congress to prohibit in the Territories those twin relics of barbarism—Polygamy, and Slavery."[1] In some ways this was the beginning of a national crusade against the Mormons.

The Saints were safely ensconced in Utah, hundreds of miles from any other state, but unfortunately for them, federally appointed judges to the territory continued to complain of Mormon noncompliance, and one of them, William W. Drummond, overtly requested that President James B. Buchanan replace Brigham Young with a non-Mormon governor and send him quickly to Utah, accompanied "with sufficient military aid." Fed alarming reports, President Buchanan came to believe that the Saints were in a state of rebellion, and he took the opportunity to demonstrate the power of the federal government where he thought he could.[2] In early 1857, mere months after his inauguration, he ordered the army to Utah to make an example of the Mormons and supplant Young as territorial governor.[3]

The "Utah Expedition" as it was officially called was a fiasco, quickly earning the apt nickname "Buchanan's Blunder." The troops departed late in the traveling season and suffered from a lack of supplies, effective leadership, and even the support of most of the American people. Although hardly pro-Mormon, Americans increasingly saw the crusade as unprovoked, unnecessary, expensive, and unjust. For their part, the Saints had no idea about the government's intentions, but with a long history of persecution, they had every reason to expect violence. President Buchanan sent no advance notification that he had appointed a new governor for the Utah Territory. All they knew is that a sizable armed force was marching straight for their kingdom.

Defiant as ever, Brigham Young saber-rattled his people into action, but ultimately elected to do what the Church had always done best: hit the road. Unlike previous exoduses, the "Move South" as it was called was more like a temporary mass evacuation than a permanent relocation. Starting in April 1858, *over 30,000* Utah Saints started traveling south to Provo, approximately forty miles away. When the newly appointed territorial governor, Alfred Cumming, arrived in Salt Lake City on April 12, months ahead of the slower-moving army, he witnessed this impressive but pathetic migration for himself and wanted it stopped, assuring the Saints that the approaching army would not harm them. Understandably skeptical of government promises, Young continued the evacuation until Salt Lake City was a virtual ghost town. He also left a rear guard in the city, with orders to burn it to the ground if the army showed any sign of hostility.[4]

Fortunately for everyone, when the Utah Expedition reached the city on June 26, 1858, the soldiers were under strict orders not to destroy any property. A few days later, as per prior negotiation, they began constructing Camp Floyd, forty miles to the southwest and thus removed from any unwelcome encounters with the Saints. The 30,000 participants of the "Move South" then began slogging back to their abandoned homes. One soldier who witnessed the returning dispossessed described them as "ragged and dirty, though some of the young girls had endeavored to make as respectable an appearance as possible, by making garments out of corn sacks."[5] Although they had avoided violence, this was yet another humiliating experience for the Saints. They had fled the world to live their religion and build their kingdom in peace. After a decade of struggle, deprivation, and sacrifice, the world had come to them in the form of an invading army—an enemy force camped menacingly a mere forty miles away.

The "Utah War" as it was also called thus ended in a literal standoff between Church and state. The Saints were now an occupied people. Although a buffer zone existed between the two, the army was clearly poised to execute with force if necessary the orders of the US government. "The Mormon quest for political autonomy, while not fully over," one historian sums up, "had suffered a crippling blow from which it would never recover."[6] Brigham Young was no longer the governor of the Utah Territory. Forced to accept federal authority, he and the Saints would not and could not control the mechanisms of government until Utah became a state in 1896, almost forty years later.

After the drama of the Buchanan administration, the Utah Saints enjoyed a season of relative peace under President Abraham Lincoln. With secession and Civil War, clearly the federal government had more pressing problems than the Mormon Church in faraway Utah. In fact, ever the pragmatic liberal, Lincoln reportedly told one Mormon diplomat in Washington: "You go back and tell Brigham Young that if he will let me alone I will let him alone."[7]

Some of Lincoln's fellow Republicans were less charitable toward polygamous Saints, but their moral crusade never got any farther than the Capitol. In 1862 Senator Justin Morrill of Vermont shepherded through Congress his Act for the Suppression of Polygamy. Wanting to send a clear and literally unprecedented message that the government would now enforce marital uniformity throughout the land, the Morrill Act did three things. As summarized by historian Sarah Barringer Gordon, it: "outlawed bigamy in the territories, providing a prison sentence of up to five years and a fine of $500; annulled the Utah territorial legislature's incorporation of the Church of Jesus Christ of Latter-day Saints; and prohibited any religious organization from owning real estate valued at more than $50,000." In the short term the bill accomplished nothing. Cash-strapped because of the war, Congress allocated no funds to enforce the law and dared not risk stirring up more hostility in another part of the country. "The act was a statement of principle from the central government," Gordon writes, but one that was effectively "stalled by the reality of resistance at the local level."[8] No polygamist was convicted under the provisions of the Morrill Act from 1862 to 1874, although it had set an important legal precedent. Thus the bill sat on the books, unenforced for over a decade; but its details—prison sentences, fines, attacks on the legal rights and property of the LDS Church—would come back to strike Mormon polygamists, and the Church itself, with a vengeance.

From the early 1860s to the mid 1870s, there was an inverse relationship between the attention the Republican-dominated Congress paid to rebels, slaves, and freed people in the South, and the attention it paid to Mormon polygamists in Utah. Fascinatingly, federal legislators even sponsored antipolygamy bills in 1866, 1867, 1869, and 1870, but none of them passed![9] "Leading politicians and preachers," Leonard Arrington writes, "had confidently predicted that the railroad would mean the end of Mormonism."[10] Once permanently connected to the Union, the theory went, non-Mormons would flood into the region, diluting the Church's control of the territory and providing a political base from which to dismantle both the theocracy and the institution of polygamy. Politically speaking, legislators reasoned, why have the federal government do what demographics and the industrializing economy would accomplish on their own? And so Congress in the late 1860s and 1870 voted down the four antipolygamy bills put before them.

Antipolygamy activists had likewise put their faith in the power of women's suffrage to undermine the institution and were likewise disappointed with the result. In 1869 neighboring Wyoming had enfranchised women in a bid to boost the population of the territory and provide companionship to the many lonely cowboys there. In January 1870 thousands of Mormon women, many of them plural wives, petitioned the Utah territorial government to grant them the same right, a request that Brigham Young enthusiastically supported. Enfranchising women entailed certain risks, but it also doubled the Mormon voting bloc. With the transcontinental railroad arriving at the same time, carrying with it a potential horde of Gentile settlers, he would take every vote he could get, and the female Saints did not let him down. The vast majority of Mormon women soon voted in lockstep with their menfolk, proclaiming defiantly their right to live their religion in peace. Antipolygamy advocates did not see this coming. They thought that Mormon women would use the suffrage as a means to escape plural marriage, not defend the institution and vote for its protection and perpetuation. However, these Mormon women largely voted to protect their status as legal—although polygamous—wives, as opposed to being mistresses or harlots; and to protect their children's status as legitimate heirs, as opposed to being bastards in the eyes of the law. Regardless, women's suffrage did not turn out to be the end of polygamy as its enemies had hoped.[11]

In the mid 1870s the crusade against plural marriage resumed with a new intensity, and this time it did not stop until the Church abandoned polygamy in 1890. Mormon leaders did not know it at the time but 1873 would prove to be a pivotal year. In September a nationwide financial crisis began that thrust the country into one of the worst depressions it had ever experienced. In the congressional elections of 1874, voters vented their rage on the incumbent Republican Party, turning their 110-seat majority into a Democratic majority of 60. Democrats had not controlled the House of Representatives for twenty years. Mormons hoped to receive more lenient treatment from the Democratic majority, but not before Republicans had fired a fatal parting shot in the 1874 Poland Act. Sponsored by Representative Luke P. Poland of Vermont, the bill was intended to give legal teeth to the impotent 1862 anti-bigamy act of his fellow Vermonter, Justin Morrill.

Federal officials had not failed to prosecute Mormon polygamists under the Morrill Act for lack of trying. It is true that they did little in the eight years from the time the bill passed in 1862 until 1870. That year, President Ulysses S. Grant appointed James B. McKean to serve as the chief justice of the Utah Territory and things were about to change. The era of Lincoln's salutary neglect was over. A devout Methodist and equally devoted Republican, Justice McKean was determined to uphold the Morrill Act and prosecute polygamous Saints for their crimes. From 1870 to 1874, however, he failed miserably. As wily as ever, Brigham Young and the Saints defended themselves, forcing Congress to pass the stronger Poland Act to deal with them.[12]

The most effective weapon in the Saints' defense against Justice McKean was their control of the territory's probate courts, which allowed them to select juries from local Utahans, who would be sympathetic to their cause. Back in 1851, the Mormon-dominated legislature cleverly wrote laws that empowered the probate courts and insulated them from outside legal meddling. Thus when Justice McKean, or any other territorial justice, wanted to prosecute Mormons for a crime, they had to go through the system that the Saints had literally written for themselves.[13]

Believing that the original 1851 establishment of the probate courts was illegitimate, Justice McKean decided to bypass them and prosecute Mormons with juries of hand-picked Gentiles, ultimately securing 130 indictments against leading Mormons, including Brigham Young, on charges from cohabitation to murder. These were seriously perilous times for the Church, but in April 1872 the Supreme Court ruled that McKean had overstepped his legal authority. All 130 indictments were thrown out, the Mormons' probate court apparatus remained intact, and Justice McKean was chastened by the highest court in the land. After the rebuke, President Grant and other antipolygamy crusaders pushed for tougher federal legislation, which they achieved with the passage of the Poland Act in 1874. The "teeth" that it added to the Morrill Act ended the jurisdiction of the probate courts and stipulated that all future Utah juries be part Mormon and part Gentile. With its passage, the Church effectively lost control over Utah's judicial system.[14]

Fatefully and at precisely the same time, Brigham Young had also lost control of his most trouble-making plural wife, Ann Eliza Webb Young. As mentioned, 1873 was a pivotal year for polygamous Saints, whether they knew it or not. In July, Ann Eliza Webb Young sued Brigham Young for divorce. The two were married in 1868, when Ann was a twenty-four-year-old divorcée and Young a sixty-six-year-old husband of at least forty other women. Ann was his last young plural wife and presumably one he regretted marrying. Her lawsuit, speaking tour, and published exposé, partially entitled *Wife Number Nineteen; or, The Story of a Life in Bondage*, revived antipolygamy sentiment throughout the country and gave the political crusade against plural marriage new life.

In truth, Young's control had been slipping for some time. In 1871 he turned seventy and confronted numerous health problems including obesity, rheumatism, and digestive and urological issues.[15] Also in the early 1870s, the husband-and-wife team of Thomas and Fanny Stenhouse, both of them Mormon critics of Young, began broadcasting their dissent. In 1872, Mrs. Stenhouse published *A Lady's Life among the Mormons*, and in 1873 her husband published *The Rocky Mountain Saints: A Full and Complete History of the Mormons*. Both took the Church to task for its theocratic authoritarianism and its institution of plural marriage. Fanny Stenhouse in particular laid bare "the secret heart-aches" and "conflicted feelings Mormon women have to contend with."[16] It was in this context of renewed dissension that Ann Eliza Webb Young first divorced Brigham Young and then told her own story to a very interested American public.

After filing for divorce in July 1873, Ann Young soon took her case to the public, speaking to packed lecture halls up and down the East Coast. Audiences lapped up her damning stories of what Mormonism's most infamous polygamist was like behind closed doors, and sympathized at her tales of suffering. When asked "where polygamy hurt the most," she famously responded: "'It hurts all over, body and soul, mind and heart... I can't tell a spot that it does not hurt.'"[17] In April 1874 she spoke in Washington, DC, to an audience that included President and Mrs. Grant, and she lobbied personally for the government to do something about the plight of Mormon women in Utah. Her crusade was so successful, in fact, that Congress passed the Poland Act just two months later, a development that must have terrified Brigham Young. Disgruntled former insiders had now joined forces with determined outsiders in an alliance that could bring down the entire polygamous kingdom, which it eventually did. Thus the real beginning of the end for Mormon plural marriage came just as much from Brigham Young's own family as it did from moral crusaders in far-off Washington, DC.[18]

Passed in part because of Ann Young's speaking tour, the Poland Act of June 1874 triggered a series of legal decisions and legislative acts that ultimately ended Mormon plural marriage in 1890. Immediately after the act's passage, federal prosecutors pushed hard to find a test case that would bring polygamists to justice. Surprisingly, Church leaders actually welcomed the showdown, confident that the Supreme Court would vindicate them just as it had when it voided Justice McKean's indictments in 1872. Devastating to the Church's case, however, this time the prosecution found a star witness in a naïve plural wife who testified that she and her husband were indeed plurally married and therefore lawbreakers.

Rather than Brigham Young or another leading patriarch, the polygamous Saint at the center of the trial was George Reynolds, the secretary to the First Presidency. Only thirty-two years old and only a polygamist since August 1874, the unassuming Reynolds seemed to be the perfect candidate to exculpate the Mormons. The problem turned out to be with his new plural wife, Amelia. Whenever asked about George Reynolds's marital status, seasoned Mormon witnesses claimed that they could not recall anything about the accused, stymying the government's search for damning sworn testimony. Frustrated by the strategy of selective memory failure and facing the possibility of losing the case, prosecutors then decided to put Amelia on the stand.

What happened next was courtroom drama of the highest order, and arguably the most pivotal moment in the government's decades-long crusade against polygamy. As one observer described the scene, when Amelia appeared in the courtroom to testify, her husband George "settled himself low in his seat with a look of hopeless terror, while the general look of dismay spread through the entire Mormon auditory."[19] Only twenty years old, "visibly pregnant," and entirely "uncoached in the strategy of obfuscation," as Sarah Barringer Gordon describes her, Amelia told all.[20] With her testimony, the prosecution proved beyond a reasonable doubt that George Reynolds had taken a second wife and thereby violated the 1862 Morrill Anti-Bigamy Act. In December 1875, the judge sentenced Reynolds to two years in prison with hard labor, and Mormon leaders scrambled to reorganize their defensive strategy.

Over two years later, in 1878 *Reynolds v. United States* made its way to the Supreme Court to decide the constitutionality of the original Morrill Anti-Bigamy Act of 1862. This was the first case on the practice of polygamy to reach the Court (their prior decision against Judge McKean had been about jury impaneling and not plural marriage), and the justices seized the opportunity to put the Mormon Church in its place. Because *Reynolds* is both so complicated and so important it merits extensive explanation.

The *Reynolds* case has many layers but the most important by far has to do with power. As the decision stated at the outset: "The inquiry is not as to the power of Congress to prescribe criminal laws for the Territories"— that power was presumed to be indisputable—"but as to the guilt of one who knowingly violates a law which has been properly enacted, if he entertains a religious belief that the law is wrong."[21] In other words, which constitutionally protected right reigned supreme: the power of the federal government to enact laws regulating the religious lives of its citizens; or the power of individuals to worship and live their religion as protected by the Free Exercise Clause of the First Amendment? Amazingly, in addition to being the first case on polygamy to reach the Supreme Court, *Reynolds* was also, ninety years after the formation of the federal government, "the first serious Supreme Court consideration of the Free Exercise Clause."[22] The Court therefore wanted to set a clear precedent and proclaim the federal government the undisputed sovereign over all potential rivals. To allow a polygamist such as George Reynolds to violate congressional legislation would be, in the justices' opinion, to "make the professed doctrines of religious belief superior to the law of the land, and in effect, to permit every citizen to become a law unto himself. Government could exist only in name under such circumstances."[23]

No, they declared in their unanimous decision, the power of the federal government must be upheld as inviolate, and the uniformity of American

Christian civilization must be maintained as good in itself and indispensable to public order. Insisting that monogamy be the national norm, it turned out, was the way to win battles on both fronts simultaneously. In the *Reynolds* decision, the Supreme Court declared unequivocally and unprecedentedly, although controversially, that the American national state had a vital interest in protecting the institution of monogamous marriage.

Here is the reasoning by which they arrived at their unanimous, antipolygamous decision. Quoting Thomas Jefferson's "Letter to the Danbury Baptists" of 1802, which declared "'that the legislative powers of the government reach actions only, and not opinions,'" Chief Justice Morrison Remick Waite concluded that "Congress was deprived of all legislative power over mere opinion, but was left free to reach actions which were in violation of social duties or subversive of good order." These last few words would prove devastating for Mormon polygamists. When religious individuals or communities held "mere opinion[s]" that might seem odd or heretical to other citizens, they were permitted by the Free Exercise Clause to do so. But whenever those opinions "'break out into overt acts against peace and good order,'" Waite proclaimed, then "'it is time enough for the rightful purposes of civil government for its officers to interfere.'" In American jurisprudence, this is the famous "belief-action distinction" that has informed Free Exercise cases ever since. Based on Jefferson's original musings on the subject, Justice Waite in *Reynolds* established a crucial legal precedent, clarifying "the true distinction between what properly belongs to the church and what to the State."[24]

Waite then explained why America should be, and henceforth would be uniformly monogamous, also revealing overtly his concern about the government's power to control the nation's marriage laws. As he put it: "according as monogamous or polygamous marriages are allowed, do we find the principles on which the government of the people, to a greater or less extent rests." Not only was the institution of marriage the foremost building block of society, it was also the foremost building block of a particular nation's political philosophy. In the United States that political philosophy was democratic republicanism, which at its most foundational level requires citizens to be virtuous, intelligent, and independent enough to responsibly choose representatives to govern in their stead. To compromise the citizenry through an institution such as plural marriage would sow the seeds of a bitter political harvest. As with the recently abolished institution of slavery, polygamy consigns the unfortunate many to abject dependence and presumed ignorance, while it dictatorially empowers the few beyond the limits acceptable in a democracy. Neither the slaveowner nor his slaves, the polygamous husband nor his plural wives could possibly possess the requisite virtues to be informed voters and responsible citizens. Plural marriage turned people into "victims," and so many of those voting victims "spread . . . over the land" would poison the republic. "So here," the chief justice concluded, "as a law of the organization of society under the exclusive dominion of the United States, it is provided that plural marriages shall not be allowed."[25]

In the aftermath of the decision Saints knew that there were going to be bad times ahead. Waite's language in *Reynolds* roused antipolygamy activists across the country to a new level of intensity, providing them with an imprimatur for their crusade against the institution. One year later, in 1880, Gentile women in Utah began publishing the *Anti-Polygamy Standard*, with clear aims for their periodical. In 1882, Jennie Anderson Froiseth, editor of the *Standard*, included the full text of the *Reynolds* decision as an appendix to her scathing four-hundred-page exposé, *The Women of Mormonism; or, The Story of Polygamy as Told by the Victims Themselves*. If her heartrending stories of abusive polygamous husbands and miserable plural wives did not move readers to action, perhaps the Supreme Court's words would. She also shamelessly stoked readers' fear of Mormon power. "If this ulcer is not to be extirpated," she wrote, "interior America will be given up to the worst phase of Asiatic barbarism."[26] Encouraged by *Reynolds*, antipolygamy activists entered the 1880s confident that their legal, political, and popular crusade would soon succeed. The *Reynolds* decision therefore established not just legal precedent but a new triumphalist and culturally chauvinistic tone in national politics. This was a case of "us versus them," celebrating all things American, Christian, democratic, and monogamous, while categorically condemning all things "Asiatic," Mormon, theocratic, and polygamous.

Federal prosecutors found out, however, that even with the Morrill Act, the Poland Act, and the *Reynolds* decision behind them, Utah Saints could still manipulate their territorial judicial system to stymie most legal cases. Witnesses continued to have lapses of memory during testimonies, the Church kept no incriminating records of plural marriages, and somehow Mormon leaders continued to empanel fellow Saints on territorial juries, where they refused to convict their peers for living their religion. And so, in 1882, yet another Vermonter, Senator George F. Edmunds, sponsored a bill to further tighten the government's control over Utah's legal system, and strike at the heart of the Church's theocratic aspirations. In 1887 the government had to ratchet up the pressure even more, granting itself the power to dismantle the LDS Church, and—perhaps most importantly—impound its material property.

In 1882 lawmakers were not ready to go this far, hoping instead that the strong provisions of the Edmunds Act would be enough. In addition to proclaiming polygamy a felony, the act empowered the government to punish Saints in unprecedented ways. It proclaimed cohabitation, which was much easier to prove in court than unrecorded polygamous marriages, punishable with steep fines and six-month prison sentences. It also barred polygamists from voting, holding office, and serving on juries; and it placed the Utah Territory's voting apparatus under the control of a presidentially appointed commission to monitor territorial elections. Nonpolygamous Saints could still vote and hold office, but federal officials in Utah interpreted the Edmunds Act to exclude from jury service not only suspected polygamists, but also those who merely *believed in* polygamy, which meant virtually all loyal Saints.[27] In 1884, with a jury of twelve trusty Gentiles, federal prosecutors scored their first conviction, Rudger Clawson. Church leaders appealed the case, but in 1885 the Supreme Court upheld the verdict, giving the green light for many more convictions to come. With Utah's electoral and judicial machinery now firmly in their control, federal prosecutors and US marshals could continue their crusade in earnest. The result is what became known as "the Raid." After the decision in *Clawson v. United States* in January 1885, federal officials swarmed the Great Basin kingdom, literally hunting for Mormon "polygs" and "cohabs," as they dehumanizingly called them.[28]

In the second half of the 1880s, Utah Saints endured unspeakable government repression, while pushing back as best they could. In March 1886, over two thousand Mormon women gathered for an indignation meeting—one of many—to protest the Edmunds Act and its enforcers. They had particularly damning things to say about the "rough and brutal deputy marshals, who watch around our door-yards, peer into our bedroom windows, ply little children with questions about their parents, and, when hunting their human prey, burst into people's domiciles and terrorize the innocent." Although Mormon women penned these words during the fever-pitch context of the Raid, they did not embellish these stories. US marshals did surveil and invade their homes, "ply" their children with questions about "the secret relations of their parents," and track down "their human prey" whenever they went on the lam.[29] "Some children," one historian writes, "bore the scars of family disruption for the remainder of their lives," enduring "a lifetime of guilt when an innocent but truthful answer led to the apprehension of their fathers."[30]

As polygamous men found out, the only way to avoid prosecution and imprisonment was to run away, or "go on the underground" as Saints called it. With no more legal protection, they were forced to resort to extralegal means of self-defense, avoiding capture by relocating regularly, holing up in the homes and barns of sympathetic Saints, or diving for cover in "polygamy pits"—hidden chambers they had dug out of their property. Prominent Church leaders often ran first, leaving their businesses, farms, and ecclesiastical offices to limp along without them. John Taylor, the Church's president after Brigham Young died in 1877, rightly sensed that he would be a prize catch for the feds and skipped town, eluding his pursuers at great personal cost. In his late seventies, Taylor lived for over two years "on the underground," rarely sleeping in one place for more than two nights at a time. Exhausted, he died on July 25, 1887, and was hailed as a "double martyr"—the first time for being shot in the Carthage jail where Joseph and Hyrum Smith were murdered in 1844. In the end, however, while the underground network succeeded at frustrating federal officers, it did not halt their prosecutorial offensive. Between 1884 and 1893 over a thousand Mormon men served time in dingy federal prisons for the crimes of cohabitation and polygamy.[31]

Authorized by the Edmunds Act, the Raid both worked and did not work. Rather than turning them into social pariahs, "polygamy sentences," one historian writes, "became a mark of status and honor."[32] Mormons regarded those convicts as heroes, suffering unjustly at the hands of an intolerant state for obeying the will of God. This was sex and sectarianism raised to a new level of intensity. As in the succession crisis of 1844, polygamy became a shibboleth—a way to distinguish the truly committed from the merely lukewarm. Back then, on the banks of the Mississippi River, plural marriage had divided the Church. In the 1880s, it unified the Saints. Defying American law became a way to demonstrate one's devotion to the kingdom. Very few Saints complied with federal officials. Most did what they could to frustrate them instead, either running away or enthusiastically aiding and abetting the fugitives "on the underground." Doubling down on their sectarian commitments, some even entered into new polygamous unions. After his release from prison, for instance, George Reynolds took a third wife on April 25, 1885. President John Taylor similarly took his last plural wife on December 19, 1886, just months before his death. Thus at the very beginning of the Raid, when the punitive consequences of their actions could not have been clearer, many Saints freely chose to flout the government and suffer, if need be, for their beliefs.

Mormon women resisted right alongside Mormon men. In the 1880s, as pressure from federal authorities increased and antipolygamy literature proliferated, Mormon women pushed back, publishing their own testimonials about the goodness and godliness of the institution. In 1884 Joyce Augusta Crocheron assembled a collection entitled *Representative Women of Deseret: A Book of Biographical Sketches,* with each contributing a testimonial about the benefits of being a plural wife. While many admitted their initial revulsion to polygamy, they also confessed their belief that "it is a principle of the Gods, it is heaven born." They likewise thanked the Lord for knowing "my heart and desires," and for being "with me in my trial, and assist[ing] me to overcome the selfishness and jealousy of my nature."[33] Thus polygamy's defenders returned once more to the theme of sacrificial selflessness.

Mormon women's propolygamy counteroffensive surprised and discouraged federal officials, forcing them to take even more drastic measures. Previously, antipolygamy activists had likened plural wives to slaves—victims of an oppressive regime. Threaten that regime with extinction, the logic went, and plural wives would run into the arms of their federal liberators in the same way that "contraband" slaves had run to the Union Army during the Civil War. When that prediction failed to materialize, antipolygamists gradually shifted their image of plural wives from being victims to being coequal perpetrators, deserving of both stigmatization and punishment along with their polygamous husbands. Thus even with the free hand they had received from the Edmunds Act of 1882 and the successes they had enjoyed from the Raid, federal officials still faced a dauntingly united Mormon front. From the patriarchal leaders at the top all the way down to the plural wives themselves, Mormons defended their institution and showed no sign of backing down. Federal lawmakers therefore concluded that if they could not break the collective defiance of the Mormon people, they would have to break the Church.[34]

On February 19, 1887, President Grover Cleveland signed the Edmunds-Tucker Act, legally dissolving the Church of Jesus Christ of Latter-day Saints, the Perpetual Emigrating Company, and the Nauvoo Legion. The act also authorized the federal government to confiscate all Church property above $50,000; it disinherited the children of plural marriages; and it rescinded polygamists' right to vote, hold office, or serve on juries if they refused to swear an oath renouncing the principle. Vindictively targeting Mormon women in particular for their disappointing insubordination, the Edmunds-Tucker Act also abolished women's suffrage in Utah. In short, the law made life miserable for every Mormon man, woman, and child, while also reducing the LDS Church to a near moneyless, powerless shell of its former self. Church leaders fretted most about the financial punishment the act inflicted upon them. With millions of dollars in assets about to be requisitioned, Church officials did everything they could to try to hold on to their property.[35]

Mormon resistance therefore continued but by this point was futile. For the next three years, the final act in the antipolygamy drama played out in the judicial system according to a familiar script: territorial courts decided for the government; the Church challenged the constitutionality of the law; and the Supreme Court rendered a crushing decision. In its ruling of May 19, 1890, an annoyed Court pulled no punches, referring to the LDS Church as "a contumacious organization, wielding by its resources an immense power in the Territory of Utah, and employing those resources and that power in constantly attempting to oppose, thwart and subvert the legislation of Congress."[36] The attention to Church "power" is noteworthy and revealing of the government's irritation at having a theocratic regime in the midst of its democratic republic. Only one power would henceforth make law in the Utah Territory and that was not going to be the LDS Church. Legally speaking, the fight was over. The Edmunds-Tucker Act of 1887 and the Supreme Court's decision in 1890 affirming the act's constitutionality had put the Church in checkmate. There was nowhere else for them to go and no more legal appeals for them to make. During the summer of 1890 the fourth president of the Church, Wilford Woodruff, gathered as much information as he could about his kingdom's situation and future prospects, and then issued his famous Manifesto. At eighty-three years of age, Woodruff was among the oldest of the old guard. He had been with Joseph Smith almost from the beginning, converting to Mormonism in 1833.

In 1890 this seasoned traveler and inveterate leader hit the road one more time, balancing out pastoral concern with pragmatic realpolitik. In August he traversed the length and breadth of the Mormon kingdom, traveling 2,400 miles (although mostly by rail) to see for himself the state of his people. He was disheartened by the misery that he found and had no desire to see it continue. Having acquainted himself with the facts on the ground, he and his entourage then traveled to San Francisco to discuss with the region's political "power brokers" whatever options remained, and he was again disheartened by what he learned. If the Church continued to practice and preach plural marriage, Utah would never become a state and the Church would never get its property and ecclesiastical powers back.[37]

Praying earnestly and wrestling mightily to discern the will of the Lord, Woodruff received an answer. In his diary on September 25, 1890, he wrote the following fateful words: "I have arrived at a point in the history of my life as the president of the Church . . . where I am under the necessity of acting for the temporal salvation of the church."[38] To his credit, Woodruff cared about more than Church property. As he warned a rapt audience at the Church's General Conference on October 6, 1890, continuing plural marriage would come "at the cost of the confiscation and loss of all the Temples, and the stopping of all the ordinances therein, both for the living and the dead." He even declared his willingness to continue suffering for the principle and "let all the temples go out of our hands, . . . had not the God of heaven commanded me to do what I did do." And so, he concluded, "I wrote what the Lord told me to write."[39]

Woodruff's 1890 Manifesto was revealing and, for the most part, conclusive. Like John Humphrey Noyes's 1879 letter ending complex marriage, the Manifesto bluntly reminded the Saints that the external forces against them had become insurmountable and that further resistance was both pointless and potentially harmful. The state had won, the Church must "submit," and, Woodruff concluded: "I now publicly declare that my advice to the Latter-day Saints is to refrain from contracting any marriage forbidden by the law of the land."[40] Crucially, the Manifesto did not command the dissolution of plural marriages, breaking up thousands of polygamous families and likely throwing Mormon society into chaos. Instead the Manifesto declared that henceforth the Church would no longer solemnize nor sanction any *future* plural marriages. Current plural families would remain intact, but be slowly outnumbered over time by Mormon monogamous families that were now the Church-mandated norm. This obviously created a confused lived reality for the Saints, as polygamists were phased out and monogamists phased in. In other words, the practice of polygamy did not die abruptly in 1890, but the Church's defense of plural marriage did. The idea and then institution of plural marriage had lived a long, somewhat prosperous, somewhat troubled life, but now its time had come. In 1890 the Church buried it.

EPILOGUE

IN THE end the world won. As early as 1870 Mormon Saints, Shaker Believers, and Oneida Perfectionists all sensed that something had changed in the society with which they, as sectarians, lived in tension. Shakers worried about their inability to win new converts, Oneidans worried about passing the torch to the next generation, and Mormons worried about the transcontinental railroad that was bringing unwelcome challenges to their intermountain kingdom. The fears of all three were well founded. By 1880 the Oneidans had ended complex marriage, in 1890 the Mormon Church declared that it would not sanction the sealing of new plural marriages, and by 1900 the United Society of Believers had shriveled to fewer than nine hundred members.[1] For many reasons this is the end of the story of Mormon polygamy, Shaker celibacy, and Oneida complex marriage.

But clearly 1880, 1890, or 1900 was not the end for the thousands of sectarians who had lived their religion sexually. Seeing themselves as characters in radically different religious metanarratives, they had condemned the world and fled into communities and identities that were defined principally by their unique sexual beliefs and practices. Over the course of the nineteenth century, those beliefs and practices had emerged, struggled, institutionalized, and faltered. In the twentieth century they would be seen as relics of a bygone era—strange religio-sexual experiments that were now over, for the most part. But what about the subjects and the legacies of those experiments? The people who participated in them lived on for decades, and the stories that we tell about them live on still. What happened to them after 1890 and how best are they to be remembered?

In many ways the story of the Shakers is the easiest to tell. Predictably, their numerical decline accelerated in the twentieth century: from 855 members in 1900, to 192 in 1926, to 40 in 1951. Villages likewise shuttered with depressing regularity—twelve of them between the turn of the century and 1947. And as their numbers continued to drop, and the average age of the remnant members continued to rise, the Believers were forced to hire even more outsiders to keep things running, erasing further their communitarian uniqueness. No longer fearing the outside world, some members had individual bank accounts, while at many villages group worship no longer took place. But as one Shaker distinctive after another fell by the wayside, celibacy remained. While clearly not good for recruitment, celibacy continued to define the United Society of Believers as a sect that was still, albeit minimally, at odds with the world, and those precious few who persisted never compromised on it.[2]

In contrast, the Church of Jesus Christ of Latter-day Saints did compromise on their sectarian sexual distinction and the Mormons' story after 1890 is in no way easy to tell. What exactly was President Wilford Woodruff's Manifesto of 1890 and what did it accomplish? Scholars have described it variously as "merely a tactical maneuver," "a tactical retreat," "a political ruse," and a document that "*evolved* to its present status as a revelation of God."[3] As historian D. Michael Quinn perfectly sums up: "the Manifesto inherited ambiguity, was created in ambiguity, and produced ambiguity." One thing, however, is clear: while not a definitive endpoint, the Manifesto was a turning point that ushered in a new era in the relationship between the Saints and their most powerful worldly adversary, the US government. As a result of the Manifesto, prosecutions of polygamists decreased, prisoners were pardoned, Church property was returned, and in 1896 statehood was granted.[4] In this sense—revelation or not—the Manifesto was a diplomatic success.

Among the Saints, however, the Manifesto's "ambiguity" elicited a range of emotional responses from relief to devastation, and a range of reactions from obedience to renewed sectarian resistance against both state and now Church. Most Saints in 1890, it is safe to say, were simply confused. Having been taught that plural marriage was necessary for exaltation, many who had not yet married polygamously feared that they would miss out on this greatest possible eternal reward. Those who were already plural wives and husbands had different anxieties. What exactly was their earthly and legal status? Were plural wives fallen women and their children bastards? Some plural wives were disconsolate and perplexed as to why the Lord would first sanction such a painful trial only to reverse course decades later. Other women felt emancipated—freed from an oppressive institution and husband. Still others felt abandoned by the Church leaders in whom they had put so much trust.[5]

Polygamous Saints were relieved, therefore, when Woodruff clarified that the Manifesto applied only to *future* plural marriages. Those unions contracted prior to 1890 would not be dissolved, and those husbands and plural wives could continue living as such. "I did not, could not, and would not promise [the nation]," Woodruff stated two weeks after issuing the Manifesto, "that you would desert your wives and children. This you cannot do in honor."[6] Polygamy as an institution, therefore, was not abruptly abolished in 1890 but would be slowly replaced by monogamous marriages throughout Utah. This compromise position apparently satisfied the US government, which virtually ceased prosecuting polygamists for unlawful cohabitation, while inflicting less trauma on existing families. Thus the pressing question of family dissolution was resolved. Utah in 1890 would not look like Oneida in 1880, with men and especially women anxiously scrambling for a monogamous partnership after the institution in which they had been joined and provided for fell apart.

But if the status of existing polygamous families was clear, the status of future plural marriages was anything but. President Woodruff issued his famous Manifesto on September 24, 1890. On April 6, 1904, subsequent President Joseph F. Smith had to issue his so-called "Second Manifesto" to more thoroughly put an end to the matter. The thirteen and a half years in between the two manifestoes were arguably some of the most "ambiguity" filled in the entire history of the LDS Church. These years also reveal just how strongly some Mormons, including Church presidents, held on to "the principle," and how painful it was for them to relinquish it. Historian Richard S. Van Wagoner, for instance, astonishingly claims that "virtually all church leaders, either by action or assent, disregarded the Woodruff Manifesto," although "most Saints knew little of the covert post-Manifesto polygamy that church leaders had been supporting."[7] Other scholars estimate that in the two decades between 1890 and 1910 the number of solemnized plural marriages ranges anywhere from a "few" to "about two thousand," with the most careful study documenting 262 such unions.[8] Regardless of the figure, the facts reveal that Saints continued to enter into plural marriages and Church authorities continued to solemnize them, which is what made the "Second Manifesto" a necessity.

Church leaders between 1890 and 1904 also did their best to get around the new laws of the nation and the stated policies of the Church. Regarding the first, one way to continue "the principle" while not incurring the wrath of the federal government was simply to leave the United States. Polygamists and aspiring polygamists therefore relocated to Mexico and Canada, where plural marriage was technically illegal but the political climate much different and the laws only rarely enforced. Many of these marriages were solemnized with the full authority of the First Presidency.[9] As Mormon historian B. Carmon Hardy sums up: "Regardless of what was said to the press, everyone acquainted with the settlements knew plural marriage was the primary reason for the Mormon presence in northern Mexico."[10]

Regarding the second—the Church's stated position on polygamy after 1890—Church leaders simply lied. Plural marriages continued to be performed under Wilford Woodruff (president from 1887 to 1898), Lorenzo Snow (1898 to 1901), and Joseph F. Smith (1901 to 1918). President Snow was the most adamant in ceasing plural marriages, including in Mexico, but his counselors in the First Presidency, Joseph F. Smith and George Q. Cannon, both "worked around the president, giving authorizations apart from Snow's knowledge or consent," Hardy writes. The result was that more plural marriages were performed in 1901, the last year of his presidency, than any year of Woodruff's presidency after 1890.[11] When Joseph F. Smith became First President, the number of plural marriages increased even more, along with the lying. "More than any other Church president after the 1890 Manifesto," D. Michael Quinn writes, "Joseph F. Smith divided the Church against itself and apostle against brother apostle over the question of new polygamous marriages." The "pattern of denying publicly what was happening privately" allowed "the principle" to continue while giving the Church plausible deniability, but the lies and the confusion of his early presidency, Quinn adds, sowed "a wind that would begin to reap the whirlwind in 1904."[12]

In 1903 the new state of Utah sent the first Mormon to the US Senate: Reed Smoot, who although a monogamist nevertheless reignited the national controversy over polygamy and power in the LDS Church. Anti-Mormon protests poured into the Capitol, petitioning the members to deny him a place in the nation's government. Compromising, the Senate allowed Smoot to take his seat but promised the public an investigation into his fitness for office. The resulting Smoot Hearings, as they became known, were an inquisition that lasted for over three years, from January 1904 to February 1907. In the end, Smoot's name was cleared and he remained in the Senate for over a quarter century, but the hearings truly killed plural marriage as an institution officially or even secretly supported by the Church of Jesus Christ of Latter-day Saints, and they killed it in the first four months of the investigation. President Joseph F. Smith was the very first witness to testify before the Senate, a confrontation between Church and State with disastrous consequences for the former. Threatened with perjury if he lied under these circumstances, President Smith admitted ongoing cohabitation with his five plural wives and immediately began "to reap the whirlwind." Senators were fed up with the

Church's duplicity and expressed no mercy for its polygamous leaders, even if they were acting to keep their families together.

But more important by far than the collective indignation of the Gentile senators was the still small voice of Reed Smoot himself. Mortified by the now publicly revealed dishonesty of the Church's leaders, Smoot wrote on March 22, 1904, that "this lack of sincerity on our part goes farther to condemn us in the eyes of the public men of the nation than the mere fact of a few new polygamy cases."[13] Less than three weeks later, on April 6, President Joseph F. Smith presented the Second Manifesto for ratification by the Church's general conference. In it he "hereby announce[d] that all such marriages are prohibited," and threatened excommunication for any Saint "deemed in transgression against the Church."[14] The result was greater clarity with the State but irreconcilable division within the Church. New plural marriages plummeted from forty in 1903 to four in 1905, and Smoot secured his place in the Senate when the hearings concluded in 1907.[15] Mormons had won for themselves a share of worldly power, but from a fundamentalist perspective they had sold their souls in the process, abandoning the sectarian practice that distinguished them as God's people in an ungodly land.

While the history of Mormon fundamentalism in the twentieth century is long, complicated, occasionally violent, and entirely beyond the scope of this book, a few concluding points bear mentioning. The most obvious is that the phenomenon is sex and sectarianism redux. Sectarians seek to live in tension with the world and the ecclesiastical institutions that have compromised with it. After 1904 the LDS Church itself became one of those compromised institutions, committed to excommunicating new or unrepentant polygamists from their ranks. In that sense the Church joined forces with the State in a united front that Mormon fundamentalists consider to be an unholy alliance. Those who remained committed to the principle now had to fight both, while trying to find safe places in which they could continue to live their religion in peace, just as their forebears had done. Mormon plural marriage therefore did not die in 1890 or in 1904; or in 1909 when the LDS Church started cracking down on polygamists; or in 1953 when authorities raided Short Creek, Arizona, and arrested approximately four hundred polygamists; or in 2011 when Warren Jeffs, the president of the FLDS Church, was found guilty of sexually assaulting girls as young as twelve years old.

Nor was Mormon plural marriage dead in 2016 when I visited the polygamous community of Rocky Ridge, about sixty miles south of Salt Lake City. The trip was organized as part of a Communal Studies Association conference and was one of the highlights of researching this book. I was struck in particular by the continuity between the polygamists I encountered in books and archives and those whose hands I got to shake. Their answers to my and others' questions (gingerly if not sheepishly asked) could have been lifted straight out of the 1840s and 1850s. When one plural wife was asked about her motivation she responded that she wanted to experience exaltation as part of her celestial family, a testimony to the power of those religious stories to move people still. Whenever a plural husband and community leader was asked what their foundational beliefs were, he always responded "agency."

The Apostolic United Brethren (AUB) who reside at Rocky Ridge are very interested in distancing themselves from Warren Jeffs and the FLDS members who have been convicted of child abuse. In those instances of inexcusable coercion, the AUB would rightly say, those children have no real agency. But the AUB's emphasis on agency is not just good public relations, consonant with American society's emphasis on choice and personal liberty. Agency is indeed one of the most foundational beliefs in the entire Mormon metanarrative: "and in the Garden of Eden, gave I unto man his agency," the Book of Moses proclaims.[16] In continuing to live "the principle," these sectarian members of the Apostolic United Brethren were thoroughly consistent with some of Mormonism's first principles.

Ambiguity about plural marriage, however, still abounds—in jurisprudence, popular culture, and the Church of Jesus Christ of Latter-day Saints itself. The fact that there was a lighthearted reality show called *Sister Wives* and another, significantly darker one called *Escaping Polygamy* running at the same time perhaps illustrates this ambiguity the most. How the LDS Church will navigate the ambiguities of its polygamous past and present is likewise unclear. Perhaps the only thing that is clear is that this particular story is not over.

The story of John Humphrey Noyes's Oneida Perfectionists is over. In 1879 they discontinued complex marriage. In 1881 they disbanded as a community and reorganized as a corporation. And on April 13, 1886, John Humphrey Noyes died. The last years of his life were spent in a kind of comfortable exile, in a nice home—the Stone Cottage—on the Canadian side of Niagara Falls. He was not alone there. His legal wife Harriet Holton Noyes joined him, along with about ten loyalists and another ten or so children, reconstituting community one last time with him as paterfamilias. There, surrounded by those who loved him most, he could contemplate his life's work and reflect on his legacy. Reportedly—and not unlike most people looking back on their lives—his moods vacillated between assured pride in his accomplishments and "deep depression" over the Oneida Community's collapse.[17] Employing yet another military metaphor, he perhaps summed things up best when he wrote: "We made a raid into an unknown country, charted it, and returned without the loss of a man, woman, or child."[18] Rather than seeing himself as a godly general conquering the forces of the world, he and his Perfectionists were more like a reconnaissance party, exploring the "unknown country" of communal sexual relations, learning what they could from the adventure, and then safely withdrawing when the group was no longer a cohesive unit. In my opinion, Noyes's assessment here is both modest and accurate in its claims.

Noyes inevitably thought in terms of success versus failure, and scholars of communal experiments often do the same; but I believe it is best to avoid such dichotomous, evaluative summations. Institutions live and then usually die. If longevity—or immortality—were the principal standard by which success is measured, only things like the Catholic Church, the English monarchy, or the Coca-Cola corporation would qualify. They have withstood the test of time and seem both wealthy and adaptive enough to endure further, although their perpetuity is hardly guaranteed. The three religio-sexual experiments explored in this book withstood the test of time for a while in nineteenth-century America, but eventually encountered challenges and changes that they could not overcome. Born in 1811, John Humphrey Noyes lived through the majority of that century and witnessed those changes firsthand. An astute observer of the visible material world and a rigorous thinker about the invisible spiritual one, he masterfully turned his ideas about the kingdom of God into institutions that both challenged and yet still fit into his historical context, at least until that context changed so much that he no longer had a place in it.

In 1879, after having left Oneida in June, Noyes actually tried to recapture and harness the spirit that had launched his extraordinary life's work back in the 1830s. Before coalescing into literal communities at Putney and then Oneida, Perfectionism had been a virtual community of scattered believers held together primarily through shared beliefs and print. After "months passed in monotonous exile," one historian describes, Noyes hoped to "rally" that diaspora one more time into a renewed, concentrated movement of God. Targeting the burgeoning Midwest, he used *The Circular*'s old subscription list to inform the faithful "that on a certain day" in Chicago "a conference of the friends of J. H. Noyes would be held, to consider the advisability of organizing a new community of Perfectionists." Only one man showed up for the "conference." The spiritual hunger for *more* that had animated thousands of seekers a half century earlier had disappeared almost entirely. Noyes and the loyalist who had accompanied him to Chicago then took a train back east and waited "on the lonely little station platform in mid-winter" to be picked up. "There is something in this picture," one biographer adds, "that suggests Lear on the Heath."[19]

The remainder of John Humphrey Noyes's life was not nearly so sad. According to his son, Pierrepont Noyes, "at mealtimes" at the Stone Cottage, from his seat at the head of the table he would watch "silently, often smilingly, the sociability of the grown folks and the animation of the children." Sometimes he would be moved to give "an old-fashioned 'home talk'" as he had at Oneida for thirty years, and then "go at once to his room . . . in order to ponder more deeply the subject discussed."[20] From that room he could gaze directly at Niagara Falls and ponder further his life and ideas. Perhaps he remembered that decades earlier, when he invented male continence, he used the metaphor of a waterfall to illustrate the three phases of sexual intercourse. Perhaps also he now looked at the cataract's unique curved form—simultaneously fixed and fluid—and also pondered "deeply" the mysterious coexistence of immutable spiritual truths and unending historical change.

NOTES

Prologue

1. George Wallingford Noyes, ed., *John Humphrey Noyes: The Putney Community* (Oneida, NY: Author, 1931), 37–38.
2. 2 Corinthians 13:12, King James Version.
3. G. W. Noyes, ed., *Putney Community*, 37–38.
4. *Doctrine and Covenants* 132:41, 62. Hereafter *D&C*.
5. *D&C* 132:17; 131:4.
6. *D&C* 132:19–20. Henceforth, the word "fulness" will be quoted without the accompanying "[sic]."
7. *D&C* 132:8.
8. G. W. Noyes, ed., *Putney Community*, 37–38.

Introduction

1. Abraham Heschel, *Between God and Man: An Interpretation of Judaism* (New York: Free Press Paperbacks, 1959), 134.
2. 1 Corinthians 7:7, 9, King James Version.
3. *Mormonnewsroom.org* (Sept. 12, 2019). The precise figure provided is 16,313,735.
4. Here is a short list of the most significant books on communal utopias, in chronological order: John Humphrey Noyes, *History of American Socialisms* (Philadelphia: J. B. Lippincott, 1870); Charles Nordhoff, *The Communistic Societies of the United States: From Personal Visit and Observation* (New York: Harper & Brothers, 1875); Arthur Bestor, *Backwoods Utopias: The Sectarian Origins and the Owenite Phase of Communitarian Socialism in America: 1663–1829* (Philadelphia: University of Pennsylvania Press, 1950); Mark Holloway, *Heavens on Earth: Utopian Communities in America, 1680–1880* (London: Turnstile Press, 1951); Rosabeth Moss Kanter, *Commitment and Community: Communes and Utopias in a Sociological Perspective* (Cambridge, MA: Harvard University Press, 1972); Raymond Lee Muncy, *Sex and Marriage in Utopian Communities: Nineteenth-Century America* (Bloomington: Indiana University Press, 1973); John McKelvie Whitworth, *God's Blueprints: A Sociological Study of Three Utopian Sects* (London: Routledge & Kegan Paul, 1975); Lawrence Foster, *Religion and Sexuality: Three American Communal Experiments of*

the Nineteenth Century (New York: Oxford University Press, 1981), later republished as Religion and Sexuality: The Shakers, the Mormons, and the Oneida Community (Urbana: University of Illinois Press, 1984); Louis J. Kern, An Ordered Love: Sex Roles and Sexuality in Victorian Utopias—the Shakers, the Mormons, and the Oneida Community (Chapel Hill: University of North Carolina Press, 1981); Lawrence Foster, Women, Family, and Utopia: Communal Experiments of the Shakers, the Oneida Community, and the Mormons (Syracuse, NY: Syracuse University Press, 1991); Donald E. Pitzer, ed., American Communal Utopias (Chapel Hill: University of North Carolina Press, 1997); Robert P. Sutton, Communal Utopias and the American Experience: Religious Communities, 1732-2000 (Westport, CT: Praeger Publishers, 2003); Robert P. Sutton, Communal Utopias and the American Experience: Secular Communities, 1824-2000 (Westport, CT: Praeger Publishers, 2004); Chris Jennings, Paradise Now: The Story of American Utopianism (New York: Random House, 2016).
5. John Lewis Gaddis, The Landscape of History: How Historians Map the Past (New York: Oxford University Press, 2002), 88 and 95. Emphasis in original.
6. William James, The Varieties of Religious Experience (1902; rpt., Liguori, MO: Triumph Books, 1991), 58.
7. Richard Lyman Bushman, Joseph Smith, Rough Stone Rolling: A Cultural Biography of Mormonism's Founder (New York: Vintage Books, 2005), 322-23.
8. Gaddis, Landscape of History, 112-14. Emphasis in original.
9. Ernst Troeltsch, The Social Teachings of the Christian Churches, vol. 1 (London: Macmillan, 1931), 334, 339.
10. Stephen J. Stein, The Shaker Experience in America: A History of the United Society of Believers (New Haven: Yale University Press, 1992), 3. See also Rodney Stark and William Sims Bainbridge, The Future of Religion: Secularization, Revival, and Cult Formation (Berkeley: University of California Press, 1985), 25.
11. Meredith B. McGuire, Religion: The Social Context, 3rd ed. (Belmont, CA: Wadsworth Publishing Company, 1992), 162.

1. MORE

1. Nathan Hatch, The Democratization of American Christianity (New Haven, CT: Yale University Press, 1989), 220, 3.
2. Ibid., 17, 6, 11.
3. Ibid., 12, 134, 16.
4. Joseph Smith, "History of the Church," 1838, in Personal Writings of Joseph Smith, ed. Dean C. Jessee, rev. ed. (Salt Lake City, UT: BYU Press, 2002), 228-29.
5. Ibid., 229.

6. Ibid., 230–31.
7. George Wallingford Noyes, comp. and ed., *Religious Experience of John Humphrey Noyes, Founder of the Oneida Community* (New York: Macmillan, 1923), 39.
8. Ibid., 15.
9. Stephen J. Stein, *The Shaker Experience in America: A History of the United Society of Believers* (New Haven, CT: Yale University Press, 1992), 70.
10. Benjamin Seth Youngs, *The Testimony of Christ's Second Appearing: Containing a General Statement of All Things Pertaining to the Faith and Practice of the Church of God in This Latter Day*, 2nd ed. (Albany, NY: E. and E. Hosford, 1810), 363, 390.
11. The full title is *A Concise Statement of the Principles of the Only True Church, According to the Gospel of the Present Appearance of Christ. As Held to and Practiced upon by the True Followers of the Living Saviour, at New Lebanon, &c. Together with a Letter from James Whittaker, Minister of the Gospel in This Day of Christ's Second Appearing—to His Natural Relations in England. Dated October 9th, 1785* (Bennington, VT: Haswell & Russell, 1790).
12. Thomas Brown, *An Account of the People Called Shakers: Their Faith, Doctrines, and Practice, Exemplified in the Life, Conversations, and Experience of the Author during the Time He Belonged to the Society, to Which Is Affixed a History of Their Rise and Progress to the Present Day* (Troy, NY: Parker and Bliss, 1812), 344.
13. John Dunlavy, *The Manifesto; or, A Declaration of the Doctrine and Practice of the Church of Christ* (Pleasant Hill, KY: P. Bertrand, 1818), 297; Brown, *Account of the People Called Shakers*, 21; Rufus Bishop and Seth Y. Wells, eds., *Testimonies of the Life, Character, Revelations, and Doctrine of Our Ever Blesed Mother Ann Lee, and the Elders with Her; Through Whom the Word of Eternal Life Was Opened in This Day of Christ's Second Appearing: Collected from Living Witnesses* (Hancock, MA: J. Tallcott & Deming, Junrs., 1816), 62. All emphases added.
14. See *A Summary View of the Millennial Church, or United Society of Believers, (Commonly Called Shakers.) Comprising the Rise, Progress, and Practical Order of the Society; Together with the General Principles of Their Faith and Testimony* (Albany, NY: Packard & Van Benthuysen, 1823), 131, 149, and 278. Emphasis added.
15. *Book of Commandments, for the Government of the Church of Christ* (Zion, Jackson County, MO: W. W. Phelps & Co., 1833; Printed Verbatim by the *Salt Lake Tribune*, 1884), 50 and 53. Emphasis added.
16. John Humphrey Noyes, *"The Way of Holiness": A Series of Papers Formerly Published in the Perfectionists, at New Haven* (Putney, VT: J. H. Noyes, 1838), 133. Emphases in original.

17. John Humphrey Noyes, *The Berean: A Manual for the Help of Those Who Seek the Faith of the Primitive Church* (Putney, VT: Office of the *Spiritual Magazine*, 1847), vii. Emphasis added.
18. See John C. Spurlock, *Free Love: Marriage and Middle-Class Radicalism in America, 1825–1860* (New York: NYU Press, 1988); and Joanne E. Passet, *Sex Radicals and the Quest for Women's Equality* (Urbana: University of Illinois Press, 2003).

2. Metanarrative

1. Anthony J. Blasi, "Definition of Religion," in *Encyclopedia of Religion and Society*, ed. William Swatos Jr. (London: AltaMira Press, 1998), 129–33.
2. Frederick W. Evans, *Religious Communism: A Lecture Delivered in St. George's Hall, London, Aug. 6, 1871* (London: J. Burns, 1871), 9. See also "The Principal Seat of Human Depravity," in Benjamin Seth Youngs, *The Testimony of Christ's Second Appearing: . . .* (Lebanon, OH: John McClean, 1810), part 1, ch. 5.
3. Genesis 1:28, King James Version.
4. *A Summary View of the Millennial Church, or United Society of Believers, (Commonly Called Shakers.) Comprising the Rise, Progress, and Practical Order of the Society; Together with the General Principles of Their Faith and Testimony* (Albany, NY: Packard & Van Benthuysen, 1823), 124.
5. Richard Lyman Bushman, *Joseph Smith, Rough Stone Rolling: A Cultural Biography of Mormonism's Founder* (New York: Vintage Books, 2005), 457.
6. Joseph Smith, *The King Follett Discourse: The Being and Kind of Being God Is; The Immortality of the Intelligence of Man, with Notes and References by the Late Elder B. H. Roberts of the First Council of Seventy* (Salt Lake City, UT: Magazine Printing Co., 1963), 9.
7. Ibid., 4.
8. Ibid., 8. Emphasis in original.
9. The version cited here comes from a footnote in *The King Follett Discourse* (1963), 9.
10. *D&C* 130:22.
11. Joseph Smith, Extracts from William Clayton's Private Book (Jan. 5, 1841), in *The Words of Joseph Smith: The Contemporary Accounts of the Nauvoo Discourses of the Prophet Joseph*, ed. Andrew F. Ehat and Lyndon W. Cook (Provo, UT: Religious Studies Center, BYU, 1980), 60.
12. Joseph Smith, *King Follett Discourse*, 16–18. Emphasis in original.
13. *D&C* 93:33, 23, and 29.
14. "Ordinances," n.d., https://www.lds.org/topics/ordinances (accessed Feb. 9, 2018).

15. Charles R. Harrell, *"This Is My Doctrine": The Development of Mormon Theology* (Sandy, UT: Greg Kofford Books, 2011), 138. Emphasis added.
16. Book of Moses 5:10. Emphasis added.
17. *D&C* 29:39. Emphasis added.
18. 2 Nephi 2:25.
19. Harrell, *"This Is My Doctrine,"* 255.
20. Book of Moses 5:11.
21. *First Annual Report of the Oneida Association: Exhibiting Its History, Principles, and Transactions to Jan. 1, 1849* (Oneida Reserve, NY: Leonard, 1849), 11.
22. John Humphrey Noyes, *Confessions of John H. Noyes: Confession of Religious Experience, Including a History of Modern Perfectionism* (Oneida Reserve, NY: Leonard, 1849), 8.
23. George Wallingford Noyes, ed., *Religious Experience of John Humphrey Noyes, Founder of the Oneida Community* (New York: Macmillan, 1923), 70.
24. Harrell, "The Great Apostasy," in *"This Is My Doctrine,"* 42; Todd Compton, "Apostasy," in *Encyclopedia of Mormonism* (New York: Macmillan, 1992), 58.
25. Richard McNemar, *The Kentucky Revival; or, A Short History of the Late Extraordinary Outpouring of God in the Western States of America . . .* (1807; rpt., Cincinnati: Art Guild's Reprint, 1968), 150.
26. Ibid., 236.
27. Hervey Elkins, *Fifteen Years in the Senior Order of Shakers* (Hanover, NH: Dartmouth Press, 1853), 36.
28. Youngs, *Testimony of Christ's Second Appearing*, part 4, ch. 1.
29. Justo Gonzalez, *The Story of Christianity* (New York: HarperSanFrancisco, 1984), 242–44, 252–57.
30. *Summary View* (1823), 305.
31. *A Summary View of the Millennial Church, or United Society of Believers, (Commonly Called Shakers.) Comprising the Rise, Progress, and Practical Order of the Society; Together with the General Principles of Their Faith and Testimony* (Albany, NY: C. Van Benthuysen, 1848), 206. Emphasis in original.
32. Ibid., 203.
33. John Humphrey Noyes, *The Berean: A Manual for the Help of Those Who Seek the Faith of the Primitive Church* (Putney, VT: Office of the *Spiritual Magazine*, 1847), 500, 504, 42. Emphasis in original.

3. Marriage

1. Lawrence Foster, *Religion and Sexuality: The Shakers, the Mormons, and the Oneida Community* (Urbana: University of Illinois Press, 1984), 239.
2. D&C 132:17.
3. D&C 132:20.
4. Jennie Anderson Froiseth, ed., *The Women of Mormonism; or, The Story of Polygamy as Told by the Victims Themselves* (Detroit, MI: C. G. Paine, 1882), 189.
5. Ann E. Young, *Wife Number Nineteen; or, The Story of a Life in Bondage: Being a Complete Expose of Mormonism, and Revealing the Sorrows, Sacrifices, and Sufferings of Women in Polygamy* (1875; rpt., New York: Arno Press, 1972), 416.
6. Orson Pratt, "Celestial Marriage," *The Seer* 1, no. 9 (Sept. 1853): 140.
7. D&C 132:52, 54.
8. Ann E. Young, *Wife Number Nineteen*, 498.
9. Augusta Joyce Crocheron, *Representative Women of Deseret* (Salt Lake City, UT: J. C. Graham, 1884), 15, 54.
10. Thomas Stenhouse, *The Rocky Mountain Saints; A Full and Complete History of the Mormons* (New York: D. Appleton, 1873), 582. Emphasis in original.
11. Maria Ward, *Female Life among the Mormons: A Narrative of Many Years' Personal Experience by the Wife of Mormon Elder Recently from Utah* (New York: J. C. Derby, 1855), 319.
12. Erastus Snow, *Journal of Discourses*, 26 vols. (London: Latter-day Saints' Book Depot, 1854–86), 26:217 (May 31, 1885), quoted in Kathryn M. Daynes, *More Wives Than One: Transformation of the Mormon Marriage System, 1840–1910* (Urbana: University of Illinois Press, 2001), 196.
13. John C. Bennett, *The History of the Saints; or, An Expose of Joe Smith and Mormonism* (Boston: Leland & Whiting, 1842), 217, 220, 222.
14. Brigham Young, *Journal of Discourses* 9:36, quoted in George D. Smith, *Nauvoo Polygamy: ". . . but we called it celestial marriage,"* 2nd ed. (Salt Lake City, UT: Signature Books, 2011), 277.
15. John W. Gunnison, *The Mormons; or, Latter-day Saints, in the Valley of the Great Salt Lake* (Philadelphia: Lippincott, Grambo, 1852), 69.
16. Matthew 6:10, King James Version.
17. Benjamin Seth Youngs, *The Testimony of Christ's Second Appearing; . . .* (Lebanon, OH: John McClean, 1810), 118.
18. "Shaker Communism," *The Circular*, new series 3, no. 4 (Apr. 9, 1866). Emphasis in original.
19. This specific quote is from Luke 20:34–35, King James Version.

20. John Humphrey Noyes, "The Battle Axe Letter," quoted in *John Humphrey Noyes: The Putney Community*, ed. George Wallingford Noyes (Oneida, NY: Author, 1931), 3.
21. "Egotism for Two," *The Circular* 3, no. 55 (Apr. 11, 1854), and 11, no. 21 (Jul. 3, 1862).
22. Frederick W. Evans, *A Short Treatise on the Second Appearing of Christ, in and through the Order of the Female* (Boston: Bazin & Chandler, 1853), 88.
23. "Christ and the Family Spirit," *The Circular* 7, no. 38 (Oct. 13, 1859).
24. *First Annual Report of the Oneida Association: Exhibiting Its History, Principles, and Transactions to Jan. 1, 1849* (Oneida Reserve, NY: Leonard, 1849), 20–21. Emphasis in original.
25. "Egotism for Two," *The Circular* 11, no. 21 (Jul. 3, 1862).
26. *A Summary View of the Millennial Church, or United Society of Believers, (Commonly Called Shakers.) Comprising the Rise, Progress, and Practical Order of the Society; Together with the General Principles of Their Faith and Testimony* (Albany, NY: Packard and Van Benthuysen, 1823), 136.
27. Ibid., 134, 136, 140. Emphases in original.
28. John Dunlavy, *The Manifesto; or, A Declaration of the Doctrine and Practice of the Church of Christ* (Pleasant Hill, KY: P. Bertrand, 1818), 280.
29. Daniel Rathbun, *A Letter from Daniel Rathbun, of Richmond in the County of Berkshire, to James Whittacor, Chief Elder of the Church, Called Shakers* (Springfield, MA: N.p., 1785), 15, 25.
30. Stephen J. Stein, *The Shaker Experience in America: A History of the United Society of Believers* (New Haven, CT: Yale University Press, 1992), 31.
31. Reuben Rathbone, *Reasons Offered for Leaving the Shakers* (Pittsfield, MA: N.p., 1800), 14–15.
32. *Summary View* (1823), 165.
33. H. L. Eads, *Shaker Sermons: Scripto-Rational—Containing the Substance of Shaker Theology Together with Replies and Criticisms Logically and Clearly Set Forth* (Shakers, NY: Shaker Manifesto, 1879), 50.
34. Evans, *Short Treatise*, 38.
35. Dunlavy, *Manifesto*, 319.
36. *Summary View* (1823), 152.
37. Ibid., 163, 149.
38. Ibid., 278.
39. Youngs, *Testimony of Christ's Second Appearing*, 112, 48, 55; Dunlavy, *Manifesto*, 278; *Summary View* (1823), 131.
40. "Shaker Communism, VI," *The Circular* new series 3, no. 9 (May 14, 1866).
41. *First Annual Report*, 37.
42. "The Object of the Sexual Organization," *Spiritual Moralist* 1, no. 2 (June 25, 1842). Capitalization in original.

43. "Shakerism," *The Perfectionist and Theocratic Watchman* 4, no. 9 (Jul. 13, 1844).
44. *First Annual Report*, 37, 29.
45. Ibid., 24.
46. John Humphrey Noyes, *Home-Talks*, ed. Alfred Barron and George Noyes Miller (Oneida, NY: Published by the Community, 1875), 352.
47. "Two Kinds of Sensuality," *The Circular* 13, no. 4 (Jan. 27, 1876).
48. "Ministering to the Whole Man," *The Circular* 8, no. 39 (Oct. 20, 1859).
49. "Organization of the Passions," *The Circular* 7, no. 23 (Aug. 22, 1870). Emphasis in original.
50. "Two Kinds of Sensuality."
51. *First Annual Report*, 28.
52. Ibid., 11, 30.
53. Ibid., 33.
54. Ibid., 31.
55. John Humphrey Noyes, *Male Continence*, 2nd ed. (Oneida, NY: Office of the Oneida Circular, 1877), 21.
56. *First Annual Report*, 33, 31.
57. Noyes, *Male Continence*, 8, 10. Emphases in original.
58. Ibid., 15.
59. "Free Love," *The Circular* new series 2, no. 47 (Feb. 6, 1865).
60. "The Three Foundations," *The Circular* new series 4, no. 2 (Mar. 25, 1867).
61. Noyes, *Male Continence*, 22.

Part II. Geneses

1. George Wallingford Noyes, ed., *Religious Experience of John Humphrey Noyes, Founder of the Oneida Community* (New York: Macmillan, 1923), 34–35; and Lawrence Foster, ed., *Free Love in Utopia: John Humphrey Noyes and the Origin of the Oneida Community* (Urbana: University of Illinois Press, 2001), Introduction, xix.
2. William James, *The Varieties of Religious Experience* (1902; rpt., Liguori, MO: Triumph Books, 1991), 36.

4. Spiritual

1. Rufus Bishop and Seth Y. Wells, eds., *Testimonies of the Life, Character, Revelations, and Doctrines of Our Ever Blessed Mother Ann Lee, and the Elders with Her; . . .* (Hancock, MA: J. Tallcott & Deming, Jrs., 1816), 3.
2. The biographical material in this and following paragraphs is largely taken from Stephen J. Stein, *The Shaker Experience in America: A History of the United Society of Believers* (New Haven, CT: Yale University Press, 1992),

3–10; Edward Deming Andrews, *The People Called Shakers: A Search for the Perfect Society* (New York: Oxford University Press, 1953), 3–14; and John McKelvie Whitworth, *God's Blueprints: A Sociological Study of Three Utopian Sects* (London: Routledge & Kegan Paul, 1975), 13–17.
3. Thomas Brown, *An Account of the People Called Shakers: . . .* (Troy, NY: Parker and Bliss, 1812), 313.
4. Stein, *Shaker Experience*, 6–7.
5. *A Concise Shaker Catechism, Containing the Most Important Events Recorded in the Bible: Also a Short Sketch of the Lives of Our First Elders or Parents, Mother Ann, Father William, and Father James* (Shaker Village, NH: N.p., 1850), 25.
6. Bishop and Wells, eds., *Testimonies*, 6, 62–63.
7. *A Summary View of the Millennial Church, or United Society of Believers, (Commonly Called Shakers.) Comprising the Rise, Progress, and Practical Order of the Society; Together with the General Principles of Their Faith and Testimony* (Albany, NY: Packard & Van Benthuysen, 1823), 9.
8. Bishop and Wells, eds., *Testimonies*, 6.
9. Eber. D. Howe, *Mormonism Unvailed* [sic]; or, *A Faithful Account of That Singular Imposition and Delusion from Its Rise to the Present Time* (Painesville, OH: Author, 1834), 258.
10. Richard Lyman Bushman, *Joseph Smith, Rough Stone Rolling: A Cultural Biography of Mormonism's Founder* (New York: Vintage Books, 2005), 50.
11. Ibid., 18–19, 27–33.
12. Ibid., 15–17, 25–26, and 36–37.
13. Joseph Smith, History [1838], in *The Papers of Joseph Smith*, ed. Dean C. Jesse (Salt Lake City, UT: Deseret Book, 1989–92), 1:10–12, 14, 18–19.
14. Ibid., 1:21.
15. Ibid., 1:26.
16. Ibid., 1:28, 30, and 46.
17. Ibid., 1:49, 53, and 59.
18. The "exaltation revelations" are today's *D&C* 76, 84, 88, and 93.
19. *D&C* 93:33, 29, 36, 30–31, 13, and 19.
20. Bushman, *Rough Stone Rolling*, 201.
21. Mormons speak not of the "founding" of their Church, but of the Church as a "restoration" of ancient religious practices.
22. Joseph Smith, History [1838], in *The Papers of Joseph Smith*, ed. Jesse, 1:69, 72.
23. See *D&C* 107:8, 5; and Bushman, *Rough Stone Rolling*, 175.
24. *D&C* 37:1, 3.
25. Bushman, *Rough Stone Rolling*, 328–41.
26. Ibid., 168–70, 178–80.

27. Lilburn W. Boggs to General John B. Clark, Oct. 27, 1838, in *Document Containing the Correspondence, Orders, &C. in Relation to the Disturbances with the Mormons; and the Evidence Given before the Hon. Austin A. King, Judge of the Fifth Judicial Circuit of Missouri, at the Court-House in Richmond, in a Criminal Court of Inquiry, Begun November 12, 1838, on the Trial of Joseph Smith., and Others, for High Treason and Other Crimes against the State* (Fayette, MO: Boon's Lick Democrat, 1841), 61. Emphasis added.
28. Stephen C. LeSueur, *The 1838 Mormon War in Missouri* (Columbia: University of Missouri Press, 1987), 161–79.
29. Bushman, *Rough Stone Rolling*, 373–84.
30. George Wallingford Noyes, ed., *Religious Experience of John Humphrey Noyes, Founder of the Oneida Community* (New York: Macmillan, 1923), 1–7; Robert David Thomas, *The Man Who Would Be Perfect: John Humphrey Noyes and the Utopian Impulse* (Philadelphia: University of Pennsylvania Press, 1977), 2.
31. G. W. Noyes, ed., *Religious Experience*, 6.
32. "Extracts from College Journal," in ibid., 20.
33. G. W. Noyes, ed., *Religious Experience*, 13–25; Thomas, *The Man Who Would Be Perfect*, 3–11; Robert Allerton Parker, *A Yankee Saint: John Humphrey Noyes and the Oneida Community* (New York: G. P. Putnam's Sons, 1935), 12–14.
34. "Extracts from Diary," in *Religious Experience*, ed. G. W. Noyes, 37–39.
35. G. W. Noyes, ed., *Religious Experience*, 40.
36. Thomas, *The Man Who Would Be Perfect*, 20.
37. John Humphrey Noyes, *Confessions of John H. Noyes: Confession of Religious Experience, Including a History of Modern Perfectionism* (Oneida Reserve, NY: Leonard, 1849), 3. Emphases in original.
38. Ibid., 4.
39. "Extracts from Diary," 39, 43, 55.
40. J. H. Noyes, *Confessions*, 2.
41. Ibid., 7.
42. G. W. Noyes, ed., *Religious Experience*, 69, 14–15.
43. 1 John 3:8, King James Version.
44. G. W. Noyes, ed., *Religious Experience*, 111; Parker, *Yankee Saint*, 25; Thomas, *The Man Who Would Be Perfect*, 48.
45. J. H. Noyes, *Confessions*, 22.
46. Ibid., 30.
47. Ibid., 2. Emphasis in original.
48. Ibid., 33, 41.
49. John Humphrey to Horatio Noyes, Jul. 2, 1834, in *Religious Experience*, ed. G. W. Noyes, 154.
50. J. H. Noyes, *Confessions*, 33.
51. G. W. Noyes, ed., *Religious Experience*, 186, 193.

52. J. H. Noyes, *Confessions*, 61–62.
53. John Humphrey Noyes to Abigail Merwin, Dec. 28, 1835, in *Religious Experience*, ed. G. W. Noyes, 352.
54. John Humphrey Noyes, quoted in John B. Ellis, *Free Love and Its Votaries; . . .* (New York: United States Publishing Company, 1870), 31.

5. SEXUAL

1. Mosiah 11:2; Jacob 2:23, 1:15, and 2:24, 27.
2. Jacob 2:30.
3. B. H. Roberts, *A Comprehensive History of the Church of Jesus Christ of Latter-day Saints*, 6 vols. (Salt Lake City, UT: Deseret News Press, 1930), 2:95, 98.
4. W. W. Phelps to Brigham Young, Aug. 12, 1861, LDS Archives, quoted in Lawrence Foster, *Religion and Sexuality: The Shakers, the Mormons, and the Oneida Community* (Urbana: University of Illinois Press, 1984), 134–35.
5. John G. Turner, *Brigham Young: Pioneer Prophet* (Cambridge, MA: Belknap Press of Harvard University Press, 2012), 88. In addition to Joseph's silence, the LDS Church has vigilantly guarded the historical record on plural marriage, often sanitizing its official history and denying researchers access to certain documents and archives. In his superb book, George D. Smith devotes two chapters to exposing "the code of silence that prevailed in Nauvoo": "A Silenced Past" and "In Search of Lost History." This and upcoming chapters are deeply indebted to these intrepid scholars of the recent Mormon historical renaissance, almost all of them practicing members of the Church who simply want to tell the story as accurately as they can. George D. Smith, *Nauvoo Polygamy: ". . . but we called it celestial marriage,"* 2nd ed. (Salt Lake City, UT: Signature Books, 2011).
6. Mosiah Hancock, Autobiography, Church Archives, quoted in Todd Compton, *In Sacred Loneliness: The Plural Wives of Joseph Smith* (Salt Lake City, UT: Signature Books, 1997), 31–32.
7. Dean R. Zimmerman, ed., *I Knew the Prophets: An Analysis of the Letter of Benjamin F. Johnson to George F. Gibbs, Reporting Doctrinal Views of Joseph Smith and Brigham Young* (Bountiful, UT: Horizon Publishers, 1976), 45, quoted in Compton, *In Sacred Loneliness*, 40.
8. Ann E. Young, *Wife Number Nineteen; or, The Story of a Life in Bondage: Being a Complete Expose of Mormonism, and Revealing the Sorrows, Sacrifices, and Suffering of Women in Polygamy* (1875; rpt., New York: Arno Press, 1972), 66–67.
9. Compton, *In Sacred Loneliness*, 36. Compton is referencing a letter Van Wagoner wrote to Linda Newell, Sept. 20, 1983, in Van Wagoner Collection, Marriott Library, University of Utah, Salt Lake City.

10. *D&C* [1835], Section CXI, "Marriage."
11. Richard S. Van Wagoner, *Mormon Polygamy: A History* (Salt Lake City, UT: Signature Books, 1989), 14n8.
12. G. D. Smith, Table 3.1, "Joseph Smith's wives," *Nauvoo Polygamy*, 223–24.
13. Oliver Cowdery to Warren A. Cowdery, Jan. 21, 1838, Cowdery Letterbook. Huntington Library, San Marino, CA.
14. *Far West Record* 163 (Apr. 12, 1838), quoted in Richard Lyman Bushman, *Joseph Smith, Rough Stone Rolling: A Cultural Biography of Mormonism's Founder* (New York: Vintage Books, 2005), 324.
15. *D&C* 132:61–62. Emphasis added.
16. See G. D. Smith, *Nauvoo Polygamy*, 40; Van Wagoner, *Mormon Polygamy*, 5; and Compton, *In Sacred Loneliness*, 35.
17. *D&C* 76:103.
18. G. D. Smith, *Nauvoo Polygamy*, 38.
19. John Humphrey Noyes, "My First Act in Sexual Freedom," in *John Humphrey Noyes: The Putney Community*, ed. George Wallingford Noyes (Oneida, NY: Author, 1931), 201.
20. George Wallingford Noyes, ed., *Religious Experience of John Humphrey Noyes, Founder of the Oneida Community* (New York: Macmillan, 1923), 238–39, 308.
21. Home-talk by John Humphrey Noyes, Apr. 9, 1851, in *Religious Experience*, ed. G. W. Noyes, 356–57.
22. John Humphrey Noyes to Polly Hayes Noyes, Jan. 21, 1841, in *Religious Experience*, ed. G. W. Noyes, 356.
23. John Humphrey Noyes to David Harrison, Jan. 15, 1837, in *Putney Community*, ed. G. W. Noyes, 3.
24. Ibid.
25. *The Battle-Axe and Weapons of War*, Jul. 1837, quoted in *Putney Community*, ed. G. W. Noyes, 4.
26. *The Witness*, Sept. 23, 1837.
27. John Humphrey Noyes, "Noyes's Farewell Lay to Abigail," in *Putney Community*, ed. G. W. Noyes, 14–15.
28. G. W. Noyes, ed., *Putney Community*, 12.
29. Ibid., 15–17.
30. John Humphrey Noyes to Harriet A. Holton, June 11, 1838, in *Putney Community*, ed. G. W. Noyes, 17–18.
31. Harriet A. Holton to John Humphrey Noyes, June 12 and 24, 1838, in *Putney Community*, ed. G. W. Noyes, 20–22.
32. John Humphrey Noyes, "Male Continence: Abstracts from Pamphlets by Noyes 1849 and 1872," in *Putney Community*, ed. G. W. Noyes, 113.
33. G. W. Noyes, ed., *Religious Experience*, 310.
34. G. W. Noyes, ed., *Putney Community*, 49.

NOTES TO PAGES 87–95   309

35. *Advocate of Moral Reform,* Dec. 15, 1837, quoted in *Putney Community,* ed. G. W. Noyes, 6.
36. Mary E. Cragin to John Humphrey Noyes, Nov. 22, 1839, in *Putney Community,* ed. G. W. Noyes, 36.
37. G. W. Noyes, ed., *Putney Community,* 38.
38. Ibid., 40.
39. Ibid.
40. Ibid., 197–98.
41. John Humphrey Noyes, "My First Act in Sexual Freedom," in *Putney Community,* ed. G. W. Noyes, 201–2.
42. G. W. Noyes, ed., *Putney Community,* 211, 196.
43. John Humphrey Noyes, "Statement of Principles," quoted in *Putney Community,* ed. G. W. Noyes, 205–6.
44. John Humphrey Noyes, "The Syracuse and Belchertown Expedition. Paper by Noyes about January 25, 1847," quoted in *Putney Community,* ed. G. W. Noyes, 215–16.
45. G. W. Noyes, ed., *Putney Community,* 302.
46. John R. Miller to John Humphrey Noyes, Dec. 7, 1847, in *Putney Community,* ed. G. W. Noyes, 324.
47. John Humphrey Noyes to John R. Miller, Dec. 14, 1847, in *Putney Community,* ed. G. W. Noyes, 340.

6. INSTITUTIONAL

1. Stephen J. Stein, *The Shaker Experience in America: A History of the United Society of Believers* (New Haven, CT: Yale University Press, 1992), 10–14; Edward Deming Andrews, *The People Called Shakers: A Search for the Perfect Society* (New York: Oxford University Press, 1953), 14–34.
2. Stein, *Shaker Experience,* 24; Andrews, *People Called Shakers,* 35–44.
3. Stein, *Shaker Experience,* 15–18, 25–31; Lawrence Foster, *Religion and Sexuality: The Shakers, the Mormons, and the Oneida Community* (Urbana: University of Illinois Press, 1984), 51–54; and Clarke Garrett, *Spirit Possession and Popular Religion: From the Camisards to the Shakers* (Baltimore, MD: Johns Hopkins University Press, 1987), 197.
4. Valentine Rathbun, *An Account of the Matter, Form, and Manner of a New and Strange Religion, Taught and Propagated by a Number of Europeans, Living in a Place Called Nisqueunia, in the State of New York* (Providence, RI: Bennet Wheeler, 1781), 4–13.
5. Ibid., 7, 13, 3, 4, 5, 9.
6. Daniel Rathbun, *A Letter from Daniel Rathbun, of Richmond in the County of Berkshire, to James Whittacor, Chief Elder of the Church, Called Shakers* (Springfield, MA: N.p., 1785), 56, 32, 15, 14, 21; Reuben Rathbun,

Reasons Offered for Leaving the Shakers (Pittsfield, MA: N.p., 1800), 4, 14–16.

7. James Whittaker, *A Concise Statement of the Principles of the Only True Church, . . .* (Bennington, VT: Haswell & Russell, 1790), 21, 23.
8. Stein, *Shaker Experience*, 41–43; Garrett, *Spirit Possession and Popular Religion*, 223–24; Andrews, *People Called Shakers*, 54–56; Theodore E. Johnson, ed., "Biographical Account of the Life, Character, & Ministry of Father Joseph Meacham the Primary Leader in Establishing the United Order of the Millennial Church by Calvin Green 1827," *Shaker Quarterly* 10 (1970): 22–32.
9. Stein, *Shaker Experience*, 43–44.
10. Ibid., 44–45. See also: Garrett, *Spirit Possession and Popular Religion*, 223–26; Andrews, *People Called Shakers*, 57.
11. Stein, *Shaker Experience*, 45–46, 114; Garrett, *Spirit Possession and Popular Religion*, 230.
12. Stein, *Shaker Experience*, 54–57.
13. Ibid., 59.
14. Richard McNemar, *The Kentucky Revival; or, A Short History of the Late Extraordinary Outpouring of the Spirit of God in the Western States of America, . . .* (1807; rpt., Cincinnati: Art Guild's Reprints, 1968), 116, 3–4. Emphases in original.
15. Stein, *Shaker Experience*, 64, 67; Andrews, *People Called Shakers*, 70–93.
16. Benjamin Seth Youngs, *The Testimony of Christ's Second Appearing; . . .* (Albany, NY: E. and E. Hosford, 1810), 61, 89, 411; *A Summary View of the Millennial Church, or United Society of Believers, (Commonly Called Shakers.) Comprising the Rise, Progress, and Practical Order of the Society; Together with the General Principles of Their Faith and Testimony* (Albany, NY: Packard & Van Benthuysen, 1823), 131.
17. *Summary View* (1823), 80.
18. Richard Lyman Bushman, *Joseph Smith, Rough Stone Rolling: A Cultural Biography of Mormonism's Founder* (New York: Vintage Books, 2005), 435; Foster, *Religion and Sexuality*, 142.
19. Bushman, *Rough Stone Rolling*, 382–84; Robert Bruce Flanders, *Nauvoo: Kingdom on the Mississippi* (Urbana: University of Illinois Press, 1965), 27–40; Glen M. Leonard, *Nauvoo: A Place of Peace, a People of Promise* (Salt Lake City, UT: Deseret Book, 2002), 41–58.
20. *D&C* 118:4.
21. Bushman, *Rough Stone Rolling*, 409.
22. U.S. Census, 1840, Hancock County, Illinois.
23. Chicago's population in 1840 was 4,470, but by 1850 had exploded to 29,963. U.S. Census, 1840 and 1850, Chicago.
24. James L. Kimball, "A Wall to Defend Zion: The Nauvoo Charter," *BYU Studies* 15, no. 4 (1975): 491–97.

25. Bushman, *Rough Stone Rolling*, 411–12; Andrew F. Smith, *The Saintly Scoundrel: The Life and Times of Dr. John Cook Bennett* (Urbana: University of Illinois Press, 1997), 1–50.
26. George D. Smith, "Table 3.1 Joseph Smith's wives," *Nauvoo Polygamy: ". . . but we called it celestial marriage"* (Salt Lake City, UT: Signature Books, 2011), 223–24.
27. G. D. Smith, *Nauvoo Polygamy*, 30, 16.
28. G. D. Smith, "Table 3.1 Joseph Smith's wives," *Nauvoo Polygamy*, 223–24.
29. The affidavits are by Joseph Bates Noble and can be found in B. H. Roberts, *A Comprehensive History of the Church of Jesus Christ of Latter-day Saints*, 6 vols. (Salt Lake City, UT: LDS Church, 1930), 2:101.
30. Zina Young, Autobiography 2, Zina D. H. Young Collection, LDS Archives, quoted in G. D. Smith, *Nauvoo Polygamy*, 75.
31. G. D. Smith, *Nauvoo Polygamy*, 73–79; Compton, *In Sacred Loneliness*, 71–82, 114–22.
32. Compton, *In Sacred Loneliness*, 123, quoting Emmeline Wells, "A Venerable Woman: Prescendia Lathrop Kimball," *Woman's Exponent* (Apr. 1, 1883): 163.
33. Martha Bradley-Evans, *Glorious in Persecution: Joseph Smith American Prophet, 1839–1844* (Salt Lake City, UT: Smith-Petit Foundation, 2016), 125; Linda King Newell and Valeen Tippets Avery, *Mormon Enigma: Emma Hale Smith*, 2nd ed. (Urbana: University of Illinois Press, 1994), 98; and Bushman, *Rough Stone Rolling*, 491.
34. Bushman, *Rough Stone Rolling*, 443; G. D. Smith, "Table 4.8 Nauvoo plural families by year of inception," *Nauvoo Polygamy*, 311.
35. G. D. Smith, "Tables 1.1 Interval between first encounter and Nauvoo marriage" and "Table 3.1 Joseph Smith's wives," *Nauvoo Polygamy*, 36, 223–24.
36. Bushman, *Rough Stone Rolling*, 407–9; G. D. Smith, *Nauvoo Polygamy*, 117.
37. Ann Eliza Young, *Wife Number Nineteen; or, The Story of a Life in Bondage: Being a Complete Expose of Mormonism, and Revealing the Sorrows, Sacrifices, and Suffering of Women in Polygamy* (1875; rpt., New York: Arno Press, 1972), 324–26.
38. "Letter to Nancy Rigdon, 1842," in *Personal Writings of Joseph Smith*, ed. Dean C. Jesse, rev. ed. (Salt Lake City, UT: Deseret Book, 2002), 538.
39. G. D. Smith, *Nauvoo Polygamy*, 147–54; Compton, *In Sacred Loneliness*, 239–40.
40. *D&C* 124:23, 27.
41. Michael W. Homer, *Joseph's Temples: The Dynamic Relationship between Freemasonry and Mormonism* (Salt Lake City, UT: University of Utah Press, 2014), 142–49.
42. Bushman, *Rough Stone Rolling*, 450.

43. Homer, *Joseph's Temples*, 160, 167–69.
44. Thomas O'Dea, *The Mormons* (Chicago: University of Chicago Press, 1957), 57.
45. Homer, *Joseph's Temples*, 242–43.
46. Bushman, *Rough Stone Rolling*, 451.
47. Anthony Wonderly, "Introduction," *John Humphrey Noyes on Sexual Relations in the Oneida Community* (Clinton, NY: Richard W. Couper Press, 2012), 15.
48. *First Annual Report of the Oneida Association: Exhibiting Its History, Principles, and Transactions to Jan. 1, 1849* (Oneida Reserve, NY: Leonard, 1849), 28–31, 18.
49. George Wallingford Noyes, undated subchapter introduction, in *Free Love in Utopia: John Humphrey Noyes and the Origin of the Oneida Community*, ed. Lawrence Foster (Urbana: University of Illinois Press, 2001), 18.
50. *First Annual Report*, 1.
51. Spencer Klaw, *Without Sin: The Life and Death of the Oneida Community* (New York: Penguin Books, 1993), 299; Foster, "Introduction," in *Free Love in Utopia*, x–xi.
52. *First Annual Report*, 43.
53. Ibid., 49–53. Emphasis in original.
54. Ibid., 1; *Second Annual Report of the Oneida Association: Exhibiting Its Progress to February 20, 1850* (Oneida Reserve, NY: Leonard, 1850), 3.
55. Foster, *Religion and Sexuality*, 109.
56. John Humphrey Noyes to John R. Miller, Dec. 14, 1847, in *John Humphrey Noyes: The Putney Community*, ed. George Wallingford Noyes (Oneida, NY: Author, 1931), 340.
57. Foster, ed., *Free Love in Utopia*, 13–14.
58. Robert Allerton Parker, *A Yankee Saint: John Humphrey Noyes and the Oneida Community* (New York: G. P. Putnam's Sons, 1935), 190.
59. Stephen R. Leonard to George W. Noyes, May 13, 1849, in *Free Love in Utopia*, ed. Foster, 33.
60. *Oneida Journal*, May 16, 1849, in *Free Love in Utopia*, ed. Foster, 33.
61. John Humphrey Noyes, "Brooklyn Talk," Aug. 12, 1850, in *Free Love in Utopia*, ed. Foster, 55.
62. "The Children's Department," Aug. 25, 1849, in *Free Love in Utopia*, ed. Foster, 53.
63. John Humphrey Noyes, "Physical Suggestions on the Subject of Amativeness: Home-Talk by Noyes," Sept. 20, 1851, in *Free Love in Utopia*, ed. Foster, 238–39.
64. For the term "leakers" see Louis J. Kern, *An Ordered Love: Sex Roles and Sexuality in Victorian Utopias—The Shakers, the Mormons, and the Oneida Community* (Chapel Hill: University of North Carolina Press, 1981), 243.

65. John Humphrey Noyes to E. H. Hamilton, Mar. 4, 1850, in *Free Love in Utopia*, ed. Foster, 224.
66. John Humphrey Noyes, "Second Lecture," Nov. 29, 1852, *Seven Lectures on Social Freedom*, in *Free Love in Utopia*, ed. Foster, 208.
67. John Humphrey Noyes, "The Campaign among the Children," 56.
68. John Humphrey Noyes, "Physical Suggestions on the Subject of Amativeness: Home-Talk by Noyes," 238.
69. John Humphrey Noyes, "The Campaign among the Children," 55.
70. John Humphrey Noyes, *Confessions of John Humphrey Noyes. Part I: Confessions of Religious Experience, Including a History of Modern Perfectionism* (Oneida Reserve, NY: Leonard, 1849), 2.
71. John Humphrey Noyes, *History of American Socialisms* (Philadelphia: Lippincott, 1870), 657.

PART III. EARLY CRISES

1. "The Children's Department," Aug. 25, 1849, in *Free Love in Utopia: John Humphrey Noyes and the Origin of the Oneida Community*, ed. Lawrence Foster (Urbana: University of Illinois Press, 2001), 53.

7. SHAKER FAMILY DRAMA

1. Eunice Chapman, *Account of the Conduct of the Shakers in the Case of Eunice Chapman and Her Children* (Albany, NY: N.p., 1817), 14, 23.
2. Ibid., 39, 54, 27, 28.
3. Ibid., 40–41. Eunice Chapman, *No. 2d. Being an Additional Account of the Conduct of the Shakers in the Case of Eunice Chapman and Her Children* (Albany, NY: I. W. Clark, 1818), 36–37.
4. Mary Marshall Dyer, *A Brief Statement of the Sufferings of Mary Dyer, Occasioned by the Society Called Shakers. Written by Herself. To Which Is Added, Affidavits and Certificates. Also, a Declaration from Their Own Publication* (Concord, NH: Joseph C. Spear, 1818), 4–5, 32.
5. Joseph Dyer, *A Compendious Narrative, Elucidating the Character, Disposition, and Conduct of Mary Dyer* (Concord, NH: I. Hill, 1818), 12–13, 32, 77.
6. Richard McNemar, *The Other Side of the Question. In three parts. I. An explanation of the proceedings of Eunice Chapman and the Legislature, against the United Society . . . in the state of New York. II. A refutation of the false statements of Mary Dyer against the said society, in the state of New-Hampshire. III. An account o the proceedings of Abram Van Vleet, esq. and his associates, against the said United Society at Union Village, Ohio. Comprising a general vindication of the Character of Mother and the elders against the attacks of public slander—the edicts of a prejudiced*

party—and the misguided zeal of lawless mobs (Cincinnati, OH: Reynolds, 1819), 140, 16, 12, 15.

7. Suzanne R. Thurman, Review of Elizabeth A. De Wolfe, *Shaking the Faith: Women, Family, and Mary Marshall Dyer's Anti-Shaker Campaign, 1815–1867, H-Communal-Societies, H-Net Reviews* (Sept. 2002), http://www.h-net.org/reviews/showrev.php?id=6787.

8. Here are Mary Marshall Dyer's publications in chronological order: *A Brief Statement of the Sufferings of Mary Dyer* (1818); *A Portraiture of Shakerism, Exhibiting a General View of Their Character and Conduct, from the First Appearance of Ann Lee in New-England, Down to the Present Time. And Certified by Many Respectable Authorities* (Concord, NH: N.p., 1822); and *The Rise and Progress of the Serpent from the Garden of Eden to the Present Day, With a Discourse of Shakerism, Exhibiting a General View of Their Real Character and Conduct from the First Appearance of Ann Lee: Also the Life and Sufferings of the Author* (Concord, NH: N.p., 1847).

9. "An extract of Mrs. Mary Dyer's deposition," in Chapman, *Account of the Conduct of the People Called Shakers*, 72. Emphases in original.

10. Dyer, *Rise and Progress of the Serpent*, 95.

11. Chapman, *Account of the Conduct of the People Called Shakers*, 56.

12. Thomas Brown, *An Account of the People Called Shakers: Their Faith, Doctrines, and Practice, Exemplified in the Life, Conversations, and Experience of the Author during the Time He Belonged to the Society, to Which Is Affixed a History of Their Rise and Progress to the Present Day* (Troy, NY: Parker and Bliss, 1812), 167, 170–73, 101, 235, 223–24.

13. Ibid., 231–24.

14. Eunice Chapman's petition to the Senate of New York, Apr. 12, 1816, in Chapman, *Account of the Conduct of the People Called Shakers*, Introduction, v; Chapman, *No. 2d. Being an Additional Account*, 38.

15. Stephen J. Stein, *The Shaker Experience in America: A History of the United Society of Believers* (New Haven, CT: Yale University Press, 1992), 87.

16. Calvin Green and Seth Y. Wells, *A Summary View of the Millennial Church, or United Society of Believers, (Commonly Called Shakers.) Comprising the Rise, Progress, and Practical Order of the Society; Together with the General Principles of Their Faith and Testimony* (Albany, NY: Packard and Van Benthuysen, 1823), iii, 165, 278.

17. Ibid., Preface, iv, 191–93, 211.

8. Polygamy and Persecution at Nauvoo

1. *D&C* 132:54.
2. Andrew F. Smith, *The Saintly Scoundrel: The Life and Times of Dr. John Cook Bennett* (Urbana: University of Illinois Press, 1997), 56–57, 78–86;

Richard Bushman, *Joseph Smith, Rough Stone Rolling: A Cultural Biography of Mormonism's Founder* (New York: Vintage Books, 2005), 460–61.
3. John C. Bennett, *The History of the Saints; or, An Expose of Joe Smith and Mormonism* (Boston: Leland & Whiting, 1842), 10, 5–7, 53, 49, 192, 293.
4. Ibid., 217–25. Emphasis in original.
5. Ibid., 226–30.
6. Martha H. Brotherton's affidavit as recorded in Bennett's *History of the Saints*, 236–38.
7. Ibid., 238–40.
8. B. H. Roberts, ed., *History of The Church of Jesus Christ of Latter-day Saints*, 2nd ed., 8 vols. (Salt Lake City, UT: Deseret Book, 1971), 4:585–86.
9. George D. Smith, *Nauvoo Polygamy: "... but we called it celestial marriage"* (Salt Lake City, UT: Signature Books, 2011), 270, 265.
10. Bennett, *History of the Saints*, 281–82.
11. Bushman, *Rough Stone Rolling*, 468–80.
12. Bennett, *The History of the Saints*, 306–7, 209.
13. Andrew F. Ehat and Lyndon W. Cook, eds., *The Words of Joseph Smith: The Contemporary Accounts of the Nauvoo Discourses of the Prophet Joseph* (Provo, UT: Religious Studies Center, BYU, 1980), 129 (Aug. 29, 1842).
14. Joseph Smith to Brother and Sister Whitney, and &c., Aug. 18, 1842, quoted in G. D. Smith, *Nauvoo Polygamy*, 143.
15. G. D. Smith, "Table 3.1 Joseph Smith's wives," *Nauvoo Polygamy*, 223–24.
16. Linda King Newell and Valeen Tippets Avery, *Mormon Enigma: Emma Hale Smith*, 2nd ed. (Urbana: University of Illinois Press, 1994), 134–36.
17. Ibid., 67.
18. Emily Dow Young, "Incidents in the Life of a Mormon Girl," 176, MS 5220, folders 1–2 and on microfilm, LDS Archives, 185, quoted in G. D. Smith, *Nauvoo Polygamy*, 176.
19. Newell and Avery, *Mormon Enigma*, 142–44; G. D. Smith, *Nauvoo Polygamy*, 172–79, 195–98.
20. Emily Dow Partridge Young, "Diary and Reminiscences, 1874–1899," 2, L. Tom Perry Special Collections, Harold B. Lee Library, BYU, Provo, UT, quoted in G. D. Smith, *Nauvoo Polygamy*, 180.
21. G. D. Smith, *Nauvoo Polygamy*, 179–82; Newell and Avery, *Mormon Enigma*, 143–45.
22. Newell and Avery, *Mormon Enigma*, 147.
23. Original in Lyman O. Littlefield, *Reminiscences of Latter-day Saints* (Logan, UT: *Utah Journal*, 1888), 46–48, quoted in Kathryn M. Daynes, "Mormon Polygamy: Belief and Practice in Nauvoo," in *Kingdom on the Mississippi Revisited: Nauvoo in Mormon History*, ed. Roger D. Launius and John E. Hallwas (Urbana: University of Illinois Press, 1996), 136–37.
24. Ibid.

25. Ibid.
26. "Helen Mar Kimball's Retrospection about Her Introduction to the Doctrine and Practices of Plural Marriage in Nauvoo at Age 15," Mar. 30, 1881, Helen Mar Whitney Papers, LDS Archives, quoted in Lawrence Foster, *Women, Family, and Utopia: Communal Experiments of the Shakers, the Oneida Community, and the Mormons* (Syracuse, NY: Syracuse University Press, 1991), 137.
27. Todd Compton, *In Sacred Loneliness: The Plural Wives of Joseph Smith* (Salt Lake City, UT: Signature Books, 1997), 123, 497.
28. "Helen Mar Kimball's Retrospection," in Foster, *Women, Family, and Utopia*, 138.
29. For bibliographic information, see notes 23 and 27.
30. G. D. Smith, "Table 3.4 Joseph Smith's inner circle of Nauvoo polygamists," *Nauvoo Polygamy*, 240.
31. G. D. Smith, *Nauvoo Polygamy*, 359.
32. Brigham Young Address, Oct. 8, 1866, quoted in Newell and Avery, *Mormon Enigma*, 141.
33. D&C 131.
34. Diary of Levi Richards, May 14, 1843, BYU, quoted in Newell and Avery, *Mormon Enigma*, 332n44.
35. Address of Hyrum Smith at the General Conference of the Church, Apr. 8, 1844, Miscellaneous Minutes collection, LDS Archives, quoted in Newell and Avery, *Mormon Enigma*, 142.
36. Newell and Avery, *Mormon Enigma*, 142.
37. William Clayton, statement, Feb. 16, 1874, published in Andrew Jenson, *The Historical Record: A Monthly Periodical Devoted Exclusively to Historical, Biographical, Chronological, and Statistical Matters* (Salt Lake City, UT: Author, 1887) 6, nos. 3–5:224–26, quoted in Newell and Avery, *Mormon Enigma*, 151–52.
38. D&C, 132:7, 15–18, 19–20, 18, 7.
39. D&C, 132:34–50, 61–63.
40. D&C, 132:53–56.
41. William Clayton, statement, Feb. 16, 1874, published in Jenson, *Historical Record* 6, nos. 3–5:224–26, quoted in Newell and Avery, *Mormon Enigma*, 152.
42. Newell and Avery, *Mormon Enigma*, 153–61; Bushman, *Rough Stone Rolling*, 494–95.
43. William Clayton, *An Intimate Chronicle: The Journals of William Clayton*, ed. George D. Smith (Salt Lake City, UT: Signature Books and Smith Research Associates, 1991), 158, 105–6.
44. See G. D. Smith, "Table 3.4 Joseph Smith's inner circle of Nauvoo polygamists," *Nauvoo Polygamy*, 240.

45. Martha Bradley-Evans, *Glorious in Persecution: Joseph Smith American Prophet, 1839–1844* (Salt Lake City, UT: Smith-Petit Foundation, 2016), 135; Brigham Young, Jul. 14, 1855, *Journal of Discourses* 3:266.
46. Bushman, *Rough Stone Rolling*, 528.
47. William Law, Diary, Jan. 1, 1844, in Lyndon W. Cook, *William Law: Biographical Essay, Nauvoo Diary, Correspondence, Interview* (Orem, UT: Grandin Books, 1994), 37, quoted in Bushman, *Rough Stone Rolling*, 528.
48. Bushman, *Rough Stone Rolling*, 500–509.
49. Ibid., 514–17, 523–25.
50. Ibid., 528, 531.
51. *Nauvoo Expositor*, June 7, 1844, 1.
52. Ibid., 3. Emphasis added.
53. Bushman, *Rough Stone Rolling*, 537–39.
54. *Nauvoo Expositor*, June 7, 1844, 1, 3.
55. Ibid. Emphasis in original.
56. Ibid. Emphases in original.
57. Bushman, *Rough Stone Rolling*, 540–46.
58. Ibid., 549–50.

9. "A Scatteration at Oneida"

1. "Manifesto of the Oneida Association," *The Circular*, old series 1, no. 66, in *Free Love in Utopia: John Humphrey Noyes and the Origin of the Oneida Community*, ed. Lawrence Foster (Urbana: University of Illinois Press, 2001), 159. Most of this chapter comes from what the compiler G. W. Noyes and the editor Lawrence Foster eventually published as *Free Love in Utopia*. The notes here, rather than simply referencing the page number of the edited volume, will instead reference the specific primary source as found in the edited volume.
2. Susan Hamilton to Putney, Apr. 29, 1852, in *Free Love in Utopia*, 176.
3. "Home-Talk by Noyes," Jul. 7, 1851, in *Free Love in Utopia*, 99.
4. "The Paper: Home-Talk by Noyes," Jul. 11, 1851, in *Free Love in Utopia*, 100.
5. "News Item Condensed from the *New York Tribune*," Jul. 26, 1851, in *Free Love in Utopia*, 104.
6. "The Sinking of the Sloop: Home-Talk," Jul. 27, 1851, in *Free Love in Utopia*, 105.
7. "Home-Talk by Noyes," Sept. 4, 1851, in *Free Love in Utopia*, 115.
8. "Home-Talk about Mrs. Cragin," Sept. 7, 1851, in *Free Love in Utopia*, 123.
9. "Hades and the Three Worlds: Home-Talk by Noyes," Sept. 1, 1851, in *Free Love in Utopia*, 121.
10. Foster, "Introduction," *Free Love in Utopia*, xlv, n. 89.

11. *Oneida Journal*, July 26, Sept. 15 and 17, and Dec. 10, 1850, in *Free Love in Utopia*, 94–96.
12. *Oneida Journal*, Oct. 2, 1851, in *Free Love in Utopia*, 137.
13. Foster, "Introduction," *Free Love in Utopia*, xxviii; *Oneida Journal*, Nov. 26, 1851, in *Free Love in Utopia*, 142.
14. "Perfectionism and Polygamy," *New York Observer*, Jan. 22, 1852, in *Free Love in Utopia*, 145–48.
15. "Coup d'Etat: Home-Talk by Noyes," Feb. 28, 1852, in *Free Love in Utopia*, 155.
16. "Manifesto of the Oneida Association," *The Circular*, old series 1, no. 66, Mar. 7, 1852, in *Free Love in Utopia*, 159. Emphasis in original.
17. *Oneida Journal*, Apr. 18, 1852, in *Free Love in Utopia*, 170.
18. John Humphrey Noyes to John R. Miller, Apr. 30, 1852, in *Free Love in Utopia*, 178.
19. John R. Miller to John Humphrey Noyes, Apr. 29, 1852; Susan Hamilton to Putney, Apr. 29, 1852; Harriet A. Noyes to Putney, Apr. 29, 1852; John Humphrey Noyes, "The Greater Miracle," Apr. 30, 1852; John R. Miller to Putney, Apr. 30, 1852; John R. Miller to John Humphrey Noyes, May 10, 1852. All in *Free Love in Utopia*, 176–79.
20. Hon. Timothy Jenkins to John R. Miller, May 24, 1852; John R. Miller to Noyes, June 18, 1852, in *Free Love in Utopia*, 181–83. *Biographical Directory of the American Congress, 1774–1927*, s.v. "Jenkins, Timothy."
21. George Washington Noyes to John R. Miller, May 28, 1852; George Washington Noyes to Brooklyn, June 25, 1852; John R. Miller to John Humphrey Noyes, June 27, 1852; John R. Miller to George Cragin, June 25, 1852. All in *Free Love in Utopia*, 182–84.
22. John R. Miller to John Humphrey Noyes, July 23, 1852; John R. Miller to George Cragin, Sept. 14, 1852; John Humphrey Noyes, "Victory of the 27th," July 28, 1852; *The Circular*, Aug. 29, 1852. All in *Free Love in Utopia*, 189–93.
23. "Manifesto of the Oneida Association," *The Circular*, old series 1, no. 66 (Mar. 7, 1852), in *Free Love in Utopia*, 158.

10. SUCCESSION, RELOCATION, AND PROCLAMATION

1. D. Michael Quinn, *The Mormon Hierarchy: Origins of Power* (Salt Lake City, UT: Signature Books, 1994), 77.
2. Richard S. Van Wagoner, *Mormon Polygamy: A History* (Salt Lake City, UT: Signature Books, 1989), 72.
3. Tertullian, *Apology*, trans. Sister Emily Joseph Daly, C.S.J., in *The Fathers of the Church, a New Translation*, vol. 10 (New York: Fathers of the Church, 1950), 125.

4. John G. Turner, *Brigham Young: Pioneer Prophet* (Cambridge, MA: Belknap Press of Harvard University Press, 2012), 413.
5. *D&C* 107:39.
6. David Vaughn Mason, *Brigham Young: Sovereign in America* (New York: Routledge, 2015), 9.
7. Ibid., 15; Susa Young Gates and Leah D. Widtsoe, *The Life Story of Brigham Young* (New York: Macmillan, 1930), 362, cited in Valeen Tippetts Avery and Linda King Newell, "The Lion and the Lady: Brigham Young and Emma Smith," in *Kingdom on the Mississippi Revisited: Nauvoo in Mormon History*, ed. Roger D. Launius and John E. Hallwas (Urbana: University of Illinois Press, 1996), 209.
8. Quinn, *Mormon Hierarchy*, 66. See also B. H. Roberts, ed., *History of The Church of Jesus Christ of Latter-day Saints*, 2nd ed., 8 vols. (Salt Lake City, UT: Deseret Book, 1971), 4:403, 412; and Turner, *Pioneer Prophet*, 83.
9. Turner, *Pioneer Prophet*, 91; George D. Smith, "Table 3.1 Joseph Smith's wives," *Nauvoo Polygamy* (Salt Lake City, UT: Signature Books, 2011), 223.
10. G. D. Smith, "Appendix B, Nauvoo polygamous families," "Table 3.1 Joseph Smith's wives," and "Table 3.4 Joseph Smith's inner circle of Nauvoo polygamists," *Nauvoo Polygamy*, 635, 223–24, 240.
11. Elden J. Watson, ed., *Manuscript History of Brigham Young, 1801–1844* (Salt Lake City, UT: Smith Secretarial Service, 1968), 171, quoted in Leonard J. Arrington, *Brigham Young: American Moses* (New York: Alfred A. Knopf, 1985), 111.
12. Brigham Young remarks to a meeting of the Quorum of the Twelve Apostles, Feb. 12, 1849, quoted in Quinn, *Mormon Hierarchy*, 156.
13. Quinn, *Mormon Hierarchy*, 154, 159, 172–73.
14. Roberts, ed., *History of the Church*, 7:234, 233; Minutes of Aug. 8, 1844, folders 21–25, General Church Minutes, quoted in Turner, *Pioneer Prophet*, 112; Quinn, *Mormon Hierarchy*, 167.
15. Scott G. Kennedy, ed., *Wilford Woodruff's Journal: 1833–1898 Typescript*, 9 vols. (Midvale, UT: Signature Books, 1983–85), 5:139 (Dec. 18, 1857), quoted in Quinn, *Mormon Hierarchy*, 168.
16. Quinn, *Mormon Hierarchy*, 152, 168, 173–74; Linda King Newell and Valeen Tippets Avery, *Mormon Enigma: Emma Hale Smith*, 2nd ed. (Urbana: University of Illinois Press, 1994), 199–209; Roberts, ed., *History of the Church*, 7:264–65; Brigham Young Journal, 1837–1845, box 71, folder 2, Brigham Young Papers, Sept. 3, 1844, quoted in Turner, *Pioneer Prophet*, 114; Brigham Young 1837–1845 diary, Aug. 31, Sept. 2, 1844, quoted in Quinn, *Mormon Hierarchy*, 170. G. D. Smith, "Table 3.4, Joseph Smith's inner circle of Nauvoo polygamists," and "Table 3.1 Joseph Smith's wives," *Nauvoo Polygamy*, 240, 223–24.

17. G. D. Smith, "Table 4.1 The widows who married LDS leaders," *Nauvoo Polygamy*, 283.
18. Marshall Hamilton, "From Assassination to Expulsion: Two Years of Distrust, Hostility, and Violence," in *Kingdom on the Mississippi Revisited*, ed. Launius and Hallwas, 215–17.
19. Ibid., 218–19.
20. *The Neighbor*, Oct. 1, 1845, quoted in Hamilton, "From Assassination to Expulsion," 223.
21. *D&C*, 124:40.
22. Tuner, *Pioneer Prophet*, 123, 141; Michael W. Homer, *Joseph's Temples: The Dynamic Relationship between Freemasonry and Mormonism* (Salt Lake City, UT: University of Utah Press, 2014), 232.
23. G. D. Smith, "Table 4.8, Nauvoo plural families by year of inception," *Nauvoo Polygamy*, 311.
24. Ibid.; Kathryn M. Daynes, *More Wives Than One: Transformation of the Mormon Marriage System, 1840–1910* (Urbana: University of Illinois Press, 2001), 35.
25. Lawrence Foster, *Religion and Sexuality: The Shakers, the Mormons, and the Oneida Community* (Urbana: University of Illinois Press, 1984), 196–99; Turner, *Pioneer Prophet*, 139.
26. Leonard Arrington and Davis Bitton, *The Mormon Experience: A History of the Latter-Day Saints* (New York: Alfred A. Knopf, 1979), 115; Richard E. Bennett, *Mormons at the Missouri, 1846–1852: "And Should We Die . . ."* (Norman: University of Oklahoma Press, 1987), 90.
27. Turner, *Pioneer Prophet*, 141–142; Mason, *Sovereign in America*, 60–61; Hamilton, "From Assassination to Expulsion," 224.
28. Van Wagoner, *Mormon Polygamy*, 82, quoting Edward W. Tullidge, *The Women of Mormondom* (Salt Lake City: N.p., 1877), 369. See also Bennett, *Mormons at the Missouri*, 194–98.
29. Mason, *Sovereign in America*, 66; Turner, *Pioneer Prophet*, 155.
30. Turner, *Pioneer Prophet*, 156, quoting Eliza R. Snow Journal, Jan. 1, 1847. Emphasis in original.
31. Mason, *Sovereign in America*, 66.
32. Melvin L. Bashore, BYU Pioneer Mortality Team, and H. Dennis Tolley, "Mortality on the Mormon Trail, 1847–1868," *BYU Studies Quarterly* 53, no. 4 (2014): Article 9.
33. Turner, *Pioneer Prophet*, 172–73; Mason, *Sovereign in America*, 80–81.
34. Turner, *Pioneer Prophet*, 195–99; Mason, *Sovereign in America*, 97–98.
35. Leonard Arrington, *Great Basin Kingdom: An Economic History of the Latter-day Saints, 1830–1900* (Cambridge, MA: Harvard University Press, 1958), 71.
36. Ibid., 97.

37. Turner, *Pioneer Prophet*, 199–204.
38. John W. Gunnison, *The Mormons, or, Latter-day Saints, in the Valley of the Great Salt Lake* (Philadelphia: Lippincott, Grambo, 1852), preface, v.
39. Ibid., 67.
40. Turner, *Pioneer Prophet*, 204; Mason, *Sovereign in America*, 102.
41. Orson Pratt, "Celestial Marriage." *Journal of Discourses* 1 (1854): 54.
42. Ibid., 54, 64, 65.
43. Ibid., 54–59.
44. Ibid., 61–62.
45. Ibid., 62–65.
46. "Theocratic Platform," *The Circular*, old series 1, no. 40 (Aug. 29, 1852), quoted in Lawrence Foster, ed., *Free Love in Utopia: John Humphrey Noyes and the Origin of the Oneida Community* (Urbana: University of Illinois Press, 2001), 192–93.

Part IV. Practices and Enforcements

1. See, Stephen J. Stein, *The Shaker Experience in America: A History of the United Society of Believers* (New Haven, CT: Yale University Press, 1992), 122, 133–39, 148.
2. John R. Miller to John Humphrey Noyes, Jan. 24, 1852, in *Free Love in Utopia: John Humphrey Noyes and the Origin of the Oneida Community*, ed. Lawrence Foster (Urbana: University of Illinois Press, 2001), 199.
3. John R. Miller to George Cragin, Dec. 27, 1852, in *Free Love in Utopia*, ed. Foster, 206.
4. George Wallingford Noyes, "Review of the Brooklyn Epoch, 1849 to 1854," in *Free Love in Utopia*, ed. Foster, 288, 290.
5. Leonard J. Arrington, *Great Basin Kingdom: An Economic History of the Latter-day Saints, 1830–1900* (Cambridge, MA: Harvard University Press, 1958), 6, 33.
6. Ibid., 199.
7. Thomas G. Alexander, *Utah, the Right Place: The Official Centennial History*, rev. ed. (Salt Lake City, UT: Gibbs Smith, 1996), 169.
8. See Arrington, *Great Basin Kingdom*, ch. 9, "Mormon Railroads," 257–92.
9. Eugene E. Campbell, *Establishing Zion: The Mormon Church in the American West, 1847–1869* (Salt Lake City, UT: Signature Books, 1988), 210.
10. Leonard J. Arrington and Davis Bitton, *The Mormon Experience: A History of the Latter-Day Saints* (New York: Alfred A. Knopf, 1979), 136.
11. Stanley S. Ivins, "Notes on Mormon Polygamy," *Western Humanities Review* 10 (Summer 1956): 230; Lawrence Foster, *Religion and Sexuality: The Shakers, the Mormons, and the Oneida Community* (Urbana: University of Illinois Press, 1984), 210.

11. Selfishness and Status

1. "Egotism for Two," *The Circular* 11, no. 21 (Jul. 3, 1862); "Christ and the Family Spirit," *The Circular* 12, no. 38 (Oct. 13, 1859).
2. *First Annual Report of the Oneida Association: Exhibiting Its History, Principles, and Transactions to Jan. 1, 1849* (Oneida Reserve, NY: Leonard, 1849), 21. Emphases in original.
3. Mary Marshall Dyer, *The Rise and Progress of the Serpent from the Garden of Eden to the Present Day, With a Discourse of Shakerism, . . .* (Concord, NH: Author, 1847), 112.
4. Report by Sarah Burt, Mary Prindle, and Mary Cragin, Feb. 2, 1851, in *Oneida Community: An Autobiography, 1851–1876*, ed. Constance Noyes Robertson (Syracuse, NY: Syracuse University Press, 1970), 331–33. Originally published in *The Circular*, Oct. 19, 1874.
5. "The Prima Donna Fever—Report of a Musical Criticism," *The Circular*, Aug. 31, 1874, in *Oneida Community: An Autobiography, 1851–1876*, ed. Robertson, 148–49. Emphasis in original.
6. Spencer Klaw, *Without Sin: The Life and Death of the Oneida Community* (New York: Penguin Books, 1993), 183.
7. "Egotism—Its Character and Cure," *The Circular* 2, no. 66 (Jul. 2, 1853). Emphasis in original.
8. "The Year's Balance Sheet," *The Circular*, New Series 3, no. 44 (Jan. 14, 1867).
9. "The Bible Argument," *The Circular*, New Series 6, no. 13 (June 14, 1869).
10. "What We Believe and Why," *The Circular*, 10, no. 18 (June 6, 1861).
11. "The Value of Certainty," *The Circular*, 10, no. 21 (June 27, 1861).
12. "A Difference," *The Circular*, new series 7, no. 7 (May 2, 1870); "Wide Apart," *American Socialist* 6, no. 11 (Mar. 13, 1879).
13. "Decadence of Marriage," *The Circular*, new series 13, no. 4 (Jan. 27, 1876).
14. "Polygamic Discussion in Utah," *The Circular*, new series 7, no. 25 (Sept. 5, 1870).
15. *Discourses on Celestial Marriage. Delivered in the New Tabernacle, Salt Lake City, October 7th, 8th, and 9th, 1869, by Elder Orson Pratt, President George A. Smith, and Elder George Q. Cannon* (Salt Lake City, UT: Printed at the *Deseret News* Office, 1869), 21; Helen Mar Kimball Whitney, *Plural Marriage as Taught by the Prophet Joseph: A Reply to Joseph Smith, Editor of the Lamoni (Iowa) "Herald"* (Salt Lake City, UT: Juvenile Instructor Office, 1882), 27.
16. 2 Nephi 2:25.
17. Elle E. Dickinson, *New Light on Mormonism* (New York: Funk & Wagnalls, 1885), 145.

18. Gottlieb Ence, Life Sketch, 36, quoted in Jessie L. Embry, *Mormon Polygamous Families: Life in the Principle* (Salt Lake City, UT: University of Utah Press, 1987), 60.
19. John Hyde Jr., *Mormonism: Its Leaders and Designs,* 2nd ed. (New York: W. P. Fetridge, 1857), 55.
20. Stanley S. Ivins, "Notes on Mormon Polygamy," *Western Humanities Review* 10 (Summer 1956): 230.
21. Leonard J. Arrington and Davis Bitton, *The Mormon Experience: A History of the Latter-Day Saints* (New York: Alfred A. Knopf, 1979), 204. Historian Jessie L. Embry disputes this claim and this first quote directly. See *Mormon Polygamous Families*, 108.
22. George D. Smith, *Nauvoo Polygamy: ". . . but we called it celestial marriage"* (Salt Lake City, UT: Signature Books, 2011), 407.
23. Richard S. Van Wagoner, *Mormon Polygamy: A History* (Salt Lake City, UT: Signature Books, 1986), 102.
24. Arrington and Bitton, *Mormon Experience,* 204.

12. Control

1. Stephen J. Stein, *The Shaker Experience in America: A History of the United Society of Believers* (New Haven, CT: Yale University Press, 1992), 44–46.
2. Eunice Chapman, *Account of the Conduct of the People Called Shakers in the Case of Eunice Chapman and Her Children* (Albany, NY: N.p., 1817), 56.
3. David Lamson, *Two Years' Experience among the Shakers: Being a Description of the Manners and Customs of That People; the Nature and Policy of Their Government; Their Marvelous Intercourse with the Spiritual World; the Object and Uses of Confession, Their Inquisition; in Short, a Condensed View of Shakerism As It Is* (1848; rpt., New York: A.M.S. Press, 1971), 212, 20, 21, 22, 40. Emphasis in original.
4. Ibid., 165.
5. Amos Taylor, *A Narrative of the Strange Principles, Conduct, and Character of the People Known by the Name of Shakers* (Worcester, MA: Author, 1782), 4.
6. William J. Haskett, *Shakerism Unmasked; or, The History of the Shakers; Including a Form Politic of Their Government as Councils, Orders, Gifts, with an Exposition of the Five Orders of Shakerism, and Ann Lee's Grand Foundation Vision in Sealed Pages with Some Extracts from Their Private Hymns Which Have Never Appeared before the Public* (Pittsfield, MA: Author, 1828), 155–56.
7. Lamson, *Two Years' Experience among the Shakers,* 27, 45, 48, 50, 170, 84, 168, 30, 56, 200, 208. Emphases in original.

8. Richard McNemar, *A Review of the Most Important Events Relating to the Rise and Progress of the United Society of Believers in the West: With Sundry Other Documents Connected with the History of the Society. Collected from Various Journals*. [E. Wright, pseudonym] (Union Village, OH: N.p., 1831), 55; Frederick W. Evans, *A Short Treatise on the Second Appearing of Christ, in and through the Order of the Female* (Boston: Bazin & Chandler, 1853), 13. Emphases in original.
9. Stein, *Shaker Experience*, 95.
10. Lamson, *Two Years' Experience among the Shakers*, 21.
11. Theodore E. Johnson, ed., "The 'Millennial Laws' of 1821," *Shaker Quarterly* 7 (1967): 54, 47–48.
12. Ibid., 45–58.
13. Haskett, *Shakerism Unmasked*, 168–84.
14. Lamson, *Two Years' Experience among the Shakers*, 209, 184.
15. Johnson, ed., "'Millennial Laws,'" 41.
16. Alonzo Giles Hollister, *Synopsis of Doctrine Taught by Believers in Christ's Second Appearing* (Mt. Lebanon, NY: N.p., 1893), 18.
17. George Wallingford Noyes, *Religious Experience of John Humphrey Noyes* (New York: Macmillan, 1923), 310.
18. *First Annual Report of the Oneida Association: Exhibiting its History, Principles, and Transactions to Jan. 1, 1849* (Oneida Reserve, NY: Leonard, 1849), 12.
19. Alan Estlake, *The Oneida Community: A Record of an Attempt to Carry Out the Principles of Christian Unselfishness and Scientific Race Improvement* (London: George Redway, 1900), 58.
20. *First Annual Report*, 10.
21. Theodore E. Noyes to Anita Newcomb McGee, Apr. 15, 1892, quoted in Constance Noyes Robertson, *Oneida Community: The Breakup, 1876–1881* (Syracuse, NY: Syracuse University Press, 1972), 16. Emphasis in original.
22. Theodore E. Noyes to Anita Newcomb McGee, Apr. 15, 1892, quoted in *Free Love in Utopia: John Humphrey Noyes and the Origin of the Oneida Community*, ed. Lawrence Foster (Urbana: University of Illinois Press, 2001), "Introduction," xxii.
23. This observation is based on my visits to the Oneida Mansion in 2012.
24. "Practical Suggestions for Regulating Intercourse of the Sexes: Home-Talk by Noyes," Sept. 22, 1852, in *Free Love in Utopia*, ed. Foster, 246–47.
25. Louis J. Kern, *An Ordered Love: Sex Roles and Sexuality in Victorian Utopias—the Shakers, the Mormons, and the Oneida Community* (Chapel Hill: University of North Carolina Press, 1981), 244.
26. "Practical Suggestions," in *Free Love in Utopia*, ed. Foster, 247.
27. John B. Ellis, *Free Love and Its Votaries; or, American Socialism Unmasked: Being an Historical and Descriptive Account of the Rise and Progress of the*

Various Free Love Associations in the U.S. and of the Effects of Their Various Teachings upon American Socialism (New York: United States Publishing Co., 1870), 133, 259.
28. Ann Eliza Young, *Wife Number Nineteen; or, The Story of a Life in Bondage: Being a Complete Expose of Mormonism, and Revealing the Sorrows, Sacrifices, and Sufferings of Women in Polygamy* (1875; rpt., New York: Arno Press, 1972), 444.
29. John Hyde Jr., *Mormonism: Its Leaders and Designs*, 2nd ed. (New York: W. P. Fetridge, 1857), 154.
30. E. D. Kane [pseudonym for William Wood], *Twelve Mormon Homes Visited in Succession on a Journey through Utah to Arizona* (Philadelphia: N.p., 1874), 114.
31. Hyde, *Mormonism: Its Leaders and Design*, 168–69.
32. Mrs. Thomas B. H. [Fanny] Stenhouse, *Expose of Polygamy in Utah—A Lady's Life among the Mormons: A Record of Personal Experience as One of the Wives of a Mormon Elder during a Period of More Than Twenty Years*, 2nd ed. (New York: American News Co., 1872), 133.
33. Hyde, *Mormonism: Its Leaders and Design*, 66, 69.
34. John H. Beadle, *Life in Utah; or, The Mysteries and Crimes of Mormonism: Being an Expose of the Secret Rites and Ceremonies of the Latter-Day Saints, with a Full and Authentic History of Polygamy and the Mormon Sect from Its Origin to the Present Time* (Philadelphia: National Publishing Co., 1870), 115.
35. Benjamin G. Ferris, *Utah and the Mormons: The History, Government, Doctrines, Customs, and Prospects of the Latter-Day Saints from Personal Observation during a Six Months' Residence at Great Salt Lake City* (New York: Harper & Brothers, 1854), 176.
36. John W. Gunnison, *The Mormons, or, Latter-day Saints, in the Valley of the Great Salt Lake* (Philadelphia: Lippincott, Grambo, 1852), 79.
37. Leonard J. Arrington and Davis Bitton, *The Mormon Experience: A History of the Latter-Day Saints* (New York: Alfred A. Knopf, 1979), 39–40.
38. John G. Turner, *Brigham Young: Pioneer Prophet* (Cambridge, MA: Belknap Press of Harvard University Press, 2012), 411–12, quoting *Journal of Discourses*, 10:295 (May 15, 1864).
39. Ann Eliza Young, *Wife Number Nineteen*, 445.
40. Stenhouse, *A Lady's Life among the Mormons*, 130.
41. Turner, *Pioneer Prophet*, 159–60, 240–43.
42. Davis Bitton, "Mormon Polygamy: A Review Article," *Journal of Mormon History* 4 (1977): 112.
43. Hyde, *Mormonism: Its Leaders and Designs*, 55. Emphasis added.
44. Ann Eliza Young, *Wife Number Nineteen*, 414.
45. Stenhouse, *A Lady's Life among the Mormons*, 52–53. Emphases in original.

46. Brigham Young, "A Few Words of Doctrine," Oct. 8, 1861, LDS Archives, quoted in George D. Smith, *Nauvoo Polygamy: ". . . but we called it celestial marriage"* (Salt Lake City, UT: Signature Books, 2011), 278–79.

13. Revival

1. I was assisted in this definition by the *Concise Dictionary of Christianity in America* (Eugene, OR: Wipf and Stock Publishers, 1995), s.v. "Revivalism."
2. John Humphrey Noyes, *Confessions of John H. Noyes: Confession of Religious Experience, Including a History of Modern Perfectionism* (Oneida Reserve, NY: Leonard, 1849), 2.
3. Constance Noyes Robertson, *Oneida Community: The Breakup, 1876–1881* (Syracuse, NY: Syracuse University Press, 1972), 46–47. Robertson is quoting a manuscript by George Wallingford Noyes, which serves as the basis for her book.
4. Leonard J. Arrington, *Great Basin Kingdom: An Economic History of the Latter-day Saints* (Cambridge, MA: Harvard University Press, 1958), 148–52; John G. Turner, *Brigham Young: Pioneer Prophet* (Cambridge, MA: Belknap Press of Harvard University Press, 2012), 254–55.
5. Turner, *Pioneer Prophet*, 254–55.
6. Ibid., 255–56; Eugene E. Campbell, *Establishing Zion: The Mormon Church in the American West, 1847–1869* (Salt Lake City, UT: Signature Books, 1988), 181–92.
7. Turner, *Pioneer Prophet*, 256; Campbell, *Establishing Zion*, 192–93.
8. *Deseret News*, Oct. 1, 1856, quoted in Campbell, *Establishing Zion*, 198.
9. Campbell, *Establishing Zion*, 198–99; Turner, *Pioneer Prophet*, 258.
10. Mrs. Thomas B. H. [Fanny] Stenhouse, *Expose of Polygamy in Utah—A Lady's Life among the Mormons: A Record of Personal Experience as One of the Wives of a Mormon Elder during a Period of More Than Twenty Years*, 2nd ed. (New York: American News Co., 1872), 185.
11. Ann Eliza Young, *Wife Number Nineteen; or, The Story of a Life in Bondage: Being a Complete Expose of Mormonism, and Revealing the Sorrows, Sacrifices, and Sufferings of Women in Polygamy* (1875; rpt. New York: Arno Press, 1972), 306, 185; Jennie Anderson Froiseth, ed., *The Women of Mormonism; or, The Story of Polygamy as Told by the Victims Themselves* (Detroit, MI: C. G. Paine, 1882), 39.
12. Stanley S. Ivins, "Notes on Mormon Polygamy," *Western Humanities Review* 10 (Summer 1956): 231.
13. Wilford Woodruff to George A. Smith, Apr. 1, 1857, Letterpress Copybook I, 439, Church Historian's Office, Outgoing Correspondence, CR 100 38, Church History Library, Salt Lake City, quoted in Turner, *Pioneer Prophet*, 257.

14. Brigham Young to Uriah Butt, Feb. 17, 1857, Copybook 3, page 408, Brigham Young Papers, Church History Library, Salt Lake City, quoted in Turner, *Pioneer Prophet*, 257.
15. George S. Ellsworth, *Dear Ellen—Two Mormon Women and Their Letters* (Salt Lake City, UT: Tanner Trust Fund/University of Utah Library, 1974), 38, quoted in Richard S. Van Wagoner, *Mormon Polygamy: A History*, 2nd ed. (Salt Lake City, UT: Signature Books, 1989), 92.
16. Ivins, "Notes on Mormon Polygamy," 232.
17. Henry Clay Blinn, *The Manifestation of Spiritualism among the Shakers, 1837–1847* (East Canterbury, NH: N.p., 1899), 15; Giles B. Avery, *Autobiography* (East Canterbury, NH: N.p., 1891), 10.
18. Stephen J. Stein, *The Shaker Experience in America: A History of the United Society of Believers* (New Haven, CT: Yale University Press, 1992), 166.
19. Blinn, *Manifestation of Spiritualism*, 84; Stein, *Shaker Experience*, 168–69.
20. Stein, *Shaker Experience*, 170–71.
21. Blinn, *Manifestation of Spiritualism*, 18, 25, 84.
22. Stein, *Shaker Experience*, 174.
23. David Lamson, *Two Years' Experience among the Shakers: . . .* (1848; rpt., New York: A.M.S. Press, 1971), 65–67.
24. Blinn, *Manifestations of Spiritualism*, 81, 61; Stein, *Shaker Experience*, 174.
25. Stein, *Shaker Experience*, 174.
26. Blinn, *Manifestations of Spiritualism*, 82.
27. Ibid., 86.
28. Stein, *Shaker Experience*, 169.
29. Ibid., 186–87.
30. Brigham Young, "The People of God Disciplined by Trials—Atonement by the Shedding of Blood—Our Heavenly Father—A Privilege Given to All the Married Sisters in Utah," Sept. 21, 1856, *Journal of Discourses*, vol. 4 (Liverpool and London: various publishers, 1857), 55.

14. Gender

1. Brigham Young, "The People of God Disciplined by Trials—Atonement by the Shedding of Blood—Our Heavenly Father—A Privilege Given to All the Married Sisters in Utah," Sept. 21, 1856, *Journal of Discourses*, vol. 4 (Liverpool and London: various publishers, 1857), 55.
2. William Hepworth Dixon, *New America* (Philadelphia: Lippincott, 1867), 337.
3. Mrs. Thomas B. H. [Fanny] Stenhouse, *Expose of Polygamy in Utah—A Lady's Life among the Mormons: A Record of Personal Experience as One of the Wives of a Mormon Elder during a Period of More Than Twenty Years*, 2nd ed. (New York: American News Co., 1872), 163–64; John H. Beadle,

Life in Utah; or, The Mysteries and Crimes of Mormonism: Being an Expose of the Secret Rites and Ceremonies of the Latter-Day Saints, with a Full and Authentic History of Polygamy and the Mormon Sect from Its Origin to the Present Time (Philadelphia: National Publishing Co., 1870), 315.
4. The Seer 1, no. 1 (Jan. 1853): 1; The Seer 1, no. 9 (Sept. 1853): 140.
5. Thomas Stenhouse, The Rocky Mountain Saints: A Full and Complete History of the Mormons (New York: D. Appleton, 1873), 582.
6. John Hyde Jr., Mormonism: Its Leaders and Designs, 2nd ed. (New York: W. P. Fetridge, 1857), 74, 71–72.
7. Pomeroy Tucker, Origin, Rise, and Progress of Mormonism (New York: D. Appleton & Co., 1867), 276.
8. Ellen E. Dickinson, New Light on Mormonism (New York: Funk & Wagnalls, 1885), 145.
9. C. P. Lyford, The Mormon Problem: An Appeal to the American People (New York: Phillips & Hunt, 1886), 144.
10. Ann Eliza Young, Wife Number Nineteen; or, The Story of a Life in Bondage: Being a Complete Expose of Mormonism, and Revealing the Sorrows, Sacrifices, and Sufferings of Women in Polygamy (1875; rpt. New York: Arno Press, 1972), 444, 390, 392–93.
11. Dixon, New America, 337.
12. Richard S. Van Wagoner, Mormon Polygamy: A History (Salt Lake City, UT: Signature, 1986), 90.
13. Jessie L. Embry, Mormon Polygamous Families: Life in the Principle (Salt Lake City, UT: University of Utah Press, 1987), 73, 137.
14. Stanley S. Ivins, "Notes on Mormon Polygamy," Western Humanities Review 10 (Summer 1956): 230; Richard Lyman Bushman, Mormonism: A Very Short Introduction (New York: Oxford University Press, 2008), 88.
15. Ivins, "Notes on Mormon Polygamy," 233.
16. Maria Ward, Female Life among the Mormons: A Narrative of Many Years' Personal Experience by the Wife of Mormon Elder Recently from Utah (New York: J. C. Derby, 1855), 302.
17. Embry, "Table 7, Husband's Age at Marriage," and "Table 8, Wife's Age at Marriage," Mormon Polygamous Families, 34–35.
18. Stenhouse, A Lady's Life among the Mormons, 78.
19. Kathryn M. Daynes, More Wives than One: Transformation of the Mormon Marriage System, 1840–1890 (Chicago: University of Illinois Press, 2001), 126.
20. Stenhouse, A Lady's Life among the Mormons, 110. Emphasis in original.
21. Embry, Mormon Polygamous Families, 55.
22. Eliza R. Snow quoted in Edward W. Tullidge, The Women of Mormonism (New York: Tullidge and Crandall, 1877), 295; Phoebe W. Carter Woodruff and Mary A. Freeze quoted in Augusta Joyce Crocheron, Representative

Women of Deseret (Salt Lake City, UT: J. C. Graham, 1884), 37, 54; Helen Mar Kimball Whitney, *Plural Marriage as Taught by the Prophet Joseph. A Reply to Joseph Smith, Editor of the Lamoni (Iowa) "Herald"* (Salt Lake City, UT: Juvenile Instructor Office, 1882), 27.

23. Ann Eliza Young, *Wife Number Nineteen*, 389.
24. Jennie Anderson Froiseth, ed., *The Women of Mormonism; or, The Story of Polygamy as Told by the Victims Themselves* (Detroit: C. G. Paine, 1882), 111–12.
25. Christopher Lasch, *Haven in a Heartless World: The Family Besieged* (New York: W. W. Norton, 1977).
26. Lawrence Foster, *Religion and Sexuality: The Shakers, the Mormons, and the Oneida Community* (Urbana: University of Illinois Press, 1984), 209.
27. See Karen Lystra, *Searching the Heart: Women, Men, and Romantic Love in Nineteenth-Century America* (New York: Oxford University Press, 1989).
28. Embry, *Mormon Polygamous Families*, 73, 78, 87.
29. Stenhouse, *A Lady's Life among the Mormons*, 75–76.
30. Hutchings interview, 13–14, quoted in Embry, *Mormon Polygamous Families*, 98.
31. Embry, *Mormon Polygamous Families*, Introduction, xvi, 122, 130.
32. Ibid., 130.
33. Stenhouse, *A Lady's Life among the Mormons*, 93. Emphasis in original.
34. Ann Eliza Young, *Wife Number Nineteen*, 291.
35. Benjamin G. Ferris, *Utah and the Mormons: The History, Government, Doctrines, Customs, and Prospects of the Latter-Day Saints from Personal Observation during a Six Months' Residence at Great Salt Lake City* (New York: Harper & Brothers, 1854), 259.
36. Embry, *Mormon Polygamous Families*, 84.
37. Ann Eliza Young, *Wife Number Nineteen*, 391, 126, 142, 292, 144, 400.
38. Stenhouse, *A Lady's Life among the Mormons*, 120, 122.
39. Froiseth, ed., *The Women of Mormonism*, 85–89.
40. Stenhouse, *A Lady's Life among the Mormons*, 115. Emphases in original.
41. Interview with Charles White, 2, quoted in Embry, *Mormon Polygamous Families*, 139.
42. John W. Gunnison, *The Mormons, or, Latter-day Saints, in the Valley of the Great Salt Lake* (Philadelphia: Lippincott, Grambo, 1852), 72.
43. Daynes, *More Wives Than One*, 173–74.
44. Beadle, *Life in Utah*, 363.
45. Dixon, *New America*, 337.
46. Genesis 1:26–27, King James Version. Emphases added.
47. Benjamin Seth Youngs, *The Testimony of Christ's Second Appearing; Containing a General Statement of All Things Pertaining to the Faith and Practice of the Church of God in This Latter Day* (Lebanon, OH: John McClean, 1808), 446, 436. All emphases in original.

48. Stephen J. Stein, *The Shaker Experience in America: A History of the United Society of Believers* (New Haven, CT: Yale University Press, 1992), 122–23, 132–33.
49. Ibid., 152–53.
50. Lawrence Foster, *Women, Family, and Utopia: Communal Experiments of the Shakers, the Oneida Community, and the Mormons* (Syracuse, NY: Syracuse University Press, 1991), 33.
51. Philemon Stewart, *A Holy Sacred and Divine Roll and Book: From the Lord God of Heaven to the Inhabitants of Earth: Revealed in the United Society at New Lebanon, Columbia County, State of New York, United States of America* (Canterbury, NH: United Society, 1843), 182.
52. "Decadence of Marriage," *The Circular* 13, no. 4 (Jan. 27, 1876).
53. Ibid.
54. "The Difference," *The Circular* 3, no. 97 (Jul. 18, 1854).
55. "Man and Woman—Their True Relation," *The Circular* 12, no. 2 (Mar. 12, 1863).
56. Spencer Klaw, *Without Sin: The Life and Death of the Oneida Community* (New York: Penguin Press, 1993), 133–34.
57. "Man and Woman—Their True Relation."
58. Klaw, *Without Sin*, 134.
59. "Our Social Position," *The Circular* 7, no. 31 (Oct. 17, 1870).

15. CHILDREN

1. Mary Marshall Dyer, *A Portraiture of Shakerism* (Concord, NH: Author, 1822), 412; Mary Marshall Dyer, *A Brief Statement of the Suffering of Mary Dyer, Occasioned by the Society Called Shakers* (Concord, NH: Joseph C. Spear, 1818), 10.
2. Eunice Chapman, *Account of the Conduct of the Shakers in the Case of Eunice Chapman and Her Children* (Albany, NY: N.p., 1817), 66, 54.
3. David Lamson, *Two Years' Experience among the Shakers: . . .* (1848; rpt., New York: A.M.S. Press, 1971), 176.
4. *A Summary View of the Millennial Church, or United Society of Believers, (Commonly Called Shakers.) Comprising the Rise, Progress, and Practical Order of the Society; Together with the General Principles of Their Faith and Testimony* (Albany, NY: Packard and Van Benthuysen, 1823), 131.
5. Stephen J. Stein, *The Shaker Experience in America: A History of the United Society of Believers* (New Haven, CT: Yale University Press, 1992), 160–62.
6. *The Seer* 1, no. 3 (Mar. 1853): 37.
7. *The Seer* 1, no. 4 (Apr.1853): 60.
8. Annie Clark Tanner, *A Mormon Mother: An Autobiography* (Salt Lake City, UT: University of Utah Press, 1969), 269, quoted in Jessie L. Embry, *Mormon Polygamous Families: Life in the Principle* (Salt Lake City, UT:

University of Utah Press, 1987), 153; Vilate Kimball, from Mrs. S. A. Cooks, *Theatrical and Social Affairs in Utah* (Salt Lake City, UT: N.p., 1884), 5–6, quoted in Richard S. Van Wagoner, *Mormon Polygamy: A History* (Salt Lake City, UT: Signature Books, 1989), 102.

9. Embry, "Table 18, Father's Relationship with Children," *Mormon Polygamous Families*, 159.
10. Embry, *Mormon Polygamous Families*, 159.
11. Attributed to Brigham Young in John H. Beadle, *Life in Utah; or, The Mysteries and Crimes of Mormonism: Being an Expose of the Secret Rites and Ceremonies of the Latter-Day Saints, with a Full and Authentic History of Polygamy and the Mormon Sect from Its Origin to the Present Time* (Philadelphia: National Publishing Co., 1870), 362.
12. Embry, *Mormon Polygamous Families*, 35.
13. Stanley S. Ivins, "Notes on Mormon Polygamy," *Western Humanities Review* 10 (Summer 1956): 236–37.
14. Brigham Young, "Plurality of Wives.—The Free Agency of Man," Jul. 14, 1855, *Journal of Discourses*, vol. 3 (Liverpool and London: various publishers, 1856), 264.
15. John Humphrey Noyes, *Male Continence* (Oneida, NY: Office of the Oneida Circular, 1872), 13.
16. "Love of Children," *The Perfectionist and Theocratic Watchman* 4, no. 14 (Sept. 21, 1844).
17. "Woman's Slavery to Children," *Spiritual Magazine* 1, no. 7 (Sept. 15, 1846).
18. *The Circular*, June 23, 1873, quoted in *Oneida Community: An Autobiography, 1851–1876*, ed. Constance Noyes Robertson (Syracuse, NY: Syracuse University Press, 1970), 353.
19. Spencer Klaw, *Without Sin: The Life and Death of the Oneida Community* (New York: Penguin Press, 1993), 132.
20. Robertson, ed., *Oneida Community: An Autobiography*, 336.
21. *First Annual Report of the Oneida Association: Exhibiting Its History, Principles, and Transactions to Jan. 1, 1849* (Oneida Reserve, NY: Leonard, 1849), 6–7.
22. Robertson, ed., *Oneida Community: An Autobiography*, 311.
23. "Community Children," *The Circular* 5, no. 29 (Oct. 5, 1868).
24. The *Circular*, May 26, 1859, quoted in Robertson, ed., *Oneida Community: An Autobiography*, 341.
25. *First Annual Report of the Oneida Association*, 33. Emphasis in original.
26. Robertson, ed., *Oneida Community: An Autobiography*, 335.
27. "Note 4," *First Annual Report of the Oneida Association*, 33–34. Emphases in original.
28. "Improved Breeding by Selection," and "Scientific Propagation," *The Circular*, new series 2, no. 2 (Mar. 27, 1865). Emphases in original.

29. "Stirpiculture," and "Stirpiculture II," *The Circular*, new series 2, nos. 3 and 4 (Apr. 3 and 10, 1865).
30. Documents quoted in Robert Allerton Parker, *A Yankee Saint: John Humphrey Noyes and the Oneida Community* (New York: G. P. Putnam's Sons, 1935), 257. These documents were later destroyed.
31. "O.C. Experience in Propagation," *The Circular*, new series 7, no. 4 (Apr. 11, 1870).
32. Parker, *Yankee Saint*, 257.
33. Klaw, *Without Sin*, 204.
34. Ibid., 204–6; Parker, *Yankee Saint*, 257, 260.
35. *The Circular*, Apr. 25, 1870 and Mar. 21, 1870, quoted in Robertson, ed., *Oneida Community: An Autobiography*, 348, 346.
36. "The Final Answer," *The Circular*, Sept. 19, 1870, quoted in Robertson, ed., *Oneida Community: An Autobiography*, 350.
37. John Humphrey Noyes, *Essay on Scientific Propagation* (Oneida, NY: Oneida Community, 1872), 30.
38. Klaw, *Without Sin*, 207.
39. John Humphrey Noyes, *Essay on Scientific Propagation*, 28–30. Quoting Sir Francis Galton's *Hereditary Genius* (1869).
40. Anita Newcomb McGee, "An Experiment in Stirpiculture," *American Anthropologist* 4 (Oct. 1891): 319–25. The term "white collar jobs" is from Klaw, *Without Sin*, 210.
41. *The Circular*, June 13, 1870, quoted in Robertson, ed., *Oneida Community: An Autobiography*, 349.
42. "Stirpiculture II," *The Circular*, new series 2, no. 4 (Apr. 10, 1865).

16. The Shakers, from Revolution to Refuge

1. Frederick W. Evans, *Tests of Divine Inspiration; or, The Rudimental Principles by Which True and False Revelation, in All Eras of the World, Can Be Unerringly Discriminated* (New Lebanon, NY: United Society Called Shakers, 1853), 87.
2. Frederick W. Evans, *A Short Treatise on the Second Appearing of Christ, in and through the Order of the Female* (Boston: Bazin & Chandler, 1853), 9; Evans, *Tests of Divine Inspiration*, 106, 123. Emphasis added.
3. H. L. Eads, *Shaker Sermons: Scripto-Rational—Containing the Substance of Shaker Theology Together with Replies and Criticisms Logically and Clearly Set Forth* (Shakers, NY: *Shaker Manifesto*, 1879), 171.
4. Evans, *A Short Treatise*, 12, 19; Frederick W. Evans, *Autobiography of a Shaker, and Revelation of the Apocalypse* (Mt. Lebanon, NY: F. W. Evans, 1869), 3, 36, 99, 92, 162; Frederick W. Evans, *Religious Communism: A Lecture Delivered in St. George's Hall, London, Aug. 6, 1871* (London: J. Burns,

1871), 31, 13; Evans, *Tests of Divine Inspiration*, 38; Frederick W. Evans, *Compendium of the Origin, History, Principles, Rules and Regulations, Government, and Doctrines of the United Society of Believers in Christ's Second Appearing. With Biographies of Ann Lee, William Lee, Jas. Whittaker, J. Hocknell, J. Meacham, and Lucy Wright*, 4th ed. (New Lebanon, NY: N.p., 1867), vi. Eads, *Shaker Sermons*, 50. Emphases in original.

The biblical misquote is Matthew 7:13: "Enter ye in at the strait gate." Neither the King James Version nor any translation I have found includes the word "agonize."

5. See *Testimonies of the Life, Character, Revelations, and Doctrines of Our Ever Blessed Mother Ann Lee, and the Elders with Her; Through Whom the Word of Eternal Life Was Opened in This Day of Christ's Second Appearing: Collected from Living Witnesses* (Hancock, MA: J. Tallcott & Deming, Junrs., 1816), 36–37, 263.
6. Stephen J. Stein, *The Shaker Experience in America: A History of the United Society of Believers* (New Haven, CT: Yale University Press, 1992), 303.
7. Ibid., 287–88.
8. Ibid., 203; William Sims Bainbridge, "Shaker Demographics 1840–1900: An Example of the Use of U.S. Census Enumeration Schedules," *Journal for the Scientific Study of Religion* 21, no. 4 (1982): 355.
9. Ms. in Hancock Shaker Village Library, Hancock, MA, Oct. 25, 1865, quoted in Priscilla J. Brewer, "The Demographic Features of the Shaker Decline, 1787–1900," *Journal of Interdisciplinary History* 15, no. 1 (Summer 1984): 49–50.
10. Stein, *Shaker Experience*, 160.
11. Bainbridge, "Shaker Demographics," 352–65.
12. Stein, *Shaker Experience*, 234.
13. Ibid., 242–50.
14. Erin Blakemore, "There Are Only Two Shakers Left in the World," *Smithsonian Magazine*, Jan. 6, 2017, https://www.smithsonianmag.com/smart-news/there-are-only-two-shakers-left-world-180961701/.
15. Stein, *Shaker Experience*, 234–35.
16. Theodore E. Johnson, ed., "Rules and Orders for the Church of Christ's Second Appearing Established by the Ministry and Elders of the Church Revisited and Re-established by the Same, New Lebanon, New York May 1860," *Shaker Quarterly* 11 (1971): 143–45.
17. Ibid., 154.
18. Stein, *Shaker Experience*, 203; Johnson, "Rules and Orders," 143, 155–58.
19. Bainbridge, "Shaker Demographics," 361.
20. Perry Miller, "Errand into the Wilderness," in *Errand into the Wilderness* (Cambridge, MA: Belknap Press of Harvard University Press, 1956), 14–15.

17. The Triumph of Bread and Butter at Oneida

1. John Humphrey Noyes, *History of American Socialisms* (Philadelphia: Lippincott, 1870), 148, 153. Emphasis in original.
2. Spencer Klaw, *Without Sin: The Life and Death of the Oneida Community* (New York: Penguin Press, 1993), 212–14.
3. Theodore Noyes, 1892 letter, quoted in Constance Noyes Robertson, *Oneida Community: The Breakup, 1876–1881* (Syracuse, NY: Syracuse University Press, 1972), 19.
4. John Humphrey Noyes to Theodore Noyes, Jul. 14, 1873, quoted in Robertson, *The Breakup*, 30.
5. Robertson, *The Breakup*, 31–32; Klaw, *Without Sin*, 216–17; Christa Shusko, "Criticizing the Dead: Spiritualism and the Oneida Community," in *Handbook of Spiritualism and Channeling*, ed. Cathy Gutierrez (Boston: Brill, 2015), 171–98.
6. Robertson, *The Breakup*, 49; Klaw, *Without Sin*, 221–22.
7. Klaw, *Without Sin*, 224–25.
8. See Robertson, *The Breakup*, 62–63.
9. Robertson, *The Breakup*, 37–38, 52–53; Klaw, *Without Sin*, 226.
10. Anonymous and undated letter, quoted in Robertson, *The Breakup*, 60.
11. Robertson, *The Breakup*, 57–64; Klaw, *Without Sin*, 226–31.
12. Robertson, *The Breakup*, 65.
13. Klaw, *Without Sin*, 236–38.
14. Robertson, *The Breakup*, 102–3.
15. Robert Allerton Parker, *A Yankee Saint: John Humphrey Noyes and the Oneida Community* (New York: G. P. Putnam's Sons, 1935), 278; Klaw, *Without Sin*, 242.
16. Frank Wayland Smith, journal entry for Feb. 5, 1879, quoted in Robertson, *The Breakup*, 91–92.
17. John W. Mears, *The Watchword*, n.d., quoted in Parker, *Yankee Saint*, 268; Michael Doyle, *The Minister's War: John W. Mears, the Oneida Community, and the Crusade for Public Morality* (Syracuse, NY: Syracuse University Press, 2018).
18. *The Circular* 10, no. 47 (Nov. 17, 1873), and 11, no. 48 (Nov. 23, 1874).
19. "The Presbyterian Synod vs. the Oneida Community II," *The Circular* 11, no. 50 (Dec. 7, 1874); "What the Presbyterians Say," *The Circular* 11, no. 48 (Nov. 23, 1874).
20. *Puck*, Feb. 26, 1879.
21. John Humphrey Noyes, n.d., quoted in Robertson, *The Breakup*, 80.
22. Parker, *Yankee Saint*, 282.
23. *Syracuse Standard*, June 21, 1879, quoted in Robertson, *The Breakup*, 110.
24. Klaw, *Without Sin*, 245.

25. Parker, *Yankee Saint*, 282.
26. Klaw, *Without Sin*, 248–49.
27. Frank Wayland-Smith letter to John Humphrey Noyes, Jul. 19, 1879, quoted in Robertson, *The Breakup*, 128–33.
28. John Humphrey Noyes to the Oneida Community's Administrative Council, Aug. 20, 1879, quoted in Robertson, *The Breakup*, 153–55.
29. Ibid., 154. Emphasis in original.
30. Frank Wayland-Smith Journal, n.d., quoted in Klaw, *Without Sin*, 254.
31. John Humphrey Noyes, *American Socialisms*, 148, 153. Emphasis in original.
32. Parker, *Yankee Saint*, 289.

18. The War on Polygamy and the Temporal Salvation of the Mormon Church

1. Kirk H. Porter, comp., *National Party Platforms* (New York: Macmillan, 1924), 48.
2. Associate Justice William Wormer Drummond to Attorney General Jeremiah S. Black, Mar. 30, 1857, quoted in Eugene E. Campbell, *Establishing Zion: The Mormon Church in the American West, 1847–1869* (Salt Lake City, UT: Signature Books, 1988), 230.
3. Information in this and following paragraphs comes from Campbell, *Establishing Zion*, 233–52; John G. Turner, *Brigham Young: Pioneer Prophet* (Cambridge, MA: Belknap Press of Harvard University Press, 2012), 265–300; Leonard Arrington, *Great Basin Kingdom: An Economic History of the Latter-day Saints, 1830–1900* (Cambridge, MA: Harvard University Press, 1956), 161–94; and Leonard J. Arrington and Davis Bitton, *The Mormon Experience: A History of the Latter-Day Saints* (New York: Alfred A. Knopf, 1979), 164–69.
4. Arrington, *Great Basin Kingdom*, 182–86.
5. Henry S. Hamilton, *Reminiscences of a Veteran* (Concord, NH. Republican Press Association, 1897), 108, quoted in Arrington, *Great Basin Kingdom*, 193–94.
6. Turner, *Pioneer Prophet*, 300.
7. Thomas B. Stenhouse to Brigham Young, June 7, 1863, Brigham Young Correspondence, Church Archives, quoted in Arrington and Bitton, *Mormon Experience*, 170.
8. Sarah Barringer Gordon, *The Mormon Question: Polygamy and Constitutional Conflict in Nineteenth-Century America* (Chapel Hill, NC: University of North Carolina Press, 2002), 81, 83.
9. Arrington and Bitton, *Mormon Experience*, 175–77.
10. Arrington, *Great Basin Kingdom*, 255.
11. Thomas G. Alexander, *Utah, the Right Place: The Official Centennial History*, rev. ed. (Salt Lake City, UT: Gibbs Smith, 1996), 178–80.

12. Ibid., 175.
13. Gordon, *Mormon Question*, 94–95.
14. The 1872 Supreme Court ruling was *Englebrecht v. Clinton*. Alexander, *Utah: The Right Place*, 175–76.
15. Turner, *Pioneer Prophet*, 310–11, 373–74.
16. Mrs. Thomas B. H. [Fanny] Stenhouse, *Expose of Polygamy in Utah—A Lady's Life among the Mormons: A Record of Personal Experience as One of the Wives of a Mormon Elder during a Period of More Than Twenty Years*, 2nd ed. (New York: American News Co., 1872), 83, 90.
17. Ann Eliza Young, *Wife Number Nineteen; or, The Story of a Life in Bondage: Being a Complete Expose of Mormonism, and Revealing the Sorrows, Sacrifices, and Sufferings of Women in Polygamy* (1875; rpt., New York: Arno Press, 1972), 108.
18. Gordon, *Mormon Question*, 112–13; Turner, *Pioneer Prophet*, 385–88.
19. The quote is attributed to General Benjamin R. Cowan, assistant secretary of the interior, in Robert N. Baskin, *Reminiscences of Early Utah* (N.p.: N.p. 1914), 66, quoted in Gordon, *Mormon Question*, 115.
20. Gordon, *Mormon Question*, 115–16.
21. *Reynolds v. United States*, 98 U.S., 147–49.
22. "Reynolds v. United States," in Paul Finkelman, ed., *Religion and American Law: An Encyclopedia* (New York, Routledge, 1999), 417.
23. *Reynolds v. United States*, 167.
24. *Reynolds v. United States*, 163, quoting *The Writings of Thomas Jefferson*. 9 vols. (Washington, DC: Taylor & Maury, 1853–54), 8:113.
25. Ibid.
26. Jennie Anderson Froiseth, ed., *The Women of Mormonism; or, The Story of Polygamy as Told by the Victims Themselves* (Detroit, MI: C. G. Paine, 1882), 364.
27. Arrington, *Great Basin Kingdom*, 358.
28. Arrington and Bitton, *Mormon Experience*, 181; Alexander, *Utah: The Right Place*, 193–94; Gordon, *Mormon Question*, 157; Arrington, *Great Basin Kingdom*, 359.
29. Arrington, *Great Basin Kingdom*, 359, 353; Gordon, *Mormon Question*, 157–58; *Memorial of the Mormon Women of Utah to the President and the Congress of the U.S.: The Outrages of Which They Complain—The Justice They Demand* (Washington, DC: N.p., 1886), 3–6.
30. Alexander, *Utah, the Right Place*, 194.
31. Richard S. Van Wagoner, *Mormon Polygamy: A History* (Salt Lake City, UT: Signature Books, 1989), 119; Arrington, *Great Basin Kingdom*, 359–60; Arrington and Bitton, *Mormon Experience*, 182; Gordon, *Mormon Question*, 159.
32. Van Wagoner, *Mormon Polygamy*, 120.

33. Augusta Joyce Crocheron, *Representative Women of Deseret* (Salt Lake City, UT: J. C. Graham, 1884), 15, 54.
34. Information in this paragraph comes from Gordon, *Mormon Question*, 147–82.
35. Arrington, *Great Basin Kingdom*, 361; Gordon, *Mormon Question*, 180.
36. *The Late Corporation of the Church of Jesus Christ of Latter-day Saints v. United States*, 140 U.S., 665, quoted in Arrington and Bitton, *Mormon Experience*, 183.
37. Van Wagoner, *Mormon Polygamy*, 138. The term "power brokers" is his.
38. Diary of Wilford Woodruff, Sept. 25, 1890, Church Archives, quoted in Arrington and Bitton, *Mormon Experience*, 183.
39. "Excerpts from Three Addresses by President Wilford Woodruff Regarding the Manifesto," *D&C*, after section 138 and "Official Declaration—1."
40. "Official Declaration—1," *D&C*, after section 138.

Epilogue

1. William Sims Bainbridge, "Shaker Demographics 1840–1900: An Example of the Use of U.S. Census Enumeration Schedules," *Journal for the Scientific Study of Religion* 21 (1982): 354–55.
2. Stephen J. Stein, *The Shaker Experience in America: A History of the Untied Society of Believers* (New Haven, CT: Yale University Press, 1992), 243, 252, 360, 251, 285, 293, 298, 352.
3. Klaus Hansen, *Quest for Empire: The Political Kingdom of God and the Council of Fifty in Mormon History* (East Lansing: Michigan State University Press, 1967), 177; Richard S. Van Wagoner, *Mormon Polygamy: A History*, 2nd ed. (Salt Lake City, UT: Signature Books, 1989), 146; B. Carmon Hardy, *Solemn Covenant: The Mormon Polygamous Passage* (Urbana: University of Illinois Press, 1992), 127, 150. Emphasis in original.
4. D. Michael Quinn, "LDS Church Authority and New Plural Marriages, 1890-1904," *Dialogue* 18 (Spring 1985): 15; Van Wagoner, *Mormon Polygamy*, 151, 154–55. See also Hardy, *Solemn Covenant*, 153.
5. Van Wagoner, *Mormon Polygamy*, 143–46; Quinn, "New Plural Marriages," 49.
6. Abraham H. Cannon Journal, Oct. 7, 1890, quoted in Van Wagoner, *Mormon Polygamy*, 145.
7. Van Wagoner, *Mormon Polygamy*, 168.
8. James R. Clark, ed., *Messages of the First Presidency of The Church of Jesus Christ of Latter-day Saints*, 6 vols. (Salt Lake City, UT: Bookcraft, 1964–75) 4:151–52, quoted in Quinn, "New Plural Marriages," 13; Hardy, "Appendix II: Mormon Polygamous Marriages after the 1890 Manifesto through 1910: A Tentative List," *Solemn Covenant*, 425.

9. Van Wagoner, *Mormon Polygamy*, 148–49.
10. Hardy, *Solemn Covenant*, 168.
11. Ibid., 187, 317.
12. Quinn, "New Plural Marriages," 95–96.
13. Reed Smoot to E. H. Callister (with copy to James Clove), Mar. 22, 1904, Smoot 1903–04 Letterbook, 813–817, box 27, Smoot Papers, BYU, quoted in Van Wagoner, *Mormon Polygamy*, 161.
14. Joseph F. Smith, "Official Statement," "General Conference of the Church of Jesus Christ of Latter Day Saints . . . Third Day," *Seventy-fourth Annual Conference of the Church* . . . 75–76, quoted in *Doing the Works of Abraham: Mormon Polygamy, Its Origin, Practice, and Demise*, ed. B. Carmon Hardy (Norman, OK: Arthur H. Clark Company, 2007), 374.
15. Hardy, *Solemn Covenant*, 317.
16. Book of Moses 7:32.
17. Spencer Klaw, *Without Sin: The Life and Death of the Oneida Community* (New York: Penguin Books, 1993), 280–81; Pierrepont Noyes, *My Father's House: An Oneida Boyhood* (New York: Farrar & Rinehart, 1937), 225.
18. Quoted in Pierrepont Noyes, *My Father's House*, 176.
19. Robert Allerton Parker, *A Yankee Saint: John Humphrey Noyes and the Oneida Community* (New York: G. P. Putnam's Sons, 1935), 293–94.
20. Pierrepont Noyes, *My Father's House*, 270–71.

INDEX

Abraham, 76, 175–76
Account of the Conduct of the People Called Shakers in the Case of Eunice Chapman and Her Children (Chapman), 125
Account of the Matter, Form, and Manner of a New and Strange Religion (Rathbun), 94–95
Account of the People Called Shakers (Brown), 123
Adam and Eve, 28–29, 32–33, 49, 94, 104, 230
Adams, Edmund, 225
Adams, Sadie, 225
adultery, 3, 79–81, 88, 143
Advocate of Moral Reform, 87–88
Affidavits and Certificates Disproving the Statements and Affidavits Contained in John C. Bennett's Letters, 134
afflatus, 259, 271
Albany Gazette, 127
Alger, Fanny, 76–82, 89, 137–38
Alger, Samuel, 77
Allen, Eliza A., 151
Almighty Father (Shaker), 218, 230
American Socialist, 187, 189
Amish, 253
Andover Theological Seminary, 23, 69–70, 89
Anglican Church, 102
antichrist, 94
Anti-Polygamy Standard, 282
Apostolic United Brethren, 293–94
Arrington, Leonard, 172, 181–82, 192–93, 204, 276
ascending fellowship (Oneida), 115–16, 199–200
authoritarianism, 20

"Babylon Is Fallen," 1–2
Bainbridge, William Sims, 255, 257
Battle-Axe and Weapons of War, 83
"Battle-Axe Letter," 83–85, 87
Beaman, Louisa, 101, 105, 138, 161
Bennett, John C., 103, 108, 130–36, 145, 156, 161–62
Berean (Oneida), 37
Berlin Heights, Ohio, 264–65
Bible Argument; Defining the Relations of the Sexes in the Kingdom of Heaven (Oneida), 110–12, 117, 188
Bilhah, 76
Bitton, Davis, 192, 204, 206
Blinn, Henry Clay, 215–17
blood atonement, 211–12
Boggs, Lilburn W., 66, 134, 136, 157
Book of Abraham (Mormon), 65, 106
Book of Commandments (Mormon), 25
Book of Mormon, 33, 62, 64, 75–76, 79, 108, 147, 161, 181, 191
Book of Moses (Mormon), 65, 294
Bradley-Evans, Martha, 145
Brattleboro, Vermont, 67, 91
Brotherton, Martha H., 132–33, 162
Brown, Thomas, 24, 123, 127–28
Buchanan, James B., 273, 275
Buell (Huntington), Presendia, 106
bundling, 1
"Burned-over District," 19, 21–22
Burt, Jonathan, 91, 110–11, 240
Bushman, Richard, 60, 63, 108–10, 222

Cahoon, Reynolds, 106
Camisards, 58
Campbell, Alexander, 64
Camp Floyd, 274
Canaan, New York, 255

339

Cane Ridge Revival, 24, 98
Canon, George Q., 190–91, 292
Canterbury, New Hampshire, 256
Carpenter, June, 256
Carthage Grays, 149
Chapman, Eunice, 124–29, 151, 185, 194–95, 235–36
Chapman, James, 124
Chicago, Illinois, 102
children: Oneida, 114–15, 238–40; Shaker, 235–37
Circular (Oneida), 150, 153, 156, 176, 187–89, 234, 240, 242, 267, 295
circumcision, 45
Clawson, Rudger, 283
Clawson v. United States, 283
Clayton, William, 144
Cleveland, Grover, 285
Commerce, Illinois, 102
Communal Studies Association, 293
complex marriage (Oneida), 4–5, 51–52, 87, 90–91, 110, 122, 153, 201, 270–72
Comprehensive History (Mormon), 76
Compton, Todd, 106, 140
Comstock, Anthony, 266
Comstock Law, 266, 268
Concise Statement (Shaker), 24
Confessions of Religious Experience (Noyes), 117
cosmology (Mormon), 29
Council of Chalcedon, 36
Council of the Fifty, 147
Cowdery, 62, 64, 78–79, 81
Cragin, George, 87–90, 114
Cragin (Johnson), Mary, 82, 87–90, 114–15, 151, 233
Crocheron, Joyce Augusta, 285
Cumming, Alfred, 274
Custer, Solomon, 77

Dartmouth College, 67
Darwin, Charles, 188, 241–42, 250
David (King), 76, 143
Daynes, Kathryn, 224, 229–30
Decker, Lucy Ann, 162

Deseret, 171–74, 181–83
Deseret News, 211
divorce, 125, 128
Dixon, William Hepworth, 219, 221, 230
Doctrine and Covenants (Mormon), 32, 63, 78, 143
Drummond, William, 273
Dyer, Betsy, 126
Dyer, Caleb M., 126
Dyer, Joseph, 124, 126
Dyer, Mary Marshall, 124–29, 151, 185, 194, 235–36

Eastman, Hubbard, 113
Edmunds, George F., 282
Edmunds Act, 283–85
Edmunds-Tucker Act, 285–86
egalitarianism, 20
ejaculation, 49–50
Elkins, Hervey, 35
Ellis, John B., 202
Embry, Jessie L., 222–23, 225–28, 237–38
endowment ordinance (Mormon), 109–10, 130, 167, 191
Enfield, Connecticut, 255
Enfield, New Hampshire, 124–27
England, 102, 161, 183
Era of Manifestations (Shaker), 214–18, 231, 253
Escaping Polygamy (reality show), 294
Evans, Frederick W., 28, 196, 251

fall of man, 28
Fielding, Mercy Rachel, 142
Fillmore, Millard, 171
Finney, Charles Grandison, 87
First Amendment, Free Exercise Clause, 280–81
First Annual Report of the Oneida Association (Oneida), 111–13, 157, 239, 241
First Presidency (Mormon), 102, 145, 147, 160, 163–64, 170, 210, 279, 292
Ford, Thomas, 148, 157, 165
Foster, Lawrence, 10, 38, 226, 231
Fourier, Charles, 26

Freemasonry, 106, 108–9, 131, 135
Freeze, Mary A., 225–26
French Prophets, 58
Froiseth, Jennie Anderson, 226, 229, 282

Gaddis, John Lewis, 11, 13
Garvin, Samuel, 154–55
Gates, Theophilus R., 73, 83
Genesis, book of, 28, 50, 230
genitalia, 44–45, 49
Goff, Anna Mariah, 215
Gold Rush, 170–72, 181
Gordon, Sarah Barringer, 275, 280
Grant, Jedediah, 210–12, 214, 217
Grant, Ulysses S., 277–78
Great Apostasy (Mormon), 35
Greeley, Horace, 111
Groveland, New York, 255
Gunnison, J. W., 41, 173–74, 204, 229

Hadd, Arnold, 256
Hagar, 76, 176
Hall, Daniel, 91
Hamilton, Erastus, 114
Hamilton, Susan, 114
Hancock, Clarissa, 77
Hancock, Levi, 77
Hancock, Massachusetts, 256
Hancock County, Illinois, 102
Hardy, Carmon, 291
Harrison, David, 83
Haskett, William J., 195–97
Hatch, Nathan, 20
Haun's Mill Massacre, 66
Hawley, Victor, 243
Heschel, Abraham, 7
Hill Cumorah, 62
History of American Socialisms (Noyes), 259, 271
History of the Saints, The; or, An Exposé of Joe Smith and Mormonism (Bennett), 131–35, 146, 153
Hobart, Ann, 263–64
holy kiss, 1

Holy Mother Wisdom (Shaker), 216, 218, 230
Hubbard, Dexter, 154, 156
Hubbard, Lucius, 154
Hubbard, Noahdiah, 151–57, 176, 201
Huntington, Zina, 106
Hutchings, Harriett, 227
Hyde, John, 203, 206
Hyde, Marinda Nancy Johnson, 106
Hyde, Orson, 102, 107, 220

Inslee, William, 180
interviews (Oneida), 201–2
Isaac, 76
Ithaca, New York, 82
Ivins, Stanley S., 212, 223, 238

Jacob, 76
Jacobs, Henry, 106
James, William, 11, 50
jealousy, 185–87
Jeffs, Warren, 293–94
Jenkins, Timothy, 154–55, 157
John, gospel of, 70
John the Baptist, 64
Johnson, Samuel, 95
Johnson, Theodore E., 198
Jones, Mary, 243

Kentucky Revival, The (McNemar), 98
Kern, Louis, J., 10, 202
Keturah, 76
Kimball, Heber C., 106, 133, 140, 164
Kimball Whitney, Helen Mar, 139–41, 191
King Follett Discourse (Smith), 29–30, 63
Kinsley, Myron, 268–69
Kirtland, Ohio, 65, 76–78
Kirtland Temple, 63
Klaw, Spencer, 187, 233, 239
Knight, Vinson, 106

Lady's Life among the Mormons, A (Stenhouse), 278
Lafayette, marquis de, 216

342 INDEX

Lamanites, 76
Lamb, Lucinda, 154
Lamson, David, 195–96, 198, 216, 236
Lasch, Christopher, 226
Law, Jane, 145, 147–48
Law, William, 145–48, 156, 163, 179
Law, Wilson, 145, 147
Lawrence, Maria, 138, 144
Lawrence, Sarah, 138, 144
Lebanon, New Hampshire, 59
Lee, Ann: life, 57–60; mission in North America, 92–97; theology, 2, 24–25, 28, 36–37, 45, 123–24, 216–17, 230, 251–53
Lee, William, 94, 96
Leo I (pope; Leo the Great), 36
"Letter to the Danbury Baptists" (Jefferson), 281
Lincoln, Abraham, 275, 277
Luke, gospel of, 42–43

male continence (Oneida), 5, 49–51, 87, 116, 202, 296
Manchester, England, 57
Mansion House (Oneida), 201
Manti, Utah, 212
Marks, William, 160, 162–64
masturbation, 50
Matthew, gospel of, 42, 85
Mayfield, Ohio, 78
McGee, Anita Newcomb, 245
McGuire, Meredith, 14
McKean, James, B., 277–80
McNemar, Richard, 35, 98, 196
Meacham, Joseph, 95–98, 194
Mears, John W., 267–68
Merwin, Abigail, 73–74, 82–85, 263
Mexican-American War, 170
Millennial Laws (Shaker), 196–98, 256–57
Miller, John R., 87, 91, 113–14, 154–56, 180, 201
Miller, Perry, 257
Missouri, 65, 76–79, 103, 134, 161
monogamy, 48, 75, 78, 83–84

Mormon Reformation, 210–14, 217
Mormons, or Latter-Day Saints, in the Valley of the Great Salt Lake (Gunnison), 173
Mormon War, 182
Moroni, 61–62
Morrill, Justin, 275, 277
Morrill Act, 275–78, 280, 282
Moses, 76, 143
mutual criticism (Oneida), 69, 88–89, 199

Nauvoo, Illinois, 66, 78, 80–81, 100–106, 130–33, 145, 147–49, 156, 159, 165, 267
Nauvoo Expositor, 147–48
Nauvoo Legion, 100, 130–32, 148, 166, 285
Nauvoo Lodge (Masonic), 108, 135
Nauvoo Temple, 166–67
Nephites, 62, 76
Newark, New Jersey, 1–2
New Haven, Connecticut, 70, 71, 73–74, 85
Newhouse, Sewell, 180
New Lebanon, New York, 97, 255
New York Observer, 152
Niskayuna, New York, 93–94, 96
Noble, Joseph Bates, 105
nocturnal emissions, 45
North Union, Ohio, 255
Noyes, Charlotte, 87
Noyes, George Wallingford, 5, 34, 69, 181
Noyes, George Washington, 87, 155
Noyes, Harriet, 87
Noyes (Holton), Harriet, 82, 85–86, 89, 114, 238–39, 260, 294
Noyes, John, 67, 71–72
Noyes, John Humphrey: communal organization, 110–17, 150–51, 153–57, 181, 198–203, 209, 259–65, 268–72, 294–96; life, 66–74; marriage/sexual teachings, 4–5, 42–43, 46–47, 81–91, 121, 176, 185, 232, 238–43, 250; theology, 23, 25, 33–34, 36–37

Noyes, Pierrepoint, 296
Noyes (Hayes), Polly, 67, 85
Noyes, Theodore, 200, 250, 252, 260–64, 266–69
Noyesism Unveiled (Eastman), 113

O'Dea, Thomas, 109
Ogden, Utah, 170
Onan (Onanism), 50
Oneida, New York, 4–5, 8, 23, 33, 81, 91
Oneida Journal, 152
Other Side of the Question (Shaker), 126, 128
Owen, Robert, 26

Palmyra, New York, 22, 60
Parker, Robert Allerton, 113
Partridge, Eliza, 138–39, 144
Partridge, Emily, 138–39, 144, 169
Paul, Apostle, 7, 42, 94, 216, 233, 271
penis, 28, 45, 47
Perfectionist (Oneida), 73
Perfectionists, 72–73, 83; antinomians, 1–2, 5; Brooklyn, New York, 112–14, 150, 201; Cambridge, Vermont, 112, 201; legalists, 1–2, 5; Newark, New Jersey, 1–2, 88, 201; Oneida, New York, 4–5, 8, 23, 33–34, 70–71, 110–12; Wallingford, Connecticut, 112, 201, 261–62
Perpetual Emigrating Company, 285
Peter, 216
Phelps, W. W., 76
philoprogenitiveness (Oneida), 186, 190, 239–40, 259
Platt, Merit, 82
Pocahontas, 216
Poland, Luke P., 277
Poland Act, 277–79, 282
Poland Hill, Maine, 255
polygamy (Mormon plural marriage), 2–5, 39–40, 75–81, 103–8, 130–49, 152, 162, 164–65, 167, 169, 172, 174–75, 183, 190–93, 205–6, 212–14, 219–28, 237–38, 250, 275–87, 290–94

populism, 20
"Practical Suggestions for Regulating the Intercourse of the Sexes," (Oneida), 201–2
Pratt, Orson, 39, 64, 132, 135, 145, 174–76, 220
Pratt, Parley P., 64
Pratt, Sarah M., 132
Priesthood, Aaronic (Mormon), 64, 109, 191
Priesthood, Melchizedek (Mormon), 64–65, 109, 191
Provo, Utah, 170, 274
Putney, Vermont, 23, 72–73, 81
Putney Corporation, 87–88, 90–91, 111

Quakers, 58
Quinn, D. Michael, 164, 290, 292
Quorum of the Seventy, 210
Quorum of the Twelve Apostles, 102, 106, 147, 160–62, 164, 166, 170, 204–5, 210

Rachel, 76
Rathbone, Reuben, 45, 95, 123, 194
Rathbun, Daniel, 94–95, 123, 194
Rathbun, Valentine, 94–95, 123, 194
Reasons Offered for Leaving the Shakers (Rathbun), 95
Reed, Clarissa, 77
Representative Women of Deseret: A Book of Biographical Sketches (Crocheron), 285
Restell, Madame, 50
Revelation, book of, 94
Revolutionary War, 93
Reynolds, Amelia, 279–80
Reynolds, George, 279–80, 284
Reynolds v. United States, 280–82
Richards, Willard, 149
Rigdon, Nancy, 107–8, 140, 163
Rigdon, Sidney, 64, 103, 107–8, 135, 140, 160, 163–64, 179
Robinson, George W., 135
Rockwell, Orin Porter, 134

Rocky Mountain Saints: A Full and Complete History of the Mormons (Stenhouse), 278
Rocky Ridge, Utah, 293–94
Rogers, Sarah Matilda, 225
Rondout, New York, 88
Root, O. P., 154–56

Sabbathday Lake, Maine, 256
Sacred Grove, 61
Salt Lake City, Utah, 169, 274
Sarah, 176
Scandinavia, 183
Second Coming of Christ (Oneida Perfectionist), 33–34
Second Great Awakening, 19, 22
semen, 45, 50
Seymour, Henry, 151–52
Seymour (Hubbard), Tryphena, 151–53, 156
Shakerism Unmasked (Haskett), 197
Shakers, 1–2, 8, 24–25, 28–29, 35–36
Sharon, Vermont, 59
Short Creek, Arizona, 293
Sister Wives (reality show), 294
Skinner, Harriet Noyes, 260
Skinner, John L., 87
Skinner, Joseph, 260–61, 263
Smith, Abram C., 88, 90, 114
Smith, Alvin, 62
Smith, Emma Hale, 39, 62, 78, 80, 89, 131, 136–45, 162, 164, 179
Smith, George D., 80, 104, 141, 192
Smith, Hyrum, 108, 133, 141–44, 146, 149, 157, 159–60
Smith, Jerusha, 142
Smith, Joseph: life, 22–23, 59–64, 71, 100–110; plural marriage (polygamy), 12–13, 37–39, 75–82, 130–49, 191–92; theology, 2–3, 29–30, 35
Smith, Joseph, Sr., 60–61
Smith, Joseph F., 291–93
Smith, Lucy Mack, 60
Smith, Mary Fielding, 142
Smoot, Reed, 292–93

Snow, Eliza Roxcy, 137–38, 169, 225
Snow, Lorenzo, 29, 292
Solomon, 76, 143
Standerin (Stanley, Standley), Abraham, 57
Stein, Stephen J., 14, 24, 45, 58, 129, 216, 231, 256
Stenhouse, Fanny, 219–20, 224, 227–29, 278
Stenhouse, Thomas, 278
Stewart, Philemon, 198
stirpiculture (Oneida), 189, 241–45
Summary View of the Millennial Church (Shaker), 36, 44–46, 100, 129
Swedenborg, Emanuel, 83
Syracuse Standard, 268–69

Taylor, Amos
Taylor, John, 149, 284
Taylor, Nathaniel William, 71
Tertullian, 159
Towner, James William, 264–65, 268–69
transcontinental railroad, 182, 249, 289
traps (animal, Oneida), 180
Troeltsch, Ernst, 14
Turner, John G., 77, 167, 205, 210
Two Years' Experience among the Shakers (Lamson), 198
Tyringham, Massachusetts, 255

ultraism, 22, 26
Union Pacific Railroad, 182
Urim and Thummim, 62, 143
Utah Expedition (Utah War), 274–75

Van Wagoner, Richard, 78, 169, 192, 221–22, 291

Waite, Morrison Remick, 281–82
Walker, Lucy, 139–40, 145
Ward, Maria, 40
Wardley, James, 58
Wardley, Jane, 58

Warsaw, Illinois, 102
Washington, George, 216
Watervliet, New York, 124–25, 214–15, 217
Wayland-Smith, Frank, 266, 269–70
Wayne County, Indiana, 77
Webb family, 78
wet dreams, 45
Whittaker, James, 94, 96
Wife Number Nineteen; or, The Story of a Life in Bondage (Young), 278
Winter Quarters (Mormon), 169–70
Witness (Oneida), 84
Women of Mormonism; or, The Story of Polygamy as Told by the Victims Themselves (Froiseth), 282
Woodruff, Phoebe W. Carter, 225

Woodruff, Wilford, 163, 213, 286–87, 290–92
Woodward, Mary, 169
Wright, Lucy, 96–100, 128, 196, 230

Yale University, 23, 33, 70
YMCA, 266
Young, Ann Eliza Webb, 202, 206, 212, 221, 225, 227–28, 278
Young, Brigham: life, 64, 102, 160–65, 179, 181–83, 198, 202–6, 210–11, 217–18, 260, 284; plural marriage (polygamy), 39–41, 76, 102, 106, 132–33, 141, 145, 167–74, 213–14, 219–22, 238, 273–79

Zilpah, 76

American Spirituality

The American Spirituality series publishes histories, ethnographies, biographies, and critical editions designed to deepen understanding of the varied ways that Americans have imagined spirituality, past and present. As such, the series advances new critical perspectives on how religious norms, practices, and institutions—including the very labeling of "religion" and "spirituality"—have been thrashed out in American culture.

www.ingramcontent.com/pod-product-compliance
Lightning Source LLC
Chambersburg PA
CBHW030604230426
43661CB00053B/1839